TIME AND METHOD

Publication Number 838

AMERICAN LECTURE SERIES®

A Monograph in

The BANNERSTONE DIVISION *of*
AMERICAN LECTURES IN PHILOSOPHY

Edited by

MARVIN FARBER

State University of New York at Buffalo
Buffalo, New York

TIME AND METHOD

An Essay on the Methodology of Research

────────────── *By* ──────────────

FERDINAND GONSETH

*Emeritus Professor of Higher Mathematics
and of Philosophy of Science
Swiss Federal Institute of Technology
Zurich, Switzerland*

Translated By

EVA H. GUGGENHEIMER, Ph.D.

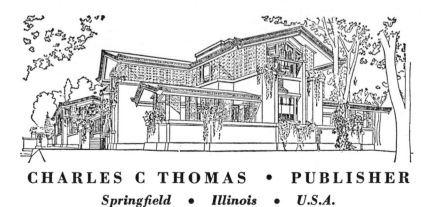

CHARLES C THOMAS • PUBLISHER
Springfield • Illinois • U.S.A.

Published and Distributed Throughout the World by
CHARLES C THOMAS • PUBLISHER
Bᴀɴɴᴇʀsᴛᴏɴᴇ Hᴏᴜsᴇ
301–327 East Lawrence Avenue, Springfield, Illinois, U.S.A.

Translated from the original French edition, *Le Probléme du Temps,*
published in 1964 by Editions du Griffon, Neuchâtel, Switzerland.

© *1972, by* CHARLES C THOMAS • PUBLISHER

ISBN 0–398–02297–6

Library of Congress Catalog Card Number: 70–175075

With THOMAS BOOKS *careful attention is given to all details of
manufacturing and design. It is the Publisher's desire to present books
that are satisfactory as to their physical qualities and artistic possibilities
and appropriate for their particular use.* THOMAS BOOKS *will be true
to those laws of quality that assure a good name and good will.*

Printed in the United States of America

B–7

INTRODUCTION

The present study is intended from the outset as a work of research—as research into the method of research. In its progress from the analysis of language to the study of atomic clocks, the argument will assume rather diverse forms. All the same, we shall never lose sight of the central question, namely: *How can arbitrariness in research be avoided?*

One may well ask whether this is really the most pressing problem. Should we not, in research, rather beware of *error*, which a correct method should permit us to avoid? Is not *truth* the constant aim of research, and is not the method designed to perceive or discover it? In the confrontation between true and false, is not the arbitrary of secondary importance?

Certainly not! In the field of research the functions are not thus divided into fundamental and incidental ones. As long as language alone is concerned, truth remains ambiguous. The truth of realistic language is not identical with the truth of idealistic language. Are we forced, then, to make a choice, to decide in favor of one and against the other? Would it then be just an act of the free will to select one's own reality? The answer is *no;* to be implemented, this freedom would have to be enforced. Is there no other tribunal before which we may take our cause?

Consider the most famous example, whose full implications do not seem to be understood as yet. The Cartesian method formulates the rules whose consistent application should have permitted steady progress, without possible error, towards truth in the natural sciences. Were these rules chosen at will? They presented themselves with the guarantee that they were obvious or necessary. What can we say of them today, now that more than three centuries have elapsed since the time they were set forth? Traveling the immeasurable distance which separates the science of that time from the science of today, have these rules been

tested by research, and have they been confirmed or proved
wrong? Each rule still retains a certain practical value, a value
at the same time stable and limited. But their most essential
claim must be abandoned without hope of return, the notion
that they must suffice, and that within their grasp they must
embrace the scientific truth in its totality. Now that this dominant idea has been abandoned, do the rules remain what they
were meant to be? Certainly not, for their dominant idea was
a vital element of their meaning. But this is not the important
point. What is important for us is to evaluate the Cartesian
enterprise from the standpoint which today may be our own,
while keeping in mind that this method necessarily involves a
certain unfairness. What the experience of three centuries has
revealed to us is the *element of arbitrariness* in the Cartesian
method. For it would be inaccurate to say, in retrospect and
out of concern for historical justice, that the assertion of holding
all the strains of truth in hand for the future was a mere hypothesis; the modern concept of hypothesis is out of place in a
system where evidence is the ultimate criterion.

A short while ago we asked ourselves whether there exists a
tribunal capable of judging the value of a language which claims
to be based upon its own legitimacy. In fact, what has just been
advanced is a judgment of this kind. The categories of the ver-
dict are not the true and the false of logic, but the idoneous and
the arbitrary. In our particular case, the element of arbitrariness
inevitably becomes clear.

What is the tribunal capable of such a judgment? It is not
common sense informed by the natural lights of the mind alone.
It is not a non-temporal consciousness capable of bringing
absolute criteria into play. It is rather a situation consciousness,
in the situation prepared for it by research, on which it depends
and without which it would not be what it is. Before this tribunal the historical or personal reasons which might explain
or even justify the main rules as well as the inspiration of the
method fade away. They leave, so to speak, a methodological
vacuum, the void in which all preciseness thereafter appears as
arbitrariness.

The above criticism transcends the individual example. It is aimed at every theory of knowledge which, proclaiming its guiding rules and ideas, does not at the same time provide the means of submitting them to the repeated test of research, i.e. of the experiment. It is essentially the autonomy of language which is thus challenged.

We shall not in this context expose the elements of arbitrariness inherent in the traditional forms of the realistic as well as of the idealistic languages. If, incidentally, they were free of such elements, how could they be so radically incompatible? The problem arising from their incompatibility is not how to make a correct choice but how to adapt both to the exigencies of their participation in the process of research.

The destinies of science and of philosophy are inseparable. Their respective laws of evolution, however, seem to be opposites. Despite their unity of intention, philosophical opinions diverge; despite their diversity of hypotheses and ways of approach, scientific opinions converge. It is therefore understandable that men have been tempted by the project of isolating and formulating the criteria capable at the same time of insuring the specificity and the reliability of scientific knowledge. But why do the attempts diverge that were made in this direction? Each of them sets up a methodological perspective appropriate to itself, but these perspectives do not agree with each other. What is missing in these attempts to form a fascicle of inquiries whose convergence may reasonably be taken for granted? They fail to represent their governing ideas as hypotheses which not only must be validated but also put to the test. Even if they were accompanied by a formal declaration acknowledging their hypothetical status it would not be satisfactory. A hypothesis which does not admit to being one clearly falls into the category of the arbitrary. But, in order not to remain gratuitous, it is not enough for it to reveal its identity. In order to be taken seriously, the hypothesis must assume a certain plausibility, which implies that it should be possible to describe, at least in a general way, the range of its presumable validity and the means of its eventual confirmation. But above all one must not rule out the contingency of failure beforehand by simply not mentioning it at all. The status of hypothesis thus has its exigencies; an assumption which does not satisfy them can only be gratuitous or arbitrary.

But how can a test be set up in the domain of methodological considerations? Take, for example, the doctrine of operationalism, to which many physicists seem to attribute a certain prominence. This doctrine essentially relates to all the quantities which the physicist is able to measure, those of *time* in particular. The physicist's time, according to this doctrine, should be reducible to its "operational definition," i.e. to *that* which the physicist does in order to measure it. For such a definition to be meaningful, one must of course be able to explain *everything one has to do* in order to obtain a good measurement of a well-defined interval of time. Will it be possible to provide these explanations in an exhaustive way, in terms of experimental procedure? Implicitly the doctrine states this hypothesis. But has the hypothesis been tested?

Nothing prevents us from carrying out the test. From water clocks to chronometers and atomic clocks, chronometry has been perfecting instruments and methods of ever-increasing precision. Here we have a ready-made field of experimentation where, in a repeat performance, the operationalist hypothesis may be tested. The matter is certainly not a foregone conclusion and requires its share of attention. On the other hand, there is no methodological obstacle to prevent it from being conducted at the very level where the operationalist makes his decision, i.e. at the level of the manufacture of watches and clocks and their use. Moreover this test is necessary, and it must be carried out in the most concrete and objective manner possible, if one wishes to clarify the value of the hypothesis.

This is precisely what we have endeavored to do in the second part of the present work. Will the operationalist thesis emerge confirmed by this scrutiny? While the thesis appears defensible in the most simple cases, it becomes less and less so as the analysis progresses toward the exigencies of increased precision, and its validity finally vanishes completely when it comes to the high degrees of precision of modern chronometry. One must not conclude, of course, that it makes no sense at all to speak of the operational aspect of research in general and of measuring procedures in particular. What becomes clear is that research cannot be reduced to this aspect, even when our only concern is to describe with complete objectivity the physicist's relation to the quantities called physical.

As far as we are concerned, we shall learn something else from this example, which enables us to make these two statements:

1. Formulated without consideration for its being put to the test, the thesis of operationalism, especially in its dominant intent, merely amounts to an arbitrary hypothesis.

2. There is, however, no difficulty of principle in carrying out this test. It is true that the result is negative.

These two statements hardly agree. Within the framework of a discipline of science, an analogous situation would never be tolerated. How can it be explained that we do not react with the same severity where, instead of such and such particular episodes, the very status of research is concerned? Do we not falsely imagine that methodological research is nothing but a purely discursive matter? The perspective changes radically if one realizes that scientific research is initiated, confirmed, and developed as an actualization of the option of openness towards experience, and that there is no reason why it should be otherwise in methodological research. To show them in the very spirit of this austere discipline is the purpose of the present work.

The terms in which we referred to discourse and discursivity could have created the impression that according to our idea the problems of language are outside the status of research discussed above. But such is not the case, as the following example will show.

The function of language is not an easy matter to understand in its totality. It is therefore not surprising that it has been the object of diverse attempts at explanation, for example, one which from a formalized system creates the ideal language, or one which advances the proposition that the sense of a word is limited to the extent of its use. But is it likewise proper not to be surprised that these explanations do not agree with each other? It often happens that, in order to explain a phenomenon,

one advances several different hypotheses not all of which could
be correct at the same time. But this is done in the hope that
some day, with the help of the experiment, the unsuitable hypotheses can be eliminated. If this hope were precluded, all the
hypotheses would lose their interest at the same time. Can the
problem of language not also be amenable to experiment, notably the experiment which consists precisely in a more or less
effective use of speech? One might then also impose the rigorous
discipline which allows to define as arbitrary a hypothesis
formulated without concern for justification and to reject one
which is proved false by the experiment.

We said before that the methods of measuring time, from
elementary processes to the advanced procedures of high precision, offer a field of experimentation where certain methodological opinions may be put to the test. The investigation of
these practices then takes immediately the form of methodological research. Now, there also exist verbal practices whose object
is to grasp, to express, and to control the temporal aspects of
our know-how. They rank from the inflected forms of nouns
and adjectives to the inflection of verbs and the structuring of
the phrase by means of adverbs, prepositions, and conjunctions.
Even when they are correct according to the most exacting
syntax, these practices are not infallibly right or effective. They
may be judged in the general context of our activities and in
particular be confronted with the exigencies of chronometrical
practices. They then likewise offer a field of experimentation
where opinions on the function of language may be put to the
test. This verbal experimentation, tending not towards logical
or syntactical correction but towards the participation of speech
in the diverse forms of our participation in our surroundings,
does not call for any special knowledge. All the same, it turns
out to be rather exacting. It excludes all attempts, one might
say even all tentative efforts to close language against one or
other of these aspects, to give it a primary information, to lend
it an invariant structure, to confer on it the capacity of immediate adequation, and so on. In a general way, the procedure
questions all the variants of a certain *analytic philosophy* which
claims to create from language a separable whole having its
intrinsic criteria of authenticity or verity. To repeat, it is not

unusual that, in a problem as difficult as that of the function of language, certain hypotheses are advanced which afterwards have to be discarded. This is no more than an illustration of one of the fundamental laws of research. But what may be surprising, if this is actually research, is that these hypotheses are formulated without the guarantee that they can be tested; which means that one is not concerned with the element of arbitrariness that might be inherent in them. This is the more striking as one has, so to speak, within his reach the field and the means of verbal experimentation, whose testimony, in certain cases at least, is immediately decisive. (This verbal experimentation, which we have called semantic positive analysis, does not come in for the criticism which has just been made against analytic philosophy, because it relates to evaluations which are not the concern of language alone.)

What may be learned from this situation? The fashion in which studies of language—and, incidentally, studies of method as well—have as a rule been conducted depends on a status which is not that of research in the actual sense.

Nothing prevents us, however, from opting for the latter; to the unity of method in this case corresponds the general coherence of cognition open to the experiment in the making.

But how can a normal status of research be introduced? Can one make it the object and the result of an investigation without running into the most immediate of paradoxes? After having made the experiment of a research project which, taking the concept of time as a pretext, travels the immense field of knowledge which extends from current language to the insights of the most recent physical science, the present work resolutely attacks the general question of the status of research. It concentrates on showing how the option of openness towards experience, replacing the method of foundation upon bases *ne varietur,* eliminates all the paradoxes of the beginning. By the solidarity which connects anticipatory research with its results and its results with its points of departure, research is perfectly capable of gradually steadying its progress and gradually defining the status which, as an open system, directs it by an anticipation which the experiment is testing and retesting constantly.

CONTENTS

TIME AND METHOD

PART I
TIME IN LANGUAGE

Chapter One

THE PROBLEM OF MEANING

PRELIMINARY REMARKS

Before we embark upon our enterprise, which is to discuss the problem of time in the spirit of open philosophy, we must consider the situation of a person who forms such a project. More specifically, it is the fundamental aspect of this situation which merits our attention. Anyone, indeed, who is faced with the task of formulating a problem can do so only by means of a language already formed. In order to be understood he must be in a position to explain what he is doing. Whatever his project, it will not take shape except through the use of a certain verbal substance. Inevitably, to formulate and treat a problem means to confer upon it a discursive form which we shall describe as inalienable, meaning thereby to indicate that, even if it does not represent the total reality of the problem, the latter nevertheless acquires reality for us only if it is presented to us in this form.

All this is nothing new. When we emphasize the rôle of language at the point where words and phrases just begin to spread the web of significations without which an author would never be understood by anyone, we merely call to mind a situation which has often been acknowledged. It is the situation of those who aim to apply reflection and all its instruments to the instruments of reflection, criticism and all its advances to the advances of criticism, research and all its procedures to the procedures of research. As far as we are concerned, we have to use language to conduct and to set forth a rather extensive study in which language itself will be implicated on the side of the object of the present study.

The situation in which we already find ourselves thus has nothing exceptional. It nevertheless presents, in the first analysis, a rather paradoxical aspect, and one may ask whether by taking it into account from the start, he does not commit himself to a

5

dead-end road. How does one manage, in fact, to escape the following dilemma:

If you intend, we shall be told, to justify in advance the use of the entire verbal apparatus which you cannot think of doing without, you will be able to accomplish this only by means of words and still more words. You will have to justify those in turn, and you will be stuck with an endless task facing you. Your intention of justifying the language you are going to speak, by means of the language which you are already speaking, deprives you in advance of the possibility of doing so, since it is from this same language where you must borrow the means for your justification.

If, on the other hand, you intend to state reservations concerning the adequacy of the discursive apparatus you are going to use, you will again be able to do so only by means of words and phrases. In order to evaluate what you are going to make them say, should you not know beforehand how to define their usage? Would it not be necessary that, in order to be understood, you should have been understood already at the preliminary level? One might conclude that there is no advantage whatever in analyzing and exposing the problematic character inherent in any exposition whose validity he does not intend to undermine beforehand.

Are we going to accept this argumentation? Of course not, since we have provoked it for the sole purpose of challenging it. It represents a certain type of objections which, at first sight, seem difficult to answer. We shall not pause at this point to discuss them, since we still have to define the means for refuting them. But it will become perfectly clear later that this argument operates with faulty reasoning and is prompted by a faulty appraisal of the situation.

Are we, then, unable to say anything about the language we are using at this very moment? Suffice it to note that this language serves to establish a bond of comprehension between the person who writes or speaks it on the one hand and the person who reads or hears it on the other, without as yet specifying the nature of that bond. The fact that it exists is undeniable. We certainly do not claim that, from the first words, the communication whose vehicle it is must be complete and perfect. Why should we assume such a thing? What would be the use of postulating such a miracle?

The existence of this bond in a fundamental way belongs to the situation in which we find ourselves, to the situation which actually is our own. Quite as fundamental is our liberty to make use of it. For this privilege we need no previous justification and no discursive demonstration. We are not here concerned with a theoretical right which has to be proved, but with a real right of which we avail ourselves each time we enter into a dialogue with another person. This right is of the order of acquired rights, just as the existence of the bond of comprehension, which was discussed before, is of the order of established facts. Accordingly it is a right we simply decide to enjoy. This is, for the moment, our answer to the dilemma in which we might have appeared to stay trapped. We have said that this dilemma characterizes the type of certain objections which, if they had to be taken seriously, would question the legitimacy of any research which takes itself as an object of research. What has been said also typifies the kind of answer which should be made to these objections; we simply note the liberty we have to benefit from the discursive bond of comprehension which we are able to establish with another person. It is of course this right, this ability, which we are using at this very moment. But it must be clear that by doing so we do not put either this right or this ability out of reach. We are not in a position to withdraw them from all investigation. By making this statement, we on the contrary define them as objects of an investigation which inevitably must revert to them. In our right to employ language, and in our ability to do so with a certain effectiveness, we still remain to ourselves a cause for astonishment and an object of knowledge. And again, it is our right and our ability not to let the matter rest here.

HEURISTIC DISCOURSE AND STABILIZED LANGUAGE OF INTERCOMMUNICATION

Our project will lead us to take language, more specifically the French language, as our first field of experimentation. But this statement might be misunderstood unless we make certain preliminary distinctions. For our purpose the term "the French language" still is not precise enough. We must proceed to a first subdivision of meaning.

1. The French language is of course the language of our report, the language of our expository treatise [in its original form]. Yet it cannot and will not be a language shared in every respect and in advance by all those who claim to "speak French." For a rather essential part it is doubtless preformed for our subject, since we already are able, before actually having started on our work, to make some statements about this project. On the other hand, this language is not everybody's language either, since for another part it is informed by that which we already know in the fashion in which we shall realize it. The means of discourse which we shall call upon, and which we cannot do without, will show this from the start. Later on we may have to modify, complete, revise, or invalidate them. At any rate, from the first words our language must incorporate a fundamental concern: it must realize its purpose by relying on means of doubtful validity. This concern includes all the elements of information and expression which will contribute to the progress of our exposition. They will evolve, more or less perceptibly, according to the course and the stages of our thought. They may even present themselves as problematic entities, wherever the progressing work is confronted with the necessity to revise its own tools.

But if this must be so, are we not going to speak a language which is our exclusive possession, which evokes no response and can only isolate us, instead of creating a link of comprehension without which our dissertation will remain a dead letter? *Non scripsit qui non legitur* ("He whose works are not read is like one who has not written anything").

One may wonder at this; one will never even wonder enough; but the situation which thus confronts us is nothing unusual. It is also the situation of all those who have set their minds on explaining and expounding anything which contains the slightest element of change. Theirs is a *didactic situation* for which the appropriate form of expression, in a more or less radical way, is the heuristic one. The language which satisfies the exigencies of a didactic situation is not completely and irrevocably fixed in advance. It may appear to be at some particular point in the exposition, but nevertheless it is modified from situation to situation, by absorbing the very process of exposition. That under these circumstances the heuristic form of expression may be intelligible and remain so, is again a fact for which we shall not try to seek a hasty explanation. While undeniable in itself, this fact still eludes the grasp of a justification intended as purely discursive. It cannot fail to reappear among the presuppositions of any language which would claim, for itself alone, the proof of its own cogency.

Thus we do not explain at present but rather state that it is typical for the function of the heuristic form of expression to operate with words and phrases whose sense is not complete and is not exactly determined as yet. Far from conveying ready-made meanings, it serves to develop meanings according to its own development. Is it not correct to say that the value of an explanation is measured by the gap which separates the meaning of the words at the start from the meaning which they assume at the conclusion?

The intention to treat the heuristic form of expression as deductive discourse is thus perfectly unrealistic. The procedure which consists in giving beforehand the definition of the words and terms one intends to use in it is illusory. This procedure is based on an erroneous conception of the didactic situation and on a much too narrow estimate of the rôle of an explanatory language, which includes the languages we have both the right and the ability to use.

To repeat: this right and this ability are ours. Why should we give them up? Besides, even if one wished to do so it would be impossible, unless at the same time he gave up every intention to explain anything at all. In fact the heuristic form of expression is the normal form of every exposition. One might use it without recognizing its nature, but it nonetheless remains what it is; and our capacity to use it with relative precision likewise remains intact. One might introduce changes and then proceed without taking proper notice of them. Likewise, without exactly realizing it, one might adapt the discursive apparatus which serves to conduct an exposition to the result which the latter brings to light. But, as far as we are concerned, as far as our project is concerned, it is important that we become clearly aware of the evolutive character of the heuristic discourse.*

2. Opposite heuristic discourse, which lets significations evolve by incorporating into them the developments it serves to accomplish, we must place the language we make an effort to fixate, in order to fashion it into a means of expression, and consequently, of intercommunication, of the greatest possible stability. Under its heuristic aspect the language must be principally open at every step to significations not yet integrated into it. Considered from this angle, the function of this language to some extent is opposed to that of a language for which one seeks, as far as possible, to define the vocabulary and to regulate the syntax. We are of course concerned with the latter kind if we propose to subject language to an investigation intended to bring out certain characteristics. This is the language which the grammarians seek to codify and to maintain in a regular usage, the language whose vocabulary is supposed to be clarified by the dictionaries. It is of course this kind we mean when we state our intention to take language, more specifically, the French language, as the field of a special investigation. The very idea of such an analysis presupposes that the language one is going to investigate be sufficiently stable and its significations sufficiently well established so as not to disintegrate under the pressure of analysis. The evolutive language of exposition and the stabilized language of intercommunication thus answer different and even contrasting needs. They represent two aspects of language which appear irreconcilable. And yet we know that insofar as it is a

---

* What has just been said concerning the language of exposition does not, of course, exhaust the subject. At this point we are concerned only with preliminary explanations whose purpose is to confirm at the same time the point of departure of our exposition and the method to which the latter will be committed. It is moreover a characteristic of this method that it is not fully justified except by the road it permits us to travel. We shall tie the loop, so to speak, by returning to the question of language at the end of our exposition and devoting to it an important part of our conclusions.

living language, French—like so many other written and spoken languages—reconciles them. How is this possible?

In reality, the grammarian's linguistic ideal remains inaccessible. The stabilization of a language whose function is not artificially restricted has something provisional and even deceptive. It is well known that one only has to shift backwards in time far enough for the feeling of achievement provided by dictionaries and grammars to fade away. A language which is truly living defies any attempt at fixation for shaping it into a completely effective tool. In the long run, the language of current use and any language of intercommunication exhibit every characteristic of the heuristic form of expression.

A science of language aiming at objectivity perhaps ought to emphasize the elements of heuristicity, of unexpectedness, of discovery constantly renewed in a common language. This science would concentrate more on that which is temporary and elusive beyond the appearance of stability and regularity of well-established languages. On the other hand, if it is within the functions of explanatory language to create adequate variations and modifications of the meanings to which the words and phrases give their *discursive form,* the language which offers itself for explanation is not therefore modified all of a sudden and uniformly throughout all its roots and its entire scope. In an evolving discursive organism, whether from the rigors of external tasks or by the play of internal causes, there is a certain stock of terms, expressions, and significations which one finds again at every stage of its evolution. It is true that the words may change; the combinations of their meanings and these meanings themselves may become more or less modified; nevertheless, if this stock of significations does not remain identical, the elements which it contains at least remain recognizable throughout the evolution which produces them and in which they participate. This process may be compared to the fashion in which an organism retains what constitutes its individuality throughout a sequence of momentary conditions which are not necessarily exact replicas of each other. The organism replaces itself "in continuity of existence" with itself, identifiable if not identical with itself, even though one or other of its parts be transformed, provided that it remains functionally integrated into the whole.

It is therefore clear that a language has the capacity of evolution, without ceasing to be this same language. One should add to this that the linguistic ideal of the grammarian, while it may be realized only in an incomplete and transitional form, nevertheless exerts a rigorous normative power. Therefore the capacity of variation of a language is contained within rather narrow limits. Must we congratulate ourselves because the language we speak has been strongly elaborated in its grammar and syntax? Yes and No. Yes, if a language of current use is concerned, a language stabilized at the level of a certain aggregate of significations which are perceived intersubjectively. No, if one expects of this language that it serve for the explanation of anything frankly new, especially if the newness is related to the language itself. Its perfection might otherwise turn into fallacy or tyranny. Thus it may be explained that a language of current usage—even though this usage be not elementary—can be taken as an object, as a milieu of analysis; it is stable or fixated enough so as not to defy investigation. But it is also clear that the language thanks to which such an analysis may be conducted will not share these characteristics; it can only be a language which has regained its capacity of evolution.

OUTLINES OF DIALECTICS IN CURRENT LANGUAGE

Our project, as already stated, is to approach the problem of time indirectly, by means of an analysis of current language. The preceding remarks have not deferred execution of this project, which is already well under way at this moment. The very intention of analyzing a language amounts to splitting it, opposing the instrument-language to the object-language of the analysis. In order to avoid inextricable confusions, one must be aware of and take into account everything that separates the active function from the passive rôle of language, which is thus used in two ways. But what do we expect from such an analysis? On this point, too, some preliminary explanations are in order.

It is convenient to confer upon the noun *dialectic* (a dialectic) the rather general significance of discourse, or part of a discourse, organized in view of certain purposes. (It is consistent with the nature of expository language to test this.) Thus, geometry may be considered as a discourse organized strictly for the purpose of a correct, as well as effective, representation of space. It is then a dialectic of space. Such a dialectic of course may have either a euclidean or a non-euclidean structure. According to the general sense which we propose, a dialectic is not necessarily unique in its genre. Must one assume that a dialectic, in its quality of discursive organism, has an autonomous existence and only displays, through the means of discourse, the exigencies of a law peculiar to it? Sometimes one interprets geometry in this sense by considering it as a purely rational discipline. This approach does not preclude a study of geometry if care is taken not to deprive it of an essential part of its signification. In its quality of effective discourse the geometrical dialectic is ordered according to a *practice* which it certainly directs, but which in turn supplies its guarantee. In the light of our present knowledge, this dialectic and this practice are revealed as being inseparably dependent upon each other: we say therefore that they are coordinated.

It is immediately clear, by comparison, that a language of current use does not require a well-organized dialectic of space, and that the activities to which this language corresponds, and according to which it is organized, do not require a systematized spatial practice. But it is also clear that any current language carries, so to speak, the traces or the more or less fragmentary outline of a dialectic of space. Vocabulary and syntax combine to provide the means for this. It would be easy to give many examples but we shall omit them at this point. In a study of geometry and the problem of space, such examples would be appropriate. On the other hand, we shall take great care to show the outline of a dialectic of time in which the system of the verb has a very special rôle. The practice which corresponds to it is implicit in all our daily activities.*

* We have explained, very summarily, the meaning we shall give to the noun *dialectic,* namely, *discursive system ordered according to a certain practice.* Dialectic and practice provide each other with mutual support to constitute themselves within a more or less delimitable whole. In order to fixate the

The dialectics of space and of time are not the only ones which current language outlines without yet forming from them well-organized discursive systems. One likewise perceives in language the traces of a dialectic of being and its modalities, a dialectic of speaking and its values of assertion, a dialectic of doing, of purposes, of effects and causes, and so on. Each of these dialectics introduces another angle from which language may be analyzed. But what is the point of doing so? Thus we come back to the question which we asked concerning the temporal aspect alone, namely: What can we expect from such an analysis?

One may imagine two eventualities which to some extent are opposites. In the first case, one would start from the idea that the *discursive formalization* of a dialectic of time can only be an

---

meaning of the adjective *dialectic,* we shall go a step further in the direction of expository discourse. An action shall be termed dialectic if it involves, at least potentially, an active turning back, a reversal, a retroaction of its effect on the situation in which it has taken place and to which it had conformed. This qualification is therefore appropriate to a discourse which is established in such a way that what it explicates can react on what it implicates, which permits a return from the results it has reached to the presuppositions upon which it was established, and which implies, in short, the integration of the acquired elements with the preliminary ones. A dialectic discourse must be open to its own renewal, precisely as a function of the tasks in which it has been engaged and of its success or failure therein. It is peculiar to this discourse that it adapts itself to the new element which it produces or helps to produce, even if the impact of the new element does not leave intact what had appeared to be a necessary substructure.

Consider now the meanings which, in our present situation, we have given to the word dialectic, first as a noun and then as an adjective. Can a dialectic, such as we understand the term, always be qualified as dialectic? The "definitions" which we have given do not seem to require it, and the example from geometry even seems to suggest the contrary. This first impression, however, must be revised. It should be remembered that one of the results of our study of geometry and the problem of space was precisely to make evident the dialectically evolutive quality of geometry taken as a dialectic of space. To anticipate, we state that the same holds true for the dialectic of time whose outline is contained in everyday language. Sooner or later, in short, every dialectic reveals that it is, and cannot but be, of a dialectic nature. This is a comeback, a justification, perhaps the most far-reaching one, from the first option to the experiment, by which the present study will be increasingly actuated and which our conclusions tend fully to elucidate. As far as heuristic discourse is concerned, what we have said about its evolutive character makes of it without further ado a prime example of dialectic discourse.

implementation of discursive tools given in advance, tools already present in the language in which the dialectic is set forth. Assuming that this idea is correct, one may expect to see how a language can produce a dialectic, how it can confer upon it both its form and its meaning. And we entertain the hope that, although this dialectic is but roughly sketched, a better adjustment of the discursive means at our disposal might suffice to complete it.*

In the second case we start, conversely, from the idea that at the moment when language is confronted with the task of giving a discursive form to the dialectic of time, its means of expression are neither completely given nor perfectly determined as yet, while that which must be expressed is determined beforehand. Is this second hypothesis more valid than the first one? In this case analysis ought to demonstrate how a language acquires its forms of expression by the very search for the correct expression. As a matter of fact, neither of these two hypotheses corresponds to the real state of affairs. The first one goes too far in supposing that the material of the discursive formulation is given in advance, while the second goes too far in supposing that *the matter* waiting to be expressed exists apart from and prior to language. What the analysis does make clear is the solidary elaboration of the several forms of expression and their capacity of meaning. At this point we can make this statement only as a preliminary remark, until our analysis produces manifest proof for it.†

The results and the evidence of the analysis thus are deployed on two fronts; they will give us access both to the problem of time and to the problem of language. One should not be surprised to see the problem of language thus placed side by side with the problem of time and claim the attention of anyone who intends to treat the latter in particular. The problem of time, its tools, and its functions, inevitably looms behind all the enterprises in which it is engaged. One may not be interested in it; it will soon

---

* Did not D'Alembert have a similar idea (in the case, it is true, of the dialectic of space) when he thought that a better definition of the straight line could correct the "scandal of the parallels"?

† At a later point we shall especially illustrate this solidarity by means of what we shall then define as a sketch in the strong sense.

establish itself in the foreground. One may pretend to ignore its presence; it nevertheless remains present behind all the words which one employs. As far as we are concerned, we shall allow it to take, quite naturally, its proper place in our studies as a problem of the first order.

FIRST OUTLINES OF A THEORY OF LANGUAGE

Our project remains the same: We shall not give up our plan to attack the problem of time indirectly by means of an analysis of current language. It has just now become clear that the problem of time is not separable from that of language. This fact illuminates the situation but is not of a nature to modify our intentions. The investigation towards which we are proceeding quite simply shall be conducted in view of a double aim, and both problems will be treated simultaneously.

In doing so we shall not be exempt from the common rule according to which it is impossible to tackle any problem without at least some preconceived idea. In our particular case, we cannot think of entering upon the practical application of our analysis without a certain previous conception of the function of language. The ideas which one enlists by engaging in an investigation certainly are not random ones. They generally are the fruit of preliminary reflection or even of previous experience. Must the latter be invested with the guarantee of absolute correctness? That would be asking too much of it: it is sufficient for it to have a certain plausibility. These, then, are hypotheses which are proved by being tested. It may happen, in the process of research, that they have to be revised. Such a revision is by no means inadmissible or illegitimate. On the contrary, it is the most common procedure.

Must and can the preliminary ideas engaged in an investigation always be clearly explained? Very often, on the contrary, the preliminary idea emerges and is defined only according to the progress of the investigation. It is then not always easy to correct it if it turns out to be inadequate.

What is our own situation? We are precisely trying, in these preliminary remarks, to explain in a provisional form some guiding ideas without which it would be most difficult to conduct our analysis. Are we asking that these ideas should be taken for granted right away, and that they should be adopted as a first outline of a correct theory of language? Without going this far, we do believe that they have an undeniable plausibility and that it is therefore reasonable to consider them.

As far as their true justification is concerned, we shall, in order to present it, await the methodological commentaries which will conclude the present work; for, according to our method, it is in the light of the results obtained that we may judge the correctness of the preliminaries in the most accurate fashion.

Our research will at all times be informed by what has just been said about the function of language. But these are only fragmentary views which are still far from constituting a theory. In the following discussions, the meaning of the term *theory* will be modified to satisfy the requirements of an open methodology.*

Let us say for the moment that a theory for us is a discourse (a discursive system) of an explanatory character, utilizing for the purposes of improved knowledge a certain number of hypotheses on a specific, more or less demarcated area of research. Taken in this sense, a theory always represents a more or less successful attempt at explanation. It cannot therefore be considered correct before it has been tested. By extension we might define as a theory even a fragmentary and inadequate attempt at explanation, provided that it tends towards organizing itself into a coherent discourse. In this sense a theory is the kind of answer, more or less complete, which is appropriate to a problem such as the problem of language. In this extended sense, we might say about ourselves that we have already laid the foundations for a certain theory of language. Thus we have marked a certain guideline for the investigation to which we must invariably return. But it is equally necessary for us to be informed about the reflections and experiments of others in the field.

---

* We should not be expected to define, at this point, what the meaning of the word *theory* will be; while the investigation continues, i.e. as long as the exposé is not complete, the proposed meaning eludes any definite prediction. This remark does not transcend our former statements; it merely allows the word *theory* to benefit from its capacity for development, which it has by virtue of being a part of heuristic discourse, viz. the discourse of our exposé. The same, of course, is true of the expression *an open methodology*.

LITTRÉ'S THEORY OF ACCEPTATION

In the context of what has just been said, one of the first questions that comes to mind is the following: How do words acquire their meaning? This is also the question, obviously, which confronts all those who plan to establish a dictionary. If someone forms the project of systematically conferring a precise meaning on all words used in a language, does he not have to explain in advance how he expects to achieve this? Should he not in advance explain his *theory of acceptation,* since it would be unthinkable for him to be without one? Every great dictionary, in our opinion, should contain an explanation of the linguistic theory on which it is based. Such an explanation would offer an opportunity to face the problems which inevitably arise from the radical antagonism between the concern for maintaining the purity of a language on the one hand and the concern for rejuvenating this language on the other. It may seem surprising, but this "preliminary chapter," the most fundamental and the most interesting part a dictionary might include, is usually missing.

This is not true, however, for the dictionary of the French language by Littré, who in his preface explains and defends the theory of language on which the entire work is based.

"Every living language," he writes, "above all every language belonging to a great people and to a great development of civilization, exhibits three stages: a contemporary usage which is the appropriate one for each successive period; an archaic usage which formerly was the contemporary one; and, finally, a neologism which may corrupt the language if managed badly, develop it if managed well, and which in turn will one day become an archaism" (Preface to the dictionary, pp. 3, 4).

Nothing could emphasize more clearly and more incisively the evolutive character of a living language.

"I wish to explain," one further reads, "defining the present dictionary, that it includes and combines the present usage of the language and the usage of the past, in order to confer upon the present usage the entire fullness and soundness belonging to it" (p. 2).

Littré moreover proposes to conduct his enterprise in an entirely positive fashion. He begins with the statement that it is necessary to transfer the language of the natural sciences (i.e. the sciences of observation) to the science of words, that the materials used by the latter are the equivalents of experimental facts, and he moreover defines the dictionary as "a collection of positive observations and experiments designed to clarify usage and grammar."

In this positive spirit Littré intends to use the observation of the evolutive movement of the meaning of words as the means par excellence for the clarification and definition of their contemporary meaning. "I was so impressed," he writes, "by the correlations between modern French and ancient French, and I noticed so many cases where the meanings and expressions of today cannot be explained except through the meanings and expressions of former times, that it seemed to me that the theory and even the practice of language are not well established unless they rest on their ancient foundations. The past of a language immediately directs the mind towards its future."

In a more definite way, Littré proposes the following rule for the explanation of words:

"This is what I call explaining a word: one completes gaps of meaning by supplying intermediary forms from the various periods of the language, and one shows how the words relate to the etymology by slender but firm connections" (p. 12).

"A word, which has nothing in its unknown original creation that would permit us to consider it as accidental, is even less so in the languages of secondary formation, such as the Romance languages, the French in particular; it is fully determined, with a primal sense, through Latin, Germanic, Celtic, or any other source from which it may originate. This is where we find the raw material of the meanings which emerge in the words. . . . If we agree on this the derivative meanings which are the achievement and the creation of succeeding generations doubtless are diverted from their point of departure, but only according to procedures which, developing either the literal meaning or the metaphorical sense, have nothing arbitrary or unsystematic." Finally, we quote the following passage: "The function of etymology is to break up a word into its radicals or parts; ascertaining the meaning of each of these parts permits us to understand how the human mind has proceeded in going from simple and elementary meanings to derivative and complex ones."

The preceding quotations clearly demonstrate how Littré defines an acceptation, or rather a contemporary acceptation. The discussion of the problem is not closed, however. What has been outlined is a "practice of the determination of meaning," and we still have to discuss its scope and its soundness.

The first obstacle, inevitable in the elaboration of a dictionary, is the vicious circle. It inevitably results if one intends to treat the explanation of the meaning of a word as a simple matter of definition. This was already noted by Pascal. The vocabulary of a language is not infinite. The number of words it contains, on the contrary, is finite. Compared to the "big numbers" of physics and astronomy it is even a small number. Now, if I define a word by means of words, the latter in turn must be defined, and so on. Then the moment will soon arrive when the total of available words, especially those which I might utilize, will be exhausted. I will thus have no choice but to fall back on words I already used: the vicious circle will be closed.

The analysis of synonyms especially tends to reveal this inevitable trap. The French *Académie*, for example, defines the word *fier* ("proud") by the synonyms *hautain, altier*, while it defines *hautain* by *fier, orgueilleux.*

In this case the definition certainly does not go far afield before undercutting itself.

Does Littré do better than the Académie? He claims that he does. For him the true link of synonymity between *hautain* and *altier* as well as, at the same time, the nuance which must differentiate between them, is made clear and precise by the connection of the adjective *haut* with the two preceding terms, *haut* being taken in its moral sense; it is then noted that all three terms have a common background of meaning determined by the Latin adjective, *altus*. As far as this latter word is concerned, Littré's method does not go any further. The word is accepted as such, being the raw material from which *haut, hautain,* and *altier* are derived.

This method in fact avoids the vicious circle of the strict definition which tends to anchor itself firmly somewhere. It is immediately obvious in what its proper value consists: the contemporary French language is illuminated and explained by the investigation of its formative process from the Latin (and, to be sure, from other languages as well, to which it owes its present form). There can be no doubt about the effectiveness of this method. For current usage it certainly succeeds in defining the contemporary connotations. But, is it capable of defining them perfectly and completely? This is quite a different question, to which we shall presently return.

But is the vicious circle actually broken? In its artificiality as a Romance language, French takes us back to Latin. Is this really a satisfactory solution? Must not Latin in turn be discovered and explained as a language of civilization, with the same justification as French, as one would also have to do with Greek if he wished to investigate it for everything the French language owes to Greek? This is an exigency to which Littré does not pay attention. As far as we are concerned we feel that this exigency cannot be dealt with except in an analysis of the significations which would implement Littré's method in the strict sense and without arbitrary limitations. Is it not in fact utterly arbitrary to terminate the analysis as soon as one reaches the Latin roots? We have no reason to assume that the analysis is completed and that, for example, the meaning of the word *altus* in Latin should not be examined in the same way as *haut* must be examined in French.*

Thus, if going back to Latin permits us to avoid the vicious circle at the level of French, it nevertheless leaves entirely unsolved, at the level of Latin, the question from which we started: How do meanings come to words—this time, to Latin words?

Littré thus avoids the vicious circle only at the price of a questionable decision: not to apply to Latin the method which he himself has devised for application to French. This decision

* It will be understood why, in the present discussion, we only made brief mention of Germanic, Celtic, and other roots. For our purposes it is of course sufficient to keep to the example of Latin.

appears to us arbitrary, but it did not seem so to him. He justified his method by the existence, by the historical and logical pre-existence of well-determined acceptations which the lexicographers would have to isolate with all desirable precision. The method thus is being completed by means of a principle which, to use a convenient term, we shall define as the *principle of determinate acceptations.*

Having thus defined the principle, we shall seek to press more closely the sense in which it must be understood. One might expect to find a clue in the acceptation which Littré's dictionary offers for the term acceptation. This is what one finds there: "manner to take a word, meaning which is given to it."

Is this a well-determined acceptation, one which would not require further elaboration in order to be complete? Apparently this is not the case. On the contrary, the acceptation appears to be incomplete and in need of a better explanation. We shall certainly be told that, by limiting ourselves to the preceding "definition," we do not really apply Littré's method. We have not proceeded to the etymological analysis which would reveal the roots from which the word has sprung. We have not followed the evolution of its actual meaning throughout its history, which could be done only by inserting the word into appropriate contexts. We have not been present at the evolution of meaning, in which we could only participate through the sequence of its contexts. Littré's method certainly would require all this. All the same, we do not get the impression that, even if we had not neglected anything, the meaning of the word *acceptation,* the meaning appropriate for today, might be delivered to us ready-made.

What troubles us is the feeling of not having sufficiently understood, even, perhaps, of not having understood at all, what is meant by a determinate acceptation. First of all we must ask how such a concept and a principle of determined acceptations can be compatible with the evolutive quality of language, a quality which in turn cannot be doubted.

In one of our quotations we have reminded the reader that Littré considered it correct to use, in questions of linguistics, the vocabulary elaborated by the natural sciences. Accordingly we feel justified to give some consideration first of all to the evolution of natural species and to the theoretical conceptions associated with it.

It is well known that the idea of a natural classification of vegetable and animal forms is not incompatible with the idea of the evolution of the species. If one assumes that every form of life has evolved from a previous form, a form which preceded it in time, one must infer from this the possible, if not completely elucidated, existence of a genealogical tree, according to which all the past and present forms of life must be able to be classified. Conversely, the actual existence of a natural classification of this type may validly be invoked in favor of an evolutive conception of the forms which life has assumed on our planet. Let us imagine this genealogical tree as established and let E be a species occupying the extreme end of a certain branch. Could we say that we are concerned with a determinate species? Why not? It is that insofar as it is possible to vindicate the idea of a species. But one might say exactly the same concerning any other form E' (species, genre, etc.) which would precede it. Would we say, concerning one form or the other or all of them together, that these forms were predetermined? That is an entirely different matter.

One may imagine here the following three ways in which to interpret the word "determinate":

a) First of all, one may assume that every form of life existing at a particular moment in history is or was the form of realization, the actualization of a potential form which therefore preexisted. For each form of life, there would thus be a form of metaphysical character irrevocably predestined for it.

This hypothesis does not necessarily exclude an evolutionist interpretation. One can still imagine that in the realm of potentialities the potential forms are ordered in such a way that the forms of life succeeding each other in time along a line of evolution thereby only actualize the atemporal order of succession.

We have a very strong feeling that, in a theory of evolution, recourse to a background of potentiality can only be a useless additional task. The other two hypotheses to be described are free from it, the first in an imperfect way, the second totally.

b) In a less rigorous fashion, one may imagine that what is proposed for actualization is not a potential form predestined for each of the forms of life following each other along a line of evolution, but only an ultimate form, a form towards which the forms of life would have to progress as if towards an aim. These ultimate forms alone would constitute the background of potentiality whose actualizations would have to be joined together across the transformations linked to environment and circumstances.

According to this interpretation, the "new" could actualize itself in transitory forms which are not predestined.

c) Finally one may note that, as far as the forms are concerned in which life presents itself today or has once presented itself, the knowledge we have of it was not acquired through the transition from a potential to an actual state. Nothing shows that we are capable of deploying the preliminary vision of a world of potentiality, the awareness of which might guide our knowledge of the actualized world. In fact, the potentialities are given to us only as a kind of understudies for the appearances of reality. And we shall make no progress as long as we do not have access to the principle permitting us to build in its autonomy the universe of actualizable potentialities. Under these circumstances it is perfectly useless to invoke the potential in order to explain or justify the actual. Notwithstanding a certain philosophic tradition, that would be no more than a sterile artifice. Should we then give up, purely and simply?

On the other hand, it is clear that by such a decision one would not elucidate the problem of evolution but only put it into another form. It makes sense to rip it out of its context, whose uselessness is known, only if one intends to treat it as a relevant problem of scientific research. One may persevere in the project of formulating an adequate theory of evolution, but it is only with the help of the disciplines of science, in their spirit, and with their means and vocabulary, that such a project will regain its chance of success.

By bending hypothesis *a* towards *b* in order to arrive at *c* we invoke, in brief, the radical conversion which the problem of evolution undergoes in passing from the purely discursive domain to the domain of objective research. The meaning of the word "determinate" is also implicated in this conversion. Of a form which one intends to describe he will always feel and say that it is determinate. But although the word remains the same, its acceptation changes. It depends on the context which in its turn changes to adapt to the transformation of viewpoints.

To return to our problem, i.e. acceptation, we shall try to make good use of this brief analysis. Not that we would establish a rigorous analogy between the evolution of living forms and that of discursive forms. We only plan to identify, for words and their acceptations, three cases where the correspondences are similar to those of the three preceding cases. In order to emphasize the parallelism we shall designate the cases a', b', and c' respectively.

a') It can be imagined that there exists, in the form of potentialities, a certain group of acceptations susceptible of actualization at a given moment in history, through a given word figuring in a given fragment of discourse.

In formulating this hypothesis, it should be stressed that we do not presuppose a univocal and reciprocal relationship between words and their acceptations, i.e. a relationship that would attribute precisely one acceptation, the correct one, to each word in particular, and one definite word, the proper one, to each particular acceptation. A living language so rigidly constructed does not exist and never has. It certainly is not in such a simple manner that words acquire their meanings. The notion of a double catalogue, one for correct acceptations and the other for proper expressions, which could simply be connected in order to say anything and to say it well, does not take into account, or rather takes into account in a highly unsatisfactory way, the complex and many-shaded interplay of expressions and significations.

But, one may object, is not this the very idea which guides the production of every serious dictionary? If such were the case the value and the explanatory power of a dictionary would be severely limited. But we shall see, by means of quotations from the *Littré*, that this is a dictionary which exemplifies a different type.

If we would stop here, the hypothesis just formulated would entail a much more flexible practice. It would simply require that, if a word is given in its context, and this context in turn is inserted into its place within the history of language, one could,

under these given circumstances, associate a well-defined acceptation with it. The task of the lexicographer would consist in dis-
covering and applying the means to isolate this acceptation and
to make it precisely understood. Would these acceptations be
fixated forever? Hypothesis *a'* does not go so far; while the acceptations are momentary in principle, it is enough for them to
represent, in practice, a certain stability.

We have said that, in the conception of Littré, the fundamentally evolutive character of language is combined with a certain
principle of determinate acceptations, while evolution somehow
takes over a certain total of predetermined acceptations. Thus
this concept might hold in the framework of the first hypothesis.

But the latter is essentially heterogeneous; it projects a practice from which no subtlety is principally excluded against a
metaphysical background whose elements appear only through
the circumstances and the peripeties of actualization—by means
of the expedient which one might call a reverse actualization.
The situation certainly would be entirely different if the acceptations could be delivered in a pure state; but this is impossible,
and we are therefore led to believe that the metaphysical backdrop is nothing but an artificial and embarrassing overload.

Hypotheses *b'* and *c'* moreover will show how we can free ourselves from it.

b') This hypothesis mediates between the preceding one and
the following one. It is arrived at by the separation of the notion
of acceptation from its metaphysical backdrop and its transfer to
the forefront of the investigation. During an investigation the
knowledge of which we are capable is not measured by the
greater or lesser distance separating it from an ideal knowledge
which is not directly accessible to us. This knowledge is simply
what circumstances permit it to be for us. It is not necessary or
even useful to imagine, after this "for us," an "as such" which
would be revealed to us only afterwards. But it is impossible completely to dispense with every reference or recourse to the idea
of a complete knowledge. This idea may remain on the horizon
of the investigation. Then it could play the rôle of a guiding idea,
without which certain minds can hardly operate.

Speaking of the knowledge which can be ours, we have in mind the acceptations which we can use; what has been said about the former may easily be applied to the latter, and to the changes and modifications affecting them.

c') One may finally go all the way to the limits of the idea according to which an acceptation can be what it is for us without having to be anchored in a universe of preexisting acceptations. What would be the advantage of this approach? We cannot at this point repeat the remarks to which case *c* has given rise; one does not elucidate the problem of acceptation by completely detaching it from hypothesis *a'* or any other hypothesis of the same type; one merely restates the problem. For a meaningful procedure we must have something to propose as a substitute for the principle of predetermined acceptations, as it is done in an objective analysis. Do we have, at this point, such a hypothesis available? In the following section we shall outline a principle of sketched acceptations likely to run counter to the principle of predetermined acceptations. It is in fact necessary, in order to be able to treat the problem of acceptation in a perspective of objectivity, to invoke a new notion, the notion of open acceptation, around which a new explanatory language must organize itself.

This is the course to which we shall commit ourselves. Our method does not imply an attempt to justify this choice, to demonstrate that it is well founded, by means of a previously existing discourse. There can be no question of proofs but rather of confirmations. It will be established that the eventuality *c'* conforms to a conception of language capable of integration into an open methodology of objective knowledge.

As far as our own position is concerned, these are the points which the preceding considerations give us occasion to specify. From among Littré's statements about language, we select two very distinct groups, one of which, as it seems to us, should be retained, while the other should be rejected. The first group implies the confirmation of the evolutive character of any living language and the practice based on it of explaining and elaborating the meaning of the words. The second group implies everything connected with the existence of predetermined acceptations.

We have sufficiently emphasized the fact that a language

which is being used also develops. We count this fact among the number of undeniable, proven facts. We add that, in order to be admitted as such, a fact does not have to be justified discursively. In order to know that a stone falls, or that it has fallen, it is not necessary for us to have conferred upon it, by means of words, its right to fall.

Neither do we intend to cast doubts upon the effectiveness of a certain practice of elaboration of the meaning of words. All the dictionaries of the world exemplify this practice, Littré in particular. We shall not hesitate to utilize this method without awaiting any further justifications other than its own success, even if that does not mean the production of completely realized acceptations. It will be all the more necessary for us to review and examine this procedure more closely in order to discover its key element, the one factor which appears to account for its effectiveness, the *procedure of the context*.

We avoid any assumptions about predetermined acceptations as being superfluous as well as inadequate. The first of these objections alone would suffice.

THE PROCEDURE OF THE CONTEXT

Throughout our critique of Littré's statements we have sought to disengage the outlines of our own method, of the method that is already ours. When all is said and done concerning this critique, what remains of it? Littré's doctrine presented itself as a kind of linguistic positivism, but we would hesitate to define it as such. We think that a method should be considered positive only if it is capable of isolating, together with its own principles, the guarantees with which it fortifies these principles, and the circumstances and means by which it proves them. This is precisely what Littré's theory of language does not do; it postulates the existence of a level of correct acceptations as if this were not a question of a hypothesis, a proven hypothesis perhaps, but nevertheless one still subject to the counter action of the experiment. In fact, the critique of Littré's views thus leaves us without a satisfactory theory of language, in particular a theory of acceptation on which we might hope to build the analytic practice to attack the problem of time. Are we then left without any resources? We already have said that there remains for us a practice of the fixations of acceptations. There even remains a practice tested a thousand times, only we should not expect that it infallibly reveal acceptations having the quality of definitive discursive entities.

In what does this practice consist? It lets a word, and the acceptation it must assume, participate in a fragment of text or even in a text of a certain importance; the sense of this text should be unproblematic. Again, this is the reason why we shall propose to call this method the procedure of the context.

This way of presenting the method cannot fail, we think, to provoke the following objection: "In order to form the project of defining the sense of a word by its insertion into a context, it is of course necessary that the meaning of this word should not yet be given with complete precision. The meaning must still be incomplete. But in that case, how can a text employing this word be unproblematic? Is not the truth rather that such a definition itself is a problematic one?" This objection appears to be embarrassing, but it is prompted by an analytical conception of language which bypasses reality.

Let us assume that I write, "The six sides of a hexagon. . . ." After having written it, I know that the hexagon is a polygon with six angles, even if I had not known it before, provided that I have some knowledge of drawing. This brief phrase, which is not even a complete sentence, could not be adapted to a definition. If it can teach a person who does not know it that the hexagon is a figure with six sides and, consequently, six angles, it does so not because it is descriptive but because it is allusive. The phrase alludes, not to all the circumstances in which written words, including the word whose meaning is unknown, might be interpreted, but to certain words among them which our memory highlights with a certain discursive halo. In its near instantaneousness, the development of this process defies analysis. But the result is no less certain: the acceptation of the word hexagon which fits into this fragment of text emerges well defined.

The following example is more sophisticated. Let us take up again the acceptation which the *Littré* gives for the word *accep-*

tation: "manner of taking a word, meaning which is given to it." Does this short phrase really define the meaning of the word *acceptation?* In a certain sense, yes. We shall not try to find out whether, thus defined, this meaning can also be called complete. We do not have any means to decide this question. Let us rather direct our attention towards the verb *to take.* The meaning it has in this case is not its most common one but rather the opposite. Let us assume that we must define this meaning clearly. How could we go about it, and how would a dictionary go about it? Is there a simpler and more effective method than just giving an example of this specific usage, the only one which furnishes the definition of the acceptation mentioned before? This definition is not problematic for the purpose in question. The verb *to take* which is being taken (it is not for a mere play upon words that we are multiplying the other usages of the verb *to take*) is thus defined through its usage, through the fact of being a part of this context. Contrary to what would be expected of a purely logical analysis, the meaning of the text, taken as a whole, confers more precision upon the meaning of one of its parts; and the sense of the latter, thus defined more clearly, in its turn confers more clarity upon the meaning as a whole.

We shall later give numerous examples of the procedure of the context. The rôle which we now attribute to it shall become more explicit but in the process shall progressively spread to all the areas which are connected with the discursive.*

But, does not the method which Littré proposes transcend the procedure of the context in this sense?

Let us recall how Littré feels entitled to proceed. The previous existence of acceptations to be isolated and defined, and the validity of the notion of acceptations itself do not represent for him any limitations. Without doubt the contemporary sense of a word represents only a moment, the last moment for us, of an evolution which may always be continued by neologisms. To fixate a mean-

---

* The method which we are now starting to discuss through the expedient of an assured practice, and which shall be progressively expanded, will also be the object of a discussion in an attempt at synthesis towards the end of the present work, viz. in our "Methodological Commentary and Conclusions." The method will then be shown in its proper position within a general methodology of open knowledge.

ing thus means to follow a line of evolution in order to arrive at an actual sense, but without the implication that this sense were to mark a point at which the evolution would stop. We disagree with Littré in this respect. He believes that the meaning to be arrived at is perfectly assured by the exhibition of its etymological roots on the one hand and by the rigor, sufficient in his view, of the laws governing the evolution of languages on the other. We believe, however, that it is necessary to proceed to a more fundamental examination of the lexicographer's actual situation and to invoke, at least tentatively, the open acceptation which shall be introduced in a moment.

So much, then, for the theoretical position of Littré. But what is its practical application? The theory operates with the help of appropriate quotations. It follows the evolution of acceptations through borrowings from authors, ranging from the Middle Ages to the nineteenth century. It has been said again and again that this is the principal contribution of Littré's dictionary. In fact it constitutes its enduring value, whereas the etymologies to which Littré attributed so much importance in many cases have turned out to be illusory. On the whole, Littré only applies the procedure of the context. The context in this case admittedly is not a simple fragment of text but rather an ordered sequence of quotations, an enlarged context having historical depth. But nothing prevents us from extending the idea and the spirit of the procedure of the context towards a context thus amplified. At this point we do not have any theory of acceptation with which Littré's theory could be replaced; the latter only offers, in our opinion, a rather artificial and even inadequate frame for the practice of the context. But this practice does not have to be theoretically justified in order to be effective. The latter is of the order of proven facts. It certainly is not an absolute effectiveness, but there is a certain level of activity where it is undeniable. Even at this point it offers us an advantage which we shall not hesitate to utilize, being free to turn back and to review the circumstances of its setup if we think it useful or necessary.

The intention by which the procedure of the context is informed may be presented in the most general way: it is to confer a higher degree of determinism or precision to a material which lends itself to it, by viewing it integrated into a certain whole. A whole deserves its name only if it is coherent. But there are various degrees in the fashion in which it can be given and, consequently, there also are degrees in the fashion in which we can consider it as coherent. There exists no rule for deciding this question in advance and forever. The rule which takes precedence over everything is that, while being engaged in a process of judgment, we have retained our liberty of reconsideration while taking into account the experiences we have gathered.

The matter to which the method may be applied is not necessarily an acceptation; it may also be a piece of information, an idea, a project, a program of action, a more or less delimited activity, etc. The definition, if it really means anything, can be viewed under this aspect. But this is only a very special example. Any other sector of our activity could serve as well, provided that our faculty of analysis may get a foothold in it.

THE OUTLINED ACCEPTATIONS

It is admittedly difficult to tell what a well-defined acceptation should be. Let us assume, improbable as it sounds, that someone does not know what a *tree* is. Will it suffice to show him a pine tree, for example, in order that the acceptation of the word be defined to its full extent? If he sees an oak, will the person immediately take it for another tree? One may doubt that he would. On the other hand, as soon as he has made the definition for an oak tree, he will then probably not hesitate to do likewise for a linden tree, for a poplar, and even for a willow. This means that the fixation of the acceptation here is comparable to a diagram which implies a rather wide margin of interpretation. But will this diagram suffice for the distinction of a tree from other tree-like forms of vegetation, such as, for example, certain arborescent ferns? Nothing permits us to assume that this would be the case. One may even say that, on the contrary, only when one starts from a more fundamental knowledge of the nature of a tree can the distinction be made at all.

In other cases, in order to attain an acceptation of a certain precision, one must consider its purpose, its mode of usage, its origin, its genesis, or its form. In short, the acceptation implies multiple aspects; it is connected with multiple notions and with multiple activities, and its determination does not exceed the determination of these notions and these activities.

This last remark at least partly facilitates our understanding of the procedure of the context. This procedure would not function if the acceptations and the discursive entities were given and grasped completely and immediately. Let us repeat that for us the effectiveness of the procedure is a proven fact. We do not have to justify it in the name of any previous theory of acceptation. On the contrary, it is this procedure which must serve as a touchstone. The problem is to know how one must conceive the acceptation so that the procedure of the context can function. Considered under this aspect, the problem has only one answer: the acceptation must be conceived as an *open* one, i.e. as an acceptation still capable of further, more exact determination.

Subjectively, the acceptation is everything which it evokes in me, while I am in expectation of all the services it will be able to render me. Intersubjectively, it is the same for others by the same capacity. Objectively, the acceptation is what it is by providing the guarantees through which objectivity is established. Is it image, scheme, outline, project, program of action, or something else still? Depending on the individual case, we conceive of it most easily under one or other of the above aspects. Each of them accordingly must be said to be open in the sense indicated above.

The following examples will permit us to illustrate the idea of openness and to orient it towards the strongest meaning we intend to give it:

The map of a country is never a completely finished thing. Not only can it never be a perfectly true representation of everything which constitutes the actuality of this country, but moreover this actuality is never completely fixated, stabilized, and crystallized in any definitive form. The map is thus incomplete in two respects:

1. Its function is not to represent everything.

2. What can be represented is only one aspect of a reality which inevitably is subject to change.

The map accordingly is the vehicle of an open representation.

The portrait of a man never gives his perfect likeness, which could not be improved by further details, and to which no further traits might be added. If this is so, the reason is not only that the painter, if he wants to include everything, is likely to miss out on what makes the essential value of the picture, but also because a portrait cannot claim to be perfectly accurate. The person represented by the portrait is not fully present in any of his momentary aspects, and one may miss an essential element by laying too much stress on the appearance of the moment. A portrait thus is likewise an open representation:

1. It is never possible to include everything.

2. What can be represented is only one aspect of a whole which is changing because of the very fact that it exists.

A sculptor who says that he has just made a sketch for a statue could take the act of sketching in one of two ways: "I had," he might say, "a very definite idea of the statue I wanted to create. It was to some extent already there, before what you might call the inner eye. Of this ideal statue, I have so far only been able to make a first approximation. I shall retouch it, I shall correct it so well that I will finally succeed in creating from it the faithful realization of the model which preexisted in my mind." Likewise, the artist might have said, "This is the sketch of a statue whose image is haunting me. But don't think that I know in advance the definitive shape it will eventually take. This shape may not even exist as yet, except in an incomplete form, in this sketch. From the sketch several statues might emerge, as it seems to me—possibly even an unlimited number of statues. Which will be the one that emerges from my efforts? I do not know yet. Perhaps this first sketch will help me create a form which satisfies me, and perhaps I shall gradually realize what I shall do, what I shall be able to achieve from this unfinished shape." We should say that the first case represents the realization, still incomplete, of a preexisting model, of a sketch which by a certain amount of effort may be approximated ever more closely towards the idea which it must represent. Of the second case we should say that it is a *sketch in the strong meaning* of a provisional expression of an idea which is still open and in the process of developing.

Here, then, are two meanings of the term *sketch* which differ widely from each other. We shall adopt the second alternative. This is the meaning in which we may speak of a sketched idea or of a meaning which has the quality of a sketch. In the same sense we would say that an idea or a notion is open. To return to the acceptation, now one single word will be enough for us to designate the quality which enables it to participate in the procedure of the context, viz. the word *openness:* the acceptation simply must have a certain capacity of openness.

Is it not sufficient for an acceptation to be capable of evolution in order to be, by virtue of this fact alone, an open acceptation? We have distinguished three ways to imagine an evolution. Figuratively speaking, one might say that, according to the first way, evolution does not outline anything but rather actualizes a sequence of preformed models; according to the second way, evolution puts to work the sketch of a predefined form which it tries to realize progressively; only according to the third way does evolution pursue, throughout a sequence of forms, a sketch in the strong meaning, whose achievement remains suspended.

It is of course easy to amplify in many directions what has just been said. Thus we may note that only in the third case which was discussed above could an evolution be characterized as open. Let us anticipate here a possible misunderstanding: an open evolution is not necessarily a haphazard evolution. It will suffice to return once more to the example of the sculptor and his statue in order to understand this fact.

THE PROBLEM OF EXPOSITION

The Acquisition of Language

The description of the procedure of the context has not clarified the problem of acceptation. The procedure can help us define the meaning of a word within a passage whose sense, as far as it is understood, is unproblematic. But how does this passage acquire its own meaning? So far we have done nothing to give an explanation for this. We have merely stated that the procedure really works. This fact may be surprising, for it is irreconcilable with those opinions about language which appear to be most natural. One might think in fact that if a text is to take on meaning, the same should first be true of all the sentences of which it consists, and the latter can only refer us in turn to the meaning of the words which they contain. Thus it seems that a well-conducted analysis of the text must begin with the well-defined determination of its elementary parts, i.e. words, in order to proceed afterwards to syntactically correct combinations of these words, and so on. Is the reversed order of procedure not contrary to all logic? According to the procedure of the context, this does not result in confusion. The first statement to be made is that if on paper the sentence consists of words which seem to be its parts or elements, this is only a semblance. The meaning of a sentence is a whole to which the meaning of each word certainly contributes, but not by simple juxtaposition or, more generally, by the fact of a purely additive principle of composition.* Certainly this is not the way in which sentences acquire their meaning.†

For a study of language and its functions, the metaphor of a machine which would be taken apart into its components and later put together again can only lead to error. The same is true of the example of the living organism, imagined as being built from molecules which in turn are built from atoms which in turn are built from still more elementary particles, in the hope of understanding and explaining everything by starting from the ultimate particles. However indispensable an analysis at a certain level of relative stability, one must beware of making inferences from it in favor of an analytic ideal guaranteed to elucidate the rôle of language from a totally analyzed situation. It is not enough to say that this ideal is unattainable; one must also realize that it leads the investigation towards faulty perspectives.

In fact—and this is another remark which we shall take very seriously—the method by which we ourselves have been put in

---

* A purely additive principle of composition would be a law combining into a whole the meaning of the elements which are part of it, while the meaning of the elements is not modified or altered by the fact of their participation.

† It is obvious that this remark comes close to a certain logical analysis of language and even overlaps with it to some extent. For a first critique, this analysis may be useful and even necessary. But for an incisive and fundamental treatment of certain questions it is absolutely inadequate.

possession of the language we are using does not conform to any analytic ideal. This is a universal experience made by one generation after another. Why not acknowledge this fact and learn from it?

We actually come into possession of a preformed language by the detour of practice. We enter this language at a certain moment of its evolution, but the practice guiding us is wholly of the present. But most important, it is not a practice of a discursivity which could be separated from our activity in general. It is not even enough to say that it is an integral part of this activity. It is rather an aspect which relates to all other aspects, penetrates all other aspects, and is in active and passive communication with all other aspects.

If one keeps gazing at an analytic ideal he will never run out of objections. He wants to invoke a different genesis of language. For him, language must not be born in ambiguity, caught in the traps of every emotion, of all ignorance, of all erroneous notions and hasty interpretations. He seeks a pure source for language.

As for us, we are content to find in language a first point of support, to emphasize among all the prerogatives of language the one to which we are called as participants: it permits dialogue. This dialogue is not exclusive, restricted to some privileged partners and covering only a reserved sector of their activity, thought, or emotions. On the contrary, this is a dialogue which may be established between members of vast linguistic communities, and which is not encumbered by any obstacles originating in its own nature. Not all persons participate in the dialogue after the same manner, but no one is excluded on principle; all things are not grasped and treated in it after the most correct fashion, but nothing appears to be out of reach. This dialogue, in a rather elementary sense which must not be pushed towards the absolute, is general and universal: general, because it is open to all; universal, because it is open to everything.

Monsieur Jourdain is surprised at having spoken in prose without knowing it, and the public laughs. But, are we so much more advanced than he is concerning the dialogue in which we naturally participate? What could we say about it before seriously thinking it over?

I speak to someone who answers me in turn, and a dialogue is established. Who would think of wondering at this? Now, dialogue reveals a fact which is fundamental not only for myself or another person but for everyone at the same time: the fact that we possess a common language assures us of mutual understanding.

The domain to which this language gives access is not defined in advance, once and forever, or for everyone at the same time, and the understanding of which it is the instrument is not total. Nevertheless, what it is capable to express about beings and things is the most certain guarantee for the coordination of those activities which are necessary to maintain life in society.

This fact is elementary and defies all objections. One might insist upon the fact that language, the vehicle of dialogue, is an imperfect instrument and that not infrequently dialogue ends in discord. This remark is certainly correct, but the fact which we have defined as elementary remains valid all the same.

It may appear paradoxical to attribute so much effectiveness to mere combinations of words before having understood how each of them acquires its meaning; as we have said before, in order to be what we are and to be able to do what we are doing, we do not need to give a coherent explanation in advance. As it presents itself this fact is undeniable; if one wished to draw a forced conclusion from our inability to fixate "as with an engraver's needle" the sense of the words before engaging them in the peripeties of the dialogue, it could only be the conclusion to which we already referred, viz. that the meaning of a word isolated from any context inevitably must retain a certain indetermination.

One may wonder how we acquire the language of dialogue, and through what kind of "osmosis" a common spoken language can become the language of each individual who speaks it; one may wonder especially why we know so little about this problem, why we have not become aware of it during the process of experience at least once while we were growing up in a preexisting linguistic milieu. This fact deserves close attention. Such a lack of immediate data about a process which has taken place in each of us and which is repeated everywhere around us must have reasons connected with the very manner in which the meaning *for us* comes to the words.

This is again one of the aspects of the problem to which we seek to give its due prominence and dimension, but it is no longer the aspect which we have emphasized so far. We are now concerned with an aspect related to ourselves, namely our capability of learning a language and the manner in which we succeed in doing so. This is the specifically psychological aspect of a question which implies many others; in a certain sense one may consider this aspect as complementary to the sociological aspect under which language appears in the capacity of a *common instrument of expression.*

This brings us back to the question, How do words acquire their meaning? It was to be expected, because this question has never ceased to be at the focus of our attention. The observations to which it has given rise so far have been of a rather eliminatory nature. We have discarded the eventuality of a cut-and-dried solution and preserved our option of an open one. But we are not as yet really engaged in the analytic investigation which must serve us as a field of experimentation; we only have announced and prepared it.

Nevertheless, in the preceding passage, brief as it is, we have just come one step further. We have done this simply by separating the psychological aspect of the problem of the *acquisition* of language from its sociological aspect.

We do not claim that these are the only aspects of the problem, or that they could be completely separated from the rest and treated each by itself. We shall explain immediately why we do not think that this would be possible. Nevertheless, the fact remains that we have just shown two angles from which the question may be approached, insofar as it belongs to two disciplines which are subject to the rules of objectivity. It cannot be denied that the psychological aspect, for example, may be discussed according to the already proven methods of genetic psychology. Likewise, it cannot be doubted that sociology is already able to provide us with some valuable indications as to the sociological aspects of the problem.

Explanatory Discourse and Heteronomous Discourse

How should the problem be understood? It seems useful to us at this point to mark the turn which our explanations will take. We must refer to what was said before about explanatory discourse. We already have sufficiently stressed its evolutive character so as not to have to repeat ourselves. Now we shall direct our attention to an entirely different aspect. The axiomatic method has produced the model of a discourse which unfolds from its own basis, without involving any experience other than this unfolding. Is it possible that this internal experience could be reversed towards its basis and be conducted so as to be reinterpreted or even revised? The example of geometry shows that it cannot be done. Let us compare with this model the passage where a rather sudden allusion is made to the psychological and sociological aspects of the problem of acquiring a language. If we ever had the notion that every explanatory discourse must conform to the geometric model, or approximate it, we cannot but recognize our error; if the passage in question has any meaning, it certainly does not come from the explanations which we have already offered, nor from the experience which we were able to make in giving them. The meaning of the passage derives from another source. It comes from whatever is specific in the knowledge and experience of the psychologist on the one hand and of the sociologist on the other.*

---

* In order to be well understood, i.e. in order to be interpreted according to our fundamental attitude, this last statement calls for some additional explanations. For anyone reading it, the meaning instantly actualizes itself as a function of the information derived from the psychology and the sociology of the information which the reader can bring into play. But this is only a provisional and incomplete actualization. It remains open towards information which transcends it in volume and depth and which might be defined as being both actual and potential at the same time: potential for our reader in whom it has not yet actualized itself completely, but actual for the psychologist and the sociologist because it is the information in which he participates at this moment. But the latter information, as well as the meaning of any statement which we could base upon it, is not definitive either; it remains open towards the experience of the future and the knowledge which shall be held by future psychologists and sociologists.

At this point in our text, the distinctions which we have described have an obvious significance, because they illustrate in a very simple fashion how the

It should be noted that the psychologist and the sociologist both need an already developed language in order to conduct and explain their research, but they cannot wait for the problem of language to be definitely elucidated and, in particular, for complete clarity to be reached on the ineluctable question of the acquisition of language. No one will deny their right to do so, since they proceed with undeniable effectiveness. Even if they do not mention it, they doubtless are not without certain preliminary views about their practice of explanatory discourse. Should their views not be correct beforehand in order to be legitimate? It is enough if they satisfy the following two conditions:

1. The views should not disagree with the practice of language which otherwise turns out to be effective.

2. They must remain open to revisions which might become necessary through the progress of the analysis.

This, then, is the turning point which we mentioned earlier; it appears that in order to transcend the elementary fact of the effectiveness of the dialogue for which the indispensable instrument is a common language, and in order to transcend the first consequences which may be drawn from this, objective research must concentrate on this language. It must do so without waiting for all the problems created by language to be solved, and even without having reached complete clarity about the process of acquiring a common language; the advancement of this research will shed light upon these problems, not all the light all at once, but a light in which the various aspects of the question shall appear with increasing clarity.

The fact which we have called elementary is then transferred from the perspective of current language to that of a language which is elaborated to correspond to certain systematic exigencies. It is not doubtful that the specialist of a discipline can acquire the mastery of a developed language thanks to which dialogue, a dialogue of increasing effectiveness, may be established between himself and other specialists of the same discipline. In order to be noticed and appreciated, this fact does not need to

---

meaning of a fragment of discourse may remain incomplete and open towards an exterior information, i.e. an information which is not inherent in the discourse and which does not develop from its unfolding alone.

be explained beforehand. The confirmation which the effectiveness of the dialogue has conferred on it at the level of the most general language is given by scientific research and its undeniable success at the level of the particular disciplines. It must be put beyond doubt even if research turns against language, against the language which it uses as well as the language of the most common usage.

As far as this fact is proven we shall not hesitate to utilize it by taking as object and milieu of analysis the language which is not yet engaged in any specialized research. Does this mean that we shall abandon forever any intention of justifying the fact upon which we propose to base our analysis? Absolutely not. But the elements of an idoneous explanatory discourse are not given in advance. We still have to isolate them and can only do so step by step. Only at the end of our study, in a review informed by all the peripeties of the road we have travelled, can these elements be properly arranged and used to formulate methodological comments and systematic conclusions.*

Nevertheless, what we have said about the participation of psychology and sociology in the problem of the acquisition of language even at this point shall permit us to evoke with greater precision the second characteristic of explanatory discourse, which we propose to emphasize. For this purpose we will introduce two new words to our vocabulary. Earlier we had contrasted the discourse capable of autonomous development with the discourse depending upon information, experience, or author-

---

* Before we proceed, we will state some of our reasons for thinking that neither psychology nor sociology is capable of specifying, in a fundamental way and independent from each other, the psychological and the sociological aspects of the problem of acquiring a language; for these disciplines cannot fail to encounter, in the light of their own progress, the problem of the language which they use. Thus both disciplines would have to take into account, either to confirm or to reject, the previous views which their practice implies. For both disciplines the correctness of these views will become part of their pursuit of research insofar as it is a preliminary condition of effectiveness.

Thus the two disciplines shall again be united in the common concern of elaborating language, as they have been at the beginning, in their common practice of a not yet specialized language. These brief explanations do not have to be interpreted as an attempt at demonstration. The dialectic structure of the method attributed to them at this point merely anticipates the results which finally will be attained by our own investigation.

ity from without. Let the former be defined as *holonomous* and the second as *heteronomous.*†

Having thus projected in our own discourse the fundamental distinction which we have to keep in mind, it is now easy for us to point out, by naming it, the character which must be associated with the evolutive character of every explanatory discourse; by virtue of its function the latter cannot but be a heteronomous discourse. At this very moment, our own exposition gives an illustration for this by the manner in which it is integrated; this is especially true for the epithet *heteronomous.* How does this word take on its meaning? We are at least partly able to tell because the meaning comes from us and through the intermediary of our own explanations. Let us first emphasize the fact that this word does not contain the experience which underlies it but only represents this experience. In a certain sense the word is only the trace of the experience. The latter thus participates in the formation of the meaning of the word only as far as we are able to keep track of it. This meaning is neither given in advance nor given once and for all, nor is it predetermined or complete. It has the status of incompleteness; it remains open to every complement and every revision of information to which, for any one or eventually for all at the same time, the practice of heteronomous discourse might give rise. This meaning inevitably must also be modified by the relations which will be established, from the fact of its being employed, between the word in question and the other words of the discourse. But all that is said here concerning the term *heteronomous* has already been said concerning psychology and sociology. We would not gain much by adding more examples at this point. It seems to us more useful to formulate some conclusions relative to the discourse of exposition. These conclusions will be far from definitive, however; they still must be subjected to the test represented by our exposition.

As we have seen, the problem of acceptation flows into the

† Holonomous discourse must not be confounded with a predicative discourse whose characteristic is that it can develop without ever questioning again what it has acquired. As we just said, it is not excluded that the structure of holonomous discourse could be dialectic; the structure of a predicative discourse never is.

problem of exposition. We have noted in fact that the meaning of a word may be defined by the method of the context. Now, this method requires the word to be part of a fragment of text. How does the latter acquire its meaning? How, still more generally, does the aggregate of texts which form an exposition assume its explanatory power? This is the problem of exposition.

But the fact that the texts of which an exposition consists represent a heteronomous discourse does not permit us to hope for the solution of the problem to be isolated at the level of discursive activity alone. Again, we are referred towards a larger context of which explanatory activity represents merely one aspect: the context of effective action in all "dimensions" whose traces a language can receive and carry. Thus it appears that language, for every sector of our activities, can play the rôle of a milieu of representation. It is true that no sector of our activities is represented in it as it is now, and even less that it might be in the future. Sometimes there is simply an allusion which would remain devoid of sense without a certain extrinsic knowledge of the *matter* in hand; or the discursive material may lend itself to a certain expressive form. But language is never a notation which could determine, by the mere fact of being that notation, a well-defined interpretation which would confer upon it *its own* signification.

One may try out a number of words to illustrate how language bears the marks, traces, and signs of what one succeeds in making it say. Those which come to mind most naturally are representation, projection, and mapping.

These words have something in common: the operations described by them may all be accompanied by a loss of extension, of dimension, of capacity of variation. As a result the "original," i.e. *that* which is being represented, *that* which is being mapped, cannot be retrieved or reestablished in its integrity without the implication of contexts of activity of which these operations are an integral part. Here we find again the quality of incompleteness which inevitably marks the heteronomous discourse. But if we would limit ourselves to the problems of representation, projection, and mapping offered by mathematics, this would not be the kind of incompleteness we try to grasp at this moment. It would be an incompleteness of a mathematical nature, rather than an incompleteness of openness relative to all possible dimensions of our activity.

For lack of a better word, we shall say meanwhile that language is a universal domain of mapping, a domain relevant to the entire context of our activities, capable of receiving, carrying, and conveying their traces in more or less accurate form, and finally being integrated with them to take its meaning therein.

This is the language which the discourse of exposition employs. The person who makes an exposé invites the one listening to it, or reading it, to share with him an experiment which could not be conducted without the help of language, but whose elements are inherent in language only to a slight degree. In a procedure whose stages the exposé points out, the mind must be ready to acknowledge not only the words but also that which the words serve to recall, to evoke, and to suggest. This procedure merges into certain judgments and conclusions which certainly shall need words to be expressed, but for which, again, these words are only traces, and which therefore shall not establish contact between these words in reality, but rather between *those things* of which they are the "discursive appearances;" in this case the experiment, thus conducted, shall be a success.

But what should be said about the manner in which relations must be established between the informational materials to which language refers us? This question would immediately lead us beyond the preliminary considerations which we felt had to be treated at such length.

As to holonomous discourse, we shall later see how it may conveniently be integrated into a procedure of heteronomous character.

Chapter Two

TIME AT THE LEVEL OF NOUNS
AND PREDICATES

INTERMEDIATE REMARK

We shall now proceed to the execution of the first point of our program of analysis, which consists in isolating the meaning, or rather meanings, which the word *time* assumes in current language. Our method shall be the method of the context; a short passage, a sentence, or even part of a sentence shall serve as "revelators." As we have seen, this is the method consistently used by Littré and indispensable for any dictionary. Our borrowings from the *Littré* will go beyond; most of our examples likewise are taken from it.

These examples will be very simple and unproblematic, at least as far as the evidence is concerned which they must furnish to us. We will be unable to reduce to still simpler forms the acceptations which will emerge. These acceptations therefore must be termed elementary and immediate, at least at the level of the activities which guarantee them. Nevertheless, one should not be deceived about the nature of this simplicity and elementarity. However simple a language, and however simple the situations to which it refers, the acceptations which this language employs and the evidence which the situation implies never constitute absolute data. Commonplaces evolve, and it is one to say today that judgments of common sense are not irrevocable but may be brought again to trial by research which is carried systematically and deliberately beyond the obvious and immediate. This is a fact nobody can dispute any more, and it reinforces to the point of paradox the other fact that a language is always the language of a milieu and a period, and is marked and dated accordingly.

If misunderstood, this fact might be interpreted to our disadvantage, against the legitimacy of our enterprise. Where, it will be argued, are the simplicity and the elementarity of the discursive material with which the analysis should be concerned? How can they be taken for granted when they yield to the pressure of the clarifying and specifying procedures of research?

But this observation is pointless. The language which furnishes the material of the analysis may in turn be considered under a twofold aspect:

1. It may be considered for its own sake, in the totality of the functions which it normally exercises, i.e. as a means of expression and communication, of explanation, exposition, and research, and so on. One may then ask all the questions concerning it which are asked about a language in general. One may ask, even if he does not doubt the fact, how it is possible that a language can satisfy all the functions which belong to it although its basic information remains scanty and incomplete; one may find food for thought in the fact that common sense may be invoked to bear down upon itself in order to revise its own judgments and transcend its own evidence. But, as we have already stated in other terms, the questions which thus occur to us cannot make our data disappear or change the practice of a language. Moreover, we have already realized that the key to the answer depends upon a single word, namely the adjective *dialectic* in the sense which was given to it in the preceding chapter. When one has understood that an activity, research in particular, can start out practically from any situation and that a reverse action may take place from perspectives newly opened towards the starting situation, one is no more surprised that the same should be true for all forms of discursive activity. In particular, one is no more surprised that the language could be engaged, from its current usage, in increasingly sophisticated pursuits and be put in the service of an experiment whose notations it does not carry in advance, but to whose results it will be able to accommodate itself.

One may then understand that this language is marked and dated by the fact that it is the language of a milieu and a period, and far from considering this as a paradox, one recognizes in it the condition, the fundamental property without which it would heavily influence the development of the activities which it penetrates, informs, and expresses.

2. It cannot therefore be doubted that the data in which we participate with the help of a current language are not absolute. Likewise, even in its elementary manifestations, the common sense which asserts itself here is not infallible. But it is not in this quality of bearing open data that this language will provide us with the material for our analysis. The latter only needs one thing in order to function: It must have access to actual significations. Whether these are open or closed, revisable or fixed, sketchy or complete, partly or entirely correct is not the function of the analysis to decide. The analysis must accept them such as they are at their present stage.

Does this mean that analysis may be applied to discursive material which is completely empty or inadequate? This eventuality may simply be disregarded, since at the level where analysis takes it up, language is guaranteed by the efficiency with which it is used.

On the other hand, would we wish to say that the interest of the researcher could stop at the significations which he discovers; that it is unimportant whether or not he is informed about the capacity of evolution belonging to everything which forms a language? By no means, for the analysis does not aim at purposes of its own. The following example will become relevant only when put in its context in the explanatory discourse of which we confirm the first steps, a discourse which aims at something completely different with greater implications. Thus the researcher has no autonomous finality but is merely one of the representatives of the exposing agent, who in turn cannot do without the qualities of development and openness of the language which he must use.

It seems to me that in the preceding chapter we have sufficiently stressed the distinction which must be made between language as an object and language as a means of analysis, to conclude our preliminary explanations here.*

---

* The method cannot fail to be clarified by the very simple applications that shall be made of it. But it will be only by a reverse operation, towards the end of our study, in the section reserved for our methodological comments and conclusions, that we shall be able to define exactly the range of our method in the general context of an open methodology.

A few more words about the acceptations of the word *temps* ("time") which the method of the context will permit us to isolate. There are some which purely and simply must be eliminated, for example those which, translated into German, do not correspond to the word *Zeit* ("time") but to the word *Wetter* ("weather"). This is obviously the case in the following example: *Hier, il a fait beau, mais ajourd'hui le* temps *se gâte.*† The *temps* with which we are concerned in this case has nothing *zeitlich* in it, nothing temporal, we will say. Moreover, this is not the only acceptation which we must eliminate because it does not belong to our problem. It is sufficient to open the *Littré* to look up those cases; we shall not try to enumerate them here.

The remainder will give rise to certain distinctions, such as the contrast between subjective and objective time, or the distinctions which permit us to separate from each other certain variants of subjective time and certain other variants of objective time respectively. The very method by which we designate them, to which we are prompted and even forced by the current usage of the French language, almost inevitably suggests the following hypothesis: According to the model of a genealogical tree, one imagines without difficulty what might be called the lexicographical tree of the acceptations which are likely to be attached to a word. One might begin by separating from each other, in the intention of treating them separately, acceptations which hardly have anything in common except that they are designated by the same word. One would thus separate, for example, the meteorological meaning of the word *temps* from its more strictly temporal sense, and it is the latter which we would assign to the trunk of the lexicographical tree to be constructed. Two ramifications would result, corresponding to objective and subjective time respectively. Each of these two ramifications would branch out independently; subjective time would sprout at least three branches, corresponding to the consciential, ideal, and existential varieties of subjective time. On the other hand, one imagines as easily what might be called the logical tree of an idea. The trunk would correspond to a notion taken in its greatest general-

---

† "Yesterday the *weather* was fine but today it is turning bad."

ity, while the ramifications of the first order would correspond to the notions issued from the first one through simple qualifications, just as the notion of subjective time seems to have to issue from the notion of time; the ramifications of the second order then would correspond to the notions engendered by a still more narrow qualification, starting from the notions that already have been qualified once, and so on. We now present, in the form of a question, the hypothesis announced earlier: Is it not the result of the analysis to reveal, behind the lexicographical tree of a word, the tree of the corresponding acceptations, or better, that of the proper acceptations, which means no other than the logical tree of corresponding notions? Certainly not! The result of the analytic effort is not to determine, for a start, a general notion (which would deliver the proper acceptation, not yet qualified, of the word *temps*) and thereupon determine a fan of subsequent qualifications. Our analysis thus will be entirely unlike any logical analysis. The acceptations which it shall discover at first as elementary and irreducible data are the same that will be placed at the extremities of the lexicographical tree. They will not present themselves as logical specifications of more general previous acceptations; they are complementary acceptations to be unified in a synthetic manner. We shall not fail to give examples of this unification process which we shall call a discursive synthesis. Behind the lexicographical tree of a word, we will thus not discover a logical, Aristotelian structure, but rather a structure of complementary aspects, which is very different from it. Thus there shall emerge a theory of language for the study and exposition of which logical analysis at this point appears to be radically inadequate.

TYPES OF SUBJECTIVE TIME

What does a title such as the above mean? It is certainly not limited in advance by the words of which it consists. Separated from their context, these words in fact do not have more than a sketchy meaning; we do not know yet what are the types of subjective time that are being discussed. Put in their proper context, restored to their function as a title, the words indicate that the acceptations which will thus be named shall be disengaged. The title accordingly belongs to the discourse of the exposition whose infinitely complex rôle is thereby underscored.

The meaning which belongs to the title is guaranteed by its integration into this discourse. Thus it does not have to be subjected to a preliminary analysis. (The texts, often very brief, to which our analytic procedure shall be applied, will be printed in italics.)

Let us examine the following brief sentence: When I say *le temps me dure* ("time seems long to me"), I may wish to express that I am bored, impatient, uneasy, tired, and so on. Why mention time? It is because my boredom, my impatience, my uneasiness, my exhaustion are accompanied in my mind by the awareness of their duration, a duration of which I am becoming increasingly conscious. My mind is like a place where the duration which I experience becomes a duration which tries me. By saying *le temps me dure,* I thus posit the existence of a time which leaves its mark on me; this mark appears to the alerted mind in the form of duration. By taking note of it, I feel that it is endowed with this quality of length or sometimes shortness; its form of existence within me implies a duration, which may last from the briefest moments to periods of endless waiting. It likewise happens that I say, knowing what I am saying because I have felt it, *I have passed bad moments,* or *I have lived joyous seconds.* But if one tries to see of consciousness only its function to make subjective time manifest for the ego; if, in other words, one excludes all those qualities which duration implies and retains only the one which in every case and invariably generates its presence in the mind, he then designates the time which we shall define as the *time of consciousness* or *conscientional time.*

There is one problem which we shall not treat here, a question we do not have to answer at this point. It is the question whether everything which time can "be" for us, for each of us, is reduced to being just that. We have made an effort to delimit the sense which the word *time* can assume under certain circumstances, but at this point nothing permits us to affirm that by isolating a conscientional time we would have discovered *the* fundamental and true significance of this word. In order to be entitled to affirm anything, we must wait for our experiment to develop—the experiment represented by the present analysis. We must be careful in particular not to embark upon a premature attempt at theorization. The following example, a quotation from Laplace borrowed from Littré's dictionary, puts into clear relief the appropriateness of this cautionary remark:

"Time for us is the impression left in the memory by a sequence of events which, according to our firm belief, have existed successively."

Is this a statement which everybody would accept? Certainly not! We shall soon have other opinions to quote, with which the preceding one is in flagrant contradiction. What strikes us is its complexity, a complexity nevertheless which remains rather superficial. Let us note first that Laplace means to explain what time is *for us*. We are thus concerned with a definition which must grasp and set forth what time *means to us*. And it is enough to refer to our former remarks about explanatory discourse in general, and about heteronomous discourse in particular, to understand the feeling of reserve and doubt with which we receive such an attempt at definition.

At this level and for an object so concealed, a definition which takes no account of the activities guaranteeing it cannot but remain a "discursive gesture" of little consequence. One may best characterize what positive elements it has or may have by saying (in a sense, it is true, which will become explicit only by what follows) that one must consider it as a theoretical sketch, as a first step towards a theory of the knowledge of time. But a premature theoretical attempt always has something adventurous, incomplete, and even artificial. The same is true for a definition, especially if it does not take note of its own hypothetical elements.

But in which respect is Laplace's definition open to criticism? In what does the time to which it refers differ from the conscientional time which we ourselves have discussed? It is certainly true that this definition refers to a subjective time, a time *for us,* even a time resulting from an impression we have received. But where the definition becomes risky is in the rôle which is attributed to the memory, which, by restoring for us the structure of our impressions, would thereby create everything time means to us. As far as we are concerned, we do not think that even a hardly admissible "definition" could be given without a more fundamental study of the structure of our subjectivity. On the other hand, the definition is inextricably complicated by invoking, besides, the certainty that the events recorded by memory have been successive.

It is necessary for us to state why we think the critical appraisal of Laplace's definition is appropriate at this point. The reason is that, in a first example, the criticism touches an aspect of the method. Let us review it. Would we want to say that in the elaboration of what time means to us, we have to eliminate the rôle of memory? By no means. And do we intend to question the feeling of certainty with which we decide that one element has preceded the other? We have no such intention. Then, what is the problem? The problem is to know whether, *yes* or *no*, a definition implies those guarantees of correctness by the mere fact of presenting itself as such; to know whether, in a more general way, a purely verbal elaboration perforce implicates thought, and the knowledge to which it is applied, in an assured channel. And if not, the problem is finally to know how, and from what point of view, the definition itself might be evaluated.

It suffices to put the question thus to know how it must be answered, at least the first part. The answer is No. The history of knowledge offers us too many examples of definitions and verbal elaborations faultily engaged (and distracting thought rather than serving it) for any justified doubts. Is the definition of Laplace, with which we are concerned, an exception? We do not know what the preoccupation was to which it answered; but today, confronted with current views on the function of memory and the limits of certainty, it appears artificial and, in sum, arbitrary. The explanation it offers us of "what time means to us" misses the point; it is a "dated" statement which did not include, at the time it was set forth, the guarantees belonging to a sufficiently reliable piece of information. At this point our criticism harks back to the distinction which we made between holonomous and heteronomous discourse. We had acknowledged that an explanatory type of discourse inevitably is a heteronomous discourse. It is not otherwise in the case of Laplace's definition. The latter puts into focus certain views about the nature and function of memory, which are not in advance evident to all who know how to read the words commissioned to evoke them. Here, then, is the answer to the first part of our question: A definition can very well be a mere attempt at verbal heteronomous elaboration and consequently does not have to imply any prerogative of correctness. But, we ask, from what point of view can it be judged? We must reconsider the meaning of the words which it employs in today's usage, in the context of our actual knowledge; above all we must confront it with what we already know about the more or less explicit theoretical aspect which every formulation necessarily implies. It is certainly true that only at the end of our investigation we shall meet again, among the four fundamental principles of open methodology, the principle of duality which refers to the connection of the level at which knowledge is set forth with the level at which it is tested. But we need not have made the entire journey for our thoughts to be informed in advance by the results we will ultimately attain. It is perfectly legitimate to anticipate future results, provided that this anticipation is not contradicted afterwards. In this sense the definition of Laplace may be viewed as an attempt at theorization, but a premature one, because at the time when it was formulated the conditions for testing it by means of reliable information did not exist. As far as our present endeavor is concerned this attempt at theorization has lost all its plausibility.

What has just been said shall permit us to measure more easily our distance from the Bergsonian concept which reduces time to a time only for us and reduces this concept in turn, in the form of duration, to a mere immediate datum of consciousness. "But this duration, which science eliminates, which is difficult to perceive and to express, is felt and is being lived." (*La Pensée et le Mouvant.*)

Let us first consider the entire distance which separates the Bergsonian concept of time from the Laplacean concept. What should be understood by the words "an immediate datum of consciousness"? It would be a highly adventurous project to reconstruct their meaning from the Bergsonian context. For a considerable part it is by the expressive rôle which the words have fulfilled in this context that they were charged with a relatively precise meaning. It will suffice, for our purposes, to keep in mind the following: When I live with the pure and simple, but vivid, consciousness of my being in the world, I have without any intermediary the feeling of my duration. This is the essence of time; for myself, I do not know of any other, I cannot know of any other; all things considered, it is by being part of *my own* duration that every interval of time becomes manifest to me.

Let us reexamine the quotation from Laplace. The duration which I attribute to the deployment of a phenomenon is viewed there as a manifestation in myself of this phenomenon, as a manifestation of the collective of impressions which this deployment has left in my memory. Thus I am only the passive agent in whom the duration of events taking place outside my consciousness is inscribed, in a form, it is true, which is my own and which is recognizable to me. This really is a time for myself, but the origin of this time is not within myself; it is not an immediate datum of my consciousness.

Earlier we have criticized Laplace's concept and argued that it must be considered as a sketch of a risky and premature theorization. Shall we now decide in favor of the Bergsonian concept? On the contrary, we shall blame it for the same fault. Time reduced to being a mere immediate datum of consciousness is likewise the product of a discursive, theorizing elaboration which does not provide its own pledge of correctness. The Laplacean and the Bergsonian concepts illuminate one another by what they have in common as well as by their contrasts. They both are meant to *tell* us what time is for us, and to give us a discursive elaboration of it; but their most important common characteristic, viz. that each is a mere partial and theorizing interpretation of the term, becomes apparent precisely in their contrasts; each concept underscores, by that which it stresses, an aspect of time for us which is missing in the other.

We think there can be no doubt whatever about the intention in which we have combined the *critiques* of the Bergsonian and Laplacean concepts of time. We have introduced these concepts in our discussion only in order to be able to move away from them, to move away in particular from any method which tends towards a purely discursive elaboration of acceptations. The analytical procedure which we have begun to follow is entirely different from such a method. We do not attempt to discover, in the current usage of language, a correct, exact, satisfactory, and final definition of what time *is*, not even of what time is *for us*.

As one learns about a fact, thus we want to learn about certain current acceptations. At the level of language these are realities of a certain order. We shall not attempt to strain the meaning but neither shall we restrict it. We must accept it such as it is: the vehicle of an undeniably effective knowledge whose limitations, however, we do not know. Thus we must receive it as an open meaning and beware of any premature theorizing rigidity. If we take this caution seriously, our analytic procedure and the method of research of which it is an integral part will assert their specificity towards any method which relies on language as a carrier of complete or perfectly elaborated meanings.

The following passage from Pascal shall permit us to go one step further:

"I say to the one: 'you are bored' and to the other: 'the time does not seem long to you.'"

It is clear that the time of which Pascal speaks is, for both persons whom he is addressing, the time we have called conscientional. This time does not have the same quality for both persons, the quality of being either long or short. Its subjective character is thereby underscored, which does not prevent it from being experienced as a duration by both persons. Would we say that it is the same duration? This is a question to which the situation apparently offers no answer. Here conscientional time seems to present itself in its pure state.

But do we have to assume that in a situation involving a real dialogue, time for us could be reduced to a mere time for the "I" and "you," while nothing permits us to compare the two with each other? We shall come closer to a clear situation if we restore to its context the preceding quotation by Pascal taken from the Littré.

"Those who judge a work without rules are, in relation to others, as people without watches are in relation to others: one

says 'it has been two hours,' while the other says 'it was only three quarters of an hour.' I look at my watch and I tell the first: 'you are bored' while I tell the other: 'the time does not seem long to you.' For actually it was one hour and a half. I laugh at those who say that the time seems long to me and that I judge it according to my imagination. They do not know that I judge it by my watch."

The situation which this text evokes does not only imply two consciousnesses enclosed within the separate worlds of their respective subjectivity, which independent of each other take note of a duration throughout which each existed in an isolated state. Both find themselves confronted with a third consciousness which refuses to be committed to the awareness of duration alone but on the contrary measures this awareness according to the objective validity which a judgment assumes for the first two consciousnesses, which does not originate in them. Thus it may be seen how within the same conciousness the time which we have called consciential enters into dialogue or perhaps even conflict with another awareness of time. What is more, one may even discern, in a person who follows the law of objectivity, a certain irony towards those who do not.

The following example is simpler than the preceding one. In it a manifest allusion to consciential time does not preclude a reference to the objective aspect of temporality: *I waited an hour which seemed endless to me.*

The time referred to has certainly been experienced in its duration. For a consciousness (i.e. for a consciousness in the process of waiting) time has assumed the quality of being interminable. This, however, is not the only form of temporality to be impressed upon one who experiences it. Such a person compares and contrasts this temporality with time that is objectivated by being measured. Thus, the example by Pascal clearly shows that the quality of being measurable with some exactness is not the result of the simple appreciation of a duration. The subject does not attain it by reverting upon himself, but, on the contrary, by participating in an activity capable of participation in the "exterior realities."

It is therefore clear that consciential time is not the only "form of realization" we must take into account. It represents only one variety among others. We have seen how conscientional time combines and also contrasts with a time which no longer responds to the circumstances of subjectivity but to the exigencies of objectivity. But we are still far from having at our disposal all the variants which the most common discourse brings into play. They form a rather large fan which we shall not deploy in its totality. Nevertheless, it cannot suffice for us merely to have opened it; we shall therefore pursue our analysis, on the problem of subjective time at first, and then continue with objective time.

Let us assume that Peter answers Paul, who invites him to play: *"I have no time for it."*

Is the time concerned here a conscientional time? Peter, of course, means that the time *at his disposal* is not long enough for him to come and play in addition to doing what he has to do. In a more differentiated fashion, he might say that the time *does not appear* long enough to him, but he certainly would not say that this time *will not appear* long enough to him. The difference between *appear* and *will appear*, the present and the future respectively which were underscored, is essential: The former introduces a judgment which aims at objectivity while not excluding the possibility of an error of judgment; the second only leads into absurdity. All the same, it is this second tense which would be appropriate, if we were concerned with a conscientional time.

Peter does not judge the time *at his disposal* by assessing in advance the quality it will assume for him of being long or short; he measures the time against the task which must be accomplished. This is not the time of someone reverting to his own consciousness but rather the time of someone facing the activities awaiting him, someone facing the engagements he has in his own milieu. It is true that this time continues to have for this person a certain duration, but it hardly makes sense any longer to say that the latter lends itself to consciousness immediately and without an intermediary. On the contrary it not only is not separable from the aggregate of our activities, but it is inseparable from the whole of all the aspects and forms of our existence.

In order to make the difference between the essential and the conscientional types of time still more evident, let us imagine the following brief dialogue between John, who is waking up, and Frank, who was not sleeping: *"Did I sleep for a long time?" asks John. "I don't think so," answers Frank. "That's true," resumes John, after a glance at the clock.*

John certainly has not admitted that while he was sleeping, time for him had ceased to flow. Does this question show that in order to be able to determine the duration of his sleep, he must invoke the conscientional time of Frank? Certainly not. It is not excluded that the latter could refer to it in his answer. But if John accepts Frank's testimony, after having checked it moreover against the evidence of the clock, it is by deriving from it a judgment which concerns him, a judgment relative to the duration of his own sleep, a judgment about his personal time of existence. Thus we have isolated, at the level of current language, an acceptation of time which does not coincide with the acceptation of conscientional time. The first of the two examples above might have suggested the term of a time of action, but the second suggests that the action may be only a manifestation of existence. Accordingly we shall define the time we are discussing at present as the *time of existence* or *existential time.*

If one says, *"He looks younger than his age,"* or *"The years have left their mark on him,"* he certainly does not mean a special reference to the time of consciousness, a time which would leave its traces within our being, by the mere fact of having been felt in its quality of shorter or longer duration. What informs our being is not simply this apperception but also everything which accompanies it, in the way of action as well as of feeling but also transcending both. It is not only consciousness, or our moral being, or our physiological being, which would testify to the time lived by us, but rather our entire being.

This is also the time discussed by Bossuet: *". . . my entire being depending on time, whose nature is forever only to exist in a moment which flees in a swift and irrevocable course."*

It is evident that the time concerned here is not, as it were, locked within the conscious. Bossuet has said explicitly that nothing of existence was foreign to him. But why does he add that the nature of time is forever only to exist in a moment that flees irrevocably? If this statement had to be taken literally, we would of course have to ask ourselves whether we must consider it as obvious. Otherwise we would have to investigate its guarantees of correctness. But it is neither evident nor guaranteed. Moreover, its function is not to say something true but to express a sentiment such as everyone experiences when he is thinking about the brevity of existence.

With regard to consciential time, we have noted, in Laplace as well as in Bergson, a theorizing intention which tends to close the meaning of the word *time* towards a discursive elaboration of the time of consciousness assisted by memory. We had rejected these theoretical outlines as being premature and arbitrarily restrictive. The same would be true of Bossuet's statement, if it had to be taken as an attempt to define the essence of time. Moreover, this is not the last attempt of this kind which we shall encounter during our present analysis.

We are trying, of course, to bring out as clearly as possible the difference between a consciential and an existential time. The analysis contrasts them with each other in order to describe them better. The same care quite naturally will extend to other variants which will have to be discussed. But we must beware of thinking that the process of specification can be carried to its extreme limits all at once. In other words, one should not expect that the variants specified by the analysis from now on present themselves as perfectly separable variants, as genuine variants which might be used independent of each other. The separative power of the analysis does not go this far, because the variants which it distinguishes remain bound up within the use which language makes of them. This fact is extremely awkward for someone who thinks that discourse operates with well-defined acceptations. We, however, attribute the greatest importance to it. Accordingly we shall at this point put more emphasis on it than we have done so far.

In this new intention we might take up and treat more thoroughly the short sentence from which we have isolated our first example of existential time. We shall replace this sentence, however, by the following one, which is as short, and which one might believe to be taken from the same context: *He is wasting his time.*

Does time which is wasted also lose its duration? On the contrary, it may be interminably long. This is not time under its aspect of consciential time. It is a time which in some way is granted to the subject in order to be validly lived. Must it be understood as being a purely existential time? In its brevity, the indication which is given of it could lead one to think so. But this indication is not univocal. We can expose its ambiguity, its latent multivalence, by completing it, for example, in the following three ways:

1. *He wastes his time without noticing it.*
2. *He felt that he was wasting his time.*
3. *He finally realized that he had been wasting his time.*

In the first of these three variants it is specified that the time under discussion is the time of the being involved in it, while the form of this involvement remains indeterminate. In the second, an explicitly consciential moment is superimposed on the moment lived. In the third example, we finally are no longer concerned with a mere consciential aspect which allies itself with, and is superimposed on, the existential moment. The wasted time certainly has been perceived by the consciousness, but not by a passive perception whose only function would be to feel the duration of the time. The consciousness entering into play here is active, imaginative, and creates at the same time the idea of time lost and of time elapsed. The imaginary, the product and also the instrument of our power to represent things to ourselves, thus has a temporal component. This time produced by the imagination and represented to the consciousness shall be called *conceptual time* or *time of the imagination.*

Do we have to say that this time is not real in the same sense as existential or consciential time is?

In fact, whatever the variant to which language is referring, it may be attached or superimposed on it. Even in the simple act of naming it and referring to it by its name, there inevitably is an imaginative element. The name evokes and recalls the thing named, and if the imagination were not capable to reproduce, in a mysteriously recognizable form, what of the thing has been inscribed in us, the name would remain devoid of meaning. As soon as the imaginary is outlined in its function, the problem of language assumes a broader scope. We have asked ourselves how words acquire their meaning. As soon as the rôle of the imaginary becomes apparent, other questions arise: How do words again take on their meaning for a person who reads or hears them? How does the imagination succeed in giving back to the words a meaning which another experience had imparted to them? How do words evoke the representation of the thing which the imagination newly creates each time? Our project is not to attack these problems directly and generally. At the moment our aim is no more distant than temporality and the power of language to express it by putting it into "discursive form." The study of this particular case, the study towards which we are now proceeding, is the only means we have to review these problems in their general aspect. Let us therefore continue with our examples: *In my time. . . . ,* or *In the time of my youth. . . .*

The reference to time lived is evident. But this lived-through time is not enough to give these expressions their full meaning. The time one remembers is evoked in its past reality only because it has reemerged from the memory, newly evoked by the imagination.

In a general way, the time of the imagination cannot fail to participate in a more or less explicit way each time a verb is put in the past or future tenses. Although we do not say so, the time of the imagination has a part in each of the two following statements: *I waited at least for an hour,* or *I shall not wait more than an hour.*

It is easy, by modifying these statements somewhat, to put into focus very clearly the imaginative component of time to which they refer. Let us assume that I say, for example, *I am afraid I'll have to wait more than an hour.*

The time thus referred to has not yet been either felt or lived. It may never be. My fear of having to wait may be unfounded. What, then, is the nature of the time I am speaking of? It is a time which I imagine and have the power to imagine, a time which compares with time really lived, as a hypothetical fact would compare with a real fact. At the end of this analysis there thus emerges a time of the imagination.

But there is more to it, and this remark has a certain generality, for this time is still capable of modification by as many contexts as one might wish. It possesses in itself all the indetermination of the possible.

In order not to deviate from the line which we have traced earlier, we now must show that, although clearly discernible, the imaginative component is not the only one that gives its sense to the preceding statement. We must call attention to the participation of an objective component which is introduced by the words "not more than an hour." We will, nevertheless, leave this point in suspense in order to take it up again in detail in connection with a later example. So far we have noted three outlines of theorizing departures: We said that Laplace theorizes by devoting a certain elaboration of the consciential variant to the rank of fundamental notion; Bergson does the same by taking time essentially as an immediate datum of conscience; Bossuet likewise yields to the spirit of theorization by reducing time to the instantaneousness of a present; the following example is a fourth attempt of the same order. It is the theory of Condillac, who acknowledges of time only its conceptual aspect: *"We judge a duration only by the sequence of our ideas."*

This statement by Condillac gives us the opportunity to make a somewhat more fundamental statement. Is the reduction made by Condillac justified? Which arguments might he advance in order to explain and make acceptable his particular concept of time? It should be noted that if Condillac is right, Laplace, Bergson, and Bossuet would all have to be wrong. Each of the four points of view which we thus have before us pretends to correctness. What means do we have to decide about this? None of these alternatives is enforced by evidence. Our analysis is not complete, but it is already clear that none of the alternatives covers all the acceptations deriving from it. Each alternative is founded on one or other of the aspects which the whole includes, but none is capable of accounting for all aspects of this whole. In this respect the last alternative does not transcend the rest. The point which seems to us most important for all of them is that none displays any reasons for us to consider it correct, or more correct than the others. What is missing for us, in the case of Condillac, for example, is an explanation which would enable us to understand how the reduction he claims would have to operate. But how could he provide this explanation? We believe, and this is what we are driving at, that he inevitably would have to turn to an analysis of language which, when all is said and done, could hardly differ from the one toward which we are proceeding.

What decision then should we make? The only conclusion which could be drawn from our commentary is the following: None of the several variants emerges privileged from the analysis. Since we do not have any discursive method for reducing them one to another, none of the variants known to common sense consequently could be eliminated or omitted without arbitrariness.

These statements already foreshadow the conclusions which we will have to accept. They may be surprising and even appear confusing. If one were to ask at this point what may be grasped of real time across the dispersion of its significations, the answer could only be a very complex one and would remain superficial nevertheless. All the same, upon a substance already scattered by analysis, considering moreover that this dispersion has not yet reached its widest scope, any answer would tend to gather everything together, to reunite all aspects under a common viewpoint of temporality. At this point one becomes aware, through the very fact that it is still eluding us but that we would remain powerless if we always had to do without, of the synthetical process without which we would be unable to explain one of the most natural functions of language, a function which to some extent is the inverse of discursive analysis, one which succeeds in reconstituting a unified and thereby effective meaning from a broad range of significations; for language would not have the power it actually has, if it were not capable of putting together again what was separated by analysis.

When I am saying, *A moment was enough for me to live through this day again,* it is certain that a *global temporality* insures the coherence of this statement. In the first place the temporality is that of the subject coming to the fore individually, with the intention of imparting to us an experience of his own. Then there must be, transferred, a temporality of each of the other selves respectively who has understood the intention of the first. But how can we recognize the elements of subjectivity of the first while they can thus be transferred and remain recognizable in the subjectivity of the rest? Partly at least, these elements are the ones with which our analysis is concerned. One may easily recognize, in this particular case, those we already have isolated and named.

The expression *to live through again* is the central articulation of this small verbal organism. In the first place it evokes the consciential variant, and only very secondarily it evokes the existential variant of subjective time. But it does not evoke it as an immediate datum of consciousness. The speaker does not perceive the past time of that day at the moment when he remembers it. It is the memory which enables the imagination to restitute this time to the conscious. In the expression *to live through again* it may thus be observed that upon the time which formerly was the time of the conscious, a time is superimposed which is the time of the imagination; but was the time which the subject remembers a purely consciential time? We cannot decide by the text alone.

The second striking term is the word *day*. It evokes a variant of time which is not properly subjective, which is not a time of the self but rather of the universe. Perhaps a certain consciential or even existential trait is involved; we might say, however, that this is only a superimposition. But here the day is not the one that is passing or that has just passed in its quality of an event of the universe. An instant has been enough to live through this day again; the imagination takes a time objectivated in one day in order to project it, with characteristic suddenness, into an instant of the self, an instant felt by the self. Have we thus exhausted all aspects of this Protean time, which nevertheless appears to be unequivocally one to the speaker? Not yet. The word "moment" calls for one further remark. As we have already said, it evokes a time which has assumed its form of duration for an individual, but it is time experienced in the speaker's past. It is thus likewise a time re-created by the imagination, a time rethought; and it is in this rethought time where the imagination succeeds in placing the representation of a different time, of this entire day of the past which has elapsed in the universe.

This, then, is what analysis makes of the short text which we had before us. But is this also the way in which the matter presents itself to the speaker? He is not in an analytic situation while he is speaking. Nevertheless, everything for him takes place virtually as if the analysis were made. The variants which we actually distinguished are at his disposal. If the distinctions to be made are not defined by an explanatory discourse *ad hoc*, the natural practice of language supplies the deficiency.

After this statement we must realize that if the analytical factor alone were concerned, the practice of language could not be what it is. If it is correct to say that things evolve as if at each moment the analysis had been made, it is proper to add that they also evolve as if every time a synthetic moment were capable of pulling everything together again. The function of language is not the same in the use which the subject makes of it in order to express himself on the one hand, and the use we make of it in order to further our procedure on the other. While the latter is mainly analyzing, the former is mainly synthesizing. The individual has at his command all possible acceptations, not to separate them in their divergences but to gather all of them together in one global signification. In order to make a statement, the individual seems unable to do otherwise than put the different variants of time in communication with each other in a discursive whole, which is the sentence itself in the oneness of its meaning.

What has just been said of the synthetic moment, however, only represents a first indication. We shall return to it later when we shall explain in more detailed form what shall then be called discursive synthesis.

The solidarity which the practice of language establishes between the possible acceptations of the word *time* has not permitted us to treat the *subjective types of time* completely apart from the *objective types of time*. We have been unable to avoid some references to the latter. For a balanced inquiry these references naturally do not suffice. We must therefore pursue our analysis on a plane to some extent complementary to that of subjectivity. But first of all we shall put our preceding remarks in a different and perhaps unexpected light. By subjecting to analysis the fashion in which language expresses subjective temporality, one also proceeds towards the analysis of the subject himself. Whether consciential, existential, or imaginative, any acceptation of subjective time stresses a corresponding character of the subject expressing himself. The discursive, taken at the most elementary level as the *milieu* of analysis, exhibits at the same time a structure of subjective temporality and a structure of the subjectivity common to all individuals. The same method thus reveals the two structures in their mutual connectedness. Words, sentences, texts capable of being analyzed, in short, the *analytic milieu,* must then be viewed as a projection, as a representation *sui generis* of the total of subjects capable of using it together.

We believe that we have done no more than sketch a way of access towards the study of subjectivity. The forms of discursivity moreover are not the only ones in which the structure of subjectivity may appear to the individual. The study of the subjective and the study of the discursive thus can support each other. But we are still quite far from having exhausted all aspects of the question. We believe, on the contrary, that a more careful examination of subjectivity might find its projection in a parallel analysis of certain sectors of discursivity. We even believe that the simultaneous study of the discursive and the subjective would bring out, in both, other characteristics of subjectivity and other variants of temporality. On the other hand, it is clear that what has been said about analysis may also be applied to synthesis, a consideration which might open up a way towards certain psychological experiments.*

---

* We attach a certain importance to the preceding remarks. We believe that they mark the point at which our study could orient itself towards phenomenology and contribute to the foundation of an *open phenomenology.* Let the following remarks suffice here:

1. Temporality, for us, is merely a privileged example. It is quite certain that the consciential, the existential, and the imaginative are not qualifica-

TYPES OF OBJECTIVE TIME

Our analysis of language will now continue in a different perspective and start from different preliminary information. Our procedure shall no longer be directed towards the self but towards those elements which are not reducible to the self. Language shall no longer be considered as an expression of the subject but as a representation of the object, i.e. of that which assumes the quality of object by being opposed to the subject. We have seen that on the part of the subject, what language contains of preliminary information, and what analysis reveals of the structure of subjectivity, seems to be rather fundamental. At first sight the same is not true for objectivity. Current language certainly conveys all elementary information which is indispensable for certain shared activities. This is the case, for example, where two simultaneous or non-simultaneous actions or events are concerned. But it is above all at the level of the adverb and of the verb that we shall see how the discursive means capable of structuring an objective time are put in operation. As for the domain of the noun and the adjective, current language is trapped in rather vague ideas which do not form an integrated whole with the practices evolved from the measuring of time, upon which the organization of our industrialized civilization is partly based.

The following images are familiar: *Time elapses, time passes, time flies.* Here time is no longer the time of an individual in whom it inscribes itself, nor even a time shared by all individuals. It is a time posited in an unconditional fashion, in an ex-

---

tions which ought to be reserved for temporality. One may find them again in other applications of discourse. We may see in this, even beyond discourse, aspects under which subjectivity puts itself, or is being put, into position.

2. The synthesis of acceptations effected by the discursive subject evokes processes, dialectizations across which the subject asserts his oneness.

3. The discursive subject is merely that which is apparent, across his discursive engagement, of the phenomenological subject. Moreover, he helps to make the latter more specific, who is not fully given beforehand.

4. The analysis of the discursive is only the starting point of a study which will not remain self-contained but will extend over a far wider area. The specification of the discursive subject thus is only one of the means of progressive specialization of the phenomenological subject, who in turn represents but one of the aspects of the subject engaged in research.

istence which owes nothing to anybody. It elapses as the water of a river flows by, or the moment passes or flies like an object carried away.

It is true that this comparison only represents one aspect of this *flux of time which never stops.* The flow is of limited scope, contained within its bed. But in all regions of the universe *the present moment retreats* into the past and is continually replaced by a new *present moment.* The image common to all the expressions we have cited is thus that of a *stationary flow* moving, not into the universe, but across the universe.

To this vision of a stationary flux of time renewing itself while yet remaining the same, we refer the idea of eternity, as it appears in the following expressions: *This has existed from time immemorial,* or *This is going to last forever.*

We shall not seek to make a list of all the expressions which refer to this fashion of imagining time. They do not constitute a coherent verbal organism. In order to set them forth in a systematic way, it would be necessary for us to make an effort at systematization which current language does not imply. One must call attention, on the contrary, to the usefulness of an image which to some extent is the opposite of the one that has just been mentioned. When one speaks of the *ancient times to which the historian goes back,* or of *the end of the world towards which we are advancing day by day,* time is represented as rolled out in its entire extent. It is like a line along which the speaker is shifting, and all the things of the world are moving with him. The present moment corresponds to the position which the speaker occupies on the line, the future moment to the position he will occupy. The duration of an existence is the distance which it travels along the line of time. It has a beginning and an end, but the time in which it takes place does not. According to this viewpoint, one may say as did the attorney in the *Plaideurs,* *"Before the birth of the world. . . ."* or invoke the end of the world without at the same time invoking the *end of time.* Thus we will say, on the other hand, *We advance in age;* or *We are entering upon a new era;* or *We are advancing towards better times;* or more simply *Let us not revert to the past;* or still more simply *Better days are in store for us.*

In one of these viewpoints, the future comes to us and the past retreats from us, while in the other we are the ones who move away from the past and proceed towards the future. Is one viewpoint more correct than the other? For the moment we do not have to decide. Moreover we would not have the means to do so. The problems of knowing whether time "is something real," and whether a certain form of expression is adequate for it, cannot be discussed at the level of language alone. What the analysis has just shown is that the solution to our problem is not fundamentally inherent in the exercise of language. The language which will permit us to attack this problem must be elaborated, and nothing permits us to believe that this can be done without recourse to an experiment which has still to be made, an experiment to which the present study contributes.

But do we have the right, if this is so, to define as objective time the two rather vague and partly contradictory acceptations which we have discussed? Certainly not if "objective" were rigorously defined as "strictly conforming to reality." But, as we have just said, this objectivity is not a preliminary datum. Like reality, it must be regained by a procedure which is not ready in advance. The definition preceding it remains beyond any possibility of actualization. For us, however, the word "objective" shall not take on its meaning from such a definition. It is guaranteed through the use which is made of it at the level of the investigation. In this respect it does not figure in the fragments of text subjected to analysis, but rather in the discourse of the explanation itself. It may assume there a somewhat weakened meaning but one which is certainly admissible.

Keeping in mind the fashion in which one may at the same time coordinate and define the two preceding representations by engaging them in a discourse informed by the scientific aspect of the universe and its evolution, we shall define as "cosmic time" the variant of objective time to which these two representations refer.

In the preceding remarks universal time to some extent was neutralized. We have not yet shown it as endowed with certain powers conferred on it by verbal expression. In statements such as the following: *We must let time run its course,* or *Nothing exists which time does not terminate,* time presents itself not only as the milieu, the indicator, or the condition of change, but as a power in constant action. It may be sometimes an outright power of evolution. *"Time,"* says Bossuet, *"is the great workman of nature."*

We do not say of this creative time that it passes or flees but rather that it progresses, and this progression is imagined as accompanied organically by a process within the changing matter. In this sense we say, *Every being carries within itself the slow work of time.*

But we must add immediately that in an exactly opposite sense, time in current language also appears as endowed with a universal power of destruction: *Nothing,* we will say, *resists the ravages of time;* or likewise, *What time has made it can unmake;* or finally, *Time obliterates everything.*

Again, it should be clearly understood that we do not present as correctly informed opinions those of which current language thus becomes the vehicle. What of the preceding argument can we keep for a more fundamental study of the contribution of language to a work of research? Perhaps not much of it would remain if other objective variants could not be added.

We shall not try to enumerate all the expressions in which time appears as an *element* of any reality, and what is more, of everything that can have sufficient presence to be given a name, albeit a void or a nothing. We may recall Pascal's expression, *"The eternal silence of these infinite spaces. . . ."*

This Protean time may be active or passive, a cause or a condition, substance or environment; one will never exhaustively define its meaning by considering it as a mere product of the imagination or as a projection of subjectivity. What the discursive subject seeks to express against the obstacles of his own implication is precisely an aspect of time for which he could not be held responsible. Under these aspects the emergence of the object from the discursive remains problematic. At the point where we are now the reason is rather simple to point out: it is because of the distinction which we have made between a holonomous and a heteronomous discourse, and it has to do with the fact that the specification of the objective facing the subjective is not properly a discursive affair. Language certainly contributes to it, even in such an essential way that nothing could be acomplished without it. It is, however, not the only element, and it is by a process connected with it, but developing from it irreversibly, that the meaning of the objective asserts itself. We shall return to this problem in the context of the variants of objective time, which still have to be discussed.

One might also be tempted to see the reason in the fact that, such as it is presented through language, cosmic time remains perceptibly engaged in the subjective, if not even in that drastic form of the subjective which is the *illusory*. It is clear, for example, that the time of which we say that it *elapses irrevocably,* or that it *advances without ever coming to a standstill,* is not given to us with the immediacy which we attribute to it. The expressions we use are heteronomous; they invoke images. This time is presented to the conscious which must take note of it through the intermediary of analogous representations. This means that the value of objectivity of this variant becomes accessible to us only with the help of the imagination, which reproduces after its own fashion, perhaps only by analogous allusions, the circumstances of the encounter of the self with that which confronts it, in the most immediate way possible, as something other than the self.*

Why not say that we have here the reason for the problematic nature of the objectivity of cosmic time, under the aspects already presented to us by the analysis? The answer is that the same reason could equally be invoked for all types of objective time. Thus, those types towards which our attention must now be directed cannot be judged after the same fashion. They emerge from the subjective and from the problematic at the same time. This is because the objectivity of speaking above all depends on its relation to the effectiveness of doing. It inscribes on the discursive plane the capacity of the self to assert itself and to

* The reader may have noticed with what caution we are referring now, and have referred earlier, to the immediate data of the conscious. The reason is that one should not prematurely close, on a felicitous phrase, the entire problem of the elementary and of the inalienable in the foundation of consciousness.

unfold in the face of that which constitutes and asserts itself as being not the self.

The two variants which will follow precisely overcome, not through language but through fact, the subjective illusion according to which time would merely be a matter of subjectivity.

We have already said that common sense is dated, and that from every angle it shows the state of the society where it reigns.* The same is true for current language, even where the objective aspects of time are concerned. Let us assume that someone says, *The hours of the day are longer in summer than they are in winter.*

Should we not point out to him that he is mistaken, that the duration of the hour is determined objectively and that therefore all hours are equal to each other? Yes, if one assumes, even without knowing it, that the hour is the twenty-fourth part of the median solar day as determined by the astronomers. No, if one is concerned with a definite place and time, with the twelve hours of the day which succeed each other between sunrise and sunset.† The latter are really meant in the biblical expression "the worker of the eleventh hour" and remain more or less understood in the current expressions *the first* or *the last hour of the day, the noon hour.* Although different, these two practical definitions of the hour have in common that they eliminate the subjective elements which cause us to say that depending on the case, an hour *appears* to us long or short. We stress the transition from the subjective to the objective by changing from the verb *to appear* to the verb *to be:* we have already pointed out that in the practice of current language, it is rare for a subjective aspect of time to present itself dissociated from any objective aspect. Let us review, in somewhat modified form, our first example, and say, *This hour seems long to me.*

Brief as the indication is, the two words "this hour" refer to an hour determined elsewhere and consequently add an objective

---

* We refrain from formulating at this point the reservations with which the expression "reigns" must be understood.

† This is not a gratuitous hypothesis; in fact, this is how the ancients used to define their hours.

element to the subjective state evoked by the sequel "seems long to me."

What link is there between the two preceding examples? None, except that both recall, the first very explicitly and the second by a mere nuance, the exterior connections projected into the objective types of time. The range of these connections is very wide, even if one considers only those forms which can be named or projected into the language. It is by no means our intention to make a detailed survey of them. This would even be impossible, because the list which could be compiled would always remain incomplete, open towards the connections which increasingly escape the judgment of common sense. This is the case in particular in technical and scientific activities directed towards the exigencies of a high degree of precision. Current language naturally will not be able to bear this out except to the extent where in a heteronomous quality, it can bear its marks. But a serious study cannot stop here; at this point we must look ahead to where the analysis must turn towards the front lines of our activities. (The analysis will continue to be supported by its own discourse, but from now on the engagement with the discursive will represent only one of the constituent moments of the specifications of which language is made the agent.)

If we wanted to keep track of everything which projects itself into current language—the language current in our time—there would thus be a multitude of cases to be analyzed, from the time of the most natural knowledge to measured time or legal time, for example. We must fear that without guidelines our study would end in failure. We shall follow a course which corresponds to a progressive emergence of the objective. Discarding any notion that we must say everything possible, we shall be free to begin with certain cases where the subject remains the subject among the objects, and afterwards discuss other cases where it is only an object among other objects. The first example of these cases is the following: If one says, *The days succeed each other and do not resemble each other*, it is clear that above all a certain feeling is being expressed. In order to express an opposite feeling, another person might say, *The days succeed each other and all are alike*. Nevertheless, the two persons thus expressing themselves accept a common objective frame of reference, that of the succession of days following each other for both persons while neither of them could change this process in any way.

We might at this point recall the quotation from Pascal in which he arbitrates a disagreement about two subjective appreciations of duration, judging time by his watch. The following case is similar: *We were to meet at noon. I thought he was late, he thought he was early. The clock striking twelve reconciled us.*

The entire case revolves around the possibility of determining a common noon. The words *late* and *early* presuppose this possibility. But without an impartial, i.e. an impersonal judge, the subjective appreciations could conflict indefinitely. The clock striking twelve takes the place of the judge. How can it be explained that the two subjects accept it as a common standard?

The matter is far from simple. It would be entirely irrelevant to explain the reconciliation as the observance of a mere convention. Besides the arbitrariness of the convention, the problem would be to know how the convention can be put into practice. The only reasonable explanation is to recognize that the two individuals benefit from a technique of measuring time whose correctness they acknowledge. Perhaps they know—but it is also possible that they don't—how and at what price this technique could be perfected. It would be pointless to say that the two persons have agreed about the time simply in order to have a common reference. This reconciliation is the fruit of a shared experience; it represents the condition without which their actions could not be coordinated in any precise manner. Thus it is imperative for them to agree under penalty of failure.

It remains for us to learn, in a somewhat complementary way, how this measurement could be established independent of the two subjects in such a way that it is convenient for both as well as for all those with whom they live. But this is a different problem. If language carries its traces, analysis such as we practise it does not suffice to solve it. The analysis must be extended and transcended by a different analysis concerned with techniques ordered according to the development of knowledge. We cannot avoid it eventually, but for the moment this is only a rather re-

mote perspective. The results of the analysis of the "case" thus
are as follows: Under penalty of not being integrated into the
milieu on which they depend, the two subjects must subordinate
their personal times to an aspect of time originating outside themselves; the exigencies of the action force them to comply with
this aspect.

In short, the analysis of language refers us to something other
than language, to something of which language is still and always an element, but not the decisive one.

Now let us examine the following case in which an instructor
describes the experiment he is conducting for his students to
show that in a vacuum all bodies fall "after the same fashion":

*"Look!" he says. "The two bodies, one a small ball of cotton,
the other a little ball of silvery metal, have started to fall at the
same moment. Their speed increases but nevertheless they remain side by side all the time. Now they have arrived at the end
of their fall simultaneously. At every moment and for every intermediate position their times of descent thus have been the
same."*

Is the instructor describing the experiment in terms of his own
time? All the expressions he uses for describing what takes place,
at the same moment, all the time, simultaneously, and so forth,
do they not take on their meaning only in relation to his own
personal view of time? This must be the opinion of all those who
would reduce the "reality of time" to its conscientional aspect.
But it is enough to imagine ourselves in the situation to which
the preceding text might correspond in order to realize to what
extent such a position would be artificial. The instructor is not
the only agent in the case. He feels entitled to speak as he does
only because he knows, with a knowledge assured by his entire
experience, that his viewpoint is also that of all his listeners, and
that consequently he is speaking for all of them. The attention
required to follow the experiment does not leave the students
free to abandon themselves to the fluctuations of their personal
impressions. Their common participation in the event has the
effect of engaging them in the same interpretation of all its temporal circumstances. For each student subjectivity thus must
yield to an intersubjectivity. This is one of the conditions, the

first, perhaps, without which the event lived through in common cannot take on the significance of an experience valid for all. But this does not enable us to penetrate to the correct acceptations of the terms in our text. Above all we must understand that the meaning of this text is not a simple matter of vocabulary and syntax—of vocabulary previously defined and of syntax previously established. The text evokes an experiment in physics and its meaning inevitably relates to this fact. But, again, in order to grasp the relevance of this fact, it is not enough to write or say that we are concerned with "an experiment in physics." The meaning of the words in quotation marks is not inherent in them. It has been derived and is still being derived from what the physicist has been able and is still able to present as "nameable in such a way" in his activity of research. Any experiment, then, which would bring into focus only a characteristic of subjectivity is not an experiment in physics. The latter cannot be divorced from an intention of objectivity.*

Accordingly all temporal references made by the teacher in our text are finally affected by an objective meaning. Their relation to the experiment, although it may be an imaginary one, is of prime importance; the process thus begun may continue as far as the reinterpretation of the subjective aspects of temporality, to the point of making them only representations approximating an objective temporality.

We are far from having reviewed all cases which might be presented under the same angle. But we shall not seek to imagine others. It seems to us that we have sufficiently illustrated the concept which we shall name *relational time* or *time of coordination.* The coordination is that towards which any subject proceeds or to which it submits in order to be or to act. It may have a thousand forms, from the strictest to the least rigorous. It may be a coordination of the simplest gestures of an isolated subject or the coordination of multiple activities for the purposes of a

---

* The word *objectivity* in this case belongs to the discourse of the exposition. We have explained in the preceding chapter how it is possible that the meaning which it here assumes be practically assured. Of course this does not imply that the meaning would not remain open and consequently capable of still being defined with greater accuracy.

concerted action. This is the coordination without which there would be no integration into a milieu, no agreement between the members of a community, no common plans, no collective intentions or realizations, no trace of organization or possibility of community life. . . . In the inexhaustible variety of these cases and of all those which are analogous to them, language has a certain group of temporal indicators which by usage are invested with an irreducible objective quality. (This statement is made at the level of the analysis and one cannot judge in advance the later results.)

We have just seen how a precise objective meaning is brought to certain uses of language if the latter is engaged in a clarifying activity, e.g. the description of an experiment in physics. Once more the fact is emphasized that the meaning of a text may very well depend on the fashion in which it relates to a situation about which it does not carry any preliminary knowledge, and whose representation it does not convey in advance. This again is just another way of saying that such a text is heteronomous.*

We have presented the objective types of time as if they had emerged from the subjective types. We are concerned here merely with a device intended to facilitate our exposition. We could have arranged the analysis in a way to have it reveal the objective types of time prior to the subjective types. At the level of the elementary action these types are simply amalgamated. At the level of the concerted action the procedure of synthesis will obliterate either one's anteriority. At this point in our exposition it would nevertheless be very inconvenient to depart from our adopted line. Let it be stated, then, that relational time along this line does not represent the last step of objectivation.

If one says, without further elaboration, *It is noon,* the state-

---

* It appears at this point that analysis of language is not separable from another analysis to which it inevitably leads, *viz.* that of the total of activities in which language participates. This means that the problem of language can only be a facet of the greater problem of the conditions and means of research and knowledge. At this point emerges the question of learning how the discursive and the activities in which it serves can support each other. To a considerable extent this question will determine the borderlines of our exposition. The answer which it requires brings into play the principles of open methodology such as will develop from our *methodological commentary* and from our *conclusions.*

ment does not convey any trace of a subject. We may, of course, direct our attention, as we have explained in the case of relational time, towards the circumstances which permit us to give to this affirmation the value of a relatively precise statement. We will be astonished at the complexity and diversity of the means to be put in action. These means range from legal and administrative dispositions regulating a society to the organization of an industrial production of great scope. But what is especially important for us here is that this immense array of means surrounds us so completely that in order to decide whether it is noon or not, a familiar motion is enough for us: We glance at a watch or a clock, or we hear the stroke of the hour, etc. The word *noon* has taken on immediate significance, identical for all who live in the same place or even in the same region. It is the objective meaning which the word henceforth assumes, even if isolated from any context.

We must add that noon is only one of the terms of the discursive structure which may be built with the help of nouns, such as *millenia, centuries, years, days, hours, minutes, seconds,* and of numerous adjectives. On this verbal system is projected the complex practice of the *determination of a common time for everybody.* Using this system as intermediary, this practice integrates itself into language and fixates, in a manner comprehensible to all, the meaning of expressions such as the following:

The Caravelle Geneva-Nice will take off at 10:25 a.m.

The world record in the 100 yards range has just been beaten by two tenths of a second.

The preceding examples immediately suggest a further one, namely the calendar. The names of the days of the week and of the months of the year, and the numerous adjectives relating to them thus form a small verbal universe and integrate the designation of any day of the year into the current language of today. Everyone will consider the following temporal indication as an objective statement: *He was born on February 29, 1900.* This objective character is of course underscored by the fact that the succession of all the days of a year materializes through the calendar with tear-off leaves, each of which carries information showing *which day corresponds to it.* We shall define as integrated time the variant of objective time suggested by the two last examples. *Measured* time is a special case of it.

Our last examples permit some complementary observations, which also could be made concerning all variants of objective time. It is clear that the time of the clocks, as well as the time of the calendars, to some extent is conventional. The very history of the calendar, from its introduction and throughout its reforms, gives direct proof of it. Concerning the time of the clocks, the fact that a legal act is enough to switch, for example, from *winter time* to *summer time*, makes the conventional element clearly manifest. Is the objective character of time thus "defined" therefore weakened? One would make an error of interpretation to assume that this is so. What constitutes the objectivity of the temporal indicators conveyed by language is that they are interpreted by means of facts which are not modified by the fluctuations of subjectivity. Whether these facts be of a natural order, such as the succession of days and nights, or of an institutional order, such as the succession of the months, makes little difference. The objective resides not only in what we suffer but also in what we build.

Is the objectivity of the variants just mentioned of a specifiable, pure character? This is a bad question, because the idea of objectivity itself is an open concept. The objectivity which is invested in the words, in the quality of meaning, can never be defined more accurately than the objectivity conveyed by our actions.

It is more important to mention that as the subject becomes indistinct, discourse becomes indirect and any reference to the speaker or writer disappears, while the part taken by a certain creative and theorizing imagination in the discursive enunciation becomes more and more decisive. The following examples illustrate this point:

1. *The first traces of man date back more than five hundred thousand years.*

2. *It is now possible to speak objectively about a duration of the order of a millionth of a second.*

The convergence of this type of imagery is not always as striking, but it is relevant for all the domains of history and even for every time when discourse evokes an event of the past or places an event in the future.

These remarks, coming as they do after so many others which our analysis has occasioned, lead quite directly, as it seems to us, to the problem which we shall now discuss: the constitution of—let us not say univocal but rather unified—meaning of a *situated text*.

But let it be well understood, before we pass on to this new stage in our study of language and the temporal expression, that we do not claim to have enumerated *all types of time* which a more complete analysis of language might reveal.

THE DISCURSIVE SYNTHESIS, OR DISCOURSE AS A SYNTHETIC MILIEU

We already have pointed out the difficulty encountered in disengaging pure acceptations. Our best examples are those involving a coincidence or agreement between several acceptations. The majority of examples in particular establish a relation between such variants and even derive their signification solely from the fact of this relation. It is true that the analysis succeeds in isolating from each other a whole roster of acceptations, but if it can distinguish between them it does not therefore establish them in perfect purity. Language does not naturally use acceptations in an isolated state. It represents "text" in the strong sense of the word. It does not tie ready-made meanings together. The fashion in which the words are integrated in language contributes to "modulate" their meaning.

But we must add, and this is a decisive statement, that analysis does not bring out, beyond the acceptations which it separates from each other, a primary sense, a sense proper from which all the rest would be derived, either by particularization or by reduction, by figuration or by modulation. Thus, a text in which several acceptations of temporality are integrated does not relate them to a sense proper, which would be given in advance, of temporality; the text establishes a global sense which analysis alone cannot provide. Any analysis pretending to grasp this sense could only destroy it.

Let us consider the following example, which will confirm our last remark: *Time, which has given us our good days and has again carried them away, will not give them back to us.* This text is not explanatory; it appeals to our emotions. Therefore an analysis aimed at separating from each other the variants of temporality which are combined in the text will not discover their real sense, which is global. Such an analysis would turn the text into a discursive analytic milieu which would provide it with a secondary, artificial reality not corresponding to its poetic character.

Nevertheless, we shall proceed towards this type of analysis, because it will inform us about the matters we are investigating. Let us try to extricate from each other the varieties of time contained in the above text. The word *days* evokes a time of the universe and even a time already measured according to the regular sequence of days. But this variant is evidently modified by the qualifying adjective *good* and the possessive adjective *our*. The former already realizes the transposition of the time of the universe to the time of the self, more exactly to a time experienced as good. The adjective *our* goes as far as to identify the universal time with the time of the self, which has become a property of our being. But later in the text we encounter the principal variant, the active type of time, which gives and takes away, and which does not give back. This is time as a dispenser of duration, which in this case may be identified as existence. An imaginative element moreover is superimposed on these variants.

It is obvious that none of these acceptations is perfectly pure; none represents a primary meaning belonging to the temporality of this text. Moreover, our analysis in no wise touches our emotional being, and consequently the real and poetic sense of this fragment, the sense we have called global, eludes us. Language does not operate by strokes of proper meaning and by cut-and-dried significations which would be combined without alterations. Through the interplay of significations connected by a text, language operates a discursive synthesis which produces global meanings.

Let us now direct our attention more specifically towards the synthetic relation in language between the subjective and the objective. We shall observe that the discursive fact realized within current language immediately assumes existential value for one who uses the discursive form. Let us consider our examples from this point of view.

We have already noted the interaction of the subjective with the objective in the interpretation of the fragment we are discussing. The following example is similar to it although shorter: *Be quick, time is flying.* It would seem at first that the time which is flying is actually cosmic, but the phrase also conveys a dramatic allusion to the time we have to live. There is no reason whatever, except for the reasons of our analysis, for separating the two parts of the sentence from each other and to consider them apart, as endowed with their differentiable significations; for the meaning of the text lies in the combination of the two parts and is not divided into *be quick* on the one hand and *time is flying* on the other. On the contrary, the meaning depends on a mutual relationship between the two parts. Thus we see emerge, even in such a short example, the synthetic effect of language, which is by no means a mere juxtaposition of significations but causes them to interact and to echo each other.

Let us now try to find out in what this echo of one part of the sentence to the other consists, for the person expressing himself. The point is that the time of the universe, which is flying, is identified with the time which is allotted to us. There is thus a connection, which may go as far as identification, between the self and the universe, and it is through this connection that, in the universe, the self is drawn towards its destiny. The acuteness of meaning which the sentence tends to assume thus depends essentially on the possibility, implied by language, of operating a close synthesis between the subjective and the objective.

Consider the following additional examples:

1. *The hours seemed short to me.*

2. *I lived again, in my imagination, through these interminable minutes of waiting.*

We do not subject them to the same analysis as we applied before. We could only repeat ourselves, at least as the emphasis on the different acceptations of temporality is concerned. It is more specifically from the angle of the relations between the subjective and the objective that these two examples must be considered. Both renew for the self the impression which it retains from an event experienced in the past. This is precisely the essence of what we have called their global sense. Thus it is clear that this sense develops only through the effect of a link between the self—even the self which becomes aware of itself—and the event into which the self is projected. Thus, in the second example the self projects its state of interminable waiting into the minutes of an exterior time. In the first example the self places the brief time of the experience within the time it knows otherwise to be the hours of the clock.

These statements could not be made in such a way if we did not have at our disposal subjective as well as objective variants of temporality. In sum, the relation with which we are concerned, through the times of the self and the times of the universe, quite naturally belongs to the discourse in which the self expresses itself. In particular, language operates a synthesis of the objective and the subjective and holds them only to make them interact; this fact among others deserves comment.

The synthesis of the self with the universe in current language is not surprising. Only someone who believes in pure acceptations would be surprised at it.

Our entire life depends on our being inserted, as acting and thinking persons, into the milieu of our activities. This process is possible only if it is guided by a just relation of the subjective categories to the objective ones. The universe must be able to project itself into the subject, just as the subject must be able to insert itself into the universe. It is precisely the prerogative of the imagination to project the self into the universe and the universe into the self. There is no self which would imagine nothing but self.

This, again, is not surprising. All the same there is a surprising aspect in the fact that language should be not only the result of this integration of the self into the universe, but also one of the most effective means for this purpose. Thus, discourse, at least as far as temporality is concerned, has the capacity to realize the agreement of the self with the outside world through the combination or opposition of the various acceptations. The syntactic bond between the significations is more than a simple grammatical fact; it also depends, more than on the structuration of language alone, on the possibilities which are given to us as really existing in the universe.

One may ask how it would be possible to describe in greater detail the fashion in which the global meanings are constituted, by the play and the affinities of the meanings which are isolated by the analysis. By way of explanation it seems to us convenient to recall at this point one of the first results from *La Géométrie et le Problème de l'Espace*. On the other hand, we have set up the rule that the present study may not be based upon any previous, even analogous, study. In fact our aim is to perform an experiment independent of any preceding studies and of results obtained elsewhere. Accordingly we shall not borrow from *La Géométrie et le Problème de l'Espace*, except for the purpose of comparison.

Anyone who studies elementary geometry will soon notice that geometrical facts present themselves under three aspects: an intuitive aspect (that of our natural view of space), a theoretical aspect (that of rigorous deduction), and an experimental aspect (that of the realization of geometric entities by objects and phenomena). These three aspects may easily be distinguished from each other. All the same, it is difficult or even impossible to make them perfectly autonomous; this is one of the essential facts which have been made evident. In its full meaning geometry constantly illustrates these three aspects. If one says, for example, that a light ray in empty space proceeds in a straight line, the words *straight line* alone do not designate any of the three acceptations which the three aspects impart to it. On the contrary, the sentence only succeeds in imparting a meaning to the words because it contains no reference to the existence of the three fundamental aspects. Geometrical discourse thus has the faculty, according to its purpose, to constitute global significations otherwise than by means of the juxtaposition of differentiated acceptations. These significations are irreducible and synthetical at the same time because they do not differentiate the differentiable; likewise one may, conversely, constitute analytical meanings by differentiating that which naturally presents itself as undifferentiated.

We have given the term of *dialectic synthesis* to this play of distinctions and identifications of geometrical concepts specifiable according to the three aspects. One of the essential results of *La Géométrie et le Problème de l'Espace* was that geometry reaches its full effectiveness only through a dialectic synthesis at the level of elementary geometry.

In our study of language we may have been informed and guided by the result just mentioned. But we have not explicitly borrowed anything from it. We are the more free now to state the analogy between the first results we have obtained here and the first results of the geometrical investigation. What we are trying to explain is that the discursive activity which constitutes the global meanings has all the characteristics of a dialectic synthesis at the discursive level. When we say, *"Time for us is measured,"* analysis could discover, under the term *time*, several of the acceptations which we have differentiated: the time of the self, existential and consciential, and the time of the universe, which has been and is being measured. Here the discourse avoids to elaborate distinctions. It confounds the meanings in order to identify them under the same term and thereby it gives to the phrase its irreducible and synthetic sense.

The analogy which we wanted to explain thus is evident, although the synthesis at the discursive level is of a different and more inextricable complexity than the synthesis at the level of elementary geometry. The latter knows only two operations, those of analytic differentiation and of nondifferentiation respectively, or, one might say, of synthesizing confusion. In the case of time, synthesis knows and practises far more varied operations; it can oppose meanings, identify them, superimpose them, or project them into each other.

We have noted the absence of a primary meaning of temporality in which all the other acceptations would participate and from which they could be derived. The nonexistence of this primary sense has raised the problem of the legitimate acceptations as taken individually and in their mutual relations. Now we have the answer to this problem: The function of this hypothetical primary sense is the dialectic synthesis at the level of the discourse which adopts it.

One may further ask whether the synthesis at the level of elementary geometry and the synthesis at the discursive level are comparable in that they suppose the equality of the levels of knowledge where they are realized. We might have prefaced the analysis of the geometric fact with an analysis of spatiality at the level of current language. Why have we not done so?

Geometrical language, which partly is prefigured in current language, possesses precise characteristics of preconstituted language. If we were to try to analyze it in the same way in which we have analyzed time, it would present itself as the language of a discipline, i.e. as a discursive organism stabilized and defined since the time of the Greeks by an entire theorizing activity. What geometrical element there is in current language does not fit into it as naturally as do its temporal elements. We realize that it is impossible today to discount the importance, during the entire history of geometry, of the teaching and the practice of the discipline, of which it may be said without exaggeration that they have descended to the level of common sense.

All the same, the fact remains that if we have been inspired by the ideas of *La Géométrie et le Problème de l'Espace,* the study of the discursive milieu towards which we have proceeded represents, conversely, a complement to the study of geometry. What is more, it is a priori the model of a complement necessary for any study of the same type.

We shall carry the present analysis of language still further, this time considering grammar as the organizer of a structured temporality.

Chapter Three

TIME AT THE LEVEL OF THE ADVERB
AND THE VERB

TIME AS STRUCTURED BY THE ADVERB

The adverb, it says in the grammar books, is an invariable word which modifies, by defining and completing it, the meaning of a verb, an adjective, or a different adverb. This definition omits the essential feature which we shall point out for the adverbs of time, viz. the function which certain groups of adverbs have in common to structurize the form, in this case, time, to which they refer.*

The adverbs are not the only group to play this rôle; prepositions and conjunctions are also capable of it. It is sufficient, in order to make this quite clear, to compare the following three statements:

1. *He has departed, and since then the house has been more quiet.*

2. *Since his departure the house has been more quiet.*

3. *Since he has departed the house has been more quiet.*

In the first example, *since* (*then*) is an adverb, in the second *since* is a preposition, and in the third *since* is a conjunction. Otherwise, especially insofar as our problem is concerned, the three statements have exactly the same meaning.

For the conclusions we intend to draw, the study of the systems of adverbs will suffice. But we shall not hesitate to treat as adverbs adverbial expressions of rather diverse form, without seeking information about whether they are listed as adverbs in the grammar books and dictionaries.

A certain grammatical tradition requires that the adverb should be treated only after the verb has been discussed. Do we

---

* The logical form of this definition, however, may be objected to; it defines the adverb by means of the verb and the adjective primarily, but also by means of the adverb itself.

have any reasons for proceeding otherwise? The following are the most important:

1. In spite of etymology, the exposition of the system of the verb, with its moods, tenses, and inflections, and the development of the system of adverbs, are *linguistic processes* which are relatively independent of each other. In certain languages, in fact, the system of the verb is far less developed than it is in the Indo-European languages and generally does not include comparable inflections. What the latter have to indicate remains expressible in such systems, but the *setting in discursive form* is entirely different. The adverbs in particular turn out to be capable of this function. For a correct understanding of the amount of *expressive power* which these two linguistic formations imply, it is useful to emphasize their relative independence. We believe that we will show this conclusively by treating the adverb before the verb and before any systematic analysis of the latter's function.

2. Verb and adverb (as we have already said, but this is a statement anyone may make and which we are using for our purpose, as we have done in other cases with other statements, with the only reservation that we will have to define it eventually by that which follows) share and even dispute each other the putting into discursive form of a *structured time*. By doing this they mutually exert an assimilating and synthesizing action upon each other.*

Now the structuration effected by adverbs is far less elaborate than that established by the intermediary of the system of the verb, i.e. far less charged with significations not belonging to time, significations related to other aspects of the process which the corresponding verb conjugates. The adverbial system is comparatively simpler, less sophisticated, but it also has a more rigorous coherence. One can easily find in it a structural model capable of serving as a guide to a critical analysis of what the verb may be capable or incapable of expressing. In this sense, and especially as far as we are concerned, the study of the adverb thus precedes that of the verb.

---

* We have just seen, in the case of discursive synthesis, what the words "assimilating" and "synthesizing" mean.

3. The assimilating power of the adverbial system recalls the analogous power of the mathematical structures relative to their applications. In this case we are concerned with more than a vague analogy. It will turn out that at the level of the adverb there exists a pattern of the theoretical time of the mathematicians. Thus it is precisely by measuring how far the system of the verb is removed from it that one may understand everything effective, but also everything unachieved and even tentative, inherent in the discursive form, through the means of conjugation, about the temporal aspects of a process.

4. The problem of recognizing what, in all possible dimensions, is the structuring power of the adverbs, certainly transcends the problem we are discussing. The same is true for subtended structures achieved through adverbs. The temporal structure is only one of their aspects. Or one might rather say that they are only one aspect of a structure that may be interpreted in a wider context. Thus, for example, *before* and *behind* can be adverbs of place as well as of time. Thus it is manifest already at the level of the adverb that an ordered structure in itself is neither spatial nor temporal but lends itself to a spatial interpretation as well as to a temporal one. We shall not pose the problem of the structuralization of language by means of the system of the adverb in its most general sense. We shall not even seek completely to analyze its temporal aspects. What we wish is to emphasize that the adverb has a structuring power and how this power is realized; this does not mean enumerating all the cases where it is exerted.

5. The verb also has a power of synthesis and structuralization. But looking more closely, which we shall not fail to do, we will notice that the verb tends less than the adverb towards the constitution of abstract structures. It acts primarily as a factor of integration of the temporal aspect with other aspects of the process, of the action, and of the activities expressed by language. In combination, these reasons hardly leave any doubt as to the expediency of treating the adverb before the verb.*

---

* These reasons, however, have become clear to us only after we had attempted, according to grammatical tradition, to discuss the verb before discussing the adverb.

Let us now proceed towards the analysis itself. We are no longer concerned, as we just said, with distinguishing and defining acceptations, but we intend to reveal the structures subtended in common by certain adverbs. The simple procedure of the context will no longer suffice, and we will have to elaborate it. We shall be unable to succeed merely by enrobing an adverb in a fragment of text, with the intention of thus fixating the meaning it assumes on its own, independent of other adverbs. What must be made clear now is the temporal structure which certain adverbial constellations are able to evoke with the help of a conveniently selected context. We are no longer concerned with meanings to be given individually to each of the elements of such an adverbial group; these meanings are given only according to the meaning of the group of elements.

Let us now consider how the preceding remarks will be taken into account in practice. The following is a first example which we deliberately leave in a state of vagueness:

Such a thing had never been seen *until then.*

We *now* are witnessing it.

From now on everyone must take it into account.

The adverbial constellation whose structuring power this example is supposed to illustrate is obvious; it consists of the three adverbial expressions *until then, now,* and *from now on.* It divides the sequence of all possible moments into three categories: one which concerns the *now,* one which concerns the moments preceding it, and one which concerns the moments following it.

At this point we must eliminate a paradox to which we would be led inevitably by a too rigorous interpretation of the meaning which the three adverbs in our example assume.

The adverb *now,* it will be said, can only designate a precise moment, which has no duration or density; for only such a moment can make a neat separation between the moments coming *before* and those coming *after.* But if this is so, the *now* of the speaker is a fleeting moment, a moment which already is not the same any more between the instant one begins to say and the instant one finishes pronouncing the decisive word *now.*

Is it necessary to state explicitly that current language does not have in its makeup such sharply defined significations? The latter are appropriate only in a language which systematically and conscientiously practises mathematical rigor. Correctness and precision must not be confounded; in order to be correct, the *now* of current language must precisely be capable of conveying a certain imprecision. This *now* is not intended to effect a cut but rather to serve as an intermediary between an *until then (so far)* and a *from now on,* both of which do not have to be imagined as being determined with ultimate precision. This is confirmed by the following second example:

Formerly these lands were not cultivated.

Now (or *at present*) they are being cultivated.

From now on they will be covered with vines.

The three adverbs, *formerly, now, from now on,* also subtend a temporal structure which likewise implies a past time, an intermediate time, and a future time, but does not determine them with mathematical precision. The following is a last example of the same type:

Not long ago we used to follow the trails to climb the Chasseral.

Today a large road goes up there.

In the future one might use helicopters.

Obviously it is not always the same words which effect the structuralization that has been pointed out. The adverbs capable of fulfilling this function fall into three categories, according to the specific tasks assigned to them. Within the same category, however, they are not automatically interchangeable. For a considerable part their selection on the contrary depends on the context in which they belong.

We shall now demonstrate how, by means of adverbs alone, language is capable of transferring this type of structuration of any *now* into a *then* of the past or future. In order to verify this, it is enough to take up again, with slight modifications, the first of the three preceding examples:

Never, *until then,* had anything like it been observed.

But it was witnessed *then* by some persons.

From then on one had to take it into account.

It is clear that the three adverbial expressions, *until then, then, from then on,* share the total of possible moments relative to the category centered around a *then* of the past, which the text otherwise leaves indeterminate. Everything we have said about the three adverbs which in a certain sense form the temporal frame of our first example is also true for the three adverbial expressions in the second. The following, on the other hand, is an example of the same transfer towards an indefinite *then* of the future:

Then we shall witness what *formerly* (*heretofore*) we did not want to believe.

After this (*henceforth*) it must be taken into account.

It is very important for us to see as a whole, as illustrations of one single fact, the first of our examples and the two variants which have just been given. What has been set forth is, on the one hand, the capacity of certain adverbs to divide the possible moments into three successive categories, and, on the other hand, to transfer this order from a *now* to any *then*.

The feasibility of the transfer belongs to the temporal structure which the adverbs subtend; it is their essential property. This is moreover the structure which mathematical time has the function to realize as perfectly as possible.

We have noted that adverbs such as *now, today, presently,* most often merely designate an intermediate time between a past and a future without a very precise delimitation. On the strength of this remark one may point out that these expressions may often be replaced by adverbial forms such as *in our day, in our times, in this era,* etc.

The temporal configuration which has been discussed here of course is not the only one which may be evoked by a triad of adverbs. Let us examine, among other possibilities, the following example:

He has left *early this morning.*

He shall return *late this evening.*

I do not know where to find him *in the meantime.*

The temporal configuration in this case corresponds to an event of the past, an event of the future, and the temporal interval which intervenes. Although centered around an implicit present tense of the speaker's, the intermediate time is something quite different from a fleeting moment. This time extends between two events situated within the day with very relative pre-

cision. It is not superfluous to point out these facts, because it is
important to understand that in order to attain the effectiveness
which one expects of it, language does not need significations as
strictly delimited as those of a mathematical discipline.

The temporal structure, subtended by the adverbs, as noted
above, implies the possibility of transferring a temporal configuration towards the past or towards the future. It is obvious that
this essential feature may easily be verified in our new example.
It is enough to add the following slightly modified versions:

1. That day he arrived *early in the morning* and left again
late in the evening. But I do not know what he did *in the meantime*.

2. One of these days he will arrive *early in the morning* and
will depart *late in the evening*. But I do not know what he will
do *in the meantime*.

Once again, we must regard as a whole the original version
and the two modified versions of our last example. We then find
ourselves confronted with a rather complex temporal configuration which we shall now proceed to analyze.

Let us start with the three adverbs, *yesterday, today,* and *tomorrow*. The meaning they assume, thus enumerated one after
the other, is clear enough without any context. The temporal
configuration underlying them is not identical with either of
those which we already encountered. In relation to the intermediate time designated by *today, yesterday* certainly denotes
the past, but it is a limited past, and *tomorrow* denotes the future, but it is likewise a limited future.

Obviously our configuration may be transferred from the present day to any day of the past or future; we only have to replace
the three adverbs used above by the three adverbial expressions
the day before, that day, the next day.

The intermediate time designated by the expression *that day*
can be any day of the past or future. Nevertheless, one must
assume that its meaning has to be defined through an adequate
context. One might, however, leave it entirely indeterminate,
replacing the expression *that day* by *a certain day* or, still more
simply, *one day*.

But suppose that *that day* be *tomorrow*, then the corresponding adverbial triad is *today, tomorrow,* and *the day after tomorrow.* If *that day* was *yesterday,* one would obtain the expressions *the day before yesterday, yesterday,* and *today.*

Thus we obtain a "temporal cell" whose centre is today and which is subtended by the following sequence of adverbs: *the day before yesterday, yesterday, today, tomorrow, the day after tomorrow.*

The rule of transfer is immediately applicable to it. The corresponding adverbial expressions are *two days before, the day before, that day, the day after, two days later.*

Here, too, the adverbial expression *that day* designates an indeterminate day of the past or future, a day which is undefined but which would be more or less exactly determined by the context. Likewise *that day* might also be left completely indeterminate; to effect this, one would only have to replace the expression again by *a certain day* or *one day.*

Grammar books and dictionaries do not include adverbs permitting amplification of a cell of five terms, such as the preceding one, into a cell of seven terms. We are not concerned here with the freedom of spoken language, where this is sometimes permissible. It is nevertheless clear that the resources of current language are not exhausted. In order to proceed further, language may resort to the numerical system (whose law of unlimited formation, as we have noted before, is integrated into language); one might then say *the third day before,* or *the fourth day after,* a certain other day. Or, invoking the calendar, one might say *a month and two days ago,* or *in another five weeks and four days,* etc.

It is on this unlimited scale of days that the operation of the transfer can finally take place; the origin of days, 0-day, may be replaced by any day upon any other day. Thus it is on this basic configuration that the adverbs *early, late,* and *in the meantime* trace, as if in a superimpression, a temporal configuration consisting of more shades of meaning and more details.

Likewise, it is here where the realignment may occur with what we said before, concerning objective time, about the finer structuring into hours, minutes, and seconds, which is actually integrated into language. In this context we can, of course, only be concerned with this structuring by adverbial contexts, with particular help, as intermediaries, of the numerous adverbial expressions referring to the hours, minutes, moments, and instants. Thus it seems, even in this restricted frame, that language is open to the exigencies arising from its participation in every defining activity, in this case the techniques of measuring time.

It is not irrelevant to state that the cells consisting of five terms, which have been discussed, are not the only ones which may be constructed. It is possible to imagine others which do not cut up time into such regular intervals; for example, *some time ago, recently, for the moment, shortly, in the near future.* Transferred to any moment chosen at random the sequence might read *formerly, immediately before, then, immediately after, later.*

Discussing the meaning of words in a context, we repeatedly have stressed the fact that the meaning of one and the same word may vary from one context to the next. This meaning is often determined by the relation of the context to a certain situation. The preceding example gives us the opportunity to make an analogous remark concerning adverbs and adverbial contexts. We find, for example, that the expression *later* is placed in the fifth position. But we have also used it in third position, in an adverbial cell with three terms. It turned out to be capable, as well, of assuming the sense which corresponds to this usage. Thus we see justified the use of the term *an adverbial context* and the rule confirmed according to which the meaning of a determinate adverb may be defined more precisely in one sense or another by its insertion into an adverbial context.

Before we close the discussion on this subject, let us reply to an objection which might be provoked by our remarks. In the following brief statement,

The sky has cleared and the rain has stopped; *since then* the sun has been shining,

there is only one adverb, *since then.* The meaning which it has here is certainly not problematic. It is therefore not necessary to find an adverbial context in order to define it more precisely. Does this simple fact not disprove everything that was said before?

Let us analyze the situation: The context refers to the fact that it has been raining during a certain period of time preceding the clearing-up, and that during a lapse of time of shorter or longer duration, the condition of the sky has changed. It is thus entirely clear that the adverb *since then* only comes in the third position. This fact may be put in evidence by means of a more explicit text: The sky having cleared up, the rain *then* stopped; *before*, it had rained in floods; the sun has been shining *since*.

The lesson to be drawn from this example is the following: The temporal indications provided by a context may be precise enough to make unnecessary the use of all the adverbs which the complete explication of the situation would imply.

The analysis in which we have been engaged suggests certain conclusions, some of which more specifically concern the problem of language while others refer to the problem of time. But before we think of formulas, we must present the following two remarks:

The adverbs of time whose structuring power we have explained form, as we have seen, a triple series. There are others, among which we want to stress those which form a fourth series, the adverbs of repetition. They are, among others, *once, occasionally, sometimes, again, often, frequently*, etc., a series which might be closed by *never* and *always*. One may add to it the degrees of comparison and the numbers which make, for example, *a hundred times* from *often* and *sixty times per minute* from *frequently*. Rather than a structuring of time, this is a structuring of the action in time which these adverbs are capable of operating. They are joined in this function by those upon which our investigation is concentrated. We would veer off our subject by dwelling on them any longer.

The second of our remarks is far more important. It does not refer to the adverb's structuring power but to its assimilating power. It may be introduced by the question, What, then, is the time which the adverb is capable of structuring? Is it subjective or objective time? Could it be one rather than the rest of the variants of either? At the level of the noun and the adjective the distinction between the subjective and the objective has presented itself as a first dichotomy. Here, this distinction loses its acuity and even its meaning. One would not hesitate to say in one breath, for example: It has rained but *soon* the sun will be shining; you are bored, but *soon* you will feel full of energy again.

If this statement were reduced to its first part, the adverb *soon* would refer to an objective time; if it were reduced to the second part the same adverb would refer to a subjective time. But, in the statement taken as a whole, this adverb connects the objective perspective with the subjective one; it permits and even invites the interpretation of one perspective through the other; it relates them to each other, unites them, and assimilates them to the ends of the unity of the person and of the effectiveness of the action.

The formation of this integral perspective, however, does not obliterate every distinction between the objective and subjective types of time. One clearly realizes this by comparing the following two statements:

1. *Before this,* I had been waiting for a long time.
2. *Before this,* the waiting had seemed long to me.

The adverb *before this* which the two statements have in common is not enough to make them identical; one cannot, in effect, blame anyone who, having waited no longer than five minutes, asserts that the waiting has seemed long to him. But one can (with Pascal) contradict him "judging by one's watch" if he asserts that he has been waiting for a long time.

These last observations barely touch the subject. But the entire question will come up again in the context of the system of the verb. We shall have to discuss it again and treat it more thoroughly. We shall do this in the section entitled "The Discursive Synthesis at the Level of the Adverb and the Verb."

Finally, here are some brief conclusions which likewise merely foreshadow the thoughts with which we shall conclude this first part of our study.

From a certain angle, the study towards which we are proceeding assumes the form of an investigation of language. What are its results so far? What the example of time makes above all manifest is the inadequacy of certain conceptions about the function of language. This is the case in particular with every system of explication which does not adapt the formation and use of language to the exigencies of an effective functioning in situations which are in constant evolution. These exigencies weigh on each acceptation of each word which must participate in any form of experience. In order to be satisfactory, the acceptation cannot remain faithful to the idea of the acceptation-outline or of the open acceptation. Henceforth all theories of language have to be considered inadequate which do not take into account its heteronomous character, i.e. which do not make adequate allowance for the dialectic process which goes from language towards its fields of application and returns from there towards everything that represents meaning and signification. In a theory of language where this articulation essential—let us not say to reality but to the open experience of reality—is missing, every criterion of correctness, whatever its nature (logical, syntactic, semantic, etc.) inevitably takes the form of a premature hypothesis on the results of the experiment and the conditions of their enunciation.

In order to justify this statement, it was already sufficient for us to have made our analysis at the level of the noun and the predicate. What has been said of the temporal structure sub-tended by the adverb, or rather by the concerted play of the usage of the adverbs, forces us to go one step further. Passing from acceptation to structure leads us still farther away from any theory which would make of language a setup of individually determined acceptations.

But in which direction are we thus being pushed? The idea which is beginning to impose itself is not that of a logically organized discourse but rather of a discursive organism of a dialectic character. This organism produces significations corresponding to the situations into which it is inserted. The rules of this production are not a special feature of language alone, of a language which could remain what it is no matter what its fields of application. The signification corresponding to a specific situation often (not to say always) is determined, for the person who responds or who receives the response, only by an engagement which emerges from the discursive, and whose integrality is not reducible to its projection into the discursive.

In many respects our exposition would have been easier if we had not systematically omitted the prepositions and conjunctions capable of a temporal signification. We nevertheless shall do without the complementary information which we could have gained by taking them into consideration.

As far as our following study is concerned, of what the verb and its inflections contribute to the discursive formation of temporal relations, it will very usefully complete, newly illuminate, and confirm the preceding considerations.

TIME IN CONJUGATION

One does not have to analyze at length the function of the verb in language in order to perceive that it is able, like the adverb, to become the expression of the engagement of the *event* (of any event) in temporality. It is enough, to convince ourselves of this, to open a grammar book and cast a glance on the tables of the tenses and moods of the conjugation. Putting the verb *to give*, for example, in the present, the future, and the past tenses, is this not situating the action of giving in the present, in the future, or in the past? Does not grammar thus design a temporal structure comparable to that which is determined by the three adverbs *now, before,* and *afterwards?* Does not this simple remark show us a way on which it would be natural to travel?

When we were studying the function of the adverb in the temporal organization of discourse, we were able to avoid seeing in it the outline of the way in which the mathematician conceives the temporal continuum. We shall quite naturally be led to the study of the latter, but it is not necessary to invoke the mathematician in order to be able to imagine it. At the present time, for almost all of us, it is a common notion, and our surroundings furnish us a thousand opportunities to become familiar with it. It is therefore not surprising that this representation of time may easily account for the temporal relations which certain adverbs or groups of adverbs have the function to establish. On the contrary, we should be greatly surprised if it were not so. And why, we will think at the same time, should it not be similar for the verb? Is it not logical to think that the conjugation is based upon the same representation of the sequence of events in time, and that its function likewise is to develop this representation by the appropriate means?

This idea is very appealing and we shall pursue it. It shall lead us to imagine a *purely temporal* model of the conjugation of the verbs. This model (which we shall call our first model) will turn out, however, as being too simple and too theoretical to be able to account fully for the complexity of the *system of the verb* such as it is realized, for example, in the French language or in any of our other classic languages.

Do we mean to say that this model of a purely temporal conjugation will be a mere play of the imagination, and that since it cannot be applied as it is to the really existing discursive "organisms," or to those having had an historic existence, it is not likely to yield much profit? We are, on the contrary, of an entirely different opinion. Despite its incompleteness, this theoretical model will serve us as a governing idea and shall not fail to illuminate with a rather vivid light the different stages of the inquiry towards which we shall proceed. Guided by this governing idea, we shall first of all seek to retrieve, in the use of the verb such as it is attested to and normalized by grammar, the temporal structure subtended by the adverbial system, which our first model takes up in its turn. Against our expectation this enterprise will turn out to be an awkward one from the very outset. Only after some effort of adjustment will our governing idea become settled in its place. But this will only be a partial success. We shall have to recognize that, such as it is realized in an existing language, the system of the verb cannot be confined within the ideal frame of a purely temporal conjugation. This frame is too narrow; in the complexity of its functions conjugation must elude it.

We shall thus have to explain the fact that the aspect of pure temporality is not the only one in which the system of the verb is engaged. What are the other aspects which may be implied by it? We shall content ourselves here with a single example, borrowed from Latin; we shall later return to it. Let us assume that an orator wishes to intimate that he has nothing more to say, that he already has said all he had to say. In Latin, a single word is sufficient for him: *dixi*, i.e. *I have spoken*, or still more explicitly, *for the moment, what I had to say has been said*. The form *dixi* is not limited to expressing the fact that the action of speaking belongs to the past but also indicates an accomplished and completed action. It puts the emphasis on an aspect of the action which does not refer to the temporal situation only, on an aspect which in some way modifies the aspect of mere and pure temporality, *viz. the aspect of completion*.

The mathematician's discourse on abstract time will give us, to some extent, the crystallization of the moment of pure temporality. But, in the nonmathematized discursive organisms, this moment appears as it were broken, interrupted, covered up, and even compromised by a hundred other exigencies expressed by the verb. This statement will lead us to imagine a second model of conjugation, a model to some extent complementary to the first. Although as theoretical as the first, this second model would be designed to "put into discursive form" the different aspects under which the action or the event may present itself or may be perceived. Its aspect of temporality certainly would not be excluded, but it would not be treated in an immediate fashion and would not appear in explicit form. It would be evoked only by indirection or by the intermediary of other aspects.

A model of conjugation corresponding to this governing idea could only diverge rather radically from the French conjugation, for example. One must nevertheless not see in it a mere intellectual exercise. Certainly the verb system of the Indo-European languages actually spoken in Europe is still farther removed from this model than it is from the model of a purely temporal conjugation. The linguists, however, hold that the system of the verb approaches this model if one goes back far enough in the history of the languages of this group. This is an indication which it will be useful to follow up later. For the moment we will be content to note that the idea of this second model likewise shall contribute to inform our analysis.

One more remark before we go into further detail. Putting the action or the event into a temporal situation through the inflections of the verb is not a universal linguistic phenomenon. This method of doing it, this discursive procedure, characterizes above all the group of languages termed Indo-European; to this group belongs almost the total number of European idioms. In other groups of languages the same or a more or less equivalent result is obtained through an entirely different structure of the language, conforming, as one might say, to an entirely different grammar. What remains universal is the capacity which every language has of evoking and expressing with more or less precision what we have termed the temporal situations of the action and of the event. What is different from some groups of languages to others, and even from language to language, are the means, procedures, and linguistic devices which make it possible to integrate a temporal structure into the discourse.

But within the restricted group of the Indo-European languages, even if one considers only those that are still living languages in Europe, the problem of the temporal structuring of language through the inflections of the verb is far too vast and too complex for us even to consider tackling it in its relative generality. Even for these languages, and despite their undeniable kinship with each other (the use they all make of verbal inflection is precisely an illustration of this), there exist from one to the next, concerning the point we are discussing, differences so numerous and often so fundamental that we can hardly think of entering into details for all of them at the same time.

Our investigation thus will concentrate above all on the conjugation of the verb in the French language. Nevertheless, we shall not be able to avoid making some borrowings from comparative grammar. For the following discussion we have consulted above all the comparative grammars by Dauzat and by Meillet.

In conclusion of our investigation of the structuring functions of the verb and the adverb in the natural languages, we shall finally ask ourselves what their relevance is for our central idea of discursive synthesis.

The Conjugation of the Verb in the French Language

Every systematic discourse has its elementary notions. Grammar builds or seeks to build into a system a certain number of aspects of a language. At no moment in the evolution of a language does the grammarian confront a completely stabilized "discursive situation." The aspects which he builds into a system he partly encounters and partly isolates. The verb is one of these elementary categories.

Is it necessary to define it? Such a definition inevitably will involve several verbs, under one or the other of the aspects which the grammarians' system of the verb implies, and if we take care so as not to infringe upon the rules of this system, such a definition thus gives us a previous, more or less clear knowledge of the matter to be defined. It therefore must be a defining discursive procedure, a procedure moreover without which discourse could not operate.

The grammarian thus has reason to seek to define, in order to determine it in its very elementarity, the category of the verb. But he will soon realize that this project engages him far beyond his original intention. His defining procedure must gradually lead to greater and greater precision and, unless he intends to stop on his way, he will finally confront a general review of language by means of language, a review at the same time theorizing and elementarizing.

Will he say, for example, that the verb is the element of discourse which is capable of *carrying* the different aspects of a process (one would say, in German, *eines Geschehens*) and that the system of the verb combines these different aspects into a whole? For the sake of clarity (and to rejoin the elementary) he cannot do without an explanatory, explicating comment of the words *process, aspect, system,* etc. He must show, for example, by selecting a variety of examples, that the term *process* covers an entire series of particular acceptations, of activity and passivity in their innumerable nuances, of being and becoming, duration and termination, arriving and departing, etc. Thus he will develop, on a grammatical level which will exist in its own right, a specifically grammatical sense (a sense elementarized for the purposes of its grammatical use), which somehow will be placed opposite the practically open total of its eventual interpretations. Do all the processes which the grammarian intends to designate by this term have a common characteristic? They do; they all are affected by a certain temporality. How can they be characterized under this aspect? There are several methods; at the grammatical level, those which above all merit our attention are precisely the ones we have discussed before, the ones which, after being conveniently elaborated, attain to a normalized grammatical existence through the intermediary of the two models of conjugation which we have imagined as possible. Let us take up again, first of all, the concept of the first of these models, *viz.* the purely temporal model.

The Double Engagement of the Grammarian

One imagines the process in the different phases in which it may appear or, what is the same in this case, one imagines the different phases which a process generally must be likely to assume: At the moment when its aspect is announced by discourse, the process must be capable of being imagined as already in duration or as not having started, about to start or ready to start, starting, having started, in duration, developing, reaching its climax, repeating itself, ceasing, having ceased, continuing in its consequences, or continuing indefinitely. This enumeration certainly is not exhaustive and does not pretend to be. Nevertheless, it suffices to show what difficulties a grammarian would face if he proposed to construe a system of the verb where each phase of a process could be expressed by a tense or by an inflection of its own. In order to realize this intention, the grammarian would have to undertake an investigation aimed at the totality of the elementary aspects under which a process may present itself. In this investigation the viewpoint of the grammarian could not be limited to a grammatical horizon where he would be able freely to install discursive elements in order to establish some more or less arbitrary system of the verb. His investigation would have to transcend this horizon. The phases of the process to which the grammarian intends to give grammatical reality must correspond to the forms of being and of appearing, at their own levels of reality, of all the *Geschehnisse* ("happenings") in which the term *process* may find an interpretation. The grammarian's investigation thus cannot be separated from another investigation, one which is not concerned with words but with what the words must be able to signify. In short, the grammarian's activity could not in itself be considered autonomous but must be seen as an aspect of an investigation conducted on two fronts, one of enunciation and one of observation. Grammar then presents itself as a theory of the event in its evolution.

This done, the grammarian would not yet be at the end of his task. The process in question, which takes its place in the discourse, is not only the process considered as real but also the process deferred, imagined, hypothetical, imaginary, or unrealizable, with all the nuances which the recapture of a reality by the intellect and the imagination may imply.

To these nuances we must add those which originate from certain subjective states of the person making use of the discourse. The process, for example, may be hoped for, wished for, wanted, ordered, feared, or rejected. These nuances are not completely absent from the conjugations prevailing in the natural languages. Thus, say the grammarians, the future tense of classical Greek derives from the Indo-European desiderative.

As far as we are concerned, we shall not even think of trying to set up an actual model of conjugation corresponding to the total of its exigencies. It will, however, be useful for us, as will be seen later, to have imagined its existence.

The Subject of Temporality

One may seek to give a framework of pure temporality to the event and to all the aspects under which it may present itself, from the subjective as well as from the objective point of view.

There shall be retained, in this aim, only temporal and elementary relations, in particular the relations of simultaneity, anteriority, and posteriority. To the first of our two models would correspond the grammatical realization of this intention. We shall seek to trace its general outline.

In order to imagine it we shall take the liberty of departing rather perceptibly from the notion of the conjugation of verbs such as French grammar, for example, presents it. We shall emphasize some suggestions resulting from our study of the adverb, especially those concerning the structure of temporality which the latter is able to express.

We had been struck by the structuring function of the series of the three adverbs *yesterday, today,* and *tomorrow* (and by the still more extensive rôle of the more complete cell of the five adverbial expressions *the day before yesterday, yesterday, today, tomorrow, the day after tomorrow*). We have noted the existence of analogous series such as *before, presently, from now on,* and especially remarked that a cell of this type can be "centered" on any day, or on any moment past, present, or future.

We thus might begin by imagining (and doing so we will merely pretend to imagine what is already realized in grammar) three simple tenses, a past, a present, and a future, to which every process, viewed as a whole, must be capable of being "adapted."

This done, and trying to derive as much benefit as possible from the example given by the adverb, we shall imagine two composite future tenses and two composite past tenses. While the simple future is taking on the rôle of the present, but for an instant "in the future," an anterior and a posterior future will then assume, relative to this future, the rôles of the simple past and the simple future respectively. In analogous fashion, if the simple past takes on the rôle of the present for an instant of the past, an anterior past and a posterior past likewise will assume, relative to this past present, the rôles of the simple past and of the simple future.

Is a system of the verb imagined in this way entirely chimerical? Is it sufficient, in order to take away all validity from the fact that it has been imagined, to state that any natural language would be rather far from realizing it? We do not think so. Taking into account the aspect of rationality, the theorizing moment from which his activity is inseparable, a grammarian would perhaps not hesitate to call such a system a rational system of the verb. He even might consider it useful to take it as a theoretical model, capable of serving as a term of comparison in the study of the natural languages. As far as we are concerned, taking into account the very special points for which we invoke the judgment of the grammarian, we do not consider it too hazardous an undertaking.

The seven tenses which have been discussed would moreover merely form a nucleus of the system of the verb, a nucleus which might be complemented by the concept of a structure analogous or more or less similar to the relation of succession in time, such as the relations of cause to effect, of hypothesis to consequence, of potential to actual, of the condition to the realization, etc. These relations, in which the structure of temporality is no longer the dominating element, are not absent from the complete table of the conjugations of the verb in the natural languages. In French grammar their structure is more or less adequately represented by the tenses of the conditional and the subjunctive. Thus the two latter moods do not directly concern us.

Regarding them, we nevertheless shall make a further remark, because it supports what we have said earlier concerning the double engagement of the grammarian, his engagement at a specifically grammatical level, where a certain formative process of language takes place on the one hand, and his complementary engagement at a level of observation or even of experimentation on the other, where he, too, must take cognizance of *that* which the forms of the language have or will have to signify. In order to clarify the situation we shall make use of the following device. Let us place ourselves in the situation of someone who would undertake to fixate the grammar and syntax of a universal language. Compared with the inexhaustible diversity of the natural languages, such a language could not be anything but artificial. We do not say a totally artificial language, since its creators will not and cannot work without the example of the languages naturally or historically spoken or written; but these languages will only have the value of more or less successful experiments for them which they will feel at liberty, if this seems best to them, to imitate or to send back to their business.

Let it now be assumed that those whom we have termed the creators of this language decide to incorporate into it, by the intermediary of the system of the verb, the structure of the relations of temporality and the structures, more or less analogous, of the other relations which have been discussed. Does the success depend only on them, on the fact that nature has given them the ability to take possession of the language spoken in their environment? Is it enough for them to have experienced their humanity and to have spoken like humans? Will they because of this, without making any conscious effort, have at their command the "potential knowledge" of the structure which they intend to actualize in discursive form? Should they not, on the contrary, also make the experience of this actualization, of its idoneousness, i.e. its suitability for correctly expressing all those things which we do not experience by means of language alone, the things which are not entirely in its discursive groove?

How should these questions be answered? What guarantee do we have against error? One could not, without contradicting himself, answer in the affirmative concerning the "potential knowledge" of the structures in question, as well as answering in the affirmative concerning the necessity of perceiving the idoneousness of their discursive actualization. These two affirmatives characterize two irreconcilable viewpoints.

In our opinion, the decision in favor of either one is not simply a matter of evidence or of rationality. One cannot eliminate experience, in a wide sense, which refers to the capacity of language to express, to enounce the structure of the levels of reality which are identified by systematic research. Our study of temporality in language may be viewed as a moment, albeit partial, of this experience. Thus, all we have so far been able to clarify and all we still have to say about the system of the verb in the natural languages (feeble testimony, moreover, which a comparative grammar of a certain scope would multiply a hundred or a thousandfold), our entire exposé, in a word, hardly permits more than one single interpretation—that of the double engagement which we have discussed. There is no discursive activity which is not also engaged, to some extent, in the research and in the experiment of knowledge, with all the risks of error and failure implied by it.

As to the creators of an artificial language, all the decisions which they shall make concerning the grammatical and syntactic organization of this language, in particular concerning the system of the verb, will represent as many judgments or prejudices in the area of the validity of this language.

One might make a means of systematic analysis of the device consisting in viewing the problems of grammar and syntax through the telescope of the creator of a universal language; this device to some extent plays the rôle of a revelator. Will this creator retain, for example, the usual range of subjects of the verb, from the precise *I* to the imprecise subjects such as *some,* to the vague subjects such as *one,* and the fictitious subjects such as the *it* in *it rains?* One might think that an objective and somewhat more fundamental study of the circumstances in which a process can take place, can produce itself, or can be produced, can be the effect of a cause, the cause of an effect, and so forth, would not leave invariable the list of possible subjects nor even the grammatical notion of subject. The same may be said concerning the three voices (active, passive, and reflexive) of French grammar, of the division of verbs into categories, etc.

In appearance these last remarks touch only rather lightly on the problem of temporality implied in the structure of language. Nevertheless, they illuminate it by integrating it into a more general problem, that of the content of experiences inherent in the verbal forms utilized by some particular language.

The above attempt to define some outlines of a rationalized grammar, one may even say of a rational or theoretical grammar, will now facilitate our return to languages which are habitual to us, notably the investigation of the system of the verb in the French language.

We have shown that the mental formulation of the process may be done according to two principal themes: that of the phases and more generally of the aspects of temporality, and that of temporality itself. One must, of course, distinguish this mental formulation (whose area, as one might say in a somewhat vague fashion, is the universe of our mental representations) from the verbal, discursive formulation taking place within, and by means of, a well-defined language. The area of this latter formulation might be termed the universe of the discourse connected with this language. On it our attention must now be focussed. But in order not to leave our list too incomplete, we must name a third universe of realization of the process, *viz.* the one where its reality proper asserts itself against the verbal representation which we can give of it, the one where its existence irreducibly emerges from the universe of all the representations and from the universe of all the discourses.

As far as the real languages are concerned, some questions almost pose themselves spontaneously:

1. Is the discursive formulation, if not completely identical, at least appreciably analogous between one language and the next?

It is enough to cast a glance on comparative grammar to see that this is not the case. The difference may be very noticeable even among related languages, such as Latin and French. We shall soon give a rather striking example for this. In the case of languages remote from each other the difference may be enormous, since there exist languages which do not contain systems of the verb in the sense in which we understand it here.

We will therefore abandon our first question and proceed to the next.

2. In a language containing a system of the verb, does the latter depend, in a fundamental way, on either of the two principles which we have defined?

The answer to this second question is likewise negative. There exists no system of the verb where the two themes are not intermingled. It hardly ever happens that a tense would be reserved for the expression of a single aspect or of a single engagement in temporality. One and the same present or past, for example, will lend themselves, as the case may be, to the discursive formulation of either of the two fundamental themes. Even in its correctly inflected form, the verb isolated from its context will thus remain ambiguous. It will assume a precise meaning, or rather a meaning made precise, only within the integrating milieu of the context. In this supplementary support of signification, usage everywhere enters into competition with the "grammatical conscience," with the latter's constant tendency towards organization and normalization. Now, usage varies, not only from one language to the next but within one and the same language, according to time and circumstances. This is the reason why the grammar of the verb is so difficult to put into precise and comprehensive rules.

Accordingly we cannot follow, even if it were only for the case of French and Latin, or French and German, the meanders of a comparison relative to the "alliances" between the verbal forms, for the purpose of illustrating either theme. The informational material, which finally we will be unable to do without, will be taken from French almost exclusively. Nevertheless, although we give up any idea of a valid comparative analysis, we shall pose a third question:

3. Languages change, and the system of the verb does not appear to be their most stable part. Would it not be possible that, along a certain path of evolution, one of the two fundamental principles might overtake the other? Does this evolution not tend towards the direction of a certain priority of the theme of pure temporality in conjugation itself, while the theme of the aspect is taken over by certain auxiliary forms? Does not the French language furnish an example for this?

Despite the difficulty of the subject, we shall later make bold to echo certain hypotheses.

Let us now examine the conjugation of the French verb, the system of the verb such as it has been formed through the history of the French language. We have already said why the conditional and the subjunctive moods interest us only indirectly. We will thus mainly be concerned with the indicative.

THE INDICATIVE PRESENT. If we consider the matter only in a very summary and superficial way, we might think that the French indicative really has the structure of the theoretical system which we have imagined to correspond to the theme of pure temporality. It includes three simple tenses which put the verb in the present, past, or future respectively, as well as the composite tenses of the past and future. But this first impression does not last if one enters into the reality of actual discourse. We have said that at the grammatical level, the present tense, like the past and the future, is an elementary notion. But one must not confound this state of being "a grammatical element" with the function of designating, in an elementary fashion, elementary matters. The real function of the present is far from univocal or easily understandable.

The following are examples of the present tense:

Je regarde au loin. A quoi penses-tu? Que fait-il cet instant? Quelqu'un vient.

(I look into the distance. What are you thinking of? What is he doing at this moment? Somebody is coming.)

These examples suggest the idea that the grammatical present corresponds, and cannot but correspond, to the present of a particular consciousness, to an existential present which would be, for the consciousness, an immediate and elementary datum. But, is this consciousness always well defined? Let us review the four examples:

1. *I look into the distance.* The grammatical present in this case corresponds to my own consciousness.

2. *What are you thinking of?* Here the matter is already less clear. Does the grammatical present correspond to the conscientional present of the *you,* to whom the question is addressed, or to the conscientional present of the person who is asking?

3. *What is he doing at this moment?* In this case the connection between the grammatical present and the present of a particular consciousness is still less univocal than in the preceding case. Is it the present of the person saying "at this moment" or the present of the one of whom it is not known what he is doing at this moment? Does not the grammatical present in this case rather correspond to an intersubjective present, a present objectivated in such a way that it can be the same for both consciousnesses at the same time?

In these two last examples we thus have, as in a superimposition on the present, tied to the subject of the verb, a second present, the present of a subject not mentioned but implicit and presupposed, the present of the general subject which is the author of the discourse. Do our two examples carry no trace of this second subject? They are formulated in the interrogative mood; the structure of the phrase, brief as it is, and the question mark at the end indicate this without ambiguity. One may see here the subtle but clear indication of a second subject. Such an indication, however, is missing in the fourth example.

4. *Somebody is coming*. Still more distinctly than in the two preceding examples, the present of the implicit subject, of the person who says that someone is coming, is superimposed upon the present of the person who comes. An exclamation mark at the end might certainly be added for the purpose of alluding to this hidden subject, but it is not necessary. Even if the subject is not indicated explicitly, it is implied through the meaning of the sentence. By their very simplicity, the four preceding examples already illustrate the difficulties encountered in the interpretation of the grammatical present. Even in those cases which seem to be most suitable, in the cases where the verb puts in the present an action by a well-defined subject, the very simple interpretation of the present of the verb by the present of the subject (even if this latter present contains no ambiguities) generally is not satisfactory.

Moreover, even in the most simple case where the present expresses, as in *je pars* ("I leave, I am leaving"), the most immediate "now" of the subject, discourse makes of it, with the greatest ease, the "now" of another person, of other persons, of a remembrance, of the imagination, of fiction. It suffices to integrate this *I am leaving* into an adequate context, as in the following example:

Il me disait: "je pars." Je l'entends encore me dire:"je pars." Je l'entends déjà me dire: "je pars." Il me dira: "je pars," etc.

(He told me: "I am leaving." I can still hear him say to me: "I am leaving." I can already hear him say to me: "I am leaving." He will tell me: "I am leaving," etc.)

In short, when the present of the verb corresponds to the "now" of a subject, there are as many ways to interpret this present as there are ways of living, feeling, imagining, conceiving a subjective, intersubjective, or collective "now."

On the other hand, a "now" may also be defined objectively, and the present of a verb may also refer to such a present, as in the following example:

Ma montre marque quatre heures. Voici quatre heures qui sonnent au clocher de la tour que je vois par ma fenêtre. Le ciel est couvert. Un mince rayon de soleil filtre à travers les nuages.

(My watch shows four o'clock. Four o'clock strikes from the belfry of the tower which I can see from my window. The sky is overcast. A thin ray of sunlight filters through the clouds.)

It is clear that the discourse very easily might take up and integrate into one context all the presents which have been expressed; at the moment when I announced them (for this instant has already passed), they all were referring to a "now" defined with a certain objectivity. In doing so (but is this not already accomplished in the preceding context?) the discourse will be able to make of them as many different kinds of "now" as there are variants of objective time and possibilities to connect objective time with subjective time. And each of these "now" likewise will furnish an admissible interpretation of the present of the verb. Nevertheless, we hardly, if at all, have suggested the variety of possible interpretations.

Let us examine the famous statement, *I think, therefore I am.*

One could certainly propose an interpretation of the two presents which this statement implies by seeking to link them to a "now" of the consciousness of the person who is speaking and thereby making it his own. But this is not automatic.

Would we say, for example, that we only define the sense of the original formula by substituting the following variant: *I am thinking now, therefore I am now.*

Certainly not. The introduction of the two "now's" profoundly alters the sense and essentially reduces the value of the original statement. Neither the "I think" nor the "I am" is reducible to "instants" of thinking or of existence.

The second variant would not be more felicitous: *When I am thinking, every time I think, I am.* Unlike the first variant but entirely in as grave a fashion, this variant compromises the original sense of the Cartesian statement.

The correct interpretation of the "I am" must eliminate any allusion to a certain precise moment, to a certain momentary state of consciousness. This "I am" has the discursive function of actualizing my presence in the world; I would not be able to feel or conceive this presence without its component of duration. It is an "I am" without temporal situation, although as far as I am concerned, I know that the temporal situation cannot be arbitrary. We shall soon return to this apparent contradiction.

The present of "I think" likewise has no determinate temporal situation. It actualizes a faculty which is mine, which is my characteristic always and by nature. The present form does not actualize this faculty by placing it in a definite instant of my existence in the world but rather actualizes it for any moment. This present form actualizes, somehow outside of time, my inalienable capacity of thinking.

But this is not all. The use of this nontemporal present (in two variants which are not entirely equivalent) corresponds to an intention which hardly has any other trace of grammar except this present: the formula of enunciation as which it must serve, for the enunciation as which it serves (note the introduction of this new categorical present) must itself assume a nontemporal validity; it presents itself as true in the mouth of every person, in every place, and at every moment of his existence.

In fact we have encountered here two variants of a present without temporal situation: a variant of indetermination for *I think* and *I am* and a variant of temporal nonlimitation for the formula *I think, therefore I am* considered as a whole.

Nevertheless, it is in the objective sense rather than in the subjective one, as we have done just now, that the nontemporal presents may most easily be reunited. The following new series of present forms will serve this purpose:

Le train s'ébranle. Il est six heures cinq minutes. Le train part aujourd'hui avec cinq minutes de retard. Il part, à l'ordinaire, à six heures précises.

(The train is starting. It is five minutes past six o'clock. Today the train departs five minutes late. Ordinarily it starts at six o'clock sharp.)

The present forms of the first two sentences are, as one might say, instantaneous presents. They both actualize their verbs in a definite temporal perspective.

The same is not true for the present of the third sentence. It actualizes the *departure of this day* as an exceptional case in a regular series of other cases. The fact of its being a "now" well defined within a well-organized temporal perspective has passed to a secondary level of importance. In the fourth example, finally, the present no longer corresponds to any definite "now." It becomes the expression of a certain regularity in the effectuation of the process.

The present of regularity or habit is but a weakened case of the present of the rule, the norm, the law, persistence, invariability, perenniality, fatality, necessity, eternity, and unconditional existence.

In one of these nuances it may be the present of the proverb or the present of the maxim:

On ne vit pas de pain seulement.

La fin couronne l'oeuvre.

(Man does not live by bread alone.

The end crowns the work.)

Or it may be the present of the statement intended to strike the listener by its brilliance or profundity:

A chaque fois que l'heure sonne, tout ici-bas nous dit adieu.

L'homme est un miracle sans intérêt.

(Every time the clock strikes, everything in this world bids us farewell. Man is an uninteresting miracle.)

It is the present of inexorable events taking their course:

Le flot sur le flot se replie,

Et la vague qui passe oublie

Léviathan comme Alcyon.

(Wave follows after wave/ And the passing crest obliterates/ Leviathan as well as Halcyon.)

It is likewise the present of the norm:

Dans le système cgs, l'unité de longueur est le centimètre.

Le mètre vaut cent centimètres.

(In the metrical system the unit of length is the centimeter. The meter contains one hundred centimeters.)

It is the present of natural law:

La terre tourne en 24 heures autour de son axe.

La vitesse d'aucun transport d'énergie ne dépasse la vitesse de la lumière.

(The earth turns around its axis in 24 hours. The velocity of no transportation of energy surpasses the speed of light.)

It is also the present of the principle or axiom:

L'énergie totale d'un système fermé ne peut que rester constante.

Par tout point donné, il ne passe qu'une parallèle à toute droite donnée.

(The total energy of a closed system can only remain constant. Through any given point there exists only one parallel to any given straight line.)

It is the present of the theorem or, more generally, of the necessarily correct statement:

L'aire du carré construit sur l'hypoténuse d'un triangle rectangle est égale à la somme des aires des carrés construits sur les deux côtés de l'angle droit.

(The area of the square erected over the hypotenuse of a rectangular triangle is equal to the sum of the areas of the squares erected over the two sides of the right angle.)

One might also add the present of the dogma, and so forth.

We certainly have no intention of enumerating all the presents which the French language implies. We are rather concerned with isolating, from all the preceding examples, an idea of the function of the present as simple, as correct, and as general as possible. Succumbing to the suggestive power of the words, we have considered, for an instant, the possibility that we might interpret the putting into the present tense of the verb by the actualization of the process, under the narrow angle of a well-defined "now." But it is clear that this idea cannot be entertained. It is far from covering most of the cases which should be accounted for.

Nevertheless, nothing forces us to link the idea of the actualization of a process to the idea of a unique and instantaneous accomplishment, of a process taking place in its entirety within one short moment. As we have already said, a process may be relived, reimagined while actualizing itself in the memory, or be actualized in advance through an expectation or project. But this extension is still much too weak. The actualization, as we have seen, may equally well be conceived under the aspect of repetition, habit, norm, or law, in the perspective of perenniality, continuity, or even eternity. Going this far, do we not strain the usual or traditional meaning of the term *actualization?* Perhaps so, but this must not stop us. The extension of the meaning of a word is perfectly legitimate if it is clearly stated and does not unduly compromise the interpretations which already have been acquired. In the present case this extension seems doubly justified for the following reasons:

1. It deepens, without really altering it, the idea of actualization.

2. It anticipates the theoretical effort of the grammarian, an effort which must find its consummation in the concept of the grammatical present.

The idea towards which we are thus led may be formulated in this fashion: Putting the verb in the present tense corresponds to the actualization, in its general sense, of the process. It should be noted that this rule itself is in the present tense.

This, then, is how the (indicative) present tense presents itself in the French language. Does the result of this analysis answer our expectations?

We had distinguished two fundamental themes which a rational grammar of the verb could have adopted more or less faithfully, it seems to us, in the discursive formulation of the process. But, we have added, in the real languages these two themes are blended together in an often very complex fashion. This is precisely what our analysis has confirmed. The idea of actualization, especially if we take it in its extended sense, does not appear exclusively either in the theme of temporality or in the theme of the schematized aspect. The two themes meet and combine here in an arbitration which varies according to the perspective of the actualization. Through the expedient of putting it into the present tense, grammar integrates into the

discourse a theme to some extent preliminary to the two fundamental themes already isolated: the theme of the relationship
between the potential and the actual.

(Through the intermediary of the presents, the French
language thus inevitably assumes the aspect of a dialectic of
the potential and the actual. This aspect certainly is not
always the dominant one, but it is never completely absent. It
is one of the governing principles to which the French language
owes its structure. On the other hand, every person expressing
himself in French speaks as if he did not and could not question the correctness of this inevitable dialectic. From here to
the conferring of a metaphysical value on the two fundamental
terms of this dialectic, and to the rational organization of the
latter, is but one step. But it is a step which we are not forced
to take and will not take. The information which governs the
organization of language has its justness, a justness proved for
a long time, but it is not necessarily an ultimate justness. It
may appear to be unreformable through the fact that nothing
could be said to reform it without its own inevitable participation. Without liberating ourselves totally from this hold, it is
nevertheless possible to ease it without compromising its value
of a first approach, while gaining the liberty of an eventual revision. The analysis towards which we are proceeding is precisely
one of the means to reach this goal.)

Although, for the moment, our attention is directed towards
the conjugation of verbs, our viewpoint is not that of the grammarian. In studying conjugation, our aim is essentially to find
in it a characterized moment of the temporality of language—
even though it may appear that we sometimes overshoot that
aim. Accordingly we are very far from proposing a complete
system of the verb at this point, even if we were only concerned
with adjusting it to our own perspective and even treating only
part of it as an example. Meanwhile it seems to us useful, before
we proceed, to make the following statement: Without its perspective of actualization the present suffers from a certain indetermination. The adverb or the adverbial expression has the
power to determine this perspective more or less univocally.
Nevertheless, it happens that the latter may be assured only

semantically, i.e. through an interpretation of text suggested by its context.

By the indirect help of certain periphrases or auxiliary verbs the present likewise may be made more precise and lend itself to the expression of more specific aspects. Thus, in the forms *Nous allons partir** or *Il va pleuvoir* ("We shall [soon] leave, It is going to rain"), it is the imminence of the process which is evoked, whereas in *Il vient de dire* or *Il vient de tonner* ("He just said, It has just thundered"), the barely completed or only just terminated process is being described.

We shall not seek to enumerate all possible uses of the present. As we have said, we must leave this concern to the grammarian. We must proceed now, for our own purposes, to the investigation of the simple future. Its analysis shall be facilitated by the analysis which has just been made.

THE SIMPLE FUTURE. One remark will be sufficient to elucidate the situation: in almost all the cases where we have put the verb in the present tense we might give rather similar examples where the verb is in the future tense.

Here is, first of all, the transposition of our first four examples: *Je regarderai au loin. A quoi penseras-tu? Que fera-t-il dans un instant? Quelqu'un viendra.*

(I shall look into the distance. What will you be thinking of? What will he be doing in a moment? Someone will come.)

Concerning these four futures we may begin by asking ourselves questions entirely analogous to those which we already asked concerning the four corresponding presents. Does not each of these grammatical futures seem to correspond to an existential future, i.e. a future imagined and lived in advance by an individual consciousness? For the first of the four examples, one might assume, the answer can be given without hesitation. It is

---

* The grammarians of the eighteenth century gave a complete conjugation in tenses and moods of the verb *aller,* "to go," in this auxiliary sense "to be about to." This conjugation has never existed in usage. In this rôle *aller* is mainly used in the present indicative and less frequently in the imperfect. We mention this fact only to underscore the normative intention of the grammarian to which we have often referred, the rôle of active theorician of language which he quite naturally assumes.

surely the self, the subject of the verb, which this verb describes as being about to look into the distance in an instant which *then* I shall live as a moment of my proper existence. But the other three examples lend themselves far less easily to an analogous interpretation. The fourth example is especially ambiguous; for the person who is coming, the process, the action of coming, will *then* be accompanied by an immediate awareness of it. But for the person who says or writes *Someone will come,* there is awareness anticipated by the intermediary of the imagining of the completion of the process.

Does not the grammatical future in this case rather correspond, as has already been the case for the present, to an intersubjective future, a future objectivated in such a way as to be able to be the same for different subjective perspectives? The ambiguity of the connection of the grammatical future with a definite existential or conscientional future may be shown still more clearly by the device of introducing direct speech in a context, as in the following examples:

Hier je te demandais: où iras-tu?

Aujourd'hui je te demande à nouveau: où iras-tu?

Demain je te demanderai encore: où iras-tu?

(Yesterday I asked you: where will you go?

Today I am asking you again: where will you go?

Tomorrow I shall still ask you: where will you go?)

But indirect discourse is hardly less ambiguous. In order to realize this it is enough to take up the three preceding examples once again:

Hier je te demandais où tu irais aujourd'hui.

Je te demande aujourd'hui où tu iras demain.

*Je te demanderai demain où tu iras la semaine prochaine.**

(Yesterday I asked you where you would go today.

I ask you today where you will go tomorrow.

I shall ask you tomorrow where you will go next week.)

At this point it is already clear that the interpretation of the grammatical future meets the same difficulties as that of the present. The grammatical future is not, in general, the expres-

---

* The second form of the future "what you would do" used in indirect speech is often characterized by an element of uncertainty.

sion of a simple temporal future. We shall not seek, however, to make a list of all its possible acceptations. Let us rather compare a list of futures with the parallel list of presents previously enumerated, or at least with some of them.

First of all, here is an instantaneous future:

Nous partirons, sauf imprévu, à six heures précises.

(We shall depart, if all goes as planned, at six o'clock sharp.)

And here are more or less indeterminate or conditional futures:

Nous partirons entre six et sept heures.

Nous partirons sans trop attendre.

Nous partirons, si le temps le permet, etc.

(We shall depart between six and seven o'clock.

We shall depart without waiting too long.

We shall depart, weather permitting, etc.)

The futures of this first group clearly lack a shift of the process (of its actualization) towards a temporal future, even if the latter is not neatly and precisely situated in the temporal perspective "of someone." In the following second group this element of temporality does not disappear, but it combines with an element of habituation, repetition, iteration, perseverance, or even perenniality:

L'an prochain cet enfant ira (régulièrement) à l'école.

Cette horloge sonnera (longtemps) sans qu'on ait à la remonter.

De plus en plus nombreux, les avions traverseront l'Atlantique.

L'homme est pécheur et le restera.

De siècle en siècle, la terre tournera autour du soleil, etc.

(Next year this boy will go to school [regularly].

This clock will be striking [for a long time] without having to be wound up.

In ever-increasing numbers, airplanes will cross the Atlantic.

Man is a sinner and will remain one.

Century after century the earth will revolve around the sun, etc.)

Now, in a third group, we show future tenses expressing the rule, the norm, the law, necessity, and fatality:

Selon le nouvel horaire, ce train partira dix minutes plus tôt.
On partira, la saison prochaine, plus tôt qu'aujourd'hui.
En ville, un véhicule ne dépassera pas la vitesse de 60 km à l'heure.
Le juge appliquera les lois avec impartialité.
Tu honoreras ton père et ta mère.
Selon que vous serez puissant ou misérable, les jugements de cour vous rendront blanc ou noir.
Demain comme aujourd'hui, la nuit viendra.
Nos jours passeront, le temps du monde passera, mais l'Eternel ne passera pas, etc.

(According to the new timetable this train will depart ten minutes earlier.

Next season we shall depart earlier than today.

In town a vehicle shall not exceed the speed of 40 mph.

The judge shall apply the laws impartially.

You shall honor your father and mother.

Depending on whether you are powerful or poor, the judgments of the court will paint you white or black.

Tomorrow as today, night will come.

Our days will pass, the time of the world will pass, but the Almighty will not, etc.)

Finally, in a fourth group, some future forms are shown in which the temporal element is replaced by the intentional, by the consequence, or by the unconditional development:

Faites un triangle rectangle dont les cathètes soit respectivement égales à trois unités et quatre unités, l'hypoténuse en vaudra cinq.

Pour n tendant vers l'infini, l'expression $\left(1 + \frac{1}{n}\right)^n$ tendra vers le nombre e.

Ce qui est vrai ne pourra pas cesser de l'être.

Je ne prétendrai pas que le monde changeant, les lois qui le régissent changeront avec lui, etc.

(Make a right-angled triangle whose legs are equal to three and four units respectively, then the hypotenuse will be equal to five units.

For *n* tending towards infinity, the expression $\left(1 + \frac{1}{n}\right)^n$ will tend towards the number *e*.

What is true will never cease to be true.

I shall not maintain that, while the world is changing, the laws governing it will also change, etc.)

We shall not stress* the fact that by being inserted into an adequate context, a simple future may assume, according to the grammarians' expression, the rôle of a future of the past or of a future of the future. This fact certainly must be taken into consideration in the search for a correct interpretation of the grammatical future. Concerning our analysis of temporality in conjugation, it would nevertheless be more significant if we could indicate two tenses to which these rôles would properly belong.

What are our conclusions so far? Above all, there is an interpretation which the list of our examples clearly does not include: Without arbitrariness one could not reduce the rôle of the grammatical future to the expression of a pure and simple temporality. The parallelism which we have just pointed out, a parallelism which is striking although incomplete, between the whole aggregate of futures and that of presents in the French language, obliges us to approximate the interpretation which we have given for the grammatical present. This present, we said, is the tense of the actualization of the process in all the perspectives of actualization which a context might suggest. The connection of the grammatical present with a temporal present generally is not an immediate one. If it is never totally absent it is because the notion of actualization and the idea of the temporal present are hardly conceivable unless in a certain interdependence. The same is not exactly true for the grammatical future. The latter is more directly engaged in temporality; a certain relation to the future is inevitably a part of it. It introduces into the perspective of actualization a temporal future linked to its essence of grammatical future.

In short, the grammatical future indicates that the process "will come about" in a certain perspective of actualization. Most often this "coming about" is of a temporal character. Nevertheless it may happen that the temporal character is weakened and transformed into an "about to come" with a different em-

---

* Note the intentional future which, in our text, might be translated by "we do not wish to stress," or "we consider it superfluous to stress."

phasis, for example, in a perspective of intentionality or of finality.

(For a more fundamental study of the grammatical future the existence of such transformations is a fact not to be ignored. They have a common structural aspect and thus bear witness to a certain tendency of the future tense to become the expression of this aspect. For our purposes it is sufficient to note that, as a rule, this structural aspect is realized in the form of a temporal future.)

There is of course nothing surprising in the statement that the grammatical future incorporates certain elements of temporality, and that it is linked to the very notion of the temporal future. Everybody knows or surmises this, and unless it had been a question of stating it beyond any doubt, our analysis would not have been necessary. What the latter has brought to light, however, is that the tense of the future could not be interpreted as the expression of a pure and simple shift of the process towards a more or less precisely defined future. Severed from its context and from the meaning it must assume therein, a grammatical future remains somewhat indeterminate. What may be surprising is the complexity of the rôle of the context and of its inexhaustible capacity to modulate the function of the verb even for tenses as simple as the present and the future.

The present, as we have said, is the grammatical tense of the actualization of the process. But, we added, the actualization may take place in the most varied perspectives, and the adequate perspective is determined by the insertion of the present into its context. The temporal element of the actualization thus may be projected towards the future or towards the past, with the grammatical present then becoming a present of the future or a present of the past. On the other hand, we have just said that the grammatical future defers the actualization of the process, that it converts it into a "coming" actualization—while the context, likewise, may convert it into a future of the past or a future of the future. Is there not a certain wobble to these definitions? Thus characterized, will the present and the future tenses not be confused in the end? The fact is that the complex and varied rôle of the context makes a certain vagueness inevitable. By defining the conditions of the actualization of the process more or less narrowly, the context is bound to enter into competition with the conjugation of the verb. Thus, the following sentence (in which the future form "will depart" was replaced by the infinitive "to depart") is incorrect but unequivocal: *Dans cinq minutes, le train partir.* ("In five minutes the train to depart.")

Thus, what characterizes the grammatical future is that it carries, in its very form, the moment of temporality which must be superimposed on the actualization of the process.

Concerning the expression of the temporal situation of the process by means of the conjugation in particular, it should be noted here that there exists a second form of the future. We have seen that the grammatical future is not always interpreted through a temporal future relative to an origin of the times determined with some precision. Nevertheless, it is hardly necessary to mention that this case is not excluded. In the following example the origin is dated: *J'apprends à l'instant qu'il ne viendra que demain.* ("I hear this moment that he will come only tomorrow.") In this example the origin of the tenses is the "now" of the speaker.

The form of the future remains the same if the origin of the tenses in turn is reported in the future in connection with a well-defined temporal origin. This is the case in the following example: *Il m'écrira, je pense, demain qu'il ne viendra que le lendemain.* ("I believe he will write me tomorrow that he will come only the following day.")

This example implies two differently dated futures. The first is dated by the adverb "tomorrow"; its temporal origin is today. The second is dated by "the following day"; its temporal origin is tomorrow.

These two examples illustrate the following rule: When a future expresses a "coming" temporal situation in connection with an origin of the tenses which in turn may be interpreted as a "now" or as an "in a certain time," moreover described in a more or less precise fashion, the form of the future is the one which already has been discussed.

But if, under the same conditions, the origin of the tenses

may be interpreted by "some time ago," the form of the future is that of the conditional. Here is a corresponding example: *Il m'a écrit hier qu'il ne viendrait qu'aujourd'hui.* ("He wrote me yesterday that he would come only today.")

Finally, here is an example where the two forms of the future are combined: *J'ai appris hier qu'il ne me dirait qu'aujourd'hui quand il viendra.* ("I have heard yesterday that he will tell me only today when he is going to come.")

We shall not investigate to what extent this second form of the future, the form of the future in the past, may duplicate the form we have studied earlier. We will simply note that, where it is possible, the two forms of the future actually enter the framework of a purely temporal conjugation, whose sole purpose would be to mark, by means of special forms and endings, the temporal situation of the process.

In order to complete our study of the tenses of the indicative we also have to consider the three tenses of the past: the imperfect, the simple past, and the composite past; and towards the three tenses which express anteriority: the future perfect, the pluperfect, and the past perfect historic. Our point of view, we repeat, is not that of the grammarian. We are studying the structure of conjugation only in order to find out to what extent it represents the discursive explication of a structure of temporality. In the same intention we shall continue, guided by our analysis of the present and future.

Our first question concerning the three tenses of the past is the following: Does any of them play, relative to the present, a rôle to some extent symmetrical to the future? Let us show, without too much detail, that this is the case for the imperfect.

THE PAST TENSES. The present, we repeat, does not systematically represent the grammatical expression of a particular aspect of the process; the process appears in it neither as about to begin nor as beginning or having just begun, neither as about to terminate nor as terminating or having just terminated, neither as a consequence of some other process nor as a continuation in its consequences, but simply as taking place. *I march* may be interpreted by *I am ready to march; The earth spins* by *The earth is in a state of rotation.* The present, as we have said, is the tense of the actualization of the process, independent of any systematic temporal surcharge; but the temporal situation of this actualization is not necessarily a "now"; sometimes it is neither the present time of an individual consciousness, nor the origin of an objectivated temporal sequence. It is a "punctual now" only in a few particular cases. The grammatical present is a present *sui generis*, a discursive present whose application may be operated, as we have seen, under the most diverse aspects.

Does this reminder clarify the function of the imperfect? Does the latter truly transpose the rôle of the present such as we just have outlined again? One might at first doubt this. In fact, a certain grammatical tradition declares the imperfect as the tense of a special aspect of the process, viz. its durative aspect. This characterization of the imperfect requires, however, that the qualification *durative* not be interpreted too narrowly; the aspect corresponding to it must not only be that of simple duration but also of repetition, habit, regularity, persistence, continuity, etc. Of course it is easy to give plenty of examples to illustrate this thesis. We shall do so in an instant. Yet we are unable to concede, after what has been said about the present and the future, that this should be a characteristic quality of the imperfect. The reason for this is simple: We were able to give, for the future as well as for the present, a complete set of analogous examples. Thus we must try to find something else. For this purpose let us go back to the investigation of the modalities according to which the actualization of the process may be viewed.

Take again our former example and this time put it in the imperfect: *Je marchais.* ("I marched, I was walking.") Let us imagine at the same time some of the innumerable indirect complements through which this imperfect may be modified and defined: *Je marchais à grands pas, je marchais de long en large, je marchais depuis longtemps, il y avait à peine cinq minutes que je marchais, je marchais sans réfléchir, etc.* ("I walked with big steps, I walked up and down, I had been walking for a long time, I had been walking for hardly five minutes, I marched without thinking, etc.") It is clear that in all these variants the expression *je marchais* may be rendered by *I was about to march, I was in a state of walking*. We might repeat in this instance everything we just said about the present; the imperfect with which we are dealing now does not represent the process either as in preparation, or as about to be completed, or as being continued, nor even as extending through a certain duration of time. The process is simply described as taking place in a certain time of the past which otherwise is not precisely defined. Since the process is not instantaneous it obviously cannot be denied that it has a component of duration: it is the duration which belongs to it and without which its actualization could not be imagined. But this durative element is not a special characteristic of the imperfect; it is not limited to it but may also be found in the rest of the tenses.

Likewise, the phrase *il sonnait midi* ("the clock struck noon") does not mean *the clock was about to strike noon* or *the clock just had struck noon,* but rather that the process of "striking noon" took place; moreover, the fact does not have to be noted especially that this "taking place" cannot be separated from a certain "taking time."

The following is another example in which the durative aspect is hardly noticeable:

Il sonnait six heures. Le train partait. C'est seulement à ce moment-là que j'aperçus mon camarade.

(The clock struck six o'clock. The train departed. Only at this moment I caught sight of my friend.)

This example leads us back to the *relation of transposition* by which the imperfect at the same time differs from the present and approximates it. The following examples will illustrate this point. As far as possible we shall each time give a present in parallel with an imperfect, in order to show clearly what they have in common. This means that we will merely confirm in greater detail what was said before.

In the following example the aspect of duration is very noticeable in the present but less so in the imperfect:

A huit heures ce matin il ne pleuvait pas encore.

Depuis neuf heures, et nous voici à midi, il pleut sans interruption.

(At eight o'clock in the morning it was not yet raining.

Since nine o'clock, and it is already noon, it has been raining continuously.)

In the following example both the present and the imperfect represent grammatical expressions of a custom:

Depuis bien des années, on sonne les cloches à six heures du matin. Autrefois, c'est à cinq heures qu'on les sonnait.

(For many years the bells have been rung at six o'clock in the morning. Formerly it used to be at five.)

Instead of custom here is established regularity:

Le train qui part depuis quelque temps à six heures, partait, selon l'ancien horaire, un quart d'heure plus tôt.

(The train which, for some time, has been leaving at six, used to leave a quarter of an hour earlier, according to the old schedule.)

The following example is in the middle between convention and natural law:

Pour nous, un jour entier va de minuit à minuit et comporte 24 heures, égales entre elles en toute saison. Pour les anciens, le jour allait du lever au coucher du soleil et comportait douze heures de jour; la nuit allait du coucher au lever du soleil et comportait douze heures de nuit. La différence entre une heure de jour et une heure de nuit variait alors suivant les saisons.

(For us, a full day lasts from midnight to midnight and contains 24 hours, which are equal to each other in any season. For the ancients, the day lasted from sunrise to sundown and contained twelve hours of daytime; the night lasted from sundown to sunrise and contained twelve hours of nighttime. The difference between an hour of the day and an hour of the night varied according to the time of year.")

We shall now combine the natural law in a modern formulation with a formulation of an earlier date:

Pour l'astronome d'aujourd'hui, la terre tourne autour du soleil.

Pour les anciens astronomes, le soleil tournait autour de la terre.

(For the modern astronomer the earth revolves around the sun.

For the ancient astronomers the sun revolved around the earth.)

In the following example the present and the imperfect place the process in a long-established state:

Le Nil coule du sud au nord. Il y a mille ans, il coulait déjà dans la même direction depuis des millénaires.

(The Nile flows from the south to the north. A thousand years ago it already had been flowing in this direction for millenia.)

In the following example the present and the imperfect put the process into perspectives at the same time unlimited and complementary:

Au commencement, le monde était informe et vide:

Depuis sa création, le monde ne cesse à se transformer.

(In the beginning the world was unformed and empty:

Since its creation the world has not ceased to change.)

Finally we shall assign to the imperfect the task of expressing, by itself, an absolute perenniality:

Dans mon rêve, le concert que j'écoutais était éternel.

(In my dream the concert to which I was listening went on forever.)

We believe that it is not necessary to add to the list of these examples. Those which have been given sufficiently illustrate what we have already called the displacement of the present by the imperfect. The latter represents, in the same way as the present, the grammatical expression of the actualization of the process, but carries it back towards the past in a somewhat indeterminate temporal situation. The perspective of this actualization is not necessarily a perspective of simple reality; its period is not invariably the yesterday or the day before yesterday or any other period of the past for an individual consciousness, nor is it a determinate interval of time of an objectivated past. We may repeat almost literally, concerning the imperfect, what we have said of the present: the past of the imperfect is a past *sui generis*, a discursive past which may be applied in the most diverse modalities. In short, one may say of the imperfect that it transposes the present (in most of its forms) by imprinting on it the seal of a past.

If we were to remain within the limited area of our present

subject and accordingly had to study the temporal status of the imperfect, the preceding considerations could suffice. But while discussing the particular problem of time in language, we can hardly avoid treating the problem of language also from a somewhat more general point of view. Accordingly the few observations which follow do not seem to us to be out of place.

Is the method which we have used to study the rôle of the imperfect not open to criticism? We have been content to examine some isolated sentences and some very brief texts. Can we be sure that this procedure does not create an artificial situation where the imperfect would be unable to deploy its entire function? Could it not happen that by separating certain sentences in the imperfect from the text in which they occur, one precludes the possibility of recognizing some essential characteristic, not of the temporal status of the imperfect but of its capacity of intervention in the discourse?

This latter problem, moreover, might recur with any other tense of the conjugation. That which constitutes the discursive function of a tense probably cannot be reduced to what remains in a few shreds of texts isolated from their contexts. It is probable, on the contrary, that the discursive reality of this tense should comprise a component of interaction, that its function implies a component of structuralization, i.e. structuralization of the discourse and not merely of the immediate surroundings of the correctly conjugated verb.

In the case of the imperfect the structuring function of the discourse, which has been discussed, is particularly evident. Putting the process in the imperfect often has the effect of sketching into the discourse what might be called a frame of reference within which other processes, conjugated in their own correct tenses, would have to take place. Here are some examples in which, as it seems to us, the verb put in the imperfect undoubtedly plays the rôle of *discursive referential*. Let us first recall one of the most simple of our preceding examples. Here it is put in the present: *Il sonne six heures. Le train part.* ("The clock strikes six. The train departs.") Do these two brief sentences call for a complement? We do not think so. In their succinctness they form a certain whole.

Let us now put them in the imperfect: *Il sonnait six heures. Le train partait.* ("The clock struck six. The train departed.") The two sentences are not self-sufficient and do not form a whole as was the case with the present tense. They call for a complement of text, as, for example, the one we already gave above: *C'est alors seulement que j'aperçus mon camarade.* ("Only at that moment I noticed my friend.")

This complement of text is not indispensable for the perspective of actualization to shift towards the past. Without it, however, one has the impression that the statement is incomplete, that its meaning not only remains in suspense but also awaits a certain information to which it is only a preparation. The statement designs a frame for something that still has to be told; it appears as a referential for the process towards which our attention must still be directed.

We should also note that, in this example, the temporal situation of the referential remains undetermined. When did the clock strike six? Was it in the morning, yesterday, a week ago, or a year ago? Nothing gives us a specific indication.

We deliberately have not started with our most convincing examples but rather with an example which requires some additional explanations. The following examples hardly need any explanation:

Un octogénaire *plantait,*

Passe encore de semer, mais planter à cet âge,

Disaient trois jouvenceaux. . . .)

(An octogenarian was planting [trees];/ One may still sow, but to plant at this age,/ Three boys were saying. . . .)

Maître corbeau, sur un arbre perché,

Tenait en son bec un fromage.

Maître renard, par l'odeur alléché,

Lui tint à peu près ce language. . . .

(Mister raven, perched upon a tree,/ Was holding in his beak a piece of cheese./ Mister fox, attracted by the smell,/ Addressed the following speech to him. . . .)

Dans un chemin montant, sablonneux, malaisé

Et de tous les côtés au soleil exposé,

Six forts chevaux *tiraient* un coche.

Femmes, enfants, vieillards, tout était descendu,
L'attelage *suait, soufflait, était* rendu.
Une mouche survient et des chevaux s'approche.
(On a steep, dusty, uncomfortable road,/ Exposed to the sun
on every side,/ Six strong horses were pulling a coach./ Women,
children, old men, all had alighted./ The horses were sweating,
panting, exhausted./ A fly comes and approaches the horses.)
Un agneau *se désaltérait*
Dans le courant d'une onde pure.
Un loup survint à jeun qui *cherchait* aventure . . . .*
(A lamb was quenching its thirst/ In the current of a clear
water./ A hungry wolf came by, looking for a chance. . . .)
But however neatly defined a grammatical function may be,
usage soon manages to modify and transfer it, to twist it towards
a thousand more or less analogous purposes. Thus the referential
may become a simple reference, or even a simple accentuation
of either of the two events one intends to relate to each other.
Here are three examples:
Comme il commençait de pleuvoir, je me mis à l'abri.
J'entrai au moment où il cessait de parler.
Je le vis qui me faisait signe.
(Since it was starting to rain, I went to take shelter.
I entered at the moment when he stopped speaking.
I saw him wave to me.)
Before we proceed to examine the other tenses of the indicative, we shall cast a glance backward and compare with our
expectations the results obtained in our study of the present, the
future, and the imperfect. We have asked ourselves whether we
would find again, in the mutual relations of the grammatical
tenses (limiting our inquiry to the tenses of the indicative), the
temporal structure which certain groups of adverbs clearly
realize. We even have imagined, somewhat playfully but also
in order to have a precise term of comparison, what might be

---

* It is certainly not by pure accident that all these examples could have
been borrowed from the same fable writer (viz. La Fontaine). In all the
preceding examples, and more might be added, the imperfect provides a
framework for an event whose emergence is characterized by the use of the
simple past or the indicative present.

a conjugation responding only to the concern of furnishing a discursive expression of the temporal situation of the process. Besides, this playfulness was not entirely arbitrary, for we let ourselves be guided, on the one hand, by the results obtained in the study of the adverbs and, on the other, by the knowledge of the structure of the mathematicians' temporal continuum. Opposite this purely temporal conjugation we likewise have imagined a conjugation in some way complementary, whose function would be to express the elementary aspects of the process and, if possible, to bring them into correlation.

At this point we might ask ourselves whether, as far as the three tenses under consideration are concerned, the French conjugation perfectly corresponds to either of the imagined models. Now, in its actual complexity, the conjugation has seemed to elude such a simplification at first. Already in the case of the present tense a grave difficulty appeared to bar our way from the very first steps. Except for certain situations the grammatical present cannot be assimilated to a simple "at the present time"; nor can it be assimilated to the "now" of a determinate consciousness or the instant of origin of an objectivated temporal perspective. It is a present tense of a special kind, a discursive present whose function cannot be reduced to the fixation of what might be called the present moment of the process. Its area of application is far more extensive and reaches from the instantaneous to the eternal, from the temporal to the unconditional. Our intention of finding again in actual conjugation at least the outline of our first theoretical model thus appears to have been totally unfounded. These statements concerning the grammatical present could also be applied to the future or to the imperfect.

Nevertheless, if it were established in this way that the project of directly translating the grammatical present by a temporal "at this time" could not be carried out, it would be absurd to conclude from this that conjugation does not carry any temporal structure. The apparently paradoxical situation becomes clear if one refrains from directly applying the grammatical tense to the process, but rather relates it to what we have defined as a perspective of actualization. The transition from the present to the future and the imperfect then may be translated by a certain transposition in the time of the perspective of actualization relative to the present.

In this roundabout fashion, our project thus may yet be realized; under this aspect it is certainly some temporal structure upon which conjugation confers a certain form of discursive existence.

But we are far removed from the simplicity of our first outline. We still are concerned only with the three simplest tenses of the indicative, and nothing gives us the right to assume that the rest could be treated and understood after the same fashion. On the other hand, we have concentrated our attention on only one aspect of the problem, i.e. on what might be called the *temporal prominence* of conjugation. The very orientation of our investigation has caused us to neglect as secondary matters the more or less apparent traces of other aspects. (They are in fact secondary as far as the principal object of our investigation is concerned; they might not be for a grammarian who would make conjugation itself the object of his study.) It is by no means certain that the thus neglected aspects would not assume much greater importance for the tenses, especially for the composite forms, which we have not considered so far.

Finally, in the case of the imperfect and the rôle of referential which it often plays in the discourse, we had occasion to remark that what makes the discursive reality of a tense may very well involve a *syntactic component* which is displayed only through the insertion into the discourse of the correctly conjugated tense.

These few remarks are not only those which it would be necessary to make if one were concerned about all the complexities of language, we might even say its analytically irreducible elements. The aim of our remarks, at this point in our exposition, is to remind ourselves of all the schematic and, in sum, theoretical elements implied in the vision we are trying to isolate. But we must come back to this point later. Let us now consider the other tenses, especially the compound tenses.

Among the imperfect, the simple past, and the composite past, the imperfect is the one which most faithfully takes on the function of the present by transferring it into some past. How do the simple past and the composite past differ from it?

It will be sufficient for us to adopt for our use the usual notations of the grammarians. The two past tenses with which we are concerned here have a common characteristic in which both differ from the imperfect, and which at this time must be pointed out. They both represent a process as being completed. Accordingly they both present, in two different nuances of meaning, a particular aspect of the process. Such as they are, they thus could not take place in a conjugation which, according to the example of our first theoretical model, would have the sole purpose of expressing the temporal situation of the process. First, here is an example where the two nuances are rather close to each other:

Il fit alors la déclaration suivante.

Il a fait alors la déclaration que voici.

(He then made the following declaration.

He then has made this declaration.)

There is, however, a perceptible difference between the two variants. The simple past somehow gathers the process up within itself to put it in its proper place; it makes of it a rounded whole but does not judge it as such from the perspective of the present, into which it would still carry its own incidences or consequences. The majority of our examples for the use of the imperfect were at the same time examples for the use of the past historic. The imperfect defined what we have called a referential while the simple past inserted the process. Generally speaking, the simple past refers to an event, an action, an activity, a more or less rigidly delimited process whose limits may be defined by an imperfect; but also, in a thousand ways, they may be defined through the context.

Conversely, the composite past represents the process as completed in a perspective which belongs to some present, although indication of this perspective often remains implicit. Through the fact of this insertion, which is strikingly different from the one discussed before, the process conjugated in the composite past somehow remains present in one or the other of its interpretations, whether it be through its consequences or through any other relation with the implicit present tense of the discourse.

For example, in the following brief statement, *On a sonné* ("The bell has rung."), the relation to the present of the discourse is particularly evident. It is clear that this past implies an urgent invitation to attend to the fact that "the bell (just) rang." The natural complement of the statement could be, "Are we expecting anyone?"

The grammarians note a general tendency of the composite past of the French language to replace the simple past, wherever this is possible without too serious a change in the mutual relations of the tenses, particularly in conversational language. However justified and instructive this statement may be for a grammarian, it stays outside our subject matter. For us it is on the contrary more interesting to note that in certain examples, the two tenses could hardly be mistaken for each other. The following is a case in point:

Le corbeau, honteux et confus,
Jura, mais un peu tard, qu'on ne l'y prendrait plus.

(The raven, ashamed and confused,/ Swore, albeit somewhat late, that he was not going to be caught in this trap again.)

In this example the substitution of the composite past *a juré* ("has sworn") for the simple past *jura* ("swore") somehow would destroy the consistency of the discourse. It would arrest its flow and would tear the action of swearing from its historical context, to confer upon it a meaning in relation to the author of the story, a meaning which to some extent would be outside the story. In its proper place in the text the simple past does nothing except preserve the tightness and coherence of the tale taken as a whole. More exactly, the simple past implies a story, an account of things seen, heard, or lived through. This is also indicated by usage; the simple past is a tense of literature and is not used in conversation. The case of the fable is quite instructive; here the change of the simple past into the composite past is impossible, because the composite past is too concrete a tense and would destroy the allegory.

As we have already noted, by insisting too much on this aspect of the analysis of conjugation we would deviate from our subject. What must be said, however, is that the two past tenses discussed above could not be placed side by side with the present, the future, and the imperfect in our first theoretical model of conjugation, but rather would belong to our second model, to the conjugation whose object would be to express, through the inflection of the tenses, the various aspects but not the temporal situations of the process.

Thus, as anticipated, but with unexpected twists, conjugation in the indicative mood operates two principal themes: the temporal transposition towards the future or towards the past, and the distinction between a process on the way to its completion on the one hand and a completed process on the other. This statement, however, is based on a scrutiny of five tenses only, viz. the three principal tenses and the two tenses which may enter into competition with the imperfect. Will our consideration of the other compound tenses not introduce a new element, an element capable of aggravating to the point of inextricability (at least from our point of view) the already very complex character of the situation? A simple remark will suffice to give a fresh start to our analysis. In order to provide scope for the development of the theme of temporal transposition, we had to resort to the expedient of an intermediate reality, the perspective of actualization. For a new start we shall again submit an intermediate grammatical material, viz. the relation of succession between two tenses.

THE THEME OF ANTERIORITY. In reviewing the composite past we should note that the grammarians consider it a *relative tense*. This means that this tense takes on its full significance only in its relation to a different tense, to the present in our particular case. The following example will explain this better:

On a pris hier la décision que je formule maintenant.

Je formule maintenant la décision qu'on a prise hier.

(Yesterday the decision was made which I am now formulating.

I now formulate the decision which was made yesterday.)

The first of these two statements puts the emphasis on the process which took place in the past, relative to which the second process then is put in the present. The second statement does the opposite, since it puts the emphasis on the process which takes place in the present, relative to which the second process is put

in the past. Thus the composite past expresses a relation of consecution which is above all, but not exclusively, of a temporal
character. In one example the emphasis is on the earlier date,
while in the other it is on the later one. Thus the relation is one
of anteriority and posteriority, the preceding date always being
in the past and the subsequent date always being in the future.
But, in making the connection between these two tenses, the
mind does not always pass from one to the other in the same
direction; it is sometimes prompted to go back from the posterior
date towards the anterior. In this way the relation of consecution
may be traveled in both directions, and it presupposes both
tenses in order to be validly established.

In brief, the grammatical nature of this relation of consecution
is determined only by the relation between the two tenses, by
the relation between the composite past and the present in our
particular case.

By saying that in the preceding discussion only a particular
case is being considered, we already have anticipated the
following. It is, in fact, quite natural to ask ourselves whether
we have not just demonstrated the conditions of a new application of the procedure of the temporal transposition. Does the
transferred relation adequately realize itself through already
existing tenses, or rather pairs of tenses?

It is obvious that transposed into the future, our relation can
only be realized through the addition of the future perfect to the
future. The following example in two parts shows this very
clearly. It introduces three persons designated respectively as
A, B, and C.

B parlera lorsque A aura lu. Et B aura parlé lorsque C lira.

(B shall speak after A has finished reading. And B will have
spoken when C reads.*

B's action is in the future in one case and in the future perfect in the other. Nevertheless, in reality, there is only one single
action. One may therefore say that, in the first part of the
example, the rôles of the future and of the future perfect may

---

* In this example the relation of succession is not merely a temporal relation;
it is accompanied by the indication, more or less imperative, of an order
which has to be observed.

correspond to their respective grammatical designation but that, in the second part, the future perfect assumes the rôle of a future, while the future should be called a posterior future. The relative character of the future perfect to the future is thus made evident.

It must also be noted that if *B's* action is not expressed through the same tense, although it is one and the same action, the reason is that it is not presented under the same aspect each time; in the future it is an action which must be effected, while in the future perfect it is an action which is considered complete. We thus see defined, in analogy to the rôle of the composite past, that of the composite future, i.e. the future perfect: It is within its function to represent the process as already accomplished.

We shall also note, without, however, dwelling on the subject, that the same relation could be realized by replacing the first form of the future by the second. Conjugation in fact contains a second form of the future perfect, whose temporal origin is in the past. The following is an example: *J'étais sûr que quand B parlerait A serait déjà parti.* ("I was certain that when B would speak A would already have left.") It is, of course, the imperfect *j'étais sûr* ("I was certain") which fixates the origin of the tenses in the past.

We shall now try to transpose our relation of succession to the past. Taking into account our previous experiences, it is quite natural for us to use, in this endeavor, the pluperfect and the imperfect. Let us recall, for this purpose, the preceding example in slightly modified form:

Ce que B disait, A l'avait déjà lu.

Lorsque B l'avait dit, C le lisait à nouveau.

(What B was saying A had already read.

When B had said it, C read it again.)

Once again, *B's* action, which is one single action, is being conjugated in the same text in two different tenses. It is in the imperfect as a posterior action and in the pluperfect as an anterior one. Should we say that here likewise the anterior tense, the pluperfect, presents the action as accomplished? A finer distinction is needed to make this statement perfectly correct. What is presented as complete is the fact that the process has been effected. For this reason, in certain cases, the function of the pluperfect in relation to the imperfect may be profitably conferred on the imperfect of the colloquial expression *avoir fini de* . . . ("to have done [with] . . ."). Thus modified, our first example looks like this: *B parlait lorsque A avait fini de lire* and *Lorsque B avait fini de parler, C lisait à son tour.* ("B spoke when A had done reading" and "When B had done speaking C read in turn").

The difference pointed out in this fashion clearly shows that the pluperfect assumes, in its proper function of expressing the relation of anteriority, if not totally at least partially, the rôle which we had attributed to the imperfect.

Let us pause for a moment to review what has been said. In a very succinct fashion—we must emphasize this fact—we have given a replica to our study of the three basic tenses. The application of the procedure of temporal transposition has given us possession, starting with the composite past, of the other two composite tenses, viz. the future perfect and the pluperfect. In order to give a complete replica to the first part of our analysis it remains for us to apply the second theme, the theme of the contrast (in a certain perspective) of the process on its way to actualization on the one hand and the completed process on the other. We shall not attempt to give an exhaustive list of all possible variants of this application. The following example shows how, in our relation of succession, the rôle of the posterior tense may be assumed by the simple past and the rôle of the anterior tense by the past perfect historic:

Quand A eut parlé, B se leva et parla à son tour et quand il eut parlé, C se leva pour en faire de même.

(When A had spoken, B rose and spoke also, and when he had done speaking C rose to speak in turn.)

Here, likewise, it is one and the same action of *B's*, viz. rising at one particular moment, which is being conjugated, in the simple past in one case and in the past perfect historic in the other. It should be noted as a new fact that in both cases the action is represented as complete, in one case as posterior and in the other as anterior to two other equally complete actions.

Finally we give an example where the relation is realized through the intermediary of the composite past and a super-composite past:

A peine ai-je eu tourné le dos qu'on m'a appelé,

(I had scarcely turned my back when someone called me,)

According to the function of the composite past this short sentence would rather naturally admit of a complement which would extend its meaning all the way into a present, such as the following:

et je sais maintenant qui l'a fait.

(and I know now who did it.)

It seems to us rather unnecessary to continue this analysis for other supercomposite past tenses.

We should note, however, that in order to realize the relation of consecution, the French language very often does something which might be called a crosswise use of the tenses of the past, in very varied nuances which need not be analyzed here but which may be accounted for from the succinctly established relations between the imperfect, the simple past, and the composite past. Here, finally, is an example of such usage:

A avait déjà parlé lorsque B prit la parole.

Lorsque B eut terminé, C s'est alors éloigné.

(A had already spoken when B took the stand.

When B had finished C then left.)

It is clear that examples of this type might easily be multiplied but they would hardly serve the intention which has prompted our study of conjugation.

The Discursive Power of the Verb

As far as we are concerned, the present investigation has now reached its goal. We are in a position to answer, in general rather clearly, the questions which we have raised. The conjugation of verbs represents the discursive expression—a fact which cannot be doubted—of a certain structuration of time. On the other hand we noted that certain groups of adverbs contain and display in discourse a temporal structure which prefigures the structure of the mathematicians' time. Does the temporal structure of conjugation belong to the same type? Does the change from one grammatical tense to another, for example, the change from the present to the future, prefigure the liberty with which the mathematician shifts a point 0 in time along the entire axis of time? The answer to this question is neither frankly Yes nor frankly No; by its very complexity it reveals to us profound insights into the expressive power of language and on what might be called the nature and limits of the *discursive faculty*.

1. It must first be noted that the group of adverbs which have been mentioned realize a temporal structure which is more devoid of any other aspect, more pure and as a whole more abstract than the one realized by conjugation. On the imaginary line which leads from current language to the language of the mathematician, the adverb is closer to the mathematical form of expression than is the verb in the process of conjugation.

2. In conjugation, grammar engages a certain number of themes. These themes do not develop independent of each other so as to form little discursive systems which would be more or less complete and autonomous. They are, on the contrary, at the same time connected and superimposed on each other in relations which are often difficult to systematize. This fact can be explained, for these relations are not simply the result of the grammarians' efforts but partly represent the actual final stage of an historical evolution still in progress.

3. It is not necessary, for the purpose we have in mind, to extend our analysis beyond the indicative mood. But it is clear that, if we had considered it useful to do so, we would have had to enlarge our starting base as well. We would have discovered that against a background of temporality, the conjugation of verbs puts into discursive form most of the themes which any theory of knowledge subsequently must isolate and develop. We shall see that against this background of temporality the verb becomes the expression, in its moods and tenses, of the motives, causes, and aims of the process as well as of its conditions and circumstances. Why have we said that the themes thus treated are in the rank of those which any theory of knowledge must deal with? We simply wished to emphasize once again the fact

that the discursive grasp at the level of the grammatical organization has nothing of a definitive formulation. In order to make this perfectly clear we must repeat at this point what we said about the outline in the strong sense and its application to the idea-outline.

An outline in the weak sense, we said, is the one which seeks, but has not yet attained, the faithful imitation of a model given in advance, one whose ideal purely and simply is the copy which perfectly conforms to the model. The outline in the strong sense, on the other hand, does not have a preformed model; it represents a search for this model by means of the formulation which it proposes for it, but it is also the model's provisional form of existence, a form which also lends itself to a modification intended to make it correspond more closely to its purposes. In this last sense, the discursive formulation is an outline in two respects: *That* which it must grasp is not offered to it as a preformed reality, as a reality which would already be given according to other modes of expression. The fashion in which it expresses what it is able to grasp is at the same time the form through which it makes of it an object of knowledge.

On the other hand, while the discursive activity tends to organize itself to become the expression of the themes we have mentioned, it seeks, retouches, replaces, and newly imagines the discursive materials which will give it the help it expects from them.

We have stated that the result of the discursive formulation at the grammatical and syntactical levels is comparable to an outline offered as such to someone who would know how to work with it. Do we have proof for this? Precisely that is the essential point which we may learn from our analysis of the indicative. To repeat its principal features: Its structuring tendency only operates on two fundamental themes, viz. temporality and the disparity between two aspects of the process, the contrast between the process during actualization and the accomplished process. The dominating theme is temporality, but to see it imposed one must push the analysis rather far and release the discursive intermediaries by means of which the temporal structuration operates. Nevertheless, although dominant, this first theme does not develop into a purely temporal system. We shall not review the way in which it combines with the second theme to form a compound system whose daily application moreover demonstrates its effectiveness.

Now, we have a very precise term of comparison for deciding whether this system has reached its stage of completion or whether it merely represents the outline of a system which it would prefigure; we mean, of course, the time of the mathematicians and the abstract temporal structure which may be imposed on it. We have repeatedly alluded to the fact that even before introducing mathematical time into our study, and even before being able to do so, we nevertheless are informed by the knowledge we have of it, which today appears as common knowledge. From a certain point of view, mathematical time presents itself without doubt as an achievement of discursive formulation of a refined temporal structure, a structure which in nonmathematical language cannot be dissociated from the compromise (between temporality and the other aspects of the process) upon which the entire system of the verb is based.

Our analysis thus is not self-contained. It cannot assume its full significance unless it extends beyond what an analysis of language by means of language could offer. It transcends, to some extent inevitably, into the field of the mathematician's activity, which even at this point presents itself as a replica of the structuring activity of the grammarian. Doubtless the grammarian does not have the same rigid strictures as does the mathematician. But it is these exigencies and the possibility of satisfying them which create the conditions of a reverse judgment about what the discursive formulation can do and what it is worth at the level of ordinary language.

Thus it is by integrating mathematical time and, more generally, scientific time, into our study that our analysis of language will be able to assume its full significance. This fact deserves to be pointed out because it sheds an unexpected light upon the analytical method. Apart from an activity extending it, this method could only be separated from our major conclusions as well.

We have found it necessary to anticipate on the results of a mathematical study of time and of the structure which the mathematician confers on it. The next chapter of the present work shall be devoted to this study.

We are, of course, far from having examined the system of the verb under all its aspects. In conclusion we offer some complementary observations. These do not touch our subject directly but rather take up again some views of the grammarians. In an indirect way, however, our remarks illuminate and confirm our statements about discursive formulation by pointing out its impressive and almost disquieting capacity of evolution. We shall be guided by the following three questions which were already asked earlier (cf. pp. 8 ff).

1. Is the discursive formulation of the process, if not entirely identical, at least appreciably analogous in all languages? Does one find everywhere the equivalent of a conjugation similar to the one we have analyzed?

2. In a language containing a system of the verb, does the verb, if not always, at least sometimes, rely predominantly on either one of the two themes which we had isolated? Can the theme of pure temporality, in particular, be separated from the theme of aspects to the point of assuming real autonomy?

3. Does it not happen that, while the two themes remain connected, one of them might overtake the other? Languages change, and the system of the verb moreover does not appear to form their most stable component. Does not the French language give an example of an evolution through which the theme of pure temporality has assumed a certain priority? Could not such an evolution be explained, if not by peremptory reasons, at least by very plausible ones?

These three questions, in this order, draw a rather sharply oriented line of discussion. It is clear that we shall answer them only in a rather succinct fashion, with the sole aim of giving, if possible, a still more solid base to our conclusions.

The answer to our first question is frankly negative. The question may even surprise a person whose linguistic training is limited to the Indo-European area of the past and the present. It is true that most languages currently spoken in Europe possess a verb system, and the same is true for the languages whose more or less direct heirs they are, as French, for example, is an heir of Latin. But the situation is quite different outside this linguistic area, whether we pass on to other groups of contemporary languages or, within the same group, we go back far enough in its linguistic history.

In fact, there exist currently spoken languages (it suffices to consider the group of the Semitic languages to find an illustration) which do not contain any verb system in the sense in which it is understood here. Do we have to conclude that these languages do not offer the possibility of expressing the relations of temporality which conjugation in particular makes manifest? This would be a fundamental misconception of the discursive power evident in any more or less widely used language. It is good to know, in order to get the right feeling for the relativity of the forms which discursivity is able to assume, that conjugation is not one of its obligatory forms. This should not come as too much of a surprise since we ourselves have noted that the system of the adverbs is capable by itself of supplying the discourse with temporal structures more simple and more bare than are those of the verb system. Temporality is not absent from those languages in which the system of the verb has not been constituted into an organized whole; the temporal element is expressed there by other devices for which a good translator is able to supply the equivalent. It is true that in a language which does not have a verb system, our analysis would have to take an entirely different route.

But what is the situation in the group of the Indo-European languages? Investigating its past, do we find that the verb system appears blurred or dimmed? Once again, this is not the way in which the situation must be understood.

In its origins Indo-European morphology was extremely complex; it lacked verbs and the principle of conjugation, as well as nouns in general and the principle of declension, in the sense in which a modern grammarian understands these terms. But it did possess inflected words which fell into two fundamental categories, precisely those which today, after a long historical effort of grammatical purification and abstraction, are called verbs and nouns. The grammatical reality which for us is attached to these terms did not exist explicitly; it rather was underlying a certain group of forms. There are no Indo-European words meaning *loup* ("wolf") independent of any context, but rather such forms as the Latin inflections *lupus, lupum, lupi, lupo*. Likewise, there is no word to signify in isolation such actions as are expressed by our verbs *prendre* ("to take") or *donner* ("to give"), but rather verbal forms which modulate this action into a function of categories (to speak in our own language) which the classical grammarians, as we know, call persons, numbers, voices, aspects, tenses, and moods. The general idea of the process is a creation by the grammarians to whom it affords the basis for the definition of the verb. The diverse modalities of the process, depending on whether it be stated, imagined, desired, wished for, commanded, and so forth, are expressed by as many special forms. As a nonorganized expression of the aspects, the verb system itself to some extent was present only through its aspects.

The answer to our first question thus is entirely negative. It merely illustrates more clearly the unique value of a discursive organization such as the conjugation of our modern languages.

We will now pass on to our second question. Why has the system of the aspects not been preserved in its complexity? We shall presently venture to formulate a hypothesis on this subject. The historians speak of a progressive decay of the system of the aspects and describe the emergence of the verb system, the transition from one to the other operating in multiple variants through the simplification of endings and through a codification tending towards rational rigor.

A striking example of this historic or linguistic phenomenon, perhaps even the most striking one, is Latin. This language has been constituted into a more rigid system than any other comparable languages. The verb system of Latin was formed by reducing, on the one hand, the variety of the Indo-European themes and by developing, on the other hand, a series of innovations. This twofold task had been accomplished by the time the first literary texts appeared. One is tempted to see in this the conscious achievement of certain craftsmen of the language.

Every Latin verb is conjugated according to two principal

themes, one of *infectum,* describing the process on its way towards completion, and one of *perfectum,* describing the completed process. Each of these themes includes, in the indicative, a present tense (*dico*), a preterite (*dicebam*), and a future (*dicam, dices*); in the subjunctive, a present-future (*dicam, dicas*) and a preterite (*dicerem*). The rest of the system of Indo-European aspects is indicated mainly through the manner in which the *infectum* and the *perfectum* are contrasted against each other. Thus, for example, *dico* contrasts with *dixi,* insofar as *dico* means "I am in the act of saying" while *dixi* means "what I had to say has now been said." This contrast is found in all forms of the two themes which thus are treated in complete parallelism. Thus, *dicebam,* "I was in the act of saying," corresponds to *dixeram,* "I had finished speaking." The entire verb system thereby is strictly regulated.

The innovation introduced by the Latin system above all consists in the ordered and regular way in which the theme of temporality, so to speak, is reduplicated through the contrast between the *infectum* and the *perfectum.*

The study we have made of the French verb system has shown to what extent the French language in this respect is the faithful inheritor of Latin. The French system (at least as far as the indicative is concerned) likewise is based on the simultaneous application of two themes, the first of which is of a strictly temporal character while the second introduces an aspect of anteriority and posteriority, an aspect of sequence which in certain cases may not remain strictly limited within the temporal frame. According to the fashion in which this relation is realized it may assume in turn the function of contrasting the *infectum* with the *perfectum.*

Nevertheless, the fact remains that the second theme of the French conjugation is farther removed than the second theme of the Latin conjugation from the system of aspects and is more involved in the discursive structuration of temporality.

Thus, despite their evident kinship, the French and Latin systems nevertheless show rather fundamental differences. French obviously has gone a step further than Latin towards a conjugation liberated from its extratemporal aspects. We know, however, how far the theme of pure temporality in the French language is still removed from complete autonomy.

Does any language go further than French in this direction? This does not seem to be the case, and so we have the answer to our second question.

We shall now go on to our third question. The means by which the French system insures the preponderance of the theme of temporality cannot fail to be noted for their subtlety. One is tempted again to see in this the deliberate efforts of experienced craftsmen of the language.

Do we have to assume that a language whose verb system breaks away from the system of the aspects is no longer the discursive expression of the latter? Evidently not; this would be a fundamental misconception of the discursive power which we discussed. Such a language has enough other ways to reach the same goal. Here are some examples of how in French the aspects are taken care of which are systematically disregarded by conjugation.

1. We have seen that it is not the temporal situation of the process itself but that of its perspective of actualization on which the tenses of conjugation are based. Now, this perspective in turn may present itself under all the aspects which a system of aspects can imply, from the most subjective to the most objective ones. Thus it may happen that depending on the circumstances, the present, the same present, or the same past serve to express very different aspects of the process; we have seen this especially in the case of the present where under the aspect of duration the process sometimes is presented as instantaneous and sometimes as forever repeating itself. But how are circumstances themselves fixated which determine the conditions under which the perspective of actualization must be considered? Partly this is done by usage, partly through the context. Now usage varies more than the rules, and context still more than usage. Both constantly enter into competition with the grammatical consciousness which, in turn, incessantly tends to impose upon the discourse an order as logical, coherent, and stable as possible.

2. In between the inflected forms of the verb and the fixation

of the perspective of actualization, there exists a certain number of periphrases which often have the function to express certain particular aspects of the process. Here are some of these periphrases: The examples *J'ai l'intention de faire* ("I intend to do"), *je me mets à faire* ("I am starting to do"), *je commence de faire* ("I have started to do") express certain nuances of the inchoative aspect; in the examples *je songe* ("I consider"), *je pense à faire* ("I am thinking of doing"), *je m'en vais devoir faire* ("I shall have to do") and *il me faut faire* ("I must do"), still other nuances are being expressed. Certain nuances of the aspect of completion may be evoked by *finir de* ("to finish doing"), *cesser de* ("to stop doing"), *avoir à peine* ("hardly having done"), etc. We certainly would not think of compiling even an incomplete list of these expressions which are particularly abundant in the French language. From the same standpoint it would be appropriate to note the rôle of the auxiliary verbs as well.

3. Vestiges of aspects still remain, in certain uses of the tenses, which are retained by usage but which, from the point of view of the rule, appear as irregularities.

All told, the system of the verb cannot be substituted for the system of the aspects. The former emerges from the latter which yields to it its own means of expression, the inflected forms of the verb. The discourse is then established on a basis of temporality, instead of a basis of aspects above all subjective.

We are now in a position to advance our explanatory hypothesis: In the emergence of the verb system whose neutrality (in the sense in which we have used this word for the adverb) is confirmed within the system of aspects often strongly engaged in subjectivity, we see the indication of a consciousness of universal time as opposed to the time of the self. This consciousness, however, in our opinion is only an aspect of the experience which the self has of its own presence in the universe. When this experience is no longer the experience of one single person but a collective experience, language cannot but carry its traces. Through this hypothesis we also anticipate the conclusions towards which we will be led by taking up again the idea of discursive synthesis.

DISCURSIVE SYNTHESIS AT THE LEVEL OF THE VERB AND THE ADVERB

This is not the first time that the idea of discursive synthesis enters into our exposition. We already used it at the level of the noun and the adjective. Let us briefly recall what the situation was at that point.

We had investigated which meanings might be conferred upon the word "time" in a language which, like French, is currently written or spoken. Would not an investigation of this type inevitably hit upon and isolate a general notion of time which this word by itself alone would have the power to evoke? This was to be expected; certain philosophies of language suggest as much. This general notion then would assure the word of a single meaning, all of whose particular significances would be nothing but qualified variants obtained by specification of the general notion through adequate qualifications. Clearly conceived, this general time would serve as a guarantee common to all the particular kinds of time which we have discussed, from the time of the imagination to the time of the universe. The problem of time would then be reduced to the clear determination of the qualities susceptible of being superinscribed over the general term.

Our analysis, however, has not answered this expectation. It has not discovered any discursive substance corresponding to a general notion of this nature. What it did discover, what language has yielded to research, is an entire spray of uses of the word "time" and an entire spectrum of corresponding meanings. It is true that these meanings do not all appear disconnected and unrelated to each other. The uses in which they are constituted do not remain apart from each other. Discourse unites them, brings them into agreement, coordinates them, and unifies them. But this unification is not achieved under the directive of a general notion which discourse would have at its disposal in advance. Insofar as it has been able to take form, an idea of this type is only a more or less advanced outline, an idea-outline in the sense we have tried to define in our discussion of open ideas and meanings.

But under these conditions, how can the different aspects, which are more or less sharply defined themselves, under which time enters into the discourse, come together in the formation of a common signification? This is the question to which the idea of discursive synthesis should provide an answer, a first answer, an answer-outline still open to the experiment of an investigation which has not yet reached its goal.

We do not intend to explain again what we said earlier on this subject.* We simply propose to examine the new elements contributed through the extension of our analysis of the adverb and the verb. Will the idea of discursive synthesis thereby be confirmed and perhaps be defined more precisely? And it is here that the first part of our study, the analysis of current language, will come to an end. But it is already clear that this study will not be self-sufficient, that it has not succeeded in conferring upon the word "time" an unique and henceforth invariable meaning, and that it has not elucidated the notion of time in a fundamental way. It appears on the contrary, even at this point, that the analysis of current language can only be preparatory, that it can only lead to a more fundamental study, the study of the clearly defined meanings in and through activities with which current language is not on the same level. We shall tell in a moment how our very inability to conclude within the analytical milieu in which we have operated so far may be interpreted positively, since it can take the form of a decisive experiment for a sequel to be added to our enterprise.

According to circumstances and intentions, discourse lends itself to either of two contrary tendencies: It may bring together the various aspects of time which are an integral part of it, going even so far as not to distinguish between them, or it may tend to separate these aspects from one another and even to contrast them. Does the system of the verb rather favor one of these two tendencies over the other? It is naturally the unifying tendency which strikes us first. Certain of its traits are so obvious that it is hardly necessary to point them out.

* "Discursive Synthesis, or Discourse as a Synthetic Milieu." Chapter Two, p. 81.

Contrary to Latin, French explicitly articulates the different subjects which the verb may require grammatically. It does not say *cogito* but *je pense* ("I think"); it does not say *dixit* but *il a parlé* or *elle a parlé* ("he or she has spoken"). Is this explicitness necessary for the clarity of the discourse? No, Latin precisely proves that the opposite is true; in most cases the inflections of the Latin verb suffice to indicate the grammatical identity of the subject, and if any ambiguity remains the context takes care of it. Under these circumstances, does not the concern clearly to designate the subject indicate an analytical tendency rather than a synthetical one? This is true only in a very superficial way. We should rather point out that the choice of the eight subjects admitted by the French conjugation, *je, tu, il, elle, nous, vous, ils, elles* ("I, you, he, she, we, you, they [masculine], they [feminine]), is not inevitably determined. English, for example, does not proceed in exactly the same manner: it economizes, in the plural, on the difference between *ils* and *elles,* while it does not do so in the singular. Should we say that in this respect English exhibits an irregularity? On the other hand, does not French grammar do as much by not including, in order to make a grammatical distinction, the difference between a masculine *je* and a feminine *je?* Might it not likewise confer a third discursive form upon the third person plural in those cases where the subjects are not of the same gender? (This is a real gap which is filled precisely by the rule of the predominance of the masculine subject.) Why not give its own discursive form to a multiple or numerous subject as well? Without leaving the grammatical plane one could easily invent many other variants some of which might not be without use. Should we conclude that the choice of the six "classical" persons and the reduplication of the third persons in French grammar is an arbitrary choice? It is obvious that such a statement would miss the point, as would also a statement to the contrary, namely that this choice would be the result of an exhaustive analysis of all the possibilities of providing a subject for a verb. The grammatical correction is based on convention and observation. The grammatical categories are the work of a *sui generis* systematization whose law is sometimes spurious. The distinction between *il* and *elle,* for example, may be considered as a discursive formulation of a real difference when two persons of different sexes are concerned, but it is purely verbal where, for example, *la lune* ("the moon") and *le soleil* ("the sun") are concerned. And yet, to be just, we should not be too heavy-handed in accounting for these shortcomings and inconsistencies. The mention of what we called the classical subjects of the verb nevertheless represents the fruit of a valid analysis of the verbal substance and of everything which constitutes the grammarian's level of reality. But, however undeniable this aspect of analysis, what counts for us above all is the inverse aspect, the aspect of synthesis towards which we now shall turn our attention.

Let us examine, for example, what becomes of the first person of the singular, the *je* (as a grammatical entity), through the fact of being engaged in the system of conjugation. We are not now concerned with the participation of a *je* in some particular tense, as in the simple expression *je pense,* isolated from any context. We are considering, on the contrary, the participation of this same *je* in two or more different tenses connected by the discourse. This connection often is not explicit or hardly so. For example, this is the case if one pronounces as a whole the following three statements:

Je pensais, je pense, et je penserai que. . . .

(I have thought, I think, and I shall think that. . . .)

As we just said, it is the same *je* which at the same time takes part in the imperfect, in the present, and in the future. At any rate it is the same *je* grammatically. Is it the same real *je,* a *je* which remains totally identical throughout the passage from an instant of the past to a present instant, and remains so throughout the passage from a present tense to the future? It would be highly audacious to assume that this is so. To which invariant of the real person could the permanence of the grammatical *je* well correspond? We do not believe that it is possible to define it except through a system of approaches of which the one we now shall try to effect through the "discursive subject" offers an example.

The preceding remarks have only a rather limited scope. We

certainly do not mean to say that a language to which a conjugation lends its structure could avoid designating a subject
for each well-defined use of the verb and could do without the
distinctions upon which the list of subjects, *je, tu, il, elle, nous,
vous, ils, elles,* confers discursive existence and legitimacy. This
list, as we have already seen, could be completed to take into
account other possible and easily imaginable distinctions.
Yielding to a tendency towards simplification one also might
shorten the list by omitting, for example, the often artificial
distinction between *il* and *elle*. Functionally this list may be
replaced, as in Latin, by the inflections of the verb and the
corresponding endings. Conversely, it is the latter which might
be omitted if the subject were always well defined. In any case,
to conjugate a verb also means to enumerate a certain group
of subjects having a grammatical reality if not always an "objective" existence. By saying that the disjunction of the subjects
for us is of secondary importance we thus do not mean to question the quite fundamental rôle of the subject in the organization of the discourse. Its quasi-general presence doubtless has
a profoundly structurizing effect in two ways. This effect in the
first place is achieved at the level of syntax, on the discursive
plane. Insofar as it is a regular syntactic procedure it fixates or
helps to fixate the norm of the correctly constructed sentence.
There certainly exist sentences without a subject and even without a verb, but these are exceptions which take on their meaning
only by implication.

But language cannot be isolated from the totality of our activities. It is one of the aspects and at the same time one of the
means of our incorporation in the universe. If it requires a certain structure it would be like an imprint which shows our hold
upon the universe as well as our being part of it. This structure
announces a form of existence of the world for us; it would certainly be an error to call this form arbitrary or conventional, but
we already know that it is only summarily adequate and in a
constant state of readaptation. In other words, the syntactic
structure of discourse expresses, admittedly in a more or less
approximate way, something which is not inherent in it; it has
an extraneous significance. To adopt it as a norm at the dis-

cursive level amounts to creating in advance a vision of what reality may be for us. As concerns the function of the subject in particular, the active and passive voices of the verb naturally do not lend themselves to the same interpretation; in the first case it exercises, and in the second it suffers, an action expressed by the verb. The level of reality upon which the discourse would be based thus appears somehow to be structured in advance, according to certain principles of affiliation; of these the principle of causality is only one example. Up to which point is this preliminary vision coherent? How can we circumscribe the activities for which it remains correct, i.e. effective? We are asking this question only in order to have an opportunity for repeating once again that it does not require a simple and immediate answer. By undertaking to treat this question, one encounters the entire problem of language; in fact, the whole of the present study (whose first part is approaching its conclusion) precisely represents a way to tackle it.

Before leaving the subject, however, we should note that the consideration of the reflexive voice alone already brings certain divisions and modifications to a too simplistic interpretation of the "exterior signification" of the syntactic norms.

Why, under these circumstances, did we say that the enumeration of grammatically admissible subjects and the disjunction caused by it are for us only of secondary importance? The reason is simple: in discourse conjugation is an agent of synthesis rather than analysis. The spectral analysis of the subject which accompanies it should not deceive us. It does not add much that is new to the spray of variants which the analysis conducted at the level of the noun and the adjective already has permitted us to recognize.

If someone happened to say, for example, *je lis, tu écris, il dessine* ("I read, you write, he draws"), he certainly would not mean to distinguish the individual times lived through subjectively by each of the three persons explicitly designated by the three subjects and the three verbs. The effect, on the contrary, would be the suppression of these three subjective times and their replacement by an intersubjective or even objective time, a general time within whose framework it would be completely unproblematic to speak of the simultaneousness of the three actions evoked by the three verbs. Of course this is a very simple example, in which the grammatical present directly corresponds to a present in time. It is adequate, however, to explain clearly the standardizing effect of conjugation. The decisive factor is that by conjugating any verb according to all the admissible subjects one establishes a general model in which the first verb may be replaced by any other verb (with few exceptions). The grammatical tense presents itself as a formal frame to which no verb is attached specifically but to which all verbs are equally attached. But, one might ask, are there not several types of conjugation? This is certainly true, but everyone knows how to put them into exact agreement. As far as anomalies are concerned they are such only in relation to the normal case. Thus the verb, in short, for the inflections imposed on it by a tense, the verb *in general*, is comparable to a variable which has a certain field of variation, and to which eight operators, the operators *je, tu, il, elle, nous, vous, ils, elles*, may be uniformly applied.

To return to our example, the grammatical present, as we have just recalled, generally is not the discursive expression of an instantaneous present, not even of a "now" of any density. Nevertheless, it is so in our example and confers upon the three actions in question an identical and immediate perspective of actualization. It is not necessary, however, that this perspective should remain thus limited. On the contrary we are entirely free to extend it to other subjects and other verbs. We could stay at first within the strict limits of the grammatical model and complete our example as follows:

. . . *elle regarde, nous comprenons, vous songez, ils attendent, elles s'ennuient.*

(. . . she looks, we understand, you dream, they [masculine] wait, they [feminine] are bored.)

As the example is extended the perspective of actualization is enlarged to include all the new additions. The nature of the actions or processes under consideration is unimportant; the distinction between objective and subjective fades, the different variants of the temporal aspect become blurred in favor of a time of synthesis, a time which envelops and synchronizes all the events mentioned above.

Starting from the well-defined model of conjugation we go a step further towards real discourse and its relative liberty by "realizing" the conventional subjects and saying, for example:

Toi, Pierre, tu lis et toi, Paul, tu songes; tandis que lui, Jean, travaille, que le soleil brille et que les heures s'écoulent.

(You, Peter, are reading while you, Paul, are dreaming of something; meanwhile John is working, the sun is shining and time is passing.)

One may see from this example how the standardizing effect of conjugation somehow permeates the discourse.

In order to regain all the variety which the use of the present implies, we must once again deploy the model of conjugation, making it more supple and more general according to our needs, in all the perspectives of actualization which are used by a real language. In all these perspectives the analysis retrieves all the variants which we know from the temporal aspect of the process. Likewise, in all of them the unity of grammatical time acts in an inverse sense, not taking into account the possible distinctions except in a measure which corresponds, not to a preliminary ideal, but to the purposes of the discourse.

In our investigation of conjugation as an agent of synthesis we have considered only the present tense so far. It would be easy but certainly tedious to study all the other tenses of the indicative after the same fashion. Except for a few details everything which has been said about the present is also valid for any grammatical tense. But discourse, even in a very brief passage, does not conjugate all the verbs in the same tense. In a very complex interplay it combines voices, moods, and tenses. We shall now consider conjugation from this angle, and while we even remain within the limits of the indicative we shall illustrate a further aspect of the phenomenon of discursive synthesis. Let us imagine that someone would say, as if it were one sentence:

Je songeais, je songe, je songerai.

(I dreamed, I dream, I shall dream.)

The fact that the same verb here appears in three different tenses but in the same person likewise has an effect of standardization, albeit in a different way. The repetition of the grammatical person evokes, across time, from past to future, the identity of the real person with himself. One might of course object that a real person is never totally identical with himself, that someone who says *I dream* is no longer exactly the same person who dreamed, and that he who will dream shall not be in every respect the same person who said *I shall dream*. Now, the practice of conjugation ignores precisely these objections. It ignores them systematically. It obliterates the distinctions which an analysis in depth would not fail to uncover, and it constitutes a "synthetic person," the one which the same *je* ("I") designates as remaining the same. Does not grammar transgress its rights by calling into syntactic existence a person to whom it lends the unreal quality of remaining identical with himself? Not at all; it only gives further proof, after having proved it so many times before, of the creative power peculiar to it. In order that a real person should not have the feeling to be somebody else from one day to the next it is necessary that something should persist in him which is profoundly characteristic for this person; the syntactic person is a theoretical form of this "something."

While a real person feels himself to be today as he was yesterday and projects himself, such as he is, into his further existence, he also makes a homogeneous whole of the time he has lived, of the time he is living, and of the time he expects to live. Is there only one specifically objective method? We certainly do not think so, and in an instant shall explain our reasons—which, incidentally, will not contain anything new. But we should ask in advance what, at the theoretical level where we have placed the syntactic person, corresponds to the homogenization of time which this person effects. One may easily understand that it is the perspective of conjugation, that the exigencies of the latter are the homogenizing factor, and that within its framework the grammatical tenses are coordinated and articulated. To remain strictly at the level of our analysis, it is still only the first person in grammar with which we are concerned. But speculation ventures much farther on its own account. The temporal perspective of conjugation is by no means reserved to any one person. It offers itself from the start as a valid, universal frame for all subjects, whether they designate persons or things. It is impervious to the distinctions which the analysis all the same is able to establish between subjective time, objective time, and their different variants; it ignores them, assuming the prerogative to ignore them. We might again ask ourselves whether grammar does not overstep its bounds by imagining syntactic devices so radically simplifying in order to be able to speak of everything at once. In principle the answer would be the same. It may be pointed out right away that the transition from the temporal perspective relative to a single person on the one hand to the universal syntactic perspective on the other can take place in several stages. This was done before in the case of the present and "universal simultaneousness," which it is able to represent. It would not be difficult at all to imagine a text in which several persons would act in different, coordinated tenses. The unity of the text would create a unity of the conjugation across the diversity of the subjects and verbs. The syntactic perspective would impose itself spontaneously in its unifying function. The text then might be selected in a still more general fashion, realizing the subjects partly through persons and partly through things, coordinating the active and passive verbs, having the persons act upon the things and the things act upon the persons; the syntactic perspective would then offer itself as the only means to maintain the unity of the text thus selected. Accordingly this unity is not the result of an arbitrary or artificial requirement; when it fails, discourse becomes the discourse of dreams or aberration.

More briefly, the coordination of the activities of persons within the same society and the same universe is established by means of a temporal perspective which mediates between all three aspects of time. Its universal syntactic perspective is the discursive formulation.

Finally, something essential is gained by not explaining the fact, a thousand times verified, of the effectiveness of this mediating perspective. The very fashion in which our analysis has developed certainly must make us cautious and guard us from taking this effectiveness as absolute. But the moment has not yet come to investigate its limits. Or rather, while we refrain from imagining it as self-evident, the fact that we can anticipate its simplifying function must enable us to evaluate its irreducible merit. But, if this simplifying rôle can be played effectively, if it emerges capable of coordination and integration, this is also because the matter which it coordinates and integrates is lending itself to it. As a matter of fact, simplification does not happen by accident or arbitrarily. It does not make its "own law" without taking into account the realities to which the law will be applied. The effectiveness of the mediation conveys a double message; it illustrates, on the one hand, the integrative power of the universal syntactic perspective, but on the other hand it equally illuminates the fact that the integrated aspects are capable of being integrated.

We have asked ourselves before whether it is permissible to imagine at the same time a homogeneous temporal perspective and a person capable of retaining his identity in it. We might have asked analogous questions at every stage of the journey whose aim is the universal syntactic perspective. We have just answered all of them at the same time. The success of the act of synthesis also conveys its justification to each of the elements entering into the synthesis.

Our preceding remarks were about the temporal aspect of conjugation. Now, this is only one of its aspects. It is through the intermediary of the "perspectives of actualization" that conjugation deploys all its effects. In order to give a complete picture of the discursive synthesis at the level of the verb, it would thus be proper to repeat everything that has been said and to extend it to its consequences. But the mind often jumps to conclusions without waiting until everything has been considered that might be said. Is it not clear already at this point that the unity of a text finds its syntactic expression in the coordination and unification of the perspectives of actualization which it creates?

Little need be added concerning the contribution of the adverb to the discursive synthesis. The adverb is capable of structuring all temporal perspectives regardless of the distinctions to which, as we know, they may give rise. The adverb thereby immediately demonstrates a structure common to all the temporal perspectives. It unifies in an abstract way. We have already mentioned this in connection with our study of conjugation. We will discuss it again when we study the time of the mathematicians.

All told, the adverb, more directly even than the conjugated verb, is the agent of syntactic unification and integration of the aspects and significations which analysis distinguishes and dissociates, the agent of what we have called discursive synthesis.

The following rather brief conclusions have a twofold aim: to recall the intentions formulated in the first paragraphs of our introduction, and to prepare the further pursuit of our enterprise.

CONCLUSIONS OF PART I

Where do we stand now in the realization of our project? Our study of time and its aspects, like a guiding thread spanned across the entire domain of knowledge, was to mark the progress of an experiment bearing on the very status of research. It is clear that we still are far from having reached our goal. We have not lost sight of it, however. More or less directly, language participates in all forms of research, from the formulation of the problems to the announcement of the results. Research makes use of language, which is one of the instruments it could not do without. The problem of language, of recognizing what its function is, of understanding how it exercises that function and how it develops in order to continue exercising it, thus is only one aspect of the problem of knowledge. Therefore it cannot contain a valid rule of research in which the rule of the effective conduct of discourse would not be included and integrated. All the same, an investigation of language does not by itself and of necessity take the form of an investigation of method unless it is oriented in that direction. How does the matter stand concerning our analysis and the views conveyed by it? Let us first take a look at language itself, insofar as it is the milieu and the means of the "discursive formulation." What it is able to grasp and to represent we ourselves have sought to grasp and to represent through a simile, that of the outline in the strong sense. Its capacity of evolution, on the other hand, recalls that of an organism capable of adaptation, whether the forces prompting it to adapt come from within or from without. Also, just as, in order to be understood, this organism must not be separated from its milieu, language must not be severed from the activities in which it participates if it shall retain its full significance.

Equipped with these characteristics and not as a more or less arbitrary hypothesis would imagine it, language must take its place within a correct method of research. This is a very simple and totally natural requirement. But how can it be satisfied? The situation does not yet arise. But we may explain already at this point why the analysis must be pursued under an enlarged perspective.

Thus the effective use of language must be integrated into the practice of a correct method; the latter encounters here a preliminary obligation which might be hard to satisfy. On the other hand, one must expect that a correct theory of language should be characterized by the fact of being only an integral part of a theory, or better, of a philosophy of research. But can the analysis of language alone provide all the elements necessary for treating this problem? The answer is not in doubt: it is negative. The analysis of language cannot teach us anything, for example, about the procedures of exact metrology. But the latter must also conform to the rule of research. This is another obligation facing the institution of this rule. But how could we account for it if we do not know what it represents? Therefore we must, leaving the domain of language, resolutely engage in that domain where the measure is law.

But is time really no more than a pretext and does that which our analysis permits us to grasp of it have no value in itself? Of course not. We shall point out two aspects under which, on the contrary, its importance is considerable. Whether it be at the level of language or of scientific research, time is an example (even a privileged one because of the scope of the field of experience in which it participates) about which one may assemble a vast body of information on the rôle of certain fundamental notions in the establishment of our knowledge.

As far as time itself is concerned it may suffice to recall here that we already had to comment on a number of philosophical works dealing with it.

Now, whether as an example or for its own sake, the texts where we identify time are only fragments of heteronomous discourses. The information by which it benefits and to which it lends a discursive appearance is at the level of all those which insure our daily activities. A serious analysis cannot stop there. It must clear a path for itself towards the most effective procedures and the most precise significations. Thus it is now the heteronomous character of a discourse involving time which forces us to start anew and to proceed with our analysis.

Only towards the end of our study, when we shall try to draw its methodological conclusion, will the questions of language and of research be revealed as connected and united by the fundamental option of being open towards experience. Only then shall we be able to explain what this option signifies and why it is imposed upon the researcher.

PART II
TIME IN THE EXACT SCIENCES

Chapter Four

MATHEMATICAL TIME

INTRODUCTION

In order to explain the rôle which the adverbs and the tenses of the verb play in the expression of temporal relations, we have often used the terms *system of adverbs* and *system of verbs*. We meant by this that the adverbs of time do not assume their meanings independent of each other, but that they all are engaged more or less directly in the discursive formulation of a certain temporal structure, and that the tenses of conjugation do not take their indicative value independent of each other, but that they, too, are solidarily engaged in the explanatory action through the means of the discourse of the general structure of the process. We already pointed out that especially where the system of the adverbs is concerned, current language carries within itself an already very sharp prefiguration of the time of the mathematicians. It is the latter which now will occupy our attention.

As a matter of fact the difference between time structured by adverbs and time structured according to mathematical exigencies is not very great. Under certain circumstances it might be useful to point out how easy the transition is from the first to the second. The mathematical imagination is quite close to the one which elaborates the temporal structure sustained by the adverbs. But we shall not proceed in this fashion; we will seek, on the contrary, to build an ordered structure which admits of a temporal interpretation, leaving to mathematical thought all the liberty and capacity of imagination which belong to it. Thus mathematical time presents itself from the start as a time of the imagination. Nevertheless, we shall have to correlate this imagination with the images of the universe which we have in us by nature and without which we would be incapable of developing even our most ordinary daily activities.

Geometry was born from our ability to imagine exact points and precise alignments of exact points. In an analogous fashion we also have the ability to imagine exact instants and unlimited sequences of exact instants preceding or following a certain well-defined instant.

The Problem of the Present Moment

At this point we must be careful not to start out in a wrong direction. It has been suggested that a *now* without duration and without density can hardly be experienced and transmitted as such to consciousness. And it is even suggested that under these conditions the precise instant can be no more than a fiction without value. This rejection of the precise instant, of course, is based on confusion. One would commit an analogous error by denying the existence of a precisely defined point, alleging that no space in the real world can exist without dimension; the existence of geometry as a mathematical discipline is unaffected by this argument. We must in fact distinguish between three levels of existence: the level of the geometrical entities, such as the point or the straight line, the level of real objects and actually drawn figures, through which we try as far as possible to realize geometrical figures, and the often forgotten level of the forms which these objects and figures assume for each of us. The real problem is not the existence of one or the other of these three levels but rather the fashion in which they can all be used for the same purpose of study.

In our specific case we must, for the sake of clarity, work with analogous dictinctions. We must not confound the forms of existence and the levels of existence of the consciously lived duration, of the measured duration, and the duration which the mathematician subjects to the rigor of his calculations. Let us recall, for example, the question of the *now*. Do we have to assume that the conscientional *now* cannot exist *for us* without a certain density? We can all the more easily assume this as the technical realization of an experimental *now* may be accomplished with a precision for which there exists no equivalent even in the most attentive and alert cognition. We shall not say that a duration whose "experimental existence" is indubitable does not have a real existence because it is too short to be a conscientional duration, and inasmuch as it is an immediate datum, it will always be a mere *now*. The experimental *now* certainly is not a *now* of ultimate precision either. But nobody would conclude from this that it would make no sense whatever to speak of a precise instant. One could not in good faith pretend to ignore that wherever time is measured accurately, the experimental aspect of the research is complemented by a theoretical and mathematical aspect. As far as the precise instant is concerned, its level of existence, the level at which its existence cannot be doubted, is the one where mathematical thought is elaborated and deployed according to the law of exactness imposed on it.

Any confusion about this point hopefully being cleared up, let us take up again the ordered structure which will subtend the idea of mathematical time. For this purpose we shall make use of a geometric model. But this does not mean that mathematical time will thereby become geometrized. The structure of order which we shall define may be separated from its geometrical support and lend itself to a specifically temporal interpretation.*

CONSTRUCTION OF THE TEMPORAL ORDER

In the same way in which we choose an origin of the coordinates on a straight line, let us suppose a first element of our structure which we shall name element zero. We do not define the nature of this first element and we shall not further define

---

* This is not the first time that we insist on the distinctions that must be made between the modes of existence of the different aspects of time. At the level of the noun we already have contrasted the time of the imagination with the time of consciousness and have shown how great a part the former takes in the organization of discourse. It seems proper to us to repeat this point in connection with the unifying rôle of the adverb and the verb; in fact this rôle does not develop at the level of consciousness but rather in a perspective where subjective time and objective time both may be projected in order to be coordinated.

the nature of the following elements. (The mathematician knows from experience that this is a liberty which he may take.) On the straight line we may select, from point 0 and according to the intervals which we will not assume to be regular, an unlimited sequence of points; nothing prevents us from naming them point 1, point 2, point 3, and so forth. Continuing in this way, we assume as belonging to our structure (and this is sufficient for giving them a mathematical existence) a sequence of elements: element 1, element 2, element 3, and so forth. At the same time we suppose the existence of an order of succession including all the elements already supposed, whose nature we shall not define except by saying that it is determined by the (numerical) order in which the elements have been numbered. On the straight line one may select in analogous fashion, on the other side of point 0 and in the opposite direction, another unlimited sequence of points which may be named point −1, point −2, point −3, and so forth. Again continuing in the same fashion, we complete our structure by the sequence of elements which we name successively element −1, element −2, element −3, and so forth, emphasizing in the thus completed structure the relation of order already indicated.

We have not assumed that the intervals between two successive points on the straight line would be of equal length.* But nothing prevents us from assuming, in superimposition upon the first, a second method of measuring the intervals, according to which the distance between two neighboring points everywhere must be equal to the unit. The distance between any two points would then be given by the difference of their ordinal numbers. For the points of the sequence and the intervals which they delimit, the requirements to which the measure of a

---

* To speak in this way of intervals which are not all of the same length naturally means to presuppose that the straight line already carries a definite measuring system. The following remarks shall liberate us from this presupposition. We shall reintroduce it later in a more fundamental sense. The characterization of the measuring system with which euclidean geometry operates quite naturally poses a difficult problem concerning the relations of our natural (phenomenological) representations with the structures superimposed on them by the formalizing axiomatization. This is precisely the problem to which our exposition will shortly lead us.

distance must answer are thus satisfied. For the sequence of elements placed outside any specific determination, the interval between any two of them has not yet been defined. Nothing prevents us from assuming that such intervals do exist and from attributing to them a measure after the example of what was done on the straight line.

We believe that by the preceding remarks we have established rather clearly how the construction on the straight line of a geometric model of a certain ordered structure may lead to construction by analogy of a similar ordered structure starting from elements whose nature is not defined except by the exigencies imposed on them. We therefore believe that we can trim down our text by discussing only what we shall further do on the straight line.

Mapping of the Structure onto Itself

Such as it has just been constructed (we shall indicate immediately how it must be systematically enriched), the sequence of numbered points admits of a group of maps onto itself, which retains its order as well as the measuring system which we have superimposed upon the euclidean measurements, but which does not concern the latter. The most simple of these operations (the one which leaves everything in place, being naturally irrelevant) consists in mapping each of the points of the sequence onto the one which immediately follows it; the inverse operation would map it onto the preceding one. The most general map, of course, would consist in the mapping of point 0 onto point n, point 1 onto point $n+1$, point -1 onto point $n-1$, and so forth.*

Division of the Intervals

We will show now a first method of procedure by whose repetition the sequence shall be progressively enriched. Let us

* Speaking of the structuration of time by means of the adverb, we already noted that the transition from one day to the following or to the day before creates a group which in every respect prefigures the one which has been discussed.

define a new point on each of the intervals delimited by two consecutive points of the sequence. Perhaps it does not lie on the euclidean midpoint of this interval. Nonetheless we shall decide, from the point of view of the measuring system which we had introduced in superimposition upon the euclidean one, that the measure of each of the two partial intervals which it determines is equal to one half. The ordered structure of the original sequence, of course, may extend to the sequence thus completed, and the latter likewise admits of a group of maps onto itself which is only the extension of the group previously considered.

The thus extended group has, in relation to the completed sequence, the same fundamental property as the original group does in relation to the original sequence; one determines exactly an application of the group by indicating for a single point of the sequence onto which point it should be mapped. The first of these points may be selected at random.

We shall give the term D (dichotomy) to the operation which has just been described. This operation, of course, may be repeated indefinitely. We shall designate as E the set of points thus created. Whichever may be, in the course of this indefinite repetition, the sequence at which we stop, the relation of order and the property of the group formulated before may immediately be extended to it.

To every point of the set E the conventions which we have introduced permit us to attribute a number, the measure of its "distance" from point 0. We shall call it its parameter and designate it by the letter t. For the points selected at first, this parameter was a simple ordinal number, counted first from 0 to ∞, then from 0 to $-\infty$. For the point selected, for example, between the point of parameter 1 and the point of parameter 2 and so that (according to our conventions) the "distance" to each of these points should be $\frac{1}{2}$, we put $t = 1 + \frac{1}{2}$. For the point selected after the same fashion between this last point and the point of parameter 2, we shall put $t = 1 + \frac{1}{2} + \frac{1}{4}$, and so forth. One may compute in the same fashion the parameter corresponding to any point of the set E: It will always be a number of the form $M/2^n$, M being an unspecified integer, either positive, negative, or 0, and n being an unspecified integer, either 0 or positive. The "distance" between any two points of the set E is measured by the difference of their parameters; this measure is also a number of the same form.

(In order not to complicate the construction of the model of the ordered structure we have in mind, we shall assume that the points of set E are distributed on the straight line in such a way that they do not leave out any interval that would not contain any of these points. It is not difficult to indicate the precautionary measures which are necessary to insure this result. For example, one must select the points whose parameters form the numerical sequence 1, $1 + \frac{1}{2}$, $1 + \frac{1}{2} + \frac{1}{4}$, $1 + \frac{1}{2} + \frac{1}{4} + \frac{1}{8}$ ... in such a way that, in the usual sense, they have the point of parameter 2 as a limit point.)

Construction of the Continuum

It is clear that the numbers of the form $M/2^n$ only form part of the set of real numbers and even of the set of rational numbers. Neither π, nor $\sqrt{2}$, nor even $\frac{1}{3}$ can be written in this fashion. Thus the set E does not have the necessary completeness for the definition of a continuous variable such as, for example, the variable t of mechanics and physics. One only has to know the elements of differential calculus in order to know by which operation the set may be conveniently completed; it is the limit process.

Assume that the sequence P_1, P_2, P_3, P_4 ... be an infinite, ordered, and bounded sequence of points of the set E. It is known to have a limit L, or in other words, there exists a point L which the points of the sequence approach indefinitely without ever surpassing it. Under the conditions assumed above, the parameters of these points likewise tend towards a limit L. The limit process consists in assigning 1 to the limit L of the points of the sequence. It may happen that the limit point L thus obtained already is a part of the set E; this is the case, for example, in the sequence considered above, of points whose parameters form, like the numerical sequence 1, $1 + \frac{1}{2}$, $1 + \frac{1}{2} + \frac{1}{4}$ ... , points which converge towards the point of parameter 2. But this is not generally the case. By adding to the set E the limits L of all possible sequences of the kind we have described, we at the same time create the geometric continuum without a lacuna of the points of the line and the numerical continuum without a lacuna of the values t of the corresponding parameter.

Through the same operation the order relation is extended without difficulty to all the points of the continuum which are thus inserted between the points of the set E, while at the same time we establish the continuous group of maps onto themselves of the geometric continuum and of the arithmetic continuum of the values of the variable t. In brief, we thus have obtained the following result:

On a straight line, and taking as our material the continuum of the points of this line, we have realized a model of an ordered structure possessing two fundamental qualities:

1. The structure carries a metric permitting us to measure the interval between any two of its elements.

2. It admits of a group of maps onto itself which at the same time preserves its order and its metric. In order to determine an operation of this group, it suffices to indicate for a single element onto which element it must be mapped.

Expressed in terms of the parameters t of the variable point P, t' of the corresponding point P', and t_o of an otherwise unspecified fixed point P_o, the group is completely given by the following simple equation:

$$t' = t + t_o$$

The latter is interpreted moreover as a simple change of origin from which the parameter t must be measured.

The Rôle of the Arithmetic Continuum

Let us return to our project, which was not to show how the geometric continuum may be coordinatized by means of the arithmetic continuum; this matter is too well known to be worth stopping for. Our project was, by taking the construction and coordinatization of the geometric continuum as a model, to propose the arithmetic construction and coordinatization of an order structure whose elements do not have any predetermined specificity. We think that it would be tedious to take up the analogy where we left it and to continue, without omitting any detail, to its explicit conclusion. Coming right to the point, we shall therefore put as known the existence of the order structure we have in mind, as well as the possibility of coordinatizing it in the most faithful way through the arithmetic continuum. This done, nothing prevents us from returning to the geometric continuum on the one hand and to the continuum of time on the other. One finds the former by assuming that the elements of the structure be "realized" by precise points, by the set of the points carried by a line. The idea of the geometrical point lends itself to this realization, while the idea of a locus of a certain extension, however small, would not. In a completely analogous way one may realize the elements of the abstract structure by precise instants, and the order relation which makes a whole of them by the relation which we are able to imagine between two precise instants, one of which would come *after* the other. Thus we bring into mathematical existence the temporal continuum which is the set of the precise instants endowed with its order relation, its metric, and the continuous group of its mappings onto itself; this continuum is the very substance of the time of the mathematicians. It represents the extension from which the arithmetic coordinatization enables us to make a measurable magnitude.

This Is Not a Spatialization of Time

Is not the way in which we have presented the problem too roundabout? Would it not be far simpler and easier to define the variable t as one defines an abscissa x on an axis of coordinates? Certainly all the results we have established from the order relation to the group of maps of the axis of the t onto itself and to the fundamental equation

$$t' = t + t_o$$

would have appeared automatically in the most elementary fashion. But we would have invited the erroneous and nevertheless so widespread conclusion that the mathematization of time is its geometrization. Our method of procedure puts the temporal continuum and the geometric continuum of the mathematician on the same level of abstraction. They are two realizations of the same order structure. They may mutually represent each other, but the specificity of one is not reducible to that of the other. The mathematician's habit of tracing, in numerous problems, a perpendicular axis of the t to an axis of the x, does not make any difference in this. At a certain level of abstraction the temporal continuum and the linear continuum are one and the same order structure; reinvested with the significance they derive from the fact of their participation in the study of the real world, the mathematical duration and distance are two notions which are mutually irreducible.

Multiplicity of Possible Models

The construction of the temporal continuum to which we have advanced gives us occasion for a remark of a certain importance and even difficulty. This remark prepares the introduction of the "time tied to the representations of the world within ourselves" to which we must inevitably refer throughout the entire study of measured time which will follow. This remark, however, will not assume its full significance before we come to the analysis of *intuitive time*, the third of the great unifying variants of our concept of time, especially when we shall have to establish a relation of synthesis between these three variants.

Thus we have realized an abstract model of the temporal order. It is a linearly ordered continuum, carrying a metric and a group of transformations onto itself; the transformations of this group leave the metric invariant. Each of the transformations of this group corresponds to a shift of the origin of the times towards the past or towards the future.

At this point we must emphasize the fact that this realization is not univocal and is not the only possible one. Operating within the first model, the constructive process which we have used naturally leads us to a second model, different from the first in general, but likewise carrying a metric and a group of transformations onto itself. These two models have the same structure; one passes from one to the other by means of a certain topological transformation of the first model onto itself (this transformation does not alter the order and does not produce any lacuna in the model). Thus the constructive procedure, given all the scope of which it is capable, creates an infinity of equivalent models, each of which may be obtained through a topological transformation of the first model onto itself. So far nothing permits us to attribute a privileged rôle to the first of these models; all the rest are equally admissible. If we had reasons for doing so we would be free to choose a different one at will from among the infinity of possible models.

Does a Privileged Model Exist?

There is a problem, however. Are these models equivalent to each other in *every* respect? Could it not be that among all the models thus constructed there exists one which is distinct from all the rest in some particular aspect, an aspect which even a mathematician would consider as relevant? Do we not give an example of such a model when we propose to represent the temporal variable t by a variable x having the value of a coordinate on a line, when we propose, in other words, to represent equal or unequal durations by segments of equal or unequal lengths respectively?

In order to give a valid answer to this question we must go back to the fashion in which the idea of a geometric continuum is defined. There is not only one single way to do this. We shall distinguish two methods which, for the purpose of clarification, we shall contrast with each other.

We shall first note that it is very easy to set up a constructive procedure exactly analogous to the one we have used. The geometric continuum thus obtained will have exactly the same structure as the temporal continuum mentioned above; ordered without lacunae, it will carry a metric and a group of transformations which leave this metric invariant. One might consider it as a first model of the straight line. Now this model gives us occasion for remarks which are exactly similar to those which have just been made; operating within this very model with all the scope of which it is capable, the constructive procedure makes it equivalent to an infinity of other models of the same structure. We pass from one of the latter to the next by a topological transformation of the continuum which they have in common.

From the point of view of the constructive procedure which was adopted, all these models are equal to each other. But repeating the question we asked before, we may ask whether they are equal in all respects. Is there none among them which stands out, for example, by the fashion in which it realizes the distances and their relations of equality or inequality?

The answer is doubtless in the affirmative. We carry within us, in our mental universe, a concept of the straight line which may be regarded as the original of which all the models which have been mentioned are only imitations. The line whose image is within ourselves by nature also carries a continuum, a metric, and a group of translations. But what distinguishes it from what we have called its imitations is not grasped through the constructive procedure. The latter does not preserve what accounts for its singularity. What no model of the structure of the line contains any longer is the form, to take only one example, in which we imagine a segment of a line, with the length proper to it, this form which our mind elaborates from our sensorial impressions.

Structuring and Schematizing Axiomatization

Does the constructive procedure, then, miss its aim? On the contrary, it reaches it, for it is inspired entirely by the intention of isolating (to the greatest possible extent) the geometrical notions of the mental images which we form for ourselves to retain only the structure of their reciprocal relations.

But it would be an error to assume that there is no other way to define the idea which we have by nature of the straight line and of the linear geometric continuum. It must be especially emphasized that on the contrary it is possible to do so by retaining the elements of forms (of representations) whose structural models have been stripped. It is sufficient, for this purpose, to construct axiomatically the geometry on the straight line, taking as the basic notions the not yet purified ideas of point, segment, orientation, distance, etc. We have tried to show, by detailed description, how such an axiomatization may be achieved, in the work already referred to.* We shall therefore not repeat ourselves here.

It is easy likewise to give to the constructive procedure the form of a strict axiomatic structure; one may then speak of a *structuring axiomatization*. The second procedure, for which the engagement in our natural representations still serves as a support, is a *schematizing axiomatization*. These two methods do not mutually exclude each other; they are placed at different levels of abstraction. It is not simply out of concern not to forget anything that we have mentioned both of them. Their inter-relatedness reveals a rather deeply hidden fact which we shall have to utilize. In the transition from the schematizing axio-matization to the structuring axiomatization, the geometrical notions thus are stripped at least of part of the value of repre-sentation (facing the tangible world) which they naturally carry in our mental universe. In the inverse process, these no-tions again assume their *intuitive form*. This coming and going for us serves as a demonstration; it illustrates the existence of that which we lose in one direction and recover in the other, the existence of the representative moment which must be im-posed on the simple order structure in order to return from the topological model to the intuitive representation used by the classical geometer.

We now may return to the temporal continuum. The example of geometry will help us answer the question we had asked before and which had remained unanswered.

First it should be noted that the temporal continuum like-wise may be axiomatized at two different levels of abstraction. We shall not dwell on the fact that we would easily have given the strict form of an axiomatic structure to the constructive procedure. As in the case of the geometric continuum, this

---

* Gonseth: *La géométrie et le problème le l'espace*. Neuchâtel, Editions du Griffon.

would be a structuring axiomatization. But this axiomatic procedure is not the only possible one. In close analogy to what may be done in geometry, we may define the ensemble of the notions relating to time by engaging them in a schematizing axiomatization. For this purpose it is sufficient to take as basic notions the notions of instant, of "earlier" and "later," of duration, of equality and inequality of two durations, and so forth, such as we conceive them in relation to our daily activities, without as yet having disengaged them from the form in which we imagine them.

Everything we have said about the straight line, of the relation between the two axiomatic procedures, may now be repeated for the temporal continuum in a rigorous analogy. Among all the structurally equivalent models of this continuum there does exist one which is different from all the others. But what characterizes it eludes the constructive procedure. This is precisely what is lost in the transition from the schematizing axiomatization to the structuring axiomatization. This is what must again be conferred upon the bare structure to return to the schematizing axiomatization. This is the form in which the temporal dimension exists in us as an element of our mental universe.

Here, too, the fact that the procedures of axiomatization are both admissible, that they may be compared and even to some extent opposed to one another, has the value of proof. Their difference is thus emphasized. We might have some difficulty in recognizing it if this expedient were not available.

Specificity of the Temporal Continuum and of the Geometrical Continuum

However close the analogy between the continuum on which a coordinate x varies and the continuum of the temporal variant t, one nevertheless must be careful not to confound them. Certainly there is no difference whatever between them from the standpoint of the structuring axiomatization. The constructive procedure valid for one also is valid for the other, without reserves or corrections. We are concerned in either case with one and the same procedure. But this is no longer true at the level of the schematizing axiomatization. If x is the measure of a space and t the measure of a time, the eventual equality of the measures must not cause us to forget the difference in the nature of these magnitudes we have to measure. The equality above all must not blind us to the fact that each of these continua is realized in our minds in a form proper to it. Mutually reducible through the measure, they remain irreducibly different through the moments of representation whose carriers they are.

It is currently said that the idea of space and the idea of time are combined in the idea of speed. Here, too, we must note the difference between speed, expressed by its measure, and the representation we form of it for ourselves. In the next chapter, studying the instruments and the procedures appropriate for measuring time, we shall have to use the notion we have of a uniform speed. This idea in itself carries an element of representation which for us constitutes its specificity. We must emphasize the fact that in this representation are combined the representation of distance and the representation of duration which have been discussed.

We might finally add (although at this point our remark could appear premature and even cryptic) that while it is invested with the quality of representation, the idea of uniform velocity in turn is connected with the idea of cause or lack of cause in the *principle of inertia* of classical mechanics.

Chapter Five

MEASURED TIME

INTRODUCTION

When we were developing in Chapter Four the idea of time towards its mathematical conclusion (the term *conclusion* should not, however, be taken too literally), our intention was a twofold one. On the one hand we have acted like a careful mathematician seeking to establish correctly the structure of the temporal continuum; but, on the other hand, we did not want to lose sight of the fact that the constitution of mathematical time is not an end in itself and could not by itself assume the totality of meanings which the word *time* already has assumed for us. The mathematician in us has stayed in the service of a methodological intention which aimed farther than he did.

We shall now examine how the objective variants of time which we discovered in current language may be taken up again and engaged in a different specification, a unifying specification which for practical reasons we shall call measured time or the physicist's time. Our intention again shall be a twofold one. On the one hand we shall make an effort to adopt the views and concerns of a person considering the problem of time in its practical aspects, a person who intends, not to define time, but to measure it, i.e. to construct an instrument or even a group of instruments capable of effecting this measurement with a certain precision.

But although it may seem to us indispensable to follow the technician of time measurement rather closely in order to learn from him how he solves his problem, we can never completely identify with him. He isolates only one of the elements of *our* problem; however close we are to him our most valid aspiration must always go beyond. We cannot do without him, but he is not the only person we need; as we have already said, the mathematician's point of view is equally important to us.

At this point we will be somewhat more specific. In order to acquire a knowledge which exceeds the informational content of current language, one must possess certain variants at the same time well-defined and well-defining, unified and unifying, of the notion of time. The time of the mathematician and the time of the physicist are the first two examples of this. We shall have to add a third variant, the variant of intuitive time. The question then confronting us will be the relations of these variants to each other and their interdependence in the practice of research. But we have not reached this point as yet. For the moment our concern is specification; we must isolate, as far as possible, the variants which we intend to use. Shall we succeed in constituting them and conceiving each one completely independent from the rest? This question will be important; it will even have a principal importance in the methodological research whose elements we are in the process of assembling. Accordingly we shall be careful not to give a premature answer. For reasons which will become clear later, we shall try above all to retain and not to compromise unnecessarily the option of a negative answer, the option of answering that the variants under consideration would not seem capable of being each based on itself. Now, this answer will only be valid if, without success, we have done everything in our power not to establish any connection between them. Our procedure from then on is very clearly defined; it is in an experimental context as far removed as possible from the discursive context which has helped us define the time of the mathematician that the time of the physicist must be established. But we must also ask ourselves, while we are doing this, whether the intended procedure of the installation of the variant deserves the qualification of "purely experimental."

Measured Time in Current Language

Let us return for a moment to current language and to what we have defined as its content of information. Is the notion of measured time integrated in this concept? Concerning the current language of the "average contemporary man" the answer is not doubtful at all; in those situations where some people say, for example, "in an instant," or "in a few moments," others will say, without further thought, "in a second," or "in a minute." It is clear that everyday language has incorporated into itself a certain vocabulary related to the measuring of time, and that the usage of this vocabulary is guaranteed by the integration in the general sense of a generalized practice of this measurement. As far as our project is concerned of establishing the physicist's time in a context as purely experimental as possible, common sense and current language thus are to some extent contaminated by our previous knowledge of the results to be established. Is it possible to disregard this preliminary information? If so, our exposition could be developed more easily.

It is, of course, possible for us to omit systematically (and provisionally) everything which, in our explanatory discourse, might be related in any way to the precise designation of a time measured by an instrument of whatever kind. It is doubtful whether this would suffice to create, at the same time, an entirely clear *situation of exposition*. For lack of anything better, however, this is what we are going to try.

The Preliminaries from the Standpoint of Language

What will be left for us? The essence of what we have said about the different acceptations implied by the word *time* and about the discursive synthesis connecting them will remain valid. The same is true of the structuring and at the same time unifying functions of the verb. Thus we are far from being thrown back to point zero. We have not lost (and we could not lose) a certain group of preliminary devices available to us through language. However far one may have pushed the analysis of language, there remains thus something anterior to any explanation. For our present purpose this anterior entity must be especially studied in its objective aspect. We shall also see in it the formulation of an element preceding activity and the procedures which specify objectifiable time as measurable time.

It is, for example, at the level of this preliminary datum that the following statements naturally take their meaning:

Emile et Paul sont partis en même temps;

Emile est arrivé sensiblement avant Paul;

Paul est donc resté plus longtemps en chemin qu'Emile.

(Emile and Paul have left at the same time;

Emile has arrived considerably earlier than Paul;

Paul thus has spent more time on his way.)

We must call attention to the expression "at the same time" in the first of these three statements. It shows that we do not have to wait until we have established a precise experimental apparatus in order to be able to conceive of two simultaneous events and to be in a position to discuss them. With certain tolerances which cannot be formulated exactly except within the framework of an activity which is well defined, the effective and correct use of a series of expressions such as *at the same time, at the same moment, at the precise moment, simultaneously,* remains preliminary to the more rigorous use which we will be able to make of it with the help of measured time.

The idea of simultaneousness, moreover, is inseparable from the idea of duration; if two events are simultaneous it must be in the framework of a duration which embraces both. In fact there is an entire group of ideas which are inseparably interconnected and involve, besides the notions of simultaneity and duration, those of the event, the instant, the beginning, the end, the interval of time, etc. We shall not seek to give a complete list of them; this would be unnecessary and would lead us too far afield.

In the second of the three preceding statements we might note the words *considerably earlier.* They could give us occasion for remarks analogous to those above. In particular, expressions such as *coming before, coming after, succeeding each other in a certain order,* might be added to the list.

In the third statement we shall note the word *thus.* It indicates a connection necessarily established at the level of the speaker between certain expressions which are available to him for preliminary use.

Our second example is very similar to the first:

Emile et Paul sont partis au même instant; ils sont arrivés en même temps; ils sont donc restés en chemin pendant le même temps.

(Emile and Paul have left at the same moment; they have arrived at the same time; thus they have spent the same amount of time on their way.)

The *thus* may be explained by the following rule, which illustrates an information somehow built into the language: Two events which begin at the same moment and end at the same moment take the same amount of time to be accomplished.

Before we continue we shall briefly point out the intention to which the preceding examples correspond. It seems to us indispensable to clarify the situation in which we shall find ourselves when explaining how measured time enters into our perspective. We had to show that, even when we omit anything that could betray the influence of a measuring instrument, we will be unable to avoid the establishment of a certain "ready made" element. This element is not introduced through circumstances but is present in advance in the language whose use must remain permitted to us.

The Preliminaries from the Viewpoint of Observation

Such is the situation in language. Let us now examine the problem from the angle of observation. Does language and its "ready-made" element correspond to it? Is it coordinated with it?

The fact that two observable events begin at the same moment (or that two sufficiently brief events are simultaneous) is equally observable. There even is evidence for this by virtue of the same qualities as for the other coincidences which play a rôle in the experimental procedures. (There even is an element of simultaneousness in the direct statement of any coincidence, since there exists no extratemporal coincidence.) The statement of simultaneousness thus is among the immediate data of observation.

The same is true of the direct statement that an event *a* precedes or follows another event *b;* this statement cannot be reduced to statements of simultaneousness without artificiality.

With the reservations already mentioned, these observations, as we know, are not incompatible with a correct use of language. They confirm in particular the transitional use of the expression *the same* of which the following statement is an example:

If the duration of the event *a* is the same as that of the event *b,* and if the duration of the latter is the same as that of the event *c,* then the duration of *a* is the same as that of *c.*

In short, our situation not only implies a certain preliminary ("ready-made") element from the standpoint of language but it also implies the validity of this preliminary element from the standpoint of observation. This may be illustrated in the following way:

Let us assume that, before a court, I must prove that Emile and Paul have spent the same amount of time to travel a certain distance. To do so I merely have to produce a first witness who can testify that they have started out at the same moment, and a second witness who can testify that both have arrived at the same time.

We have noted that the simultaneousness of two events, for example, may be observed through the facts. This does not mean, of course, that it is observable under all circumstances. It is clear that the situation must be suitable, as in any other kind of observation.

A more serious objection might be made. It may happen that a spectator in a race, however alert and well placed, is unable to determine the first arrival. He might say, "It seems obvious to me that the first two have arrived together." Nevertheless, a film of the arrivals might contradict him and reveal, through its proper evidence, that the evidence invoked by the spectator was only an optical illusion.

Does this objection not discredit the immediate data of observation which can yield direct statements of simultaneousness or of consecution in time?

It must at least remind us that there exists a problem of the evidence of the senses; that it would be simple to resolve this problem by supposing that in the last analysis there must exist a relation of adequation between the object which gives occasion to the perception and the meaning which the latter will assume for the observer. But we do not consider it useful to expand this part of our exposition. We shall limit ourselves here to the following remarks:

Concerning all the immediate data of observation we may make statements analogous to the preceding one. To suppose that an experiment cannot be made without a certain immediate perception, one may always assume that some day it will be possible to build an experimental device capable of improving and correcting the result of this perception.

But recourse to evidence therefore is not absolutely blocked. In one form or another, directly or indirectly, evidence must be reintegrated into its inalienable function, if only in the arrangement or in the regulation of the experimental mechanism. In this sense it is irreplaceable and inalienable.

The Time of Language Anticipates Measured Time

We now proceed to our third example. It will show that in the possibly somewhat artificial situation which we are trying to elucidate, language almost inevitably anticipates the guarantees which may be derived from observation; for example:

Emile et Paul ont refait aujourd'hui en sens inverse le trajet qu'ils avaient mis hier le même temps à parcourir.

Cette fois encore ils sont partis ensemble, mais Emile est arrivé sensiblement avant Paul.

Emile a cependant mis plus de temps aujourd'hui qu'hier.

Il en est donc de même de Paul.

(Emile and Paul today walked back the way which they both made yesterday in the same amount of time.

This time they also started out together but Emile has arrived considerably earlier than Paul.

Emile, however, has taken longer today than he did yesterday.

Therefore the same is true for Paul.)

Can the total of these four statements give occasion to remarks other than the two examples discussed above? At first glance this seems hardly so. Nothing collides with our common sense or with the current usage of language. All the same, from the viewpoint of observation the situation no longer appears in exactly the same fashion. In order to show the differences, we will use the same device as we did before. How could the correctness of the fourth statement be attested to before a court?

For the first and second of these statements it would suffice again to produce witnesses capable of testifying (on the strength of having verified it themselves) that Emile and Paul have started at the same instant and that Emile has arrived before Paul did. If the third statement can be verified by witnesses of equal credibility, the court certainly would not hesitate to recognize the validity of the fourth statement, which would have to be considered as a necessary sequel to the three preceding ones. Thus our third example so far has not contributed anything new.

We have set aside the validity of the third statement, or rather the possibility of basing it on the data from immediate temporal observations. This statement compares intervals of time which have nothing to do with each other and do not have any instant in common. Now, it is clear that direct observation can only be applied to two intervals which overlap, either completely coinciding or one projecting over the other. Concerning the testimony which must be given before the court, the third statement therefore poses an entirely different problem and is far more difficult than the first two statements. In order to solve this problem it would certainly suffice to glance, "yesterday" and "today" and at the place of arrival as well as at the place of departure, at the clock of a steeple or even at a sun dial. But what could be done in the absence of all such indications?

We shall not go so far as to claim that under these conditions, the third statement for us cannot assume any definite significance; but the situation must be examined and analyzed in an entirely different fashion. We must try to discover certain regularities capable of providing a context into which the circumstances of our statement can be inserted. Our subjective appreciation of duration naturally is based upon such contexts so as not to be irreducibly individualistic and not to remain unrelated to the subjective durations of others. The following conclusions seem to us inevitable:

We must abandon the idea of isolating a situation in which the measuring of time could be introduced in an entirely autonomous manner, from point 0 on. Nothing can change the fact that language is a carrier of a coherent ensemble of ideas and representations which prepare and anticipate our utilization of the measuring device.

We may account for the fact that language cannot be stripped of this function by observing that it is ordered according to the activities through which we are firmly incorporated in the realities of the world and of society.

HOURGLASSES AND WATER CLOCKS

We have already noted that we are not incapable of judging durations of time with a certain objectivity, provided that they are neither too long nor too short. But we do not intend to emphasize this natural ability. As a method, it shall have as little free play as possible for the benefit of the instrument. Nevertheless, after having given its full due to the latter, we shall return to our own personalities and restore all its proper significance to the variant of time which we shall name intuitive time. This will be the subject of Chapter Six. For the moment, then, we shall be concerned with the techniques for the realization of time.

First, how can we define a duration for an observer (or for a group of observers) in a well-defined location? If we leave aside our concern for the greatest possible precision, the hourglass is adequate for this purpose. (The hourglass could be replaced, of course, by any other vessel equipped with an orifice and filled with a certain quantity of water or any other substance capable of flowing out evenly.)

The Preliminaries of the Hourglass

Each time the hourglass empties itself, or rather, each time a particular hourglass empties itself, the time of the discharge is a determinate one; this is a duration proper to this particular hourglass; but why am I entitled to assume that the duration will remain the same, that tomorrow I shall find it identical to what it is today?

If the repeated observation of the time of discharge does not take place in an experimental context whose regularity would be assured in advance, the only reason we could give is the following: As far as we can judge it the hourglass is still the same, identical with itself, and the circumstances under which it empties itself likewise remain the same from one observation to the next.

In all its simplicity this answer gives us a great deal to think about.

1. We first put as a principle that if the vessel really remains identical with itself, and if the circumstances do not change, then the durations of the discharges inevitably must likewise remain equal. At the level of knowledge (i.e. of explicit knowledge) where we are operating, we are not in a position to justify this principle by anything more elementary and more certain than it. It is incorporated into our current activities as well as in our natural view of reality. For a craftsman (we shall reserve for a later time the testimony of the physicist) the duration of the discharge is above all a property of the instrument, a property which circumstances can modify in a secondary manner, as the color of an object is above all a property of this object, a property which the luminous atmosphere likewise can modify in a secondary manner.

The application of this principle will not be limited to particular cases. In all the cases where we shall successfully produce, through an experimental device of our own making and under well-defined conditions, an event, a phenomenon, or an effect of a certain duration, we will surely assume that as long as the device and the circumstances remain identical, the effect produced cannot have a duration different from that of the first time. If this duration were to vary, our first step would be to seek the causes, either in a modification of the device, in a variation of the circumstances, or in both at the same time. Quite simply, we shall not say that we are able to produce a specific effect unless we also are able to repeat this performance, i.e. unless we are able to reproduce the device and the exactly defined circumstances which lead to the effect. (Will the vicissitudes of a more exacting research some day cause us to abandon this idea? At the point where we are at present nothing gives us reason to think so.)

2. If the main idea is clear, that the duration of the discharge is a function proper to the hourglass (that particular one from among all hourglasses) which we are using, then its evaluation and application encounters a series of technical problems of increasing complexity. Can the craftsman who has constructed the instrument guarantee the stability of this proper function? Will the latter resist the wear and tear of usage, will it not fluctuate according to the circumstances, and will it not change by itself as time goes on? It is clear that the craftsman can answer these questions only within the limits of his own experience and that most often he does not even outline the research required for procedures of manufacture, materials used, variability of circumstances and factors influencing them, etc. From the very first steps we find ourselves forced to depend on a complementary knowledge or even to create it. If anyone believes that we could cut short these difficulties by deciding to take as a standard measure the duration of the emptying of this particular hourglass, under the conditions realized at this moment, he would nevertheless need an entire science to insure permanently the identity of this standard with itself.

But such a science is not made in advance, and as far as we are concerned we do not have one. (Its development is itself tied up with the progress of the measurement of time.)

Therefore the progress of one and the progress of the other must be coordinated.

For the moment we can only accept the guarantees of the craftsman and assume, at least on a provisional basis, that the instrument preserves a certain duration; that it preserves it from day to day, in the same place or when transported elsewhere, provided that the conditions of its use do not change perceptibly.

Verification Through Other Hourglasses

We just said that the instrument thus is installed in its function *on a provisional basis*, but are the conditions of a genuine test realized in this case? We must admit that this is not yet the case; as long as the instrument exists in only one exemplar it cannot be verified except for our subjective estimate of the duration. Thus the problem is precisely to set up a criterion better than the latter. We have to conclude that an entire series of analogous instruments is indispensable from a twofold point of view:

1. In order to give different observers the option of effecting measurements which are not unrelated to each other but between which there exists in advance a possibility of identification.

2. In order to establish the conditions of a control of the measurement instituted by the first instrument.

Therefore we must first ask the craftsman for two exemplars of the same instrument, i.e. two hourglasses having the same duration of discharge, which we would call two synchronous hourglasses. How would the craftsman fulfill this requirement?

Perhaps, after having constructed the first instrument, he would seek to make a second one identical to the first in every respect. But is he master enough of his craft to succeed without any doubt? This is hardly probable. We will be closer to reality by admitting that once the work is completed, be it ever so carefully done, it must still be tested. In order to make the test we must, of course, be able to open both orifices of discharge simultaneously. This is a technical problem whose degree of difficulty essentially depends on the requirements of precision. For the moment we must be content with the degree of precision with which the craftsman can solve the problem. Moreover we also must be content with the precision with which he can verify that two discharges end, or do not end, at the same moment.

Thus the craftsman must fear that under inspection, however painstaking his precautions, the two durations of discharge turn out to be appreciably unequal. In this case he must make some adjustments. We may assume that the apprenticeship and the very exercise of his profession have given him a good judgment and a sure touch for this purpose.

Will the two hourglasses thus constructed remain lastingly synchronized? We can make the test, which simply confirms what everyone has to admit: The two hourglasses remain synchronized, provided that the environmental conditions remain appreciably the same for both.

The result thus explicated was implicitly contained in the craftsman's art and in his success through his procedures of manufacture.

With three hourglasses which we shall designate s_1, s_2, and s_3, the experiment may go a decisive step further. Let it be assumed that by construction s_2 and s_3 both were synchronized with s_1. The experiment proves at the same time that s_2 and s_3 also are synchronized. In other words, we establish through the experiment that the equality of the durations of discharge is transitive.

(One should note that in order to be objectively valid, any relation of equivalence or of equality must be transitive. Transitivity, as we have already noted, is also one of the conditions for the correct use of the term "the same.")

The experiment may be repeated; or it may be extended to include more than three hourglasses; the transitivity of the equality of the durations is merely confirmed thereby.

We may repeat our remark that the result thus explicated is likewise incorporated in the craftsman's procedures of manufacture which he informs and directs.

The Significance of These Remarks

The above observations are of the most elementary nature and do not teach anything new. But at this point in our exposition they do have a certain importance. We should recall that our intention is to introduce a measurable type of time (together with the instruments and procedures with which to measure it) through methods as strictly experimental as possible. We must therefore try to point out the most elementary experimental data upon which our project might be based. One could hardly imagine simpler data than those described above.

In the preceding passage we have emphasized the difficulties inherent in a comparison of two durations which are not contemporary. In particular, as long as the equality of the two non-contemporary durations remains unobservable, the project of measuring the time cannot be realized. But what practical means are available to us to preserve a duration? We must decide, as we already noted, to make a hypothesis and to test it; the hypothesis is that the duration of the emptying of an hourglass is a property of that instrument. But this hypothesis would not lead to anything acceptable if we should observe that the two hourglasses found synchronous once do not remain so with certainty; for at least one of the hourglasses the duration of discharge would then have to be variable and accordingly could not be attributed to it as a real property. But for which hourglass? One realizes that the preservation of synchronicity itself is a condition *sine qua non* if the project to realize a standard of time through the duration of the discharge of a specific hourglass is not to be condemned to immediate failure. The fact that observation permits us to confirm the transitive character of the durations could give rise to remarks entirely analogous to the preceding ones.

Elementary as they may be, the experiments discussed above contribute to our project an empirical guarantee without which it could not even be formulated. If this guarantee were missing, any attempt to measure time would fail immediately. If, on the other hand, we have this guarantee to support us, we may be sure that we will not be stopped at the outset in our attempt to establish an operational time, whatever other difficulties this attempt may run into later.

To sum up, on the basis of the elementary procedures of manufacture which benefit as much as possible from the observations we have discussed, we may assume that the craftsman is able to provide us with an entire battery of hourglasses which realize the same duration as any hourglass taken as a model.

The Water Clocks and Their Time Scales

We may now proceed to the realization of a limited time scale. For this purpose we shall use (mentally) an instrument somewhat more flexible than the hourglass, viz. an elementary clepsydra (water clock). We shall imagine it in the form of a glass cylinder which is prolonged downwards by a cone perforated at its apex by the opening for the discharge. The operator must be imagined as free to change the water level in the cylinder, capable of releasing or suspending the flow at any moment, and able to mark by a clearly visible line any level at which he would choose to stop.

Now let c_1 and c_2 be two water clocks which we assume to be synchronized, i.e. both marked with a line corresponding to the same duration of discharge. We shall say that we have arranged them in a series if we are able to start the discharge of the second clock at the exact moment when the discharge of the first stops. In realizing the arrangement in a series with some precision we naturally have a technical problem to solve, but we shall not discuss it. Connected through this arrangement the two water clocks form a composite water clock which has a double duration of discharge.

Under these circumstances we may ask the craftsman to manufacture a new water clock marked by two lines, one corresponding to the duration t chosen first, and the second corresponding to the double duration $2t$, etc.

Now we shall try to realize the duration $t/2$. We shall do this by successive approximations. Let us return to the two water clocks c_1 and c_2 and let the water flow out of them simultaneously through a duration which we estimate as equal to $t/2$. (The observation of the water level remaining in the clock could assist us in this appraisal, but nevertheless it does not have to be exact.) We mark with a line on c_1 the level a where we have thus chosen to stop. Water clock c_1 then shall be filled up again as far as its original level. By opening thereafter for the second time the mouths of discharge of the two water clocks, we wait for the second clock to attain the level corresponding to t. We then mark on c_1 the corresponding level b. The correct level will lie somewhere between a and b.

It remains only to repeat the procedure, choosing a level a_1, at a guess, between a and b. Repeating the entire operation, we fixate an interval $a_1 b_1$ contained in ab, and so forth in the same way. After a certain number of attempts the level $t/2$ will be fixated with an irreducible margin of imprecision which is due to the instrument as well as to the procedures.

On a water clock where the levels t_2, t_3, and so forth are already marked, the same procedure would permit us to determine the levels $t/2$, $3t/2$, $5t/2$, etc. It would then permit us to construct a time scale whose successive intervals would have the duration $t/4$, and so forth in the same fashion.

In principle the process might be continued indefinitely. In practice the graduation cannot be carried beyond a certain sharpness.

Could one not consider completing it by "interpolation"? Certainly, but this would mean invoking a different representation, a principle which we have not used so far but will discuss later.

Why a Uniform Time?

One might ask why we have chosen, in order to calibrate our water clock, such a complicated procedure, instead of simply marking some regular graduations on the instrument, and why we have not arbitrarily decided that time would be measured by that particular water clock.

The first answer we could think of is that the flow from the simple water clock is not constant because the speed of the discharge depends on the pressure, that the pressure depends on the level of the liquid and that this level decreases as the liquid is discharged.

But at this moment nothing permits us to argue in such a way. We want to establish operationally an instrument for measuring time, without resorting to a standard clock. How shall we verify that our water clock is slowing down if we do not have a clock for reference? Are we suspecting it for theoretical reasons? Certainly not; we want to limit ourselves to the operational process, and moreover it is probable that the theory which would be required could not be established and verified without an instrument for measuring time.

We therefore have only one option open to us; we may verify that something changes during the functioning of the water clock, and we may assume, according to the principle of sufficient reason which will be invoked later, that this change might have some influence upon the development of the process. Accordingly we try to eliminate this possible cause of irregularity by measuring the duration each time from the same level.

But, to repeat, why is such a precaution necessary? Could we not declare at will that time shall be measured by a simple water clock which is graduated regularly (by volume)? Could we not construct a water clock that would empty itself every 24 hours, mark it with 24 divisions, put it into operation at midnight, and decree that it should be one o'clock when the water level has reached the first division, two o'clock when it has reached the second, etc.? The first of these 24 hours certainly would be shorter than the last, but no matter: if only the definition is rigorous and reproducible. Can we not define time as we wish, choosing as a reference any phenomenon, even if it accelerates or slows down, provided these changes are always regular? Did not the ancients have hours that varied according to the seasons and the latitudes and even differed between day and night?* The only requirement we must retain is that the phenomenon should neither stop nor slow down.

One may certainly define a time scale in an arbitrary fashion. But one cannot do so with impunity; he must pay for this arbitrariness with serious inconveniences. In fact, this regularly irregular clock would have the consequence that the phenomena would not obey the same laws at one o'clock in the morning or at eleven o'clock in the evening. One would thus have to insert, in the expression of the natural laws, the hour of the day, which would be rather inconvenient—not only inconvenient but unjustified, since the variations of the laws would not result from the phenomena themselves but from our arbitrary decision.

Meanwhile, nothing prevents us logically from maintaining our decision and to have the hour of the day represented in the expression of the natural laws. One would then realize very quickly that these laws could split up into two terms, one depending on the hour and the other independent of it. One would

* The ancients divided the day (from sunrise to sunset) into twelve hours and the night (from sunset to sunrise) likewise into twelve hours. Thus they did not have hours of equal length by day and night except at the time of the equinoxes; at the time of the solstices, especially in the extreme North and South, the duration of the hours of the day and of the night differed considerably.

also realize that the term depending on the hour is identical for all natural laws, and that this is precisely the law which permits us to pass from nonuniform time to uniform time. Is it not wiser, under these conditions, to integrate once and for all this transcription into the definition of time and to adopt *uniform time?*

Uniform time accordingly is the time relative to which the law of evolution of phenomena as similar as possible remains similar, whatever the moment when the phenomenon starts to develop.

Is Universal Time Uniform?

And what if this time is not uniform? Would it not be possible that the time thus defined should accelerate and with it, inevitably, all the natural phenomena (their law of evolution remaining the same)? Would we be equipped to notice it?

At first glance it would seem so. A movement appearing to be uniform relative to an accelerated time would in fact cease to be uniform and instead would likewise be accelerated. We must keep in mind, however, that time cannot be defined outside the phenomena which serve to measure it (this, of course, includes the biological phenomena which serve as a basis for our subjective appraisal of durations). This movement perhaps could be metaphysically accelerated, but we would be unable to verify it, since the clocks which would measure the time would accelerate at the same rate.* In order to demonstrate the acceleration of time, we need at least one phenomenon whose evolution is not subject to this acceleration, and in which we have confidence enough to take it as a reference for determining a scale of time. If all the phenomena accelerate at the same time and in

* The possibility considered here—and this must be pointed out—is not the case where all the phenomena would accelerate *in the course of their own evolution,* their speed of evolution being the function of the time elapsed since the beginning of this evolution, and the instant of the beginning not being the same for all phenomena. We are concerned, on the contrary, with the case where the speed of evolution of all phenomena would be an identical function of the duration elapsed since a certain moment, fixed once and for all and for all the phenomena together. (More generally, the speed of evolution would be a function both of the duration elapsed since a universal date line and of the duration elapsed since the beginning of the phenomenon.)

the same measure, including those which serve for measuring time (and we shall see that any phenomenon sufficiently well defined may serve this purpose), the acceleration would become undetectable. In that case, would it even make sense to speak of acceleration? Acceleration relative to what? Relative to a time independent of any phenomenon, relative to a metaphysical time? From the fact that time may be defined on the basis of any phenomenon, and that it is not linked to any phenomenon in particular, we must not conclude that time may be defined independent of *every* phenomenon.

It is unimportant whether, from a metaphysical viewpoint, time elapses regularly or irregularly. We declare as uniform a time in relation to which the laws governing the phenomena do not vary, or relative to which the expression of these laws does not involve "absolute cosmic moments" but only intervals of time (or eventually, which is the same thing, instants measured according to guide marks particular to the phenomena themselves, for example, referring to the beginning of the phenomenon). And it is doubtless more correct to say that it is the phenomena which are well defined, repeatable, and as identical as possible by which time is determined than to postulate as a natural principle that the evolvement of well-defined phenomena does not depend on the moment in which they take place.

Does a Universal Time Exist?

Nevertheless we must make a reservation. It is certainly not a priori a natural law that the laws of the phenomena would not vary in the course of time. We seek to define time in such a way that these laws remain unchanged. But nothing guarantees us in advance that the definition of such a time will be successful for all phenomena, or even that the uniform times thus defined from different phenomena will coincide. Nothing guarantees us in advance, for example, that the electromagnetic phenomena follow constant laws relative to the same time as the mechanical phenomena. And yet it is a law of nature, based on experimental evidence, that this is really the case, and that the uniform electromagnetic time is neither slow nor fast relative to the mechanical time.

We can imagine a world which would have several times, defined on the basis of different phenomena. This would not be a catastrophe, provided that the classes of phenomena obeying the same time would be well delimited; one could then establish laws of transformation between the different times and make tables of conversion.

We could likewise imagine a universe where each phenomenon would permit us to define a different time, relative to which its law of evolution would remain constant. It might then be convenient to take, more or less arbitrarily, the time of one of these phenomena as a reference; the law of this single phenomenon alone would then remain constant in the course of time; the law of the other phenomena would have to impose the moment when the phenomenon unfolds.

Our universe is not built like this. The sequel of our exposé will show clearly that clocks constructed according to the most diverse principles agree with each other, allowing for a certain margin of indetermination. And experience shows that it is not necessary to include the instants in the expression of the natural laws (unless, of course, if in these instants detectable physical influences come into play; but then it would not be the instants themselves which would play a rôle). One may thus confirm that there exists a universal time, at least in a first approximation.

Natural Control of Graduations

We have indicated how c_1 may be equipped with a time scale. Should we proceed in the same fashion to graduate c_2? For the construction of this second scale two principally very different methods suggest themselves:

1. The simpler method is to "carry over" the scale from c_1 to c_2, during the simultaneous discharge of the contents of both water clocks. The two scales would then be synchronized by construction.

2. One may also repeat the entire procedure with the rôles of

c_1 and c_2 exchanged. One may then ask whether the two scales thus constructed independent of each other will likewise be synchronized. Nobody will doubt it, provided that the two scales could be established with some precision. From a strictly experimental point of view, however, we have only one hypothesis which moreover is strictly conforming to our representation of the course of elementary phenomena. Is this hypothesis really justified? Nothing prevents us from testing it. Again, the result of this test will not teach us anything; repeated at will, the test does not disappoint our expectation of synchronicity.

Is the experiment therefore useless? Within the framework of our exposé it assumes, on the contrary, an importance which must be underscored.

The simple carrying over of the time scale of a standard water clock to all the rest could lead us to believe that thereby we have artificially "defined" a lapse of time connected by construction with the standard clock, as its other properties are connected with it. The second method, and the experiment which it permits and implies, entitle us to detach the time scale from the standard clock and to perceive in it the representation of the passing of a time which would be, by nature, the same for all the water clocks. In other words, this method provides an elementary experimental basis for what will be, in the final analysis, the time of the physicist. The correctness of this last remark moreover is reinforced by the fact that the experimentation may be extended to an ensemble of several water clocks.

Arithmetization of the Measured Duration

But it is under this somewhat different angle that it assumes its full significance. We have already said that the control of the synchronicity of the scales established according to the second method is an experiment at the same time elementary and essential. But it is not the only possible one. A different experiment would be, for example, as follows: Let t_1 and t_2 be the durations of two discharges which immediately follow each other. The total duration, which shall be designated as $t_1 + t_2$, may be realized by the formation of a series with two suitable water clocks. The same may be done with a single water clock equipped with a time scale. It is quite as easy to realize the total discharge of the duration $t_2 + t_1$, in which the durations of the preceding discharge are switched. Whether done directly with a series of water clocks or done with the aid of scales, the experiment will show that the two durations $t_1 + t_2$ and $t_2 + t_1$ are equal.

We understand immediately where this example leads us. It tends to make of duration an arithmetizable magnitude. We shall not examine in detail all the experiments one would have to make (and could make) with this intention. Everyone can imagine them without difficulty. We may limit ourselves to announcing their result. The systematic testing of time scales justifies the following rules:

1. Every duration may be viewed as a certain multiple of an otherwise undetermined standard duration. This multiple is its measure.

2. One may "define operationally" sums and differences of durations and multiply durations by a numerical coefficient. These operations are translated by corresponding arithmetical operations effected on the measures.

To sum up, one may verify empirically the conditions necessary and sufficient for *the duration* to be considered and treated as a measurable magnitude.

For the aims we set for ourselves, in examining so closely the real procedures of the measurement of time, this is already a fundamental statement. It seems to us remarkable that this statement could have been made with the help of instruments as rudimentary as hourglasses and water clocks of the most simple type. The very elementary nature of the instruments, however, must caution us against a too "literal" interpretation of the preceding statements. We must not overlook the fact that all the experiments which were discussed, all the observations which were judged possible, all the verifications which were said to be repeatable, only attain a rather low degree of precision. The evaluation of circumstances which "must remain perceptibly the same" and whose variations could alter all the results likewise must be very provisional. Under these circumstances it would be totally illusory to strive for a precision of a higher order. It would be impossible to establish a more stable result since all the statements to be made could vary within a relatively wide margin of imprecision. We must emphasize that the very possibility of announcing the results of the experiment depends on a certain moderation of the requirements of precision, the precaution of not pushing these requirements further than our "operational means" permit.

Under these conditions it is clear that the results just announced (where we have singled out the experimental basis of the measurement of time) must not be taken purely as results of observation. The concept of a time measurable with indefinite precision does not necessarily follow from it. Suggested through the experiment, this concept itself is an organizer of this experiment; at the same time it contains an exigency directed toward future experiments and may orient their development.

But it is not certain in advance that this exigency can always be satisfied. In other words, we are not entitled *through the experiment* to affirm in advance that while the "operational definitions" of the duration become increasingly precise, we shall infallibly prosper in applying them with increasing success. To attain higher precision is a problem (confronting the technician of measurement) which is by no means solved in advance; we cannot even be certain in advance that it can always be solved.

The Necessity to Resort to Other Instruments

If we ever thought that we would successfully elucidate the problem of measuring time by considering only the most simple instruments, we are now undeceived. The problem of precision cannot be separated from it. In order to begin, even to be able to begin, we had to relegate it to a level of secondary importance.

After having investigated the simple water clock we must proceed to other instruments. Are we planning a review of all the categories of instruments which are used or could be used for measuring time? Our first example has already shown that the instrument itself is the means for the specification of objective time as measured time. It is thus natural and even inevitable that our exposé should dwell on the investigation of the instrument in its diverse concrete realizations and the particular procedures of its application. Our project is not, however, to write a history of the measuring of time, and still less to draw up a list of all the known variants of clocks. For the moment our attention is directed towards the institution of an "operational time" (as operational as possible), as it already had been directed towards the definition (as purified of experience as possible) of mathematical time. But this is only part of our project. After having analyzed and specified, we will have to show how the elements thus dissociated may again be united into an organic whole. At the level of current language the discursive synthesis already has offered us the example of such a remodelling. The latter, however, is not our final aim. As far as time is concerned, it is a methodological experiment in which we are engaged, an experiment which aims at the formulation of the main outline of a methodology of research. It is towards this aim, in all the vicissitudes implied by it, that our study must be oriented.

For this reason our investigation of the various instruments for measuring time in each case shall serve a twofold purpose; on the one hand it will contribute to the progressive specification of objective time as measured time, and on the other hand it will give us an opportunity to discuss a small number of specially selected topics, each of which will have significance beyond the particular case.

Let us now review the case which was discussed before. Is the preceding remark already applicable to it? Have we made use of the opportunity to discuss some of these themes? This is exactly what we did, although we have not said so explicitly. What, then, is this theme, and would it not be appropriate to announce it?

The Sketch and Its Summary Character

We are concerned with the still summary character of the preliminary knowledge and the first observations upon which the

measurement of time may be based. By "summary" we neither
imply "doubtful" nor "inconsistent," "elusive," or "obscure."
What is summarily conceived or announced is like something
outlined; its correctness does not depend on the precision of
detail.

The idea of the sketch which has just been introduced enables
us to show that this first theme necessarily calls for a second,
that of a certain duality between the statement and the experiment. It is not for the first time that this second theme emerges,
and it will not be for the last time; its significance, on the contrary, will be confirmed as our inquiry proceeds.

Let us assume that a designer has made a sketch of a palace,
for example, in order to explain its proportions to us. This sketch
is here, in front of us, and we will call it E. It is not an exact
image of the building it represents. If we would ask that this
palace be built again in a different place, from this sketch alone,
and would expect total similarity between the two buildings, our
demand could not be satisfied. The sketch determines the second
palace only in its broad outlines; the architect who must work
with the sketch will retain a partial freedom of execution. Any
other sketch E_1 moreover could serve him equally well, provided
that it is not too different from the first one.

The designer and the architect in this case personify two
activities which are partly opposed and partly attuned to each
other. If I need a summary representation of the building I shall
turn to the designer for help. The nature of this representation
depends on his sketch and will be defined by it. The sketch is
the very device through which the representation will assume
its summary validity. In short, the summary exists only through
an activity which confers on it form and validity.

In the case where the character of summary refers to a text,
a statement, or an announcement, we speak of an enunciatory
activity and of a level of enunciation. (We shall not investigate
here to what extent the visual memory can play the rôle of an
experienced designer. Neither shall we attempt to learn whether
any representation which we are able to make would not have
more or less the character of a sketch. We prefer, for the
moment, to leave these questions unanswered.)

But if I must know whether the sketch may serve as a basis for a real construction or reconstruction, whether the indications it contains are sufficient as well as compatible, whether it will not be necessary to complement or to retouch them, it is the architect to whom I shall address myself. He will judge the matter as a professional, on the strength of his experience and possibly of additional tests he might consider useful.

(The fact that the designer and the architect may be united in the same person does not obliterate the duality of their functions. One operates on the side of representation, of a necessarily summary formulation, while the other operates on the side of realization, of a more or less accurate placing into position.)

Beginning of the Sketch

We have noted that for our purposes, the sketch E could be replaced by any sketch E_1 which would not be too different from it. We now make an assumption which might appear artificial as long as we are concerned with the dialogue between the designer and the architect. Let us assume that among all possible sketches we select one, and that we confer on it the following privileged rôle: We hand it over to the architect, who should follow its indications "literally." If he departs from the sketch it will not be because he has taken the liberty of claiming as his right a certain margin of interpretation. We assume precisely that we do not give him this liberty and do not permit him to consider the sketch selected from among all the others as an equivalent to any of them. Thus, if he departs from the sketch, he does so because he is unable to do any better. If his technical means were improved, enabling him to work more carefully and accurately, this would only cause him to follow the imposed sketch more closely.

Under these conditions, which are artificial at the moment but will assume their full significance later, two eventualities must be taken into consideration:

1. The discipline thus imposed on the architect will not be intolerable to him. Within the rules of his profession, within the requirements of his craft he will not find any reason to revolt and to reject sketch E as unsuitable.

2. The very requirements of the execution will force him one day to recover his liberty, when the sketch E cannot be fully complied with any longer.

In this last case, unless we change the method, the sketch E must be replaced by a sketch E^*.

Dialogue Between Measured Time and Mathematical Time

We now return to the "operational definition of time" which was occasioned by our first instrument. So far we have tried to emphasize the experimental aspect of the operation. Is it possible to find in it the conditions of a dialogue similar to that of the designer and the architect? We would then have to admit that even in the most elementary procedures, the experimental aspect of "the operational" cannot be made totally autonomous but is inseparably tied to a representation in which the mental activity predominates. This is not the first time that we call attention to the traces of a principle of duality likely to account for this fact at the level of a methodology of research. Hardly perceptible at this point, this principle will be more clearly isolated later.

With our attention thus sharpened, let us again examine how we have introduced the measure of a time in the process of objectivation. We shall not repeat the planned observations in every detail; it will suffice to repeat the result which sums them up, on the possibility of constructing and utilizing a time scale. We can dispense with discussing again its aspect of "fabrication" which we have pointed out sufficiently. It is the aspect of articulation which must be brought out from the obscurity where we have left it.

What, then, is the outcome of our entire experimental effort? We actually take possession of it only in announcing it; the scale imprints its structure upon the time which is being measured. More explicitly, the time thus measured is linear, additive, and homogeneous. It may be measured, being identical with itself, from any well-defined starting moment; to do so it suffices to use two equal scales, one of which is properly shifted along the other. In short, the scale presents itself as a realization, albeit of imperfect precision, of the abstract time of the mathematician. (We introduce the time of the mathematician at this point only in order to abridge the announcement of the properties of the time scale. In this context it would still be possible to omit our reference but we would have to make it later.)

Briefly, then, these are the articulations (the enunciatory verbal forms) which are set up in contrast to the experimental activity, sum up the latter, and confer upon it its clearest meaning. But is it worthwhile to point them out? Are they not simply the inevitable expression of the results obtained through experimentation? It would be a great error to judge the matter in this way. As we already know, the articulations thus formulated have only a summary validity. To return to our simile, they accordingly have only the value of a sketch. It becomes clear at once what was meant by our dialogue between the designer and the architect. Between the articulation and the experiment which share the rôles in our example (however elementary the latter may be) there exists an interdependence, a duality similar to that which combines into a whole the sketch and the actual building.

However clear the matter may be, there is one further point which merits our attention. Is ours the case 1 or the case 2 of the immediate present? Is the statement which figures in our example one from among all possible statements or is it privileged? There can be no doubt that it is a privileged statement. This is what we meant by our allusion to the time of the mathematician. It is suggested to us and imposed, if not through the concept of purified mathematical time, then at least through the representations already carried by current language, which have found their realization along a certain line of specification, in the mathematical time. But can we foresee, as in case 2, that this privileged statement might one day be contested and rejected for reasons based on the experiment? For the moment we do not have any reason to assume this. Therefore ours is the case 1.

Will we have to decide, some time, to proceed to case 2? This could only be for reasons entirely unforeseen at this stage of our exposé.

The Objectivity of Time

Each of the examples treated must permit us, as we have said, to direct the discussion towards a theme of a certain methodological significance. At first sight our second example will differ little from the first. Upon closer examination, however, we shall see that it is based on an entirely different principle. This will provide for us the occasion to raise the question about the objectivity of measured time, a question which has already been touched upon but which will properly be treated in greater detail.

The duration of the discharge of the hourglass, of *an* hourglass, at first has presented itself as a property of *this particular* hourglass. If every one of them were to measure only its own time, independent of any other hourglass, we would not and could not say that time might be measured objectively. In order to be able meaningfully to speak of objective measurement, it is not enough that the observations made on a certain instrument be independent of the fluctuations of the personal status of the observer. As a minimal condition things must present themselves as if all instruments would measure the same time, however different the methods of measuring it. (The relevance of the "as if," which has been emphasized, shall be discussed and defined more clearly later.)

Briefly, the criterion of the objectivity of the measurement of time is and must be its universality. This means that whatever the instruments under consideration and whatever the phenomena utilized to realize them, their time scales should be capable of being permanently synchronized.

But how can we establish this universality of the measurement? By experimental methods? It is clear that we shall never realize all the instruments which could be constructed if all possible phenomena were taken into consideration.[*] Even if this

---

[*] It must be noted, however, that even though we do not construct clocks on the basis of these phenomena we nevertheless seek to establish their temporal law. And if we have the temporal law of a phenomenon at our disposal, nothing is easier than to establish tables permitting us to use it as a clock. This is exactly what was done to establish the time of the astronomical tables, as we shall see in one of the following chapters. One might object that the

were feasible we would not do it. Universality, the guarantee of objectivity, thus is not directly demonstrable. What, then, is the method through which it will finally be confirmed?

In the strictly logical sense this will never be accomplished. The universality of measurement will be sufficiently insured in the same way and to the same degree as all results obtained by experimental methods. The method will take the form of a procedure of extension. It already has made its first appearance in the preceding section; there we have not entrusted the measurement of time to a single hourglass or to a single elementary water clock but have discussed the use of a group of hourglasses *and* water clocks, with diminishing emphasis on their material shapes, the similarity of their forms, the identity of the materials used, and with increasing emphasis on the equivalence of their functions, i.e. the synchronicity of their scales. Thus we have already obtained the result that the correct measurement of time is not the prerogative of a specific instrument, or of a battery of instruments as similar to each other as possible. By stressing the equivalence of function, i.e. the equivalence realizable in spite of all the differences of form, we have taken a step towards universality and consequently towards objectivity in the measurement of time.

We only must persevere in the same track, increasing the number of examples and submitting the instrument to increasingly fundamental variations. Each time a new instrument has been added to the ensemble of the already existing instruments, and especially if it refers to a phenomenon not yet utilized, we

---

clock here is taken as a norm and that it never occurs to the scientist to verify his clock by means of the phenomena which he is studying. This may be true as long as he does not study a phenomenon more constant and more precise than his clock. But if the case did occur, if the law of the phenomenon became increasingly simple and precise as better clocks were being used, would the idea of taking this phenomenon as a new standard not irresistibly suggest itself to the scientist? The establishment of the temporal law of the phenomena thus may likewise be considered as an operational consolidation of time furnished by the clock as a reference. (The methodological significance of this remark will become clear only when we tackle the problem of the autofoundation of a discipline.)

have taken a further step, not only towards the objectivation of the measurement of time, but also towards the objectivation of time itself. When will this procedure of extension have reached its term? Principally never. In practice one must observe moderation. In a situation of well-defined knowledge, it is useless to increase indefinitely the possibilities of control and of synchronicity.

But what gives us the right, we might ask, to stop the process of extension at this point? If one does not admit the existence of an objective and universal time, is it not a fault of method to assume that the controls of synchronicity which have been erected would guarantee those which were not yet erected? Is it admissible to exclude as impossible the case of an instrument still "unpublished" which could not be easily fitted into the group of clocks presently in use?

We have already answered this question indirectly. It is not necessary to construct all possible clocks; it suffices to establish the temporal law of the phenomena. As long as this temporal law does not vary with regard to the moment when the phenomenon begins (this variation certainly could not be attributed to any momentary influence or to any more or less concealed evolution of the system which is the seat of this phenomenon), we have no reason whatever to abandon the hypothesis of a universal time, and every phenomenon whose law does not vary in the course of time confirms this hypothesis. What more can we ask of a natural law?

At this point we shall conclude the discussion about the objectivity of the measuring of time and about the means to be used in order to base it upon increasingly solid foundations. One might judge that our discussion has considerably exceeded the exposition of the technical aspect of the question. Was it necessary to go this far, to proceed so manifestly beyond what may be expected of elementary clocks, which alone have been described up to this point?

The discussion of the theme of objectivity certainly has moved ahead, but it will soon be joined and even overtaken by the necessary discussion of the experimental aspects.

The Water Clock with Uniform Discharge

It is now time for the description of a new type, the water clock with uniform discharge.

We have not tried to find out whether the flow in the elementary water clocks was uniform or not. Even in the case of a uniform discharge the procedure could not be utilized (except, perhaps, at the moment of dividing the intervals of a partially constructed scale into equal parts). In order to proceed from the first water clock to the second we must above all be careful to insure this uniformity. Without being overly concerned about precision we may attain this end (principally) by keeping the reservoir in a stationary condition. (For example, we shall maintain the water of the reservoir at a constant level by adding to the water which, while not remaining constant, nevertheless will remain above the point of loss, and by draining off the surplus through a secondary opening.)

Let us now assume that the conditions of a uniform flow are satisfied. We must be careful at this point not to be caught in the vicious circle which would consist in defining the uniformity of the discharge by saying "a discharge is uniform if its outflow is constant, i.e. if the quantity of the liquid which is being discharged is in proportion to the time of discharge." With such a definition as a starting point we should already have a watch of some precision in order to verify that our water clock is well made. We would then merely carry over on it the measurement of time which this watch would have furnished to us in advance. As far as our project is concerned (of giving an increasingly solid foundation to objectivity) the construction of such a water clock would be without interest.

The notion of uniformity must be conceived at a more elementary level. A uniform discharge is simply a discharge which remains permanently equal to and even identical with itself. And the guarantee that this should be so is again that the conditions of the discharge likewise remain the same.

In the representation which we have of it by nature (not through an explicit definition) this uniform discharge takes on the value of a figuration, of a realized model of the uniform flow of time. It is this representation which informs the following statement, which takes, from this fact, the value of evidence; for two (quantitatively) equal, uniform discharges the durations of discharge are equal. Valid for any (uniform) discharges, this statement involves the proportionality of the quantities of liquid discharged to the time of their discharges. On the basis of our representation the measurement of time is thus reduced to a different, more directly realizable measure.

Should we measure the quantities discharged by their weight or by their volume? This is a technical question which will not be discussed here; moreover it pertains rather to the theme of precision, to which we shall return later, than to the explication of the principle on which the construction of a clock with uniform discharge is based.

Likewise we shall not dwell on the precautions which are necessary for a discharge to remain genuinely uniform. They also belong to the theme of precision.

The second variant of our water clock, as we have said, reduces the measurement of time to the measurement of a certain quantity of liquid; this measurement may be effected by weight or by volume. The duration, transitory by nature, thus becomes materialized; the comparison between two durations then offers neither more nor less difficulty than the comparison of two elementary physical magnitudes. We thus run into the general problem of measurements. As far as we are concerned, may we consider it as clarified? We can limit ourselves to these few remarks:

Our project to take hold of time in its physical reality has engaged us in two orders of considerations, rational and operational. Both are indispensable to us, and the exigencies of increasing precision will force them increasingly to support each other. The same is true for our understanding of any other physical magnitude. In the case of a linear measure, for example, which is one of the most simple, the rational aspect is insured by geometry insofar as it is a deductive discipline. But geometry, an abstract discipline, does not solve the problem of the designation of realized linear measures or, what amounts to the same thing, the problem of measuring lengths in the physical world. We cannot avoid taking the operational aspect of the question into consideration. It will then be of interest, as in the example of time, to confer on it the greatest possible autonomy and to specify it to the highest possible degree.

At the elementary level the problem is first reduced to the formulation of a graduated rule. It may be treated in the same way as we had proposed for providing our first water clock with a time scale. The construction of a scale of volumes or a scale of weights will turn out to be hardly different.

As we have noted before, we shall not examine in this context the means by which one could make of this second variant of the water clock an instrument of considerable precision.

Objectivity Revisited

On the other hand, we cannot avoid reviewing, in a few words, the theme of objectivity which must be increasingly involved in the measurement of time.

In what respect does the construction of the water clock with uniform discharge contribute to this project? It must be remembered that despite certain appearances, the two variants of the water clock are based upon fundamentally different principles.* If the function of "universal metronomes" of the evolution of phenomena connected, in our representation, with objectivated cosmic time did have merely the value of a subjective

---

* It should be noted, however, that although the two water clocks which we have mentioned pose very different methodological problems because one has linear scales while the other does not, they nevertheless are both based upon the discharge of a liquid through an orifice; because of this fact, the same causes may produce similar effects, to the degree that the perturbations may be parallel and therefore unnoticeable. This is true especially of the principal agent of the irregularities of the water clock, namely, temperature (the coefficient of viscosity varies from 1 to 2 between 0° and 25° Centigrade); it would therefore be useless to attempt to check against each other a simple water clock and a water clock with continuous discharge by maintaining both at the same temperature; one might conclude that both run well while actually both could show considerable departures when checked against a clock which is maintained at a constant temperature.

vue, why should the scales of our two instruments be synchronizable? If they were so by accident, what would be their chance of being synchronizable in a regular and permanent way? Would these chances not have to be judged very weak or even poor? The experiment of synchronicity therefore is not gratuitous. On the contrary, especially if it is followed through, it assumes a decisive validity. We know the result; provided that we do not exaggerate the exigencies of precision, the two scales may always be synchronized in a relatively permanent fashion.

Proceeding towards the investigation of clocks based upon still other principles, we do not return explicitly to the theme of "operational objectivity" of the measurement of time. We do not mean that this subject necessarily has been abandoned. It will continue, on the contrary, as one of our basic themes. It will be carried over from one example to the next and we shall never lose it from sight. Because of the explanations which were given above, however, we do not have to refer to it explicitly each time.

The Theme of Correctness

We now embark on the discussion of a new fundamental theme, the theme of correctness.

The theme of correctness could not be treated as totally independent of the theme of precision. The "experimental context" of the water clocks hardly lends itself to a discussion of the latter theme. On the contrary (and without any paradox) it is the positive aspect of a certain imprecision, accepted because it is inevitable, which we had to emphasize in order to explain how it is possible to begin with the summary and the elementary aspects. To repeat, the precision with which these first instruments may be equipped can only be approximate. By carrying the requirements of precision too far one could only cast doubt again on the (relative) validity of the results obtained. In this context we must make a general observation:

The precision of an instrument clearly depends on the technical means applied for its construction. If one stays with these means, or if no better ones are available, the precision of the instrument thus is one of the fundamental data. It is therefore unnecessary, it is even a mistake, to ask more of the instrument than it can deliver. There is no point in expecting of it results of an accuracy which it cannot attain. Beyond a certain degree of accuracy the supplementary indications which may be gained from it are problematic. Unless we treat them as such there is no reason why they should converge towards a precise result.

For the theme of precision to be reviewed and treated properly in our exposé, it is therefore necessary that this exposé in turn be based on measuring instruments of increasing precision.

The Paradox of the Standard

From the operational standpoint, to which for the moment and by method we seek to give as much autonomy as possible, the problem of correctness and that of precision run into the same paradoxes: How can we judge whether a clock is correct unless by comparison with another clock whose correctness has already been verified, and how can we ascertain that a clock is precise unless by comparison with another clock whose precision is already certain? If this paradox had to be taken seriously we would be unable to use the "operational definition" of objective time in a progressive procedure. But will this paradox actually stop our progress? We might have run into it even earlier. We might have mentioned it already before the establishment of any time scale. How can we establish such a scale, we might have argued, unless we use a time scale already validated? To a considerable extent, our detailed investigation of water clocks was done for the purpose of defusing this paradox and overcoming it, and to show the operational procedures through which the measurement of time may be inaugurated. It is true that in our exposition we have not yet reached the high precision of the modern clocks. But we are headed in its direction and it is one of the stages through which we must pass. For this purpose, we must for the second time deal with the paradox and again point out the principles which permit us to do so.

Invoking Intuitive Time

It is, of course, through the construction of new clocks that the technique of clockmaking acquires the means of progress. But as far as the principles are concerned which permit increased correctness and precision (and to ascertain them) without having a control clock at one's disposal, it is tempting, perhaps even useful to develop them in a context as elementary as possible. For the time being we therefore shall be content with the example of the water clocks. What idea shall we form about the correctness or the precise running of such a clock? It is sufficient for us to return to the representations on which the projected measuring procedures are based. Among our natural representations there are those of the uniform flow of time. Accordingly we assume that a clock is the more precise and dependable the more exactly it realizes the idea which we have formed of the regular flow of time. But how can we apply this "definition" in practice?

First of all we must eliminate the following very natural objection: Is such a representation not essentially subjective and its realization by a particular instrument totally artificial? We could answer in a general way that the representations involved in our daily activities are never completely gratuitous, and that the realizations of which they are capable are never completely fortuitous. But the situation requires a more detailed as well as a more concrete answer.

Let us assume that the two water clocks *a* and *b* have been synchronized and equipped with corresponding time scales. During a certain time (a time lived through by a certain observer) the two water clocks thus have run on a par, their eventual differences remaining within the margin of their inevitable imprecision. Now, let us assume that their indications do not remain concordant but that, on the contrary, we suddenly notice perceptible differences. We would then conclude, according to the concept of correctness which has been discussed, that at least one of the clocks is out of order. Supposing that one of the clocks is still functioning properly, is it enough to compare the two in order to decide which one it is? And if both clocks have been impaired, will it be possible to decide whether one of the two (and which one) has remained more correct than the other?

It is clear that if we are limited to the comparison of the two water clocks, without being able to use any supplementary information, we shall be unable to decide anything at all. What we know of the clocks are the circumstances under which they were manufactured and synchronized. Unless we are able to complete or to correct our knowledge of these circumstances, we cannot arrive at any differentiated judgment about their correctness. Must the problem be abandoned? No, because we do not have to interpret it so narrowly.

Recourse to a Larger Context; Search for the Possible Causes of Variation

One may *open up* the problem by placing it in a properly selected context. This opening up may present several aspects.

1. Within the range of common sense it may happen that certain causes can be detected. The water of one of the water clocks has been contaminated, for example, and carries sand with it; one of the water clocks was exposed to the sun while the other remained in the shade, etc. If one of the circumstances which could thus be pointed out differs perceptibly from the circumstances under which the water clocks have been synchronized, we shall not hesitate to see in this the cause, if not certain at least very probable, of the observed divergences. In certain cases the search for the causes of deviation thus can lead to a differentiated judgment of correctness for which at first there would seem to be no justification. For example, if only the source of the water for one of the clocks was contaminated while the other circumstances remain perceptibly the same, it is naturally the uncontaminated water clock which we declare the more correct of the two.

This decision may be analyzed. It anticipates the result of an experiment which should be made so that the presumed cause can be properly established. We would have to confirm that once this cause has been eliminated, the two water clocks are again synchronous. When the situation has thus been corrected, we could make an argument similar to that by which we presented the possibility of synchronizing the two water clocks as a guarantee of the objectivity (and consequently of the correctness) of their common measurement of time. If the suspected cause is not the actual cause of the divergence, what is our chance that we merely have to reestablish the *status quo ante* to correct the fault?

To sum up, we conclude that since the two water clocks were constructed synchronous, they cannot vary relative to each other without a cause for this variation. It may happen that such a cause is "discovered" in a rather immediate context. A differentiated judgment of correctness is then possible, without recourse to another clock whose correctness and precision would inspire more confidence.

2. These reasons of immediate common sense do not suffice. Our position will not be modified fundamentally; we will continue to believe that the variations observed must have their causes. Quite simply, these causes are less obvious, but our concern for correctness can only urge us on to search for them. If our observation at the level of common sense remains without results, we shall have to embark on a systematic search, but our aim will remain the same; we wish to explain the variations, give one or more causes for them, whether external or internal ones. Hypothetical at first, these causes will be acknowledged as being responsible if their elimination suffices to eliminate the variations and if their intentional reintroduction causes the variations to reappear.

It is not appropriate at this point to describe how the systematic search for causes may be conducted. It is the very basis of the experimental method which we must explain once more. We must in particular insure its proper position in the procedure of the four phases in which one may see the most simple outline of a complete experimental approach. Nevertheless, we do not want to be more specific; we could only repeat what was already said elsewhere.* But there is another point

* Cf., among others: F. Gonseth: De l'homme, médecine et philosophie. *Praxis* 45, 24:545–551, 1956.

which must be mentioned. Will the search for causative factors which we have discussed remain true to the operational intention which we seek to illuminate? In the procedure of the four phases, where the hypothesis is combined with the experiment, are we sure in advance that we can always avoid theoretical, explicit statements and the governing ideas which they express and propose? Nothing proves this in advance. Accordingly we must consider a third possibility:

3. We must finally reckon with the eventuality that the search for causes must be based on theoretical considerations and must take as guidelines certain ideas evolved from a theorization of phenomena on which the realization of the instrument is based. This is doubless the case in practice; we shall soon have an opportunity to verify it. But is the theoretical element indispensable, and could it not be suspended, just as we try to suspend it in this part of our exposé? If this intervention of the theoretical element could not be delayed any longer, if there came a moment when our search for correctness could not attain its full acuity except through a combination of the rational and the operational elements, we would have to realize that the autonomy of the operational aspect is ended. We have not yet reached this point. But the question will emerge as soon as our exposé will proceed to the investigation of clocks and watches of considerable precision.

Method of Regularization

Thus we see emerge the governing idea of a method aimed at correctness through research and at the elimination of the causes of variation. This governing idea is the following:

If the instruments for measuring time would answer exactly to the representation and concepts on which they are founded, they would have to be capable of functioning with a certain regularity, a regularity which in itself would represent the guarantee of their correctness. That they do not is because their functioning does not remain sufficiently identical with itself. In other words, the instrument varies but its variations are not without cause.

The variations can be revealed through the desynchronization of two or more clocks. The causes will give rise to a more or less systematic search. The culminating point of their demonstration will be their elimination. The progressive elimination of the causes of irregularity will progressively insure the good functioning of the instrument.

This procedure will have reached its aim when the conditions of a group synchronicity have thus been isolated and established for all types of clocks and all circumstances under consideration.

In this method the strongest guarantee is thus furnished by what we have just called the synchronicity of the group. It is certainly not absolute and still depends on several factors which it would be useless to enumerate in advance. But two of them must be mentioned right away, because they are at the level of the remarks which we are currently presenting.

The first factor is the state of the techniques of manufacture and of observations used, especially in the matter of precision. The second factor is the more or less great variety of instruments involved in the testing of overall synchronicity, especially concerning the diversity of the principles on which they are based.

Whatever this diversity may be, we could not exclude a priori the possibility of an overall variation provoked by an unknown cause which, acting on all members of the group at the same time, might have no detectable effect of desynchronization.

At this point we have occasion for a very important remark to which we shall come back later. The probability of a *residual* overall variation certainly becomes increasingly feeble in proportion to the progress of the procedure considered above. In spite of this we might be tempted to reason as follows: You have just acknowledged, we might say, that an overall synchronicity at a certain stage of our knowledge and of our techniques never excludes, with total certainty, the eventuality of an overall variation of the group. Does this reservation not remain valid to the extreme limits of our knowledge? Would not doubt persist, would it not have to persist, even in the (certainly imaginary) case where the science of watchmaking could have acquired knowledge of, and accounted for, all possible causes of variation for all possible types of clocks? In this limit case we would have exhausted forever the experimental means for detecting an overall variation of the group; this inability to observe, however, does not give us the right to maintain that what is unobservable is unrealizable. (There are those who might not hesitate to go even further than this, maintaining that consequently one can never know with absolute certainty whether observed time is also "the real time.")

The answer is this: In the extreme case that has been described there would no longer be any sense in imagining a time more real than the time observed; *for us, the time of the universe, metronome of all real phenomena whose seat the universe may be, would then be the time of the clocks.*

The Use of a Standard

In the practice of watchmaking there seems to be no clear understanding of the *method of regularization* which has just been outlined.* It is not difficult to understand the reasons for this; we shall return to this problem shortly. As far as our exposé is concerned this method has a principal importance. Let us explain it.

The entire procedure of regularization, of course, is simplified if one already has a *good clock,* i.e. a clock which is at the same time regular and precise. This clock may serve as a standard and the entire system of clocks may finally be compared to it. This clock determines the norm relative to which the divergences may be evaluated; the correctness of a different clock is then merely a correctness relative to this model clock.

In certain treatises on watchmaking, the problem of correctness (especially the problem of regulation) is presented under this narrow angle. These treatises, above all, examine the procedures and techniques permitting us to compare the functioning of any clock (i.e. any clock that has to be regulated) with that of a precision time piece, e.g. a good chronometer. But it is clear that this method does not treat the problem fundamen-

* Cf. Léopold Defossez: *Théorie générale de l'horlogerie.* La Chaux-de-Fonds, 1952, Vol. II, Chapter XI.

tally and in fact only scratches the surface. The entire problem turns up again unchanged as soon as our attention shifts from the clock that has to be regulated to the standard clock. The following two questions then emerge again with undiminished acuity:

1. How do we know that the standard clock merits our full confidence? How has its correctness been demonstrated?

2. A simple regulation by comparison can neither dispute nor confirm or increase the correctness of the standard clock. The maximal correctness possible therefore must somehow be inherent in it. But, whether the correctness be natural or constructed, what methods do we have to verify its exceptional rôle?

Principally the method outlined above answers these two questions. It is not tied to the previous existence of a standard clock. It does not even involve the notion of such a clock. It must, on the contrary, conduct us to the search for concrete procedures, which are likely to surpass in correctness any clock which for practical purposes might be proposed as a model.

The answer to our first question accordingly is this: The method considered also includes the investigation of the standard clock, the mother-clock. And the following is our answer to the second question: As long as we have not completed our inspection of all possible phenomena and have not exhausted the knowledge to which they may give rise, the problem of the most correct of all possible clocks must remain an open question.

It has been useful, we believe, to establish this point of method, before setting up in its place (in our exposé) the standard clock, which had to be and to remain for a long time the apparent motion of the celestial sphere.

The Principle of the Integrating Context

Does the method which we have discussed transcend the framework of the measurement of time? It is, in fact, only the application for special purposes of a general principle of research, which particularly belongs to the preexisting doctrine of research, that science thus accepts and adopts without explicitly announcing it. In this context (and in the analysis of the operational element to which we will turn our attention in connection with the measurement of time) it is evident that such a principle must be explained as fully as possible. We must moreover draw the parallel with the principle of the *integrating context,* to which we have attributed a fundamental rôle in the problem of acceptation (of how the meaning comes to the words), as well as in the problem of exposition (of how discourse assumes an explanatory quality). Let us recall what this principle is. The meaning of a word does not belong to that word like a property invariably and inseparably attached to it. Historically every actual signification is the result of an evolution of which we have no reason to think that it has already come to an end. Discursively the exact shade of meaning of an expression, of an element of discourse in general, derives from the rôle conferred on them in a discourse, in an integrating context. And as far as the latter is concerned, its content of meaning does not come either to it or to the words from the simple fact of "being such." To a great extent the meaning of the discourse is only the reflection of the effective activities in which we are engaged and according to which it is ordered.

The following, then, is the general principle of research to which we have alluded and for which the name of principle of the integrating context will also be appropriate: Every statement gains in validity and every experimentation gains in security if they can be integrated (so as to form an effective and coherent whole) into a larger context.

The most simple and widespread application of this principle is, of course, the testing of a certain hypothesis or procedure. To test a theory, for example, simply means to integrate it into a nonproblematic context at one's own level.

The application of this principle to the problem of correctness may have the purpose of (1) formulating a differentiated judgment of correctness, or (2) recognizing and insuring (stabilizing) the conditions of a correctly functioning measurement.

The Context of the Battery of Clocks

The following is an example for the first of these two eventualities. Let us return to the case of the desynchronization of the two water clocks. The correctness of at least one of them must be challenged.

But, as we already noted, in order to be able to form a differentiated judgment of their correctness, we must be able to place the two water clocks in a situation which provides supplementary indications, i.e. in what we have called an integrating context. This context may be naturally given; in most cases, however, it must be established artificially.

In our case the consideration of a third water clock (selected from among those which had been synchronized with the first two) suffices for the constitution of such a context. If it should happen, in fact, that this third clock had remained synchronous with one of the contested clocks, we would not hesitate to affirm that the chances are for these two clocks to be more correct than the third one. (Here, again, is the reasoning that would justify such an affirmation: If the three water clocks had been upset by random causes there would be little chance for two of them to remain synchronized. But if they had been upset by systematic causes there would be as little chance for one of them to be diverging very differently from the two others.)

If, on the other hand, it should happen that the third water clock ceased to agree with the two first ones, we would certainly put the blame on irregular causes of interference for all three clocks.

The introduction of a fourth water clock would create an even larger integrating context, which would allow certain judgments, according to circumstances, to go as far as a quasi-certitude.

The Experimental Context

The following is an example for case 2. It suffices to take again the case of the two water clocks, supposing that, in a visible way, the water of one of them would be carrying grains of sand.

The integrating context then includes, in addition to the knowledge which we already have about the two water clocks and the circumstances of their manufacture, the observation of grains of sand whose presence is justified only by "exterior" reasons and by statements of common sense about the fashion in which the sand may interfere with the discharge by entering the orifice, for example. In this case the differentiated judgment of correctness cannot be in doubt. But nothing forces us to stop here, for our information reaches still further. A procedure of correction is immediately suggested by it; it will suffice to filter the water of the divergent clock (by letting this water flow, for example, through a basin where the sand would be deposited at the bottom).

In short, not only does the method of the integrating context, properly applied, permit us to formulate differentiated judgments of correctness which may go as far as quasi-certainty; it can likewise provide the framework for certain procedures of correction capable of insuring an increasingly stable measurement, which consequently is increasingly correct.

As we have pointed out, it has seemed useful to us to present the preceding remarks on the theme of correctness before engaging in the investigation of instruments in which the concern for precision will become all-important. But it is clear that these remarks cannot assume their real significance except in a technical climate into which this concern for precision has been integrated.

THE MEASUREMENT OF TIME THROUGH A UNIFORM MOTION; THE REACTION WHEEL CLOCK

We have said, in discussing the theme of the objectivity of the measurement of time, that one of the fundamental guarantees of this objectivity must be sought in the plurality of the principles on which the manufacture of clocks may be founded. Thus we remain within the scope of our exposé when we now examine how a uniform motion may serve to measure time.

Definition Leads Nowhere

Are we going to depart from the definition of uniform motion? In order to avoid the difficulties of excessive generality we must limit ourselves first of all to the rectilinear and circular motions.

In the case of the rectilinear motion the definition of the uniform motion should, in order to be precise, take the following theoretical form: *On a straight line a point moves in a uniform way when it traverses equal spaces in equal amounts of time.* This statement is equivalent to the following: *On a straight line a point moves in a uniform way when it traverses distances in proportion to the time it uses for traversing them.*

In the case of the circular motion the definition could be as follows: *A point on a circle moves in a uniform way if the arcs which it traverses on the circle, during equal amounts of time, are themselves equal, or if the angles described by the radius of the corresponding circle in equal intervals of time are likewise equal.* As in the case of the rectilinear motion, this definition could also be replaced by the one which states that the arcs traversed (or the angles described) are proportional to the corresponding intervals of time.

These definitions are completely clear, but only on condition that we know beforehand what a distance carried on a line or on a circle is and what a duration is. Nevertheless, turning to these definitions at this point in our exposé would give rise to rather grave principal difficulties. These statements are concerned with the point, the line, and the circle, not to mention the durations. They are statements of a mathematical character which assume their full precision only at the abstract level of mathematics. In order to apply them in the construction of clocks one must confer on them a validity in the physical world, through the intermediary of adequate materials. But how can we base a real procedure of measurement on such a definition? In order to decide whether the latter is applicable in a particular case, we would first have to be able to evaluate the corresponding distances and amounts of time. Accordingly we would find ourselves back in the same situation as we were with water clocks; we would explain how we could measure time only by assuming that we already have the possibility to do so. Moreover, we have been so careful in our treatment of the case of the water clocks especially to show how we may escape from this vicious circle. This precedent permits us to hope that we shall be able to do as well again.

The Operational Consolidation

But is it really necessary to start all over again? Now that we have explained how a water clock may be equipped with a time scale, we no longer are completely helpless in the face of the practical problem of measuring time. Why should it be forbidden to use this example in order to state that a certain motion is really uniform?

There can, of course, be no question of forbidding its use. All the same, there are two reasons for not using it, one principal, the other practical. The principal reason has to do with what we already said about the *operational consolidation* of the objectivity of time: The latter increases each time a new clock is introduced, a clock based on a principle other than that of the already constructed clocks. But this test of objectivity would lose its value if the new clock could not be constructed autonomously but would derive its validity, on the contrary, from one of the already existing clocks. The practical reason is equally decisive; the precision of the clocks which we will investigate clearly must surpass the precision of the water clocks. The indications which the latter could give would therefore not suffice.

Foundations of Elementarity

If in an exposé such as the present one the uniform motion cannot be introduced through the intermediary of its definition, what means do we have to bring it into play? The answer is the same as in the case of the water clocks; we are not without a representation of it (at the level of our elementary activities), and it is this representation which we can still enforce as we see fit.

More generally, every normal person has at his disposal, in order to integrate himself actively and effectively into the universe of things, a certain ensemble of representations bearing not only on the fashion of existence of things but also on the modalities of their changes. Without much effort these representations let the person formulate comparative, differentiated judgments not only between invariable things but also between variable ones. For example, everyone is naturally in a position to understand statements such as the following: *These roses have opened more rapidly than those others; the grain this year has ripened more slowly than last year; the speed of a falling body increases; at the equinoxes the days increase or decrease the most.* We all are able, some of us more clearly than others, to conceive of motion and more generally of change as of something which in turn may remain unchanged or may change. In other words, all of us are capable of superimposing, on the representations concerning things, representations concerning what might be called their state of change. And this state of change in turn may be viewed as something to which the contrasting categories of the variable and the invariable can again be applied.

The idea which we form of a uniform change moreover is closely linked to the idea of the uniform flow of time; if something measurable changes in a uniform way, the amount of change must itself convey an adequate measurement of the time; in other words, this amount must be in proportion to the time. (We believe that this is how we must interpret Aristotle's statement: motion is the measurement of time.)

On this concept of the relation of uniform change to the uniform flow of time is superimposed the general idea that every disruption of uniformity must be caused by some "exterior" factor, i.e. a factor in addition to those which maintain the uniform change.

Thus formulated—they must be formulated so that they may be referred to—the representations in question seem to obey a principle in which we may discern a certain generalization of the limited principle of inertia, according to which a moving body in a stationary condition preserves this condition unless subjected to an outside force.

One might also see in this a variant of the principle of sufficient reason which would then take the following form: The invariable cannot begin to vary unless some agent is responsible for it.

The preceding statements doubtless represent a theorization, a theorizing explication of what our representations are and what they are worth. It is correct to note this, but how could we do without? What must be kept in mind above all is the fact that the operational aspect could not be well founded without its support.

Thus we may find in our representations the starting point we could not seek in a definition of uniform motion. The practical application of these representations nonetheless remains a difficult problem. The reason is that the state of motion and more generally the state of change (in any of their particular realizations) are not data of our representation unless very roughly sketched ones. For example, it is not in our representations that a moving body which is displaced in a straight line, with constant velocity, must be viewed as being in a state of invariable motion which would not change if nothing would interfere with it.

The matter will appear surprising to someone who thinks that all the knowledge about the universe which we carry within us can only be adequate to its object. It is not so for someone who sees in the ensemble of notions which come to us naturally (and, consequently, also in the representations which have been discussed) an organized ensemble of devices provided for the purposes of natural activity. If one adopts this second interpretation he cannot be surprised that the means remain at the level of their end. The surprising thing, on the contrary, is that they may be improved and straightened out to the point of becoming suitable for an activity such as scientific research.

Uniform Rectilinear Motion

The fact is that nature hardly offers us any uniform rectilinear motion. All the rectilinear motions which come to our attention are either accelerated or decelerated by nature. (This also explains why the principle of inertia of mechanics was formulated so late. It is sadly lacking in the entire physical science of the ancients, who could only engage in impracticable tracks as long as it was unknown.)

If, on the other hand, we would form the project to realize artificially a uniform motion by taking as a model, for example, the motion of a billiard ball, we would have to deal with a series of technical problems whose solution would require the acquisition and development of an entire field of complementary notions. We would have to realize a plane surface completely smooth and completely horizontal, manufacture a ball if not perfectly at least adequately spherical, assemble the means for locating the centre in a sufficiently precise fashion, and so forth. Can the examination of all these problems, and the technical solutions which could be found for them, be incorporated in our exposé without compromising its basic purpose, which for the moment is to specify as far as possible the operational aspect of the measurement of time? To be assured of this we would have to establish, with regard to the measurement of other magnitudes, "texts" analogous to the one we are presently developing and perhaps as copious. This is for us an impracticable project.*

The total of difficulties to overcome in order to realize artificially a rectilinear motion also underscores how few in number and how crudely approximated are the examples of such motions as we realize or of those which we find realized at the level of our current activities. The structure of mechanics is a miracle accomplished in spite of this fact.

Uniform Rotation

As far as motions of uniform rotation are concerned, the difficulties remain principally the same. Nevertheless, the fact that these motions must be periodic permits us to imagine more easily the practical procedures through which we may avoid these difficulties.

---

* As far as geometrical magnitudes are concerned, the attempt to specify them by experimental or rather operational methods, has already been made and is explained in *La géométrie et le problème de l'espace.* The result of this attempt gives us some indications which must make us cautious; it is true that the measurement of geometric magnitudes has an undeniable operational aspect capable of progressive specification, but nothing permits us to think that this operational aspect could be specified to the point of autonomy. In every concrete situation it is on the contrary by a synthesis between the theoretical, the operational, and the intuitive aspects that the measurement of geometric magnitudes becomes effective.

(We must later return to the utilization of the periodic motion in the manufacture of watches and clocks. At that point we shall investigate in a much more fundamental way the very concept of periodicity and the difficulties encountered in its practical realization for the purposes of measuring time. For the moment a periodic motion for us is "defined," only so far as is possible at the level of common sense, on the basis of the representations which ensure the effectiveness of our activities at this level.)

Without having to clarify beforehand, by a theoretical analysis, what must be understood by angular velocity, and without the means as yet to define its measurement operationally, we are able, as we already noted concerning rectilinear uniform motion, to make certain statements naturally, without fear of being mistaken. Everyone understands, for example, what the following contrasting statements mean: *This wheel is turning more and more rapidly,* and *This wheel is turning more and more slowly.*

Everyone is likewise capable of verifying with his own eyes whether these statements are true or not, provided, of course, that the variations of the angular velocity are not too insignificant and that the wheel carries sufficiently distinctive marks so that its motion may be followed. The extreme cases, the starting and the stopping of the wheel, especially lend themselves to this immediate observation.

It is clear, however, that the judgments which we have thus formed about the state of the motion of a body revolving around an axis are of very relative precision. If we intend to apply them in the construction of a clock, we must therefore seek to integrate them into procedures of a certain experimental exactness.

Our project is not inspired by a simple analytical intention. We do not propose an "operational definition" of time based on a uniform motion of rotation which would be supposed as already realized. This procedure would entail precisely the methodological vicious circle which must be avoided. Our method will be as follows:

1. To imagine some experimental process permitting us to

verify whether rotatory motion is uniform or not, without the help of any previously constructed clock.

2. To propose afterwards (at least schematically) the technical realization of a certain instrument permitting us to translate the uniform rotation into a measurement of time.

Neither the manufacture, nor the starting, nor the regulation of the new clocks must be copied from an already existing clock. But, as far as our exposé is concerned, nothing forces us to consider the preceding chapter as cancelled. We do not have to pretend to be ignorant of the road already travelled in the study of our problem. On the contrary we shall seek to profit by it in the execution of the program whose main points we have just indicated. We must take into account, in particular, how little use we can make of the observation of a single phenomenon or process separated from their context.

On the other hand, we must refer to the generalized principle of inertia already discussed. It will become rather prominent. We shall therefore begin by repeating and complementing what has already been said about it.

State and Change

Let us review, at the level of common sense, the concepts of state and change. They are complementary ideas; if one says that something changes he cannot fail at the same time to imagine a momentary state of this something. We imagine the change as the transition from one state to another, as the genesis of one state from another. We can imagine that this transition occurs suddenly, but we may also imagine it as a continuous evolution. However brief and elusive in any one precise moment the state of a changing thing may be, it depends only on us, not to bring about but to imagine that it remains as it is.

But the simple term of change nevertheless does not suffice to express that certain groups of states form a whole. Such groups are, for example, the different positions in space of a body caught in a well-defined motion; the successive determinations of its velocity or of its acceleration; or, finally, the ensemble of all the states through which this body passes during a certain interval of time, considering at the same time all the aspects under which it is likely to present itself. In the development of a phenomenon it could be the different phases whose succession, in a certain rhythm, makes this phenomenon manifest. In a mechanism "in the state of running" the particular states of the mechanism are integrated not only as phases but as conditions for the functioning of the whole. What would be the word capable of evoking this organized ensemble of states, in which the states follow each other not only in a certain temporal order but also according to a certain rhythm? In some cases we might use the word "process," which is used in grammar and which we have widely employed while studying the temporal structure of the conjugation of the verbs. The term "procedure" might be still more apt in certain other cases. At any rate it is this word which must be contrasted with the word "state" in order to emphasize the integrated aspect of the whole in the course of time, as opposed to complementarity with its momentary aspects.

A phenomenon or a process thus may be considered in turn as "entities" to which the complementary categories of permanence and of change are likewise applicable. One may speak, for example, of the regular motion of a watch and consider the circumstances susceptible of interfering with it, either by sudden variation or by continuous variation. This is also what the watchmaking industry has to do constantly and systematically in its most immediate practice. (We shall have to explain this in one of the following chapters.) In an analogous sense one could also speak of an oscillatory, more or less regular motion and investigate the means through which its regularity might be disturbed systematically at first and then irregularly; this is precisely the case of the quartz clocks. We should note, moreover, that the idea of a *systematic disturbance* merely superimposes the idea of a regular process of perturbation on the oscillatory process mentioned before. We shall lose no time over the investigation of the conditions under which we would be entitled to speak of a process, even of a regular process, as of an objectively tested reality. The question, we believe, will not arise in the few cases which we have to take into account. It may be useful to recall, however, presenting it in a somewhat more general fashion, an argument which we already have given in our discussion of the water clocks.

Every Well-Defined Phenomenon Is a Timepiece

Let us assume that a process is so well determined and at the same time so well realizable that it may be repeated at will and even be "copied." For a process limited in time and for two conforming copies the simultaneous start of the initial phase entails the parallel development of the process, phase after phase, until the exact moment when in both copies the terminal phase is reached. It is easy to imagine, with the example given for the water clocks, that a process of this type could benefit from a numerical scale which in the absence of any preliminary measurement of time would not yet have to be a regularly established temporal scale. But it would again be easy to show how these scales might be corrected and normalized so as to insure the synchronicity of the development of the process in all its reproductions.

In short, every process and every phenomenon whose reality is sufficiently assured for us to make copies of it is in principle a time piece. It seems naturally attuned to an objective and normal flow of time.

This result appears to us particularly striking. But are there not, behind the reasoning, some "preliminaries" which have remained implicit and which it would be worthwhile to isolate?

Principles of Sufficient Reason and Generalized Inertia

These preliminaries are not hard to spot. A phenomenon is repeatable only if it is practically possible to realize copies of it, and if it can be defined by the fulfillment or the realization of certain conditions. One may therefore not speak of repeatability or of identical copies without presupposing the validity of the principle that *a process must be repeatable if the con-*

ditions of its genesis are. This is one form of the principle of sufficient reason.

On the other hand, the representation according to which two processes created from "identical" situations necessarily have parallel developments implies still another presupposition: A process, once it is established in a state of stationary change, cannot vary except through the intervention of a supplementary cause. Evidently this is only a corollary of the principle of sufficient reason, applied to the same process. *If a process, evolving from a certain initial stage, returns to it, including all circumstances, after a certain time, then it can start again to evolve in identical fashion.* This is the corollary which we call the "generalized principle of inertia."

This latter principle (in connection with the former) thus is the "announced form" of one of our most fundamental representations concerning *the ways in which something is likely to change.* For this reason, and because we will have to refer to it again, we think it useful to comment on it in a few words.

May a change be produced without a cause? Our first impulse is to answer, No, a change is always the effect of the cause which provokes it. We know and have already emphasized that this answer is not accurate. Classical mechanics is wholly based on the principle of inertia in the restricted sense, according to which a mass on which no force is exerted does not necessarily remain motionless but generally shifts its position by moving along a straight line with constant velocity. In this case the change of position (is it not a real change?*) is effected thus without any cause being responsible for it. And moreover, what do we have to understand by "cause"? Is it not necessary to be more specific? especially so, as the principle which we have proposed has turned out to be inapplicable in certain cases and the task awaiting us is to delimit carefully the domain of its validity.

Should we say that by "cause" we must understand "exterior cause"? No, this is still unsatisfactory, for certain changes are due to internal causes; an example is the slowing down, i.e. the change of velocity, of a rotating body. Under these

* Let us recall that Aristotle postulated a cause for a change of this sort.

conditions, how can we delimit the causes of the change, the causes whose absence would guarantee uniformity?

It seems that there is only one way to achieve this; we must abandon the plan to define the cause through the state itself or through the action itself. We must search, on the contrary, for the causes of *differences* in the course of the processes, these causes being in turn differences of states or differences of action.

We are thus back at our principle of sufficient reason: Every difference in the evolution is due to a difference either in the initial state or in the exterior actions.

Can the Principle of Inertia Be Specialized A Priori?

What can we conclude from this principle? We have seen that we may draw from it a generalized principle of inertia. Shall we also be able to draw from it more specialized principles, such as, for example, the restricted principle of inertia of mechanics? Unfortunately not. In the first place, our generalized principle of inertia applies only to stationary processes; in order to apply it to a particular phenomenon we must first verify experimentally that the latter is truly stationary. This is not an easy thing to do; nature hardly offers us any stationary phenomena of inertia. Strictly speaking they do not exist at all, except for those which are more or less close approximations: the earth turning around its axis or around the sun, the moon turning around the earth, etc. But in order to be studied, these examples need a relevant context which must be experimental as well as theoretical, and they need it already for simple observation.

But how was the restricted principle of inertia arrived at? Perhaps the reason was the celestial movements, but it was surely not they alone. It seems that we have arrived at this principle through successive approximations by verifying that a motion becomes increasingly uniform as we remove the frictions which cause retardation. We then have boldly extrapolated by declaring that if all causes for slowing down were eliminated, the motion would be rigorously uniform. And the celestial movements confirmed this assumption. If one grants that they are unrestrained (we have reasons for assuming this: the celestial bodies neither glide nor roll; on the other hand, the extrapolation of the barometric formula inevitably leads us to the conclusion that a practically absolute void reigns in the interplanetary spaces), the principle of inertia suffices to explain the persistence of their rotation; it was therefore no longer necessary, as was done sometimes before Galileo, to postulate a tangential action exercised upon the planets by the sun.

One might likewise follow a perhaps more rigorous method, that of trying to establish the law of slowing down due to friction and resistance by the air; the form of this law could indicate whether, if these resistances become zero, the slowing down is nil. But this second method is less purely operational than the preceding one; it goes through the intermediary stage of the establishment of a law, which again involves certain risks that cannot be completely eliminated.

The *restricted principle of inertia* therefore can only have an experimental origin. Even if one would make of the *principles of sufficient reason* and of *generalized inertia* principles a priori—something which would be highly debatable—one could not derive from them the restricted principle of inertia, because nothing indicates a priori what changes and what remains constant, whether it is the place, the speed, or the acceleration; moreover, nothing guarantees that in a process left to itself, any magnitude will remain constant.

After these considerations behind the scenes of the operational enterprise, we return to our project to utilize the uniform motion of rotation.

Uniformity of Rotation at the Level of Common Sense

First, what is to be gained from the observation of a single body carried along in a rotatory motion? Very little, presumably, if one intends to examine it in isolation, without considering an eventual "experimental context" or an eventual integrating milieu. The example of the water clocks is rather discouraging in this respect.

Nevertheless, the principle of inertia and the representations of which it is an "announced form" might serve as a basis for certain considerations, such as the following:

Let us assume that by appropriate technical measures which an experienced craftsman would know by experience, it had been possible considerably to reduce all actions, in particular all frictions, which could impede the motion of this body. If left alone, the latter must nevertheless come to a stop, after a longer or shorter time, since its loss of energy cannot be reduced to zero. It may happen, however, especially when a heavy body is concerned, that a perceptible reduction of its speed occurs only after a considerable amount of time.

But the observer, in order to estimate this duration, must not yet have a clock at his disposal. Thus he will be reduced to a subjective estimate which can only yield rather imprecise orders of magnitude.

This observer will be able nevertheless to apply the representations which have been discussed. They go beyond the formulation of the principle of inertia. They imply, for example, that the speed of a rather heavy body cannot suddenly change without an action of some power. They also imply that if actions "go in the same direction," their effects cannot mutually cancel each other. On the basis of these representations the observer therefore will reason thus: The actions reducing the speed of the body which I am observing are always of the same nature and always go in the same direction. They remain weak; in fact a considerable length of time is required for the loss of speed to become perceptible. I may therefore assume that for a relatively short period of time the effect of these actions will be still less manifest and that during this time the speed will remain apparently uniform.

Perhaps the observer will not commit himself to this analysis. The judgment he makes, according to him, will be one of simple common sense. In practice the analysis in fact is unnecessary. It could only interfere with the good "functioning" of common sense. But it is by virtue of its position in our exposé that it becomes important; it is in relation to the experiment *sui generis* which this exposé represents that it is effective. It illuminates the basis of objective knowledge of which common sense benefits.*

For the manufacture of a measuring instrument this analysis of common sense has no immediate use. Its usefulness is of a methodological order. It deepens the problem of the operational definition. It shows that the latter is not as conventional as might be supposed at first, and that on the contrary it is based upon certain "preliminaries which do not elude all evaluation," that its validity thus is not guaranteed beyond the precognitions inherent in the representations which it cannot avoid using.

Comparisons of Speeds of Rotation

As far as the justified realization of a clock is concerned, the revolving body, taken in isolation, thus does not give us a satisfactory basis. Utilizing the example of the water clocks, we shall now approach the problem by a detour, through the comparative evaluation of the speeds of two bodies animated by a rotatory motion.

Without for the moment discussing how the inevitable losses of speed could be compensated, we shall assume that the two bodies to be compared are in a constant *state of rotation*. We shall not, however, form any supplementary hypothesis about their respective speeds.

Let us assume, for example, that the two discs D_1 and D_2 rotate before our eyes. How can we decide whether or not they are rotating *in identical fashion*? An essentially very simple solution suggests itself quite naturally; we might count the revolutions effected by the discs *during equal amounts of time*.

But before examining in greater detail the practical applica-

---

* Common sense thus makes use of a number of preliminary cognitions. Are they, through this fact alone, perfectly certain? They are certain only at the level where common sense uses them effectively. They may not be assured at the level of a more "refined" cognition. The same is true of all the representations to which we are inevitably led by the study of the measurement of time. Common sense is at the same time inalienable and revisable; this must be stated but it must also be explained. The open methodology, which in our study is put to the test, easily achieves this aim.

tion of this device, let us pause for a moment in order to formulate and to eliminate an objection which can hardly fail to present itself. As we have said very explicitly, the utilization of these uniform rotations for the manufacture of a clock must be autonomous. We deny ourselves the use of any previously established clock. Without this precaution we would relapse into the vicious circle which the *definition* through the instrument is precisely meant to avoid. But does the device in question not lead us directly into this vicious circle? In order to count the turns effected by either disc *during equal amounts of time,* do we not have to determine these equal times by measuring corresponding durations?

At the moment when it comes, this objection is rather embarrassing. But it collapses almost by itself as soon as it is examined more closely. In fact, we merely have to observe simultaneities or orders of succession, for which no preliminary measuring system is required. We shall return to this problem shortly.

Let us assume that during a series of successive temporal intervals we have counted the revolutions effected by both discs; the numbers obtained for the first are $n_1, n_2, n_3 \ldots$ and those for the second are $m_1, m_2, m_3. \ldots$ What conclusions can we draw from a comparison of the first series with the second?

If the two discs would constantly rotate *in the same fashion,* and if their speeds of rotation were persistently equal without necessarily being constant, every number n_1 of the first series would have to be equal to the corresponding number m_1 of the second. The finding of a single inequality would therefore suffice as positive proof that the two discs do not persistently rotate with equal speed.

But however decisive such observations may be under certain circumstances, they are not the ones that are most useful for our purpose. It is above all the equality of the speeds of rotation which we must be able to verify. In this case, as we have noted, all numbers n_i should be equal to the corresponding numbers m_i, but this necessary condition is not sufficient. It only permits us to affirm that during each of the intervals of observation the discs have turned with the same average speed. But it cannot ascertain the uniformity of the motion, neither from one interval of observation to the next, nor even within one and the same interval.

On the other hand, taken by itself and independent of any other consideration, the equality of the numbers cannot tell us anything about the fashion in which the discs will continue to turn, once our series of observations is completed. But this is precisely what we must know if we intend to utilize the motion of either disc for the construction of a clock.

The procedure accordingly has two gaps which, of course, cannot be bridged completely. Nevertheless, it is easy to imagine for the first arrangements of increasing precision, permitting us to elaborate (i.e. to enumerate one by one) the turns, half-turns, quarter-turns, the tenths and even the sixtieths or thousandths of turns. We might, for example, for each rotating system cut regularly spaced slots into a cylindrical casing forming part of the system. Passing in front of two sources of light placed judiciously, these slots would emit a series of rapid flashes which could be registered on a rapidly unreeling film. It is on this film where the series of flashes would afterwards be compared.

If we had to insist that the film should unreel at a constant speed, we would again be caught in the vicious circle mentioned before. But this is not necessary; the speed of unreeling may remain unspecified, provided it has no sudden stops.

In a still more simple way one might compare the motions of the two arrangements thus prepared according to the principle of the stroboscope.*

One must thus be able to divide the time of observation into relatively short intervals, during which the (mean) angular velocity will be the same in each part. But what should our answer be to someone who refuses to accept this result, even if it is practically useful, and who maintains that the situation is not clear enough in principle?

We might then imagine a somewhat more sophisticated device permitting a continuous registration of the relative posi-

* We would look at one of the cylinders or would light it up across the slots cut in the other; for equal speeds the first cylinder would appear motionless.

tions of the discs. Let us assume that the latter rotate facing each other and that one carries a source of light which emits a thin ray in the direction of the other disc. We assume that the other disc carries a mirror inclined at an angle of 45°, which reflects this ray in a radial direction. This mirror, however, would not be 45° exactly in all places; its inclination would continually and periodically vary several degrees; it would accordingly have a slightly helicoid form around an axis and would be constituted by a circumference concentric with the axis. The purpose of this device is to let the angle of the reflected ray vary in relation to the disc, according to the position of the mirror where it is reflected. If the two discs rotate at the same speed, their relative position will not be changed and the ray will describe, on a cylindrical photographic plate concentric with the axis, a circumference situated in a plane perpendicular to the axis. Conversely, if the relative positions of the discs are changed, the trace on the cylindrical photographic plate will not describe a circle but on the contrary a sinuous, helicoid, or other line. In this case the problem of interpolation is absent because the registration is continuous.

But no physicist will ever construct such a device. He will on the contrary depend on his interpolations and justify them by resorting to the restricted principle of inertia and to the fundamental law of dynamics that if the discs are heavy enough, considerable force will be required to change their speed quickly; the physicist will make sure that his equipment is incapable of exerting such force, which will vindicate the quality of his interpolation. It must be noted, however, that such an argument borrows heavily from theory and cannot therefore be considered as purely operational.

In short, it is not necessary to have a previously constructed clock at one's disposal, an *observation clock*, for deciding whether two rotating devices have equal angular velocity or not. It is sufficient to invoke what might be called a certain *operational common sense.**

---

* It is hardly necessary to emphasize that this *operational common sense* is not absolute. Its validity is not unlimited. We should not, however, question it as long as the results of our using it remain consistent. We have made analogous remarks already on several occasions.

Identity as a Guarantee of Uniformity

We must go one step further; we have to show how the consideration of two or more rotating devices can enable us to go as far as to affirm that they rotate with constant speed.

We shall not separate these devices from their "experimental context." On the contrary, we shall assume that everything possible has been done to insure their uniform speed, and that accordingly measures were taken to compensate, in agreement with the principle of inertia, the forces which might decelerate or accelerate their motion. We shall not examine at this point the means by which this may be accomplished. Suffice it to assume that it has been done. We will soon explain the principle of a device conceived for this purpose.

As we have seen, we are in a position to decide whether our devices rotate with equal speed. Assuming this to be the case, can we affirm that they rotate with the same *constant* speed? No, not yet. It could happen, if the devices are located in the same area and thus subject to the same influences, that they suffer the same disturbances and so remain coordinated, although their speed is not uniform. We would have reason to believe that their speed is really uniform if coordination were maintained even though one of the two devices were in a situation very different from that of the other concerning temperature, pressure, gravitation, etc. If the speed of rotation of one device is not constant there must be some cause whose effect is the variation of speed. The compensation of the forces acting on the device is still imperfect, which is in no way surprising. It is not at all certain that a perfectly compensated device could be easily realized.

The same may be said of any other device, in particular those used as "witnesses" for the first. Nor should we be surprised that their speeds of rotation are not perfectly constant.

At any rate it is improbable, if the devices are constructed each by itself, that the deficiencies of compensation should be the same for all of them. The practical cases show that they rather are accidental. Then the probability that the variations should be and remain the same must be extremely slight. If the equality of speeds consistently remains and if it extends to more than two devices, then this probability must be considered negligible—unless there exists a systematic cause which produces identical effects on all the devices at the same time. This possibility, of course, cannot be excluded a priori. It may be eliminated more or less reliably through an investigation of the integrating milieu. As a last resort the process thus realized can be tested by a comparison with some other well-defined process. (This confrontation is the very means through which the objectivity of the measurement of time may generally be verified.)

Other Solutions

One may, of course, consider many other ways of establishing whether the rotatory speed of a revolving device is uniform. In particular one may propose to measure this speed directly. This can be done successfully by observing (or measuring) the state or the variation of a process which depends on the speed. In a very general fashion it suffices for the rotating device to have, besides the amplitude of the rotation, a supplementary degree of latitude. We will preferably use devices of such a type that to a well-defined variation of the speed of rotation corresponds an equally well-defined variation of a second observable magnitude. The latter might be a linear or angular divergence, a tension, the amplitude or the period of an oscillation, some characteristic of an electric current or of an electromagnetic field, etc.

On this principle in its different variants is based the construction of speed recorders or *speedometers*. Combined with a retroaction or feedback, a device of this type may moreover serve as a *speed regulator*.

We have thus considered the question from every angle, in thought at least and in a schematic way. We have identified the method by which the forbidden methodological circle may be avoided. Recourse to certain representations integrated into our most ordinary daily "doing" can, in fact, free us from the necessity of using an observation clock previously constructed or a definition of time previously formulated. It remains for us to learn how, concretely and materially, a clock corresponding to the conditions which have been analyzed could be manufactured.

In principle we would have as many technical solutions to the problem of the clock using uniform motions as there are technical solutions to the problems of the regulator of speed. But, as far as our exposé is concerned, the majority of these solutions have no interest for us. The construction of a speedometer, even a simple one, requires knowledge of a certain group of mechanical and physical laws. Up to which point are they independent of an already defined notion of time and of measuring procedures already established beforehand? In order to find out we would have to subject each of these solutions to an analysis analogous to the one in which we are presently engaged. We would thus have to establish, each time, additional texts of which we could not know in advance how far their ramifications would extend. We would not consider using this method; it is impracticable. The sequel to our analysis will explain this more fully.

The Reaction Wheel Clock

We must be content here with a very simple example, simple enough to enable us to emphasize clearly the results of the analysis we have conducted. This explains our choice of the example of the reaction wheel clock, whose functioning we shall now schematically explain. This clock certainly has nothing of a high precision clock, and far more accurate clocks no doubt could be imagined on the model of some speed regulator. But the point is not now to embark on the theme of high precision. The opportunity to treat it properly will offer itself later. For the moment our main concern is further to elucidate the idea of the "operational definition," and to show in an example which may be fully elucidated how one may realize this idea in an adequately circumscribed experimental context.

We shall imagine the water reaction wheel in the following form: A vertical tube is extended into a certain number of horizontal arms, which are bent at right angles. The tube is held in such a way as to be able to turn around a vertical axis. The following figure represents the schema of the reaction wheel with two arms. One may suppose that it is connected with a device for counting the revolutions or fractions of the revolutions which it effects.

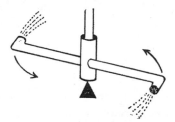

Let us imagine that the vertical tube contains a water column of height h. If the orifices of the horizontal arms remain closed the entire device remains motionless. Assume that they could be opened suddenly; the water would burst out with some violence, which would be proportionately stronger as the water column exerting pressure on it is higher. As a reaction the wheel will sustain a sudden jolt which sets it in motion unless, of course, this jolt is too weak to overcome the inevitable frictions at the start. Suppose that the water level h has been sufficient to put the device in motion. If the water which escapes from the horizontal arms is not replaced, the vertical tube will empty itself, the thrust on the reaction wheel will cease, and the latter, slowed down by friction, will soon come to a stop. To maintain the motion it is therefore necessary to replace the escaping water constantly.

Is the Rotation Uniform?

Do our natural representations permit us to make additional statements? In the case of the water clocks they have enabled us to form a decisive judgment; it was sufficient, to secure a constant flow and a regular measurement of time, to maintain a constant water level in the reservoir, all other circumstances remaining the same. Is it certain again this time that if the water level of the column in the central tube remains unchanged, the reaction wheel would permanently remain in a state of uniform rotation? Does not the thrust which it sustains depend upon its momentary speed of rotation as well as on the height of the column of water? How can a stable equilibrium be established between the flow of the ejected water, the speed of rotation, the thrust on the reaction wheel and, finally, the total of resistance to be overcome? At the level of our natural representations, this question must remain unanswered.

Thus, the project to realize a reaction wheel clock puts us in a position principally different from the one in which we could envisage the manufacture of a water clock. We do not have at our disposal, at the level of our daily activities and of the judgments which ensure them, the knowledge necessary for our new enterprise. Our previous representations are no longer sufficient; how and by what should they be completed?

Here is a quite natural idea: The reaction wheel is nothing but a very elementary water turbine; why not treat it as such? Why not treat it by applying all the means at our disposal to that effect, at the level of the knowledge and the actual procedures used by manufacturers of turbines? To do so we must, of course, invoke a certain number of theoretical considerations and a certain group of empirical statements, both relating to the mechanics of fluids. The problem then loses its elementary character. It appears on the contrary as a difficult and complex problem which may be solved only through a collaboration and even a compromise between theory and practice, between a theory which only partially accounts for the experiment and an experiment which has only partially found its theoretical formulation. But if the engineer can accommodate himself to this solution, why should we have to reject it?

This solution is the following: If the height h of the water column is maintained at a constant level, the angular velocity of the reaction wheel is stabilized. The state of motion is then stationary, the angular velocity being proportionately greater as the water column in the central tube is higher.

(In its general form the principle of inertia which we have formulated suggests itself, as we have seen, with a certain obviousness.* But we do not have at our disposal any natural representations corresponding to the case where this principle applies. It is even against a certain evidence that the most fundamental one of these cases, which is the subject of the principle of inertia of classical mechanics, has been formulated and tested. One may imagine that, once stabilized, the process of which the uniform rotation of the reaction wheel is only one aspect belongs to the cases where the generalized principle of inertia applies.)

Theoretical Justification

If, at this point in our exposé, we were only concerned with justifying our intention to construct a reaction wheel clock and to establish beyond any doubt the phenomenon upon which the manufacture of such a clock could be based, we obviously would not have to be dissatisfied with the "solution" discussed above. For the sake of completeness we would have to show everything that must be borrowed from theory and accepted from experience in order to come to a conclusion. This would be a very difficult and delicate task. We do not plan to carry it out. Why not?

Our intention, needless to repeat, above all is of a methodological rather than practical order. What we wish to study about the reaction wheel clock and the measurement of time it is capable of delivering, is the way in which time thereby is introduced and "defined". Can the preceding solution serve this purpose? To elucidate the methodological situation we would first have to discuss a number of points of which at least three would put our entire project in trouble. They are:

1. In the borrowings we would have to make from theoretical mechanics we could not fail to invoke certain laws of motion formulated as a function of the variable t, i.e. of mathematical time. In order to recognize the exact function of this variable, its significance, and the way in which this significance is acquired, we must investigate the very foundations of mechan-

---

* We must recall that this obviousness is not a guarantee of certitude at those levels of reality which are not "on our scale."

ics. We would have to investigate how the fundamental concepts are determined upon which it is based; the most fundamental one of these concepts is precisely the one represented by the variable *t*. This would throw us back, not to a point of departure already well clarified, but to the very object of our study.

2. By using certain empirical statements we inevitably invoke results obtained by means of calibrated instruments, among which there cannot fail to be a clock of some precision. What time does this clock measure? How is it defined and determined? Is not this the very function of a time piece? Again, we are back at the very question we are studying.

3. By combining the theoretical considerations with the empirical statements we would practice a mixed method which inevitably would imply a connection between the temporal variable *t* and the times furnished by some measuring technique. Are we entitled in advance to assume that this interpretation does not pose any problems? The truth is that for the third time, under a third aspect, we are led back to the very problem which occupies our attention.

Unless we want to abandon at this point our plan to examine to what extent a measured amount of time is "defined" by the instrument measuring it (and by the phenomenon on which the realization of the measuring instrument is based), we do not have the right, methodologically speaking, to adopt the solution which has been suggested and to take it as a basis for the manufacture of the reaction wheel clock. At this point any introduction of the mixed method must be considered premature; it only adds for the moment one more complication to untangle.

Experimental Justification

But do we have another solution instead? Of course we cannot think any longer of anchoring the entire procedure (supposed to result in the manufacture of the reaction wheel clock) in our natural representations alone. Nevertheless, one cannot go far astray by resorting to systematic experimentation. Anyone who has played with a garden sprinkler, pressurized it in various fashions, regulated its range and speed of rotation, may have formed some idea of the fashion in which the device works; without a clear knowledge of the reasons and without being able to explain, one may to some extent foresee the solution which the mixed method offers as a certainty. Our experience thus suggests to us a certain representation of the process, a representation which cannot be said without arbitrariness to be necessarily among our natural representations. Do we mean that this representation already deserves our full confidence, to the same degree as those which inform our daily activities, and whose correctness is confirmed by our actions each day? Certainly not, since it is still merely an assumption, an hypothesis whose plausibility can only be vaguely evaluated. But nothing prevents us from taking it as the object of a series of long and varied tests.

The method of this experiment, of course, is not a random one. Lest it revert to the difficulties (to the methodological vicious circle) which we have discussed, it may not involve the use of any previously established clock, and it must be independent of any previously defined technique of measuring time. This methodological requirement rather narrowly limits our freedom of action. Is it possible to comply with it without equivocation? To evaluate this question, it suffices to apply to the case of the reaction wheel the general considerations about uniform motions which we made in the first paragraphs of the present chapter. The answer is yes; the group of procedures which we have imagined avoids recourse to mathematical definitions as well as the use of control clocks. It is true that we must form the hypothesis that the motion of the garden sprinkler, once it is stabilized, is one of the processes to which the generalized principle of inertia would apply, but nothing contradicts it when we use the procedures which it suggests.

What Does the Reaction Wheel Clock Teach Us?

We have not considered the problem of the reaction wheel clock under the aspect of an eventual technical application. We have not worried about the difficulties which its actual manufacture would face without doubt, especially if a precision instrument is intended. In the history of the measurement of time this solution apparently never entered into competition with that of the clock with discharge. The watchmaking industry, on the other hand, seems never to have been interested in the principle of a clock with reaction wheels. Does one have to assume that the realization of such a clock would create particularly difficult problems for the technician? We do not think so, but the fact is that from the technical point of view the project has no interest. But this is no concern of ours.

We must decide above all whether the principle of uniform rotation can serve as a basis for an "operational definition" of time. We mainly wished to determine the price that must be paid for such a definition, the presuppositions that would be its concomitants, the representations on which it has to be based; for we have never believed and we think it less and less probable that grasping in an effective and accurate way *the concept of what time is for us* could somehow be gratuitous or could even be meaningfully reduced to the indication of some steps or operations to make. The steps necessary for measuring time must themselves be assured and guaranteed. Are these guarantees at the same time so clear, so easily reached, and so certain that it is unnecessary to pay attention to them? And if, as in the case of the water clocks, we recognize them as part of a natural common basis shared and used by all human beings, is it certain that the situation will be the same in all cases, especially when we attempt to overcome the difficulties of high precision?

Among the results of our analysis so far nothing seems to justify a definitive answer. It is true, provided we do not circumscribe too narrowly and critically what constitutes the value and the range of what we have called a *natural basis* of effective representations, that the concept of defining time as being measured through the method by which one measures it seems to have successfully passed its second test; everything considered, the example of the reaction wheel apparently agrees with it. But is the success of our analysis and of its application to this example really convincing? Is the enterprise as a whole not somewhat artificial, and does its justification not appear a little strained? Is it really correct to say that the analysis has been completed, that it has clearly succeeded, and that it has paid off by an undeniable success? Should we not rather say that, tested in this fashion, our project of defining the concept of time operationally has not miscarried, that the idea governing it has not been disproved, but that the very fashion in which we were able to defend, or rather protect it, does evoke certain doubts concerning its capacity for survival?

What should we do if these doubts were confirmed? We must admit that this is a question which we are not yet ready to answer. We shall therefore continue to pursue our project, without changing our plans for the moment, but also without knowing for certain that we would never have to do so.

THE APPARENT MOTION OF THE CELESTIAL SPHERE

We have noted before that nature hardly offers us any examples of rotatory motions which could be considered uniform. There is, however, one exception which probably has occurred to everyone: the apparent motion of the celestial sphere. For us who know that the earth turns around its axis in one day and who have learned that as a simple planet it completes in a year its revolution around the sun, for us who have made the effort to imagine the distances which separate us from the stars and galaxies, the expression "the celestial sphere" is merely a simile. But for an observer who believes and feels himself immobile (even if he is able to make observations of considerable precision), everything takes place as if the constellations were invariably attached to a sphere of vast dimensions which turns around itself on an axis of practically unchanging position. Every fixed star appears to describe a circumference in a plane perpendicular to this axis around the point where the axis and this plane intersect. As to the moving stars (the sun, the planets, etc.), they seem to be bound to follow on this sphere the paths which are theirs and which must be imagined as included within the collective motion. The trajectory of the sun is particularly simple (much simpler than that of the planets); it is a large circle, the ecliptic, which it covers in a year.

Principle of the Determination of Astronomical Time

Every fixed star may therefore serve as a timepiece. Assume that we could determine with some accuracy its passage at the observer's meridian, i.e. the instant when it reaches its highest elevation on its trajectory above the horizon; the duration separating two successive passages at the meridian then gives us a natural unit of time: the sidereal day. It is not difficult to imagine a device which would permit us to follow the star in its course. A straight line following the star from a fixed centre would describe a cone of revolution whose axis would be parallel to the axis of revolution of the universe. Let us imagine that this cone is intersected by a transparent plane perpendicular to this axis. The circle of intersection would then give us a homothetic projection of the circle described by the star. Subdivided into equal parts, even if our range of observation would not permit us to use it in its totality, this circle would represent a timepiece equipped with a time scale.

It is, of course, pointless to discuss the technical means which would enable us to realize such a device. Instead of tracing a star in its nocturnal course we might follow the sun in its diurnal course. Let us assume that we know how to determine the moment (noon) when it is highest on its trajectory. (Unless a very high degree of precision is required, the curve of the shadow cast by a small object onto a horizontal plane permits this determination.) The duration between two successive noons may also be taken as a natural unit of time; this is solar time. The gradation of the shadow curve or of the trajectory of a small luminous point obtained by letting through a thin thread of light could likewise serve as a time scale, as it does in the sun dial. We know why the sidereal and the solar days are not exactly equal: the reason is that the sun is a moving star and at two successive noons does not occupy exactly the same point in its trajectory on the celestial sphere. Its speed on the trajectory moreover is not perfectly uniform but varies in the course of the seasons. In order to be as exactly equal to itself as the sidereal day, the solar day must be replaced by a mean solar day (a somewhat artificial concept) whose difference with the sidereal day remains constant.

The preceding examples show that all told, it is not difficult to establish natural time pieces based on the course of the stars. Why have we postponed for so long to study them? Are they not as elementary and as easy to construct as the water clocks? From a historical viewpoint, has not the sun dial with its more or less rudimentary variants preceded the water clock?

We shall leave these questions unanswered; they are entirely outside the area of our exposé. The reasons for our decision are not hard to understand; they depend on our constant concern to disengage the operational aspect of the measurement of time.

Is the Earth a Regular Timepiece?

The first of these reasons is that the timepiece constituted by the celestial sphere in motion is not an instrument which we would know for having made it ourselves. Are the sidereal days which it adds to each other equal among themselves? Since the system is unique in its genre we would not have any operational means to compare these days to each other, unless we had another timepiece at our disposal. None of the procedures which we have discussed so far can be applied. Being unique, the system in particular leaves us without any means for checking the uniformity of its rotatory motion, a uniformity which we might take for granted from the invariance of the sidereal day.

If we had decided to postulate this uniformity at the beginning of our exposé, how could we have justified this decision? Could we have quoted as our authority the generalized principle of inertia which was discussed earlier? Would it have been correct to say, for example, since we are unable to point out any action being exerted upon the celestial sphere capable of changing its state of motion, we are entitled to assume that this state does not change and the speed of rotation consequently remains constant?

This attempt to apply the generalized principle of inertia,

however, cannot be entertained. It does not take into account at all the existence of moving stars. The latter seem to shift, not only with the celestial sphere but also relative to it; some of them, the planets in particular, describe more or less slow and more or less elaborate trajectories across the constellations. At the level of immediate observation, which does not reveal to us any cause capable of acting upon and modifying the state of motion of the celestial sphere, the causes which might be held responsible for the change of the state of motion of the moving stars likewise remain impenetrable to us. Under these conditions, why would the generalized principle of inertia apply to the fixed stars but not to the moving stars? Nothing at the level of immediate observation enables us to explain this. We must therefore look for something else.

We cannot limit ourselves to *verifying* the regularity of the rotatory motion of the celestial sphere around the axis of the universe. Assuming, at this point in our exposé, that the speed of this rotation is a natural constant, we can only form a hypothesis. Is this hypothesis plausible? Shall we be able to verify it? Let us put aside our own projects for a moment, especially our concern for pure operationality. Let us turn to the astronomer and ask him how, in his field, this hypothesis can be justified.

Theoretical Justification

This justification requires a combination of a number of very complex devices, theoretical as well as practical. The essential stages are the following:

1. The motion which we analyze is the *apparent* motion of the celestial sphere. We must first give due prominence to the fact that we are dealing merely with an appearance and proceed as best we can to the study of the natural phenomenon which gives rise to it. In order to succeed we must be able to account for two categories of facts: (1) the motion of the apparent involvement of all the fixed stars and consequently the constant shape of the constellations formed by them; (2) the supplementary displacements of the moving stars, viz. the sun, the moon, the planets, and the comets.

The solution is given by cosmography; everything is clear if one assumes

—that the earth is a spheroid (almost spherical) revolving with constant angular speed around its axis, the axis being conceived as a straight line piercing the terrestrial surface at both the north and south poles;

—that the fixed stars are only images which we project onto a fictitious celestial vault, images originating with stars situated at enormous distances from the earth;

—and finally, that all the moving stars together, including the earth, form the solar system whose moving configuration need not be explained here.

As far as the regularity of the apparent motion of the celestial sphere is concerned in particular, the problem thus boils down to the explanation of the earth's rotatory motion around its axis.

2. The second stage is to consider the earth as a rigid body and apply to it the laws of classical mechanics. In order to succeed we must take into account the forces acting upon it. We shall then apply the so-called theorem of the center of mass, according to which all its forces may be replaced by a single force applied to its center of mass, and by a single moment of momentum M. The force F will be responsible for the curvature of the terrestrial orbit; the moment M alone will be responsible for the variations of the rotatory motion.

Concerning the forces acting upon the earth, we must account for them according to Newton's law of gravitation. (It is unnecessary at this point to consider the corrections to Newton's laws in Einstein's gravitation theory.) Newton's law of attraction is formulated as follows: Two material points attract each other in a fashion directly proportional to their mass (to the product of their masses) and inversely proportional to the square of their distance. One must add up all the forces which act, according to this law, upon all the points of which the earth consists, emanating from all the points of which the other stars consist. Considering the enormous remoteness of the fixed stars it is unnecessary to go beyond the solar system at this point. The sun will play the most important rôle; we must then consider the moon and the larger planets.

The computation is also simplified by the fact that even within the solar system, the distances to be considered are relatively large. With a very high degree of approximation (whose accuracy may be evaluated later) the overall result, besides yielding a force F which need not concern us here, yields a moment of momentum M equal to zero.

We are thus referred to a rather specialized chapter of mechanics, a particularly simple case of the theory of the gyroscope.

3. This special case of the problem of the gyroscope may be elucidated mathematically. It has been completely treated by Euler. Its solution is the following:

Let C be a cone of revolution to which the gyroscope is assumed to be attached in an unchanged position. Let C' be another cone of revolution which is assumed to be fixed (or shifting by parallel translation). The motion of the gyroscope may then be obtained by positioning the cone C to touch the cone C' along a generator (the two vertices coinciding) and having C roll on C' with constant speed. The gyroscope then moves, at any moment, with a rotatory motion of constant angular velocity around an instantaneous axis which is the very generator of contact between the two cones at that moment. Taking the gyroscope as a system of reference, one may therefore also say that the instantaneous axis of rotation describes, with constant velocity, a certain cone invariantly connected with the gyroscope. This is called nutation.

Applied to the earth, these calculations yield two cones C and C' of very small aperture. The "instantaneous poles" thus would describe, each on its side, a circle of small radius around a fixed center which would be called a geographic pole.

For the period of nutation the calculations determine a value of 300 days. This result unfortunately is rather inaccurate. Chandler has shown experimentally that the period in question is 427 days. The problem therefore must be attacked again in an effort to press the data of the experiment more closely.

4. The earth certainly is not a rigid body. How, and later Klein and Sommerfeld, proposed to treat it as an elastic body. Their fundamental hypothesis is that the shape assumed by

the earth, while it changes its form under the influence of the centrifugal force, at every instant is a figure of equilibrium. The ellipticity of this figure of equilibrium is the actual ellipticity of the earth. The results of the calculations may be summarized as follows:

The period of nutation corresponding to these hypotheses is the same as that of a rigid spheroid subject to the same exterior forces as the earth, a spheroid which would be no other than the figure of equilibrium which the earth would assume if it did not turn. The value of the period of nutation is then 427 days, roughly in agreement with Chandler's observations.

Klein and Sommerfeld moreover have shown that in the same hypotheses, one must attribute to the earth, considered as a homogeneous body, a rigidity coefficient 24 percent higher than that of steel. Is this secondary result admissible?

If one assumes that the earth contains a liquid center, one may show that taking into account the very high pressure inevitably acting on this center, the Klein-Sommerfeld hypothesis of elasticity is quite plausible and offers an acceptable explanation for the considerable difference which separates the theoretical value calculated by Euler from the value observed by Chandler. As far as our problem is concerned, the fact to remember is that the corrected theory still attributes to the earth a uniform rotatory motion within a rather narrow margin of precision.

Other theoretical attempts may succeed in reducing the difference which still exists between the theoretical value and the observed value of nutation. For our purposes they hardly affect the situation. We shall therefore not study them.

5. Would the above results be modified if in the evaluation of the forces acting upon the earth we would proceed towards a second degree of approximation? The moment M, especially regarding the attraction of the sun and the moon acting on our globe, is not exactly nil. If we take this into account, calculations show that (the moment M being perpendicular to the axis of rotation) the gyroscopic motion must be completed by the global drive of the cones C and C' in a very slow motion of precession of a very long period (about 27,000 years). But

as far as the motion of the earth around its axis is concerned, the uniformity of rotation is not thereby affected.

This, then, sketched in very large outlines, is the fashion in which the astronomer can justify, insofar as the earth conforms to the model which he sets up, if not the invariance, at least the regular variation of the direction of the earth's axis (and consequently of the axis of the celestial sphere) and the regular rotation of the earth around this axis (and consequently the regular rotation of the celestial sphere around its axis).

One cannot fail to be struck by the predominance of theoretical elements in this justification. This aspect would even be reinforced if we would enter into the details of the second step of the procedure of approximation which has been discussed. In any case the problem of the terrestrial gyroscope, through the estimation of the moment of momentum M, is linked to the theory of the solar system and to the determination of the gravitational field (of the Newtonian potential) by whose introduction the entire theory may be treated. At the level of the second approximation the separation of the problem of the terrestrial gyroscope is much less easy than at the level of the first. In fact, the explanation we asked of the astronomer is an inseparable and integral part of the theory of the planetary system, to which the earth belongs.

In the preceding sketch of the astronomer's answer we have passed over in silence a certain group of mathematical devices whose importance for our problem may be secondary, but which nevertheless are indispensable and whose introduction even reinforces the predominance of the theoretical elements; these are the devices borrowed from geometry and trigonometry, without which an accurate observation of the positions of the stars on the celestial sphere would not be possible, and without which the position of the stars in space could not be related to these observations.

Nevertheless, by insisting too much on the theoretical aspect, one can only give a false impression of the question as a whole. A theory is not erected in a vacuum; it needs concrete data to which must be applied. These concrete data are the distances between the celestial bodies, their form, their mass, their moment of inertia, etc. How can they be determined with some degree of precision? We shall return to this question in a moment.

The Model Is Not Perfect

Before we make use of the preceding statements there remains a point for us to emphasize. It is clear that it is never possible to determine all the concrete data which we have discussed, those concerning the earth in particular, with ultimate precision. But even if they could be so determined, they still would give only a summary description of the material realities on which the theory rests. Thus, for example, the distribution of the masses on the surface of the earth varies according to the seasonal transfer of the water of the ocean to the glaciers and from the glaciers to the ocean, which causes variations in the moment of inertia and therefore in the speed of rotation; its mass varies from the continuous fall of innumerable asteroids; its impulse must vary according to the dissipation of energy caused by the motions of the waters and of the atmosphere; its moment of inertia varies according to the displacement of the axis of rotation, etc. (Fermi estimates that the existence of the great maritime currents might be responsible for the considerable displacement of the pole, for which rather conclusive geological evidence is being discovered.)

Principally, all these factors more or less put a strain on the theory of the terrestrial gyroscope. To what extent can they be disregarded? A geophysicist may already have the means to evaluate their order of magnitude. What appears certain is that although all these factors cannot be disregarded, their influence can only be very slight.

The chronometrical observatory of Neuchâtel (Switzerland) informs us that the increase in the length of an average day is actually 1.64 milliseconds per century, but that the total and partly very irregular variation in one day may be as high as a half millisecond. At the stage where we are now in our discussion we are still unable to imagine the consequences of this observation.

Is Recourse to Theory Legitimate?

You have raised the question, we may be told, how it could be possible to decide whether the motion of the celestial sphere is uniform or not. Do not your remarks precisely answer this question? Are the preceding explanations not enough? Are the requirements with which you have approached the problem not satisfied?

Certainly not! First it should be noted that the justification which has been offered is far from being a careful and approximately complete exposition. It remains inconclusive, in particular, about a fundamental problem which we have not even touched upon: the connection between the theoretical and the experimental aspects in the interpretation of astronomical observations. From the theoretical standpoint we have stated the law of universal attraction, speaking in terms of distance and of mass. We have by no means explained, however, how these notions are *realized*, through what procedures we may confer an operational meaning on the "distance separating two real bodies," by what measures and calculations we can attribute a well-defined mass to some of these bodies, e.g. the moon, the sun, and the planets. For all the notions announced (from the theoretical standpoint) and applied (from the experimental standpoint) the analysis is not even outlined and remains uncertain in every aspect. For each of these notions we would have to establish an additional text. For each, the problem of the specification of the rational and the operational, as opposed to each other, would crop up again. Nothing assures us in advance that these texts could guarantee the autonomy (the methodological purity) of the operational in all the directions where we would have to engage ourselves. On the contrary, in one case at least and precisely the one with which we are concerned, viz. the case of time and its measurement, we would abandon without possible return the search for a better, more distinct, and more accurate specification of operational time if we would consent to base the sequel of our exposé upon the preceding explications. This is because evidently the laws of mechanics on which we would have to depend, which inform the astronomer's methods, cannot be formulated without invoking mathematical time. The laws of mechanics, especially Newton's law of gravitation, are not valid a priori. In order to be assured, their validity must be proved by the experiment. But the test can only be made with the help of astronomical observations which in turn presuppose an already advanced technique of measuring time. Thus we would be caught in an obvious methodological circle; to define the measurement of time through the techniques and procedures to be used would require, in order to be successful, that we would be able in advance to effect this measurement. The project therefore cannot be realized.

Does this mean that we have exposed a methodological vicious circle, which ought to discourage us in advance from thinking of a *mixed method* where the rational and the operational would be combined, without even waiting for their mutual independence to be perfectly realized? The contrary is true; if the methodological circle in question could not be avoided, it is precisely the track in which we are engaged which we would have to abandon. Is there any other choice? Whether we like it or not, we would then have to return to what we just called the mixed method. So far we have not seriously examined it. We would then have to do so, and our one remaining alternative might be to adopt it.

This result would not be a genuine surprise. We would simply find ourselves in a situation analogous to the one occasioned by our analysis of current language. The solution in that case was found through the concept of discursive synthesis. Why could the methodological solution, in an analogous case, not be provided by an analogous concept?

But we have not yet reached this point, if indeed we shall ever reach it. As long as we are not forced to change our plans we shall persevere in our present project: to pursue the idea of an operational time through the exigencies of increased precision, a precision radically superior to that of the instruments considered so far.*

---

* In the perspective of our exposé the work repeatedly cited, *La géométrie et le problème de l'espace,* might be considered as a complementary text for the analysis. It is a specialized treatise on the geometrical magnitudes, and it

It is therefore entirely deliberate that we (for the moment at least) decide to disregard the suggestions and justifications derived from an already well-established astronomy based on the considerable theoretical apparatus of celestial mechanics.

Test by Means of Another Clock

The timepiece realized through the apparent motion of the celestial sphere thus apparently departs from the outline we have traced so far. It seems improbable that without any additional ideas, we could use it in our search for a purely operational time. There is, however, one very obvious idea which we have not utilized so far. Why do we disregard the measuring of time by the reaction wheel clock whose operational character we have pointed out so carefully? Why do we not consider its use for testing the uniformity of the celestial timepiece? Have we not explained how the synchronicity of the two rotatory motions may be established?

The answer is quite simple. Certainly, nothing prevents the testing of the celestial timepiece against the reaction wheel clock, but this test would not be very useful. It would surely demonstrate that the celestial timepiece runs as regularly as the best water clocks, but the new and important fact is missing. What makes the confrontation meaningless is that the celestial timepiece gives us access to an accuracy and to a precision radically superior to those of the clocks which would be used

---

investigates with particular care how we must understand the relation between their theoretical and experimental aspects. The question of a purely operational geometry is explicitly investigated. The conclusions reached in this work are clearly unfavorable to the project which, as we have said, we shall not give up without being forced to do so. If one intends to establish geometry in its full practical significance, without neglecting any of its essential aspects, he must resort to a mixed method. The radical separation of the rational elements from the operational ones then turns out to be impracticable.

But the present study must continue regardless of this result. We think, of course, that we shall be able to confirm it. But in order to assume its full value, this confirmation must use its own methods. For this reason we shall act "as if" the results of our study of geometry were still unknown to us. We shall even go so far as to suppose that they are different from what they actually are. Our conclusions, when they are made, will thereby be reinforced.

to supervise it. It is this increase in accuracy and precision which now must be incorporated into our project. But this is precisely the point which the supervision could not grasp and define, and concerning which it would thus remain inoperative.

Provisionally: An Arbitrary Standard

At the point where we are now, we thus do not have any procedure which through an operational approach could assure us of the uniformity of the celestial timepiece. Unique in its kind and out of our reach, we must accept it for what it is, in order to utilize it (at least until further notice) without being in a position to test it. It is thus in its capacity of *imposed metronome* (imposed by the limitation of our operational grasp on nature) that we have to introduce it.

Here we must beware of possible confusion; the word "operational" should not create any illusions. It is true that the measurement of time on the celestial timepiece thus introduced could not be effected without a certain experimental apparatus and a certain number of operations carried out with its help.

A measuring unit which cannot be verified and whose invariability cannot be ensured is not an *operational standard;* it is a norm whose selection is for the most part arbitrary and whose soundness, at least for the moment, is guaranteed by nothing. For we know—we already noted the fact in connection with the water clocks—that the standard of time cannot be defined arbitrarily but must satisfy certain requirements in order to qualify as a standard of universal time, the time relative to which the laws of the phenomena remain constant. Does the time which is given by the terrestrial timepiece satisfy these requirements? This is a problem to which we must return later, when we have the means to treat it.

In practice the sidereal day certainly has had this normative function in the manufacture of precision clocks for a considerable time. We shall have to demonstrate that in measurements of the highest precision, this function today is obsolete. We cannot therefore describe the normative character which the sidereal timepiece in fact has assumed during a certain period of time, as if the measurement of time could be practically and permanently based on it. Our exposé at this point must cross a sort of threshold beyond which the operational character of the measurement of time must be able to be reconstituted. If such were not the case we would have to retract our argument and to use the method of this measurement in an entirely different approach, the only one remaining open to us, viz. the double reference (to the rational and the operational at the same time) already discussed above.

This, then, is our situation at present; the consideration of the means by which the measurement of time has in fact been developed towards the great accuracy of which it is capable today introduces an obviously disturbing element into our search for a purely operational grasp of time. In order to eliminate this element, it is necessary that the provisionally arbitrary normative character of the last measurement can be retained and reintegrated into an operational viewpoint. This will not happen spontaneously; a new idea must provide the means for it. Accordingly we are faced with the following principal question: On what condition and under what circumstances can an aspect of normativeness be reinterpreted as a (constitutive) moment of an operational procedure? This is, of course, a principal question which could be accommodated to the analysis of the very idea of the operational. We must show how it may be answered within the particular frame of our study. But is it methodically sound at this point already to ask this question in its general form? The moment seems to have come for us to make a remark of some importance, which may shed light on the methodological attitude to which, as we are increasingly led to believe, we must adhere.

Definition of the Operational

The reader will certainly have noticed that, although we have formed the project of isolating (as far as possible) the purely operational aspect of the measurement of time, we have not immediately defined exactly what the word *operational* would mean for us. Why not? Because this word does not convey in advance, through the letters of which it is composed, the meaning which might be conferred upon it. On this point our analysis of the significations which the word *time* may assume cannot leave any doubt for us. In order to assume a meaning of some precision the word *operational* must be used in procedures which perceptibly and increasingly diverge from the practices of current activity. In a more or less decisive way the content of meaning of the word "to be defined" is a function of the development of these procedures, their nature, and their effectiveness.

Of course we do not pretend that the concept of the operational could not become the object of a special study, e.g. a monograph dedicated especially to this purpose. We merely wish to emphasize the fact that such a study could not be conducted in a vacuum, before the development of effective procedures through which the word *operational* is invested with its significative substance and its discursive power. Our text has given us the opportunity of illustrating this statement by a rather clear example. Could someone who wants to define the operational in advance and in a definitive way, so as to be able always to find the idea, such as he has defined it, in all the possible uses which would occur, have foreseen the episode which forces us to stop momentarily our encounter with the normative element? Would this person have been able in advance to state, in his definition, the ready-made solution of the problem facing us, or at least the elements from which this solution would be derived? We do not think so. As far as we are concerned this episode is welcome but it was not anticipated. It is welcome because it will give us an opportunity to take a step forward in the very determination of the concept of the operational. The latter, as we precisely realize at this moment, had not found its completion so far. We will say, repeating the expression which was explained at length in Chapter One ("The Outlined Acceptations"), that it was only an outline-idea. As one might take up again the model of a statue in order to perfect it or to remodel it, we shall have to take up again the still unfinished concept of the operational, to confer upon it certain traits which, for us at least, it has not implied so far.

Can We Return to the Operational?

Let us return to the question we asked earlier: Is it methodically sound to ask, in general, under which conditions one will find the possibility of reinterpreting a decision of a normative character, to make of it a moment of an operational aim? The answer can only be informed by the same methodological views as the preceding explanations. Since the very experiment which we are attempting to a considerable extent is constitutive of the operational (and, at the same time and by indirection, of the normative), it is clear that the relation between the normative and the operational cannot be instituted in advance in its most general form. On the other hand, experience contributes to form (and to inform) ideas of which it makes use only when it tends to express and to formulate itself. A certain expressive action thus is necessarily inherent in it, an action which because of its nature inevitably has some generalizing effect. The single fact can deliver its "experiential content" only when it is integrated into some effort at generalization. If thus in our case we formulate somewhat generally the circumstances under which a normative choice may be reinstated in an operational function, the reason is simply that our formulation successfully implements our effort better to grasp that particular case.

What, then, are these circumstances? In a general way we may say that a normative choice takes an operational meaning when one is able to use it, actually and effectively, to orient the search for greater precision in the construction of experimental machinery, especially in the manufacture of measuring apparatus. For our case it is especially relevant that the decision to take the sidereal day as a basic unit for measuring time derives its operational character from the fact that it has played and still plays a leading rôle in the manufacture of clocks, first in the manufacture of precision clocks and gradually in the entire watchmaking industry.

It is this aspect of the question which we must investigate now. We must likewise return to the consideration of the problem of precision, which is becoming increasingly important for us.

THE MEASUREMENT OF TIME BY MEANS OF A PERIODICAL PHENOMENON; PENDULUM CLOCKS AND BALANCE WHEEL CLOCKS

One might feel that our exposé is very slow in coming to the "real" timepieces, i.e. clocks based upon a periodical process. This delay, of course, was deliberate, since we considered it necessary to treat the problem of measuring time in its most elementary aspects. It will now be easier for us to attack the problem of high precision.

In our preceding discussion we have noted repeatedly that the measuring of time is not inevitably linked to a periodical phenomenon. It was rather uniform processes which were considered. Clocks with uniform rotation of a certain accuracy could nowadays be manufactured if there were a demand for them. Some of the reasons why the watchmaking industry preferably uses periodical motions are too obvious to be discussed. Others, however, are less so. The watchmaker prefers a system with a clearly defined period of its own, rather than a system allowing of any kind of period, such as the reaction wheel clock, for example. If this period can be made independent of the amplitude, the situation is still more favorable; the irregularities of oscillation will appear only in a very weak form in the running of the clock.

Definition of a Periodical Process

How shall we define a periodical process? Shall we say that it is a process which, for any period of time t, and for a determinate duration ω (i.e. its period), at time $t + \omega$ is again the same as it was at time t? This definition would be useful only if it would permit us to decide experimentally whether a certain phenomenon given in reality is periodical or not. But, in order to make the experiment we should be able to measure the period ω. We would thus be again caught in the same difficulties which we have pointed out and discussed several times before. We must repeat at this point that if we want to remain true to our intention, we must have a different starting point at our disposal. Otherwise we do not have to devise methods different from those which have been useful to us so far. Even before we give to it its exact mathematical definition the idea of periodicity is anchored in our natural representations at the level of common sense. At this level any process repeated in identical form is periodical. The existence of the period is implicit in the concept of "identical form"; when a periodical process again passes through a stage in which it had been once before, with all its characteristics according to the representation we have of it, we imagine that it is starting over again its evolution from this stage in the strictest form possible.* In practice the problem is then to recognize or to induce the phenomena whose evolution corresponds to our representation of periodicity. Let us imagine, for example, a freely swinging pendulum whose course might be described as follows: Having moved upward as far as the extreme position A, it swings back and moves upward symmetrically as far as the position B; from there it swings again back to return exactly to position A, where we had observed it in the first place. Under these conditions we would not hesitate to state (all circumstances remaining equal) that the pendulum cannot fail to repeat again the same motion from A to B and back to A, and so forth.

Unfortunately an actual pendulum which is left to oscillate "freely" does not exactly correspond to this ideal model; in swinging back from A it reaches a position B' which is not exactly at the same level as B; the extreme position A', which is reached on the way back from B', will never be on the same level of elevation (little as it may differ from it) as the position A. The amplitude of the pendulum's oscillation, if left to itself, thus will steadily decrease, and the pendulum finally will stop. The same is true for all oscillatory motions we can induce by mechanical means. None of them realizes in a perfectly adequate way the idea we have of a phenomenon which is repeated "in identical form." This is not surprising; the same was also said of all rotation clocks manufactured by man. We noted that in

---

* Of course the fact that such is our representation of a periodical process, particularly its deterministic character, does not suffice to guarantee the existence of a universal physical determinism. We are no less entitled to make this our starting point.

order to be permanent, the rotatory motions which we are able to induce must also be maintained. The same is true of oscillatory motions. It is nevertheless the latter, particularly the elastic oscillations besides pendular ones, which are used by the watchmaking industry almost exclusively. Under these circumstances, what is the actual position of the expert? Is his first concern about operationality?

We shall investigate the problem. This will enable us, through some change of illustrations, not to become too repetitious. Naturally we cannot think of displaying here all the problems confronting the manufacturer of a good watch or clock. By attempting it we would moreover risk to lose from sight the aim of our own study. We must therefore be content with some indications, all selected with this aim in mind.

Let us begin by asking how the operational approach could develop its requirements in watchmaking. We go back to what should be an "operational definition" of time. The time thus conceived should be defined by being measured, i.e. by the application of certain well-defined experimental procedures having the capacity of instituting a model of a temporal evolution. Such a definition implies, in fact, the designation of a standard duration. It must be completed by the indication of the procedures through which the durations to be measured could be related to the durations counted on the standard scale.

The construction of a standard clock would give the operator the right to say quite simply, "Time is *what this* timepiece measures." It is well known that the watchmaking industry produces clocks and chronometers of high accuracy. Can these clocks and chronometers be made into standard clocks? in the sense of an operational definition, of course.

The watchmaking industry makes use of two temporal evolutions, that of oscillation of the pendulum and that of oscillation of the balance wheel. Where must we seek the first suggestions that have led to their use? Our daily activities might furnish a few examples for the pendulum. The knowledge of elastic oscillations, on the other hand, certainly is not on the same level as common sense. The project to establish a standard clock therefore is not readily feasible in either case.

Whatever those first steps, moreover, the research of the watchmakers has been informed very early, not by the possibility of obtaining in advance a standard duration, but by two concepts of a mathematical nature: the mathematical pendulum and the harmonic oscillation. These two concepts belong to the domain of rational mechanics (i.e. the mathematical level of classical mechanics).

Deferment of the Operational Approach

It must be noted that by investigating these mathematical models of periodic motions we are hardly making any progress towards an operational definition of time. The variable t which figures in the equation of the motion does not represent a measured amount of time but rather the mathematical variant of imaginary time. What has thus been made clear is not the operational aspect of the realization of a periodical motion but its rational aspect. Nevertheless, these abstract models are the ones which guide the entire practice of watchmaking.

To what extent can an oscillating mechanical system (which is part of the physical world) be considered as a realization of a mathematical pendulum or of an ideal harmonic oscillator (which belong to the mathematical universe)? This is a very awkward question, not for the watchmaker but for someone who intends to explain how the watchmaker's work may contribute to the definition of operational time. What, in fact, is the reason behind the obstinate search for such a definition? It is to avoid, at least as far as time is concerned, the problem (a philosophical problem par excellence) of the relation between the things imagined and the things realized, the relation in particular between mathematical entities and physical entities, which it helps us to understand. The acquisition of an operational time would exempt the experimentor from taking sides concerning this problem. Or rather, it would give him an unexceptionable practical solution, a solution whose elements would all be guaranteed at the very level of the experiment. But the reintroduction of mathematical time, of rational mechanics, and of abstract kinematic systems must make it doubtful whether such a solution can be found.

For us who are trying to base measured time as closely as possible on the requirements of the experimentor, this reintroduction likewise is disappointing. If we want to follow the watchmaker in his practice and examine with him how he is able to satisfy the requirements of ever-increasing accuracy, we must let ourselves be guided, as he is, by the kinematic models of rational mechanics. How would we do it without admitting that this mechanics can be applied, and without having any idea how it is applied? How would we do it, in particular, if we did not have the liberty to assimilate mathematical time to a measured time? What can we expect, under these conditions, of a study of watches and clocks? One thing is already certain; the watchmaking craft will be useless in our search for the emergence of a purely operational time. The irreplaceable function which in watchmaking is attributed to the abstract kinematic models excludes this eventuality. The more detailed study which we shall presently make of it can only confirm this. What, then, is the doctrine of time to which the craft of watchmaking will give evidence of its effectiveness? It illustrates the fashion in which, through a sustained technical effort, mathematical time and measured time may be combined in an effective practice.

Does this mean that our search for an operational definition is already doomed to failure? We must beware of hasty conclusions. The watchmaking craft cannot fail to invoke certain experimental guarantees. Perhaps the latter could be clearly isolated. We may still hope that this will be possible. We would thus recover the conditions of a recapture of the operational approach. For the time being, however, this approach must remain uncertain. (This is moreover not the first time that we find ourselves in such a situation. In order to justify the hypothesis of the uniformity of the rotatory motion of the earth around its axis, disregarding the minor divergences which we could not and cannot at present evaluate, we already have been forced, once before, to break with operational orthodoxy.)

The Practitioner's Attitude

Our next question shall be what a practitioner is and what his (more or less openly acknowledged) attitude towards this problem is.

Obviously the practitioner does not simply have to be a man engaged in manufacturing good clocks and using established and tested procedures. His procedures do not remain invariable. They have not always been what they are today, and everywhere efforts are being made to improve them. Thus the practitioner likewise is someone for whom *the problem of a better clock* has always existed and continues to exist. It is clear that all practitioners do not and cannot have the same attitude towards this problem. One may assume, nevertheless, that a work such as the *Traité de l'Horlogerie** was not written without any considerations of general usefulness to satisfy the inclinations of some theoretical minds. Its purpose, on the contrary, is to be put into the hands of teachers and students of vocational schools and, more generally, to help the technicians faced with the practical problems arising from the constant updating of the procedures of manufacture. One may therefore assume that a treatise of this kind formulates, not an ensemble of commonly accepted requirements, but rather the requirements resulting from experience, as far as the education and activity of the craftsman are concerned. The collection and the arrangement of the materials suggest, if not a standard activity, at least an exemplary one, an activity which some of the best-informed professionals consider more correct and effective than any other. One may therefore say, without straining the meaning of the words, that such a work implies a certain doctrine about the correct and normal attitude of the practitioner. We may now repeat our question: Is this doctrine inspired by a concern for operationality, a concern which admittedly would not have to be explicitly stated in order to be real? This concern is nowhere apparent; there is not even a careful separation between the rational and the operational. Paradoxical as it may appear,

* *Léopold Defossez: Théorie générale de l'horlogerie*, éditée par la Chambre Suisse de l'horlogerie, La-Chaux-de-Fonds (Switzerland), 1952. 2 vols.

the practitioner is not interested in stating clearly in what their difference consists. In fact he combines both aspects in his work. His activity realizes their practical synthesis, but he does not even stop to think about it.

The Doctrine Underlying the Treatise on Watchmaking

Before we open the *Treatise,* let us state right away what we shall not do. We shall by no means try to describe all the material contained in it. Neither shall we seek to retain the order in which the material is arranged. We believe that it is more useful to emphasize what might be called its *underlying doctrine.* The latter is not formulated explicitly, and we may well make it appear more schematic and rigorous than it really is. We shall make every effort, however, to give a faithful account of the essentials.

The following, then, is the method which in the *Treatise on Watchmaking* is offered to the practitioner for solving the problem of measuring time.

Let us repeat that if the mathematical pendulum or the ideal harmonic oscillator could be perfectly realized through a mechanical system, the operational definition of time would be achieved. But we must be careful not to confound the existence of abstract mathematical models with that of their concrete realization. There exists no mechanical system which could be assimilated fully and without reservation to a mathematical model which it would have to follow. But if total and unconditional fidelity is unattainable, we may nevertheless decide to attempt a fidelity as complete as possible. The execution of this project will naturally require three categories of research:

1. A (mathematical) study sufficiently thorough of the mathematical pendulum and the harmonic oscillator.

2. A search for all the causes (of a physical character) liable to compromise the fidelity of the concrete realizations.

3. The discovery of appropriate means to compensate for or to correct the divergences which inevitably must emerge between the model and its realizations.

In principle this is a very clear program; its execution, however, presents numerous difficult problems. We illustrate the method through one of these problems whose solution, to some extent, has opened the way for watchmaking.

The program which we have schematized thus includes, in phase 1, the study of the mathematical pendulum and of the harmonic oscillator. These are two problems which rational mechanics is perfectly able to treat. It is, of course, impossible to explain the details of the solution at this point. We shall merely announce the principal results.

Theoretical Models of the Balance Wheel Spiral and the Pendulum

Let us first concentrate on the balance wheel spiral whose motion is defined by the equation

$$I \frac{d^2\phi}{dt^2} + C\,\phi = 0$$

ϕ designates here the elongation, i.e. the angle formed by the arm of the balance wheel relative to its position of equilibrium; I represents the moment of inertia of the balance wheel in relation to the axis of rotation and C a magnitude characterizing the spiral as far as its form and its material are concerned.

The solution of I may be formulated in the following way:

$$\phi = \phi_0 \sin \sqrt{\frac{C}{I}}\, t$$

This is a harmonic oscillation of amplitude ϕ_0 and of the period

$$(1) \qquad\qquad T = 2\pi \sqrt{\frac{I}{C}}$$

Note that the oscillations are isochronous, the amplitude ϕ_0 not figuring in the expression of the period. The amplitude ϕ_0 itself is retained throughout the motion.

The mathematical pendulum follows a more complex differential equation:

$$(2) \qquad\qquad l \frac{d^2\phi}{dt^2} + g \sin \phi = 0$$

where l designates the length of the pendulum and g the terrestrial acceleration.

If the maximal elongation ϕ_0 is very small, the case is reduced to the preceding case; the motion will be harmonic and the oscillations isochronous $(T = 2\pi\sqrt{l/g})$.

For any maximal elongation ϕ_0, the integration of the equation is reduced to the calculation of an elliptic integral. In this case the period is given by

$$T = 2\pi \sqrt{\frac{l}{g}} \left[1 + \left(\frac{1}{2}\right)^2 \sin^2 \frac{\phi_0}{2} + \left(\frac{1.3}{2.4}\right)^2 \sin^4 \frac{\phi_0}{2} + \ldots \right]$$

The expression between brackets [ ] is called the series of the pendulum. One may see clearly that here the oscillations lose their character of isochrony.

One more remark, to emphasize the first and irreducible difference between the mathematical models and their concrete realization: The swinging motions of the mathematical pendulum and the harmonic oscillator are perpetual. We mean, of course, that the mathematical laws of these motions are expressed as a function of the variable t, of mathematical time which we may imagine as variable from $-\infty$ to $+\infty$.

Damping and Maintenance of Motion

We continue now, concerning exactly this point, with phase 2 of our program. As we have already noted, there exists no real pendulum and no real oscillator whose free-swinging motions could be perpetual. Sooner or later the motion stops. Can we point out the reason for this essential difference from the mathematical models? The answer, anticipated by common sense, this time is provided by the mechanics involved in these applications; apart from the inevitable erosion of the mechanisms, the stopping of the motion is caused by a combination of frictions and the constant loss of (kinetic) energy which they entail.

Point 3 of the program therefore must include the introduction of a complementary mechanism capable of counterbalancing these losses.

A clock based on an oscillatory motion thus must contain, besides the oscillating device itself, two complementary devices, one for counting the oscillations, the other for giving to the intended rhythm the impulses necessary to maintain the oscillating motion. In order to function, these devices must both have some source of energy. They might easily be constructed separately. Neither of them would involve any difficulties that could not be overcome with the help of contemporary technology, the electronic techniques in particular. It is almost self-evident that a feedback solution would be especially suitable for the second device.

But we shall not investigate the clocks which could be constructed in this fashion. Our main reason is that their manufacture involves the use of a body of knowledge of physics and instrumental devices too complex for us to analyze at this point. We shall return to them later,* in our discussion of the quartz clocks. For the moment it is the classical solution, upon which the entire watchmaking craft is based, on which we will concentrate our attention.

The Watchmaker's Solution

The "watchmaker's solution" is highly ingenious; it combines into one the two sources of energy which have been discussed, and it realizes, by means of a single device, the escapement, the register of oscillations, and the connections to be established between the source of energy and the oscillating system.

A conventional watch or clock thus contains three fundamental elements: an instrument of motion, an instrument of regulation, and an intermediary instrument, the escapement.

The instrument of motion has a twofold function; it drives through successive connections the entire system of wheels, starting with the wheel on which it acts immediately. It drives, in particular, the wheel of the escapement and the wheels whose axes carry the hands which move on the dial. Its secondary function is to provide the regulator with the compensatory energy necessary for maintaining the oscillation.

* See page 352.

The function of the regulator is to insure the regularity of the motion which under the impetus of the instrument of motion is finally translated into the measurement of time. It is therefore necessary for the motor to be controlled by the regulator.

The escapement effects the connection and mutual subordination of the two previously mentioned devices. On the one hand it superimposes the rhythm insured by the regulator upon the drive of the instrument of motion; on the other hand it transmits to the regulator, in the same rhythm, the compensatory impulses from the instrument of motion.

The watchmaking industry has developed several forms of escapements; the following is a more detailed description of the functioning of an anchor escapement.

The manufacture of a watch or a clock naturally cannot be undertaken under the aspect of accuracy and precision alone. Nevertheless, this is the only aspect which we have to consider. Consequently we shall again have to concentrate our attention on the regulator and on the oscillatory system. But we now must take into consideration the fact that the regulator is no longer an isolated system but a system upon which the reaction of the other instruments is registered. In its general outline the three point program which we mentioned will not be modified by this fact. Point 1, however, can no longer simply involve the study of the free and uninhibited motion of the mathematical pendulum or the harmonic oscillator. We must replace this study by the study of a pendulum or oscillator subject to repeated impulses. How will these impulses be applied, in what rhythm, at which moment in the course of the pendulum or the oscillator, with what degree of conciseness, and so forth, so that the oscillation should be kept as regular as possible and differ as little as possible from the ideal oscillation?

This problem, of course, is not as simple as the problem of the free pendulum or the free harmonic oscillator. All the same it may likewise be treated as a problem of rational mechanics and be solved mathematically. This is the solution which will guide the watchmaker in the practical realization of points 2 and 3 of the program.

Nothing prevents us from moderating the mathematical rigor

of this first phase by a certain group of experimental investigations or even by tests of empirical rules. Our aim nevertheless remains, not the manufacture of a prototype, but the constitution of a model from which the practitioner can derive inspiration and which he may seek to realize as closely as possible.

In other words, the practitioner is guided by the idea that the regularity of the mechanism, especially of the oscillatory system, can be guaranteed by the invariability of a certain number of characteristic elements. The model in question has as its fundamental function the task of making these characteristics evident. In this particular case they are the elements characteristic of an oscillation with compensated loss of energy which after having been isolated, will define to some extent a point of convergence for the phases 2 and 3 of the program.

Causes of Perturbation

At present phase 2 of this program may be introduced by the following questions: What are the causes capable of changing the characteristic elements of this oscillating system and therefore capable of disturbing the rhythm of its oscillation? What, in particular, are the causes capable of changing the magnitudes which determine the period of this oscillation?

This is the list of causes given in the *Treatise on Watchmaking:*

1. Frictions.
2. The escapement.
3. Jolts.
4. Deficiencies in the equilibrium of the balance wheel.
5. Deficiencies in the equilibrium of the anchor.
6. Deficiencies in the equilibrium of the spring.
7. The motion of the spring.
8. Modifications in the elasticity of the spring.
9. Variations of temperature.
10. The centrifugal force.
11. Inertia of the spring.
12. Variations in the atmospheric pressure.
13. Magnetic fields.

The moment of inertia of the balance wheel is modified by the factors 9, 10, 11, and 12. The factors 7, 8, and 9 alter the elastic moment of the spring, while the factors 1, 2, 3, 4, 5, 6, and 13 alter the harmonic motion of the balance wheel by introducing forces not proportional to the amplitude of the oscillating motion.

It is clear that we cannot follow the *Treatise on Watchmaking* in its investigation of all these factors of perturbation. Moreover, not all of them are analyzable to a similar extent. The influence of jolts, for example, could hardly be studied except as a function of certain statistic hypotheses. As far as we are concerned, i.e. as far as the contribution is concerned which the practice of watchmaking can make to the elucidation of the problem of measuring time, it will suffice for us to study one especially instructive example, the compensation of the *thermoelastic effect*.

Let us review for this purpose the three-point program of the procedure. Point 1 does not have to be reviewed; we remember that it has clarified in the model the effect of certain magnitudes such as the moments of inertia or the modules of elasticity, on the period of oscillation. The practitioner therefore will seek to keep as invariable as possible the magnitudes which correspond to them in an actually realized watch. We may therefore go on to point 2 and ask which might be the effects to be compensated. The thermoelastic effect is one.

The Effect of Temperature

An increase in temperature increases the dimensions of the balance wheel and consequently its moment of inertia. This is translated (according to point 1) into a lengthening of the period of the balance wheel spring, i.e. a retardation of the watch.

By equally increasing the dimensions of the spring, the same increase in temperature reinforces the spring's moment of elasticity, reduces the period of oscillation, and thus causes the watch to run faster.

The watchmaker, however, has no great interest in compensating this effect because the predominant effect of a change in temperature on the functioning of a watch results from the variation of the module of elasticity of the spring.

This point being clarified, we may proceed to the third point of the program and ask how this predominant effect may be corrected.

The first solution (conceived as early as the eighteenth century) was the bimetallic balance wheel.

The clamp of this compensating balance wheel is made of a double metal plate using two unequally dilatable metals, usually brass and steel. If the temperature rises, a straight double plate bends, the more dilatable metal (in the case of steel and brass it would be the latter) being on the side of the convexity. For a double plate already bent in this direction, an elevation of the temperature would further increase the curvature.

In utilizing this property for the watch one first cuts the balance wheel to permit it to dilate. The brass layer forms the exterior part of the double plate. A rise in temperature consequently has the effect of increasing the curvature of the clamp. The balance wheel becomes smaller, its moment of inertia decreases as well as its period, and the watch runs faster. One may thus compensate the delay (from ten to eleven seconds as per each degree Centigrade per day) resulting from the diminution of the module of elasticity, which in turn is a consequence of an increase in temperature.

The compensation thus obtained is not the same for all divergences of temperature. It was noticed rather early that a watch, equipped with a compensating balance wheel of steel and brass and a steel spring having the same speed at two different temperatures t_1 and t_2, advances at an average temperature $\dfrac{t_1 + t_2}{2}$. More generally, the divergence between the average of the speeds at two temperatures t_1 and t_2 and the speed at the average temperature $\dfrac{t_1 + t_2}{2}$ has received the name of secondary error. (The existence of this secondary error is explained by the fact that the expansion of metals does not follow a linear law.)

Can the second error be compensated? It may be in a relatively satisfactory fashion by means of the integral balance wheel or Guillaume wheel. This wheel is made of a double plate consisting partly of a certain ferronickel and partly of brass. The introduction of the Guillaume wheel in chronometers has made it possible to reduce the secondary error by 90 percent.

The Guillaume wheel is used when the spring is made of steel. Instead of seeking to compensate indirectly (by means of the integral balance wheel) the variation of the module of elasticity of the steel springs, one may direct the investigation towards the spring itself. Since the discovery (also by Charles Edouard Guillaume) of the properties of the iron and nickel alloys, attempts have been made to manufacture springs which would permit avoiding the use of the costly bimetallic balance wheels. Guillaume succeeded in compounding an alloy which reduces the secondary error to one second for a divergence of 30° Centigrade. This alloy of iron, nickel, and chrome, known as *élinvar Guillaume,* has a module of elasticity which remains practically invariable between the temperatures of −10° +30° Centigrade. The spring made of this alloy is named the autocompensatory spring.

But metallurgical research has not stopped here. The alloys derived from the *élinvar Guillaume,* such as *métélinvar, durinval, nivarox,* and so forth, contain hardeners, e.g. tungsten, molybdenum, beryllium, and titanium, which after hypertempering produce the effect known as structural hardening. These admixtures have notably improved the elastic qualities of springs, keeping the secondary error to a minimum. These springs, however, still have some drawbacks which specialists in metallurgy seek to eliminate.

For a rationalized manufacture it is essential to have springs which in one standard series have uniform properties. But the elements used in the composition of the *élinvar* derivatives are numerous. Some change as early as during the melting process; others are difficult to blend, which may impair the homogeneity of the alloys. Once melted, and until the moment when it is formed into a spring, the alloy undergoes an entire series of thermal and mechanical treatments which are not without effect on the final product.

If we wanted to give a complete account, we would also have

to consider the latest progress made in this field by the watch-making metallurgists and the manufacturers of springs. But for our purposes this is unnecessary. It will suffice to emphasize that the pursuit of increasing accuracy engages research in ever new directions and in fields of increasingly extensive scope. What has been said about the compensation of the thermoelastic effect amply demonstrates this fact.

Neither shall we seek to learn more about the fashion in which other perturbations could be effectively compensated. Having especially discussed the watch we shall leave aside the problems connected with the pendulum clock. Not that everything essential had already been said, but the preceding remarks are sufficient for the purposes of our exposé. We shall now draw the conclusions.

The Lesson of This Study

In our treatise we can see that the practitioner is faced directly with the theoretical exigencies which his situation involves, his situation as a practitioner relating to the effectiveness rather than to the purity of the means applied. The treatise contains a succinct exposé of rational mechanics. But this is not the only point where theory intervenes as a necessary partner. We have just mentioned the research in mechanics, physics, chemistry, and metallurgy which the search for greater regularity necessitates. In order to describe this research one would have to establish an "additional text" for each of these fields. We have already asked whether, in these additional texts, the rational elements could always and everywhere be clearly separated from the operational elements. We already have expressed doubt that this could be done. For the moment, however, we are not concerned with methodological questions but with the actual method of the practitioner. Whether research in physics or in metallurgy is concerned, the practitioner's attitude is always the same; it could be that the theoretical aspect of his activity sometimes remains secondary while at other times it becomes preponderant; at all times the two aspects are combined, as if their essential difference ought to be forgotten and as if no effective practice were possible except under this condition. Faced

by this factual situation, how can we return to our methodological problem and reestablish our operational approach? Should
we attempt likewise to reestablish it in all the additional texts
which we would have to use to do justice to practice, especially
to the practice involved in the search for precision? We may
hardly think of doing so. At this point we must make a rather
serious concession. We shall abandon the plan to carry our
project as far as these detailed texts. Do we mean by this that
we intend to profit from an analysis which we have not made but
whose success appears to us as certain? The fashion in which our
exposé is developing should rather suggest the opposite. If we
have been able to believe in the possibility of completely and
definitively specifying the operational as opposed to the rational,
this hope now is beginning to fade. The hypothesis which becomes increasingly plausible as our exposé proceeds is not that
our project will succeed but that it will fail. But we have already
said that we shall accept this hypothesis only if compelled to
do so. Therefore our decision not to analyze the additional texts
which a complete exposé should not neglect must be interpreted
as follows: in fact, we are far from being convinced that our
project could include them and be successfully completed. We
are rather convinced of the opposite. In spite of this conviction
we shall act as if the additional texts did not present any problem, as if one could achieve through them the specification of
the operational procedures. We shall therefore return to the
main line of our analysis as if it alone were decisive. Following
this direction we shall finally be confronted with one of the
following alternatives:

1. Our project can be carried to a successful conclusion; in
this case our analysis must be complemented by additional
analyses along the secondary lines traced across all the additional texts.

2. We would have to admit our inability to realize this intention; in this case the question may be settled without the necessity of using the suspended texts. The experiment which we are
conducting by means of the present exposé then would have
settled the problem in favor of a mixed method, a method which
we would have to investigate more fully.

Return to the Operational Approach: The Theme of Precision

How can we decide operationally whether a process is periodical or not? This is the counterpart to the question we had to ask about every phenomenon and every process which we intended to utilize in measuring time. Principally the answer does not differ from the one we have already given; an oscillatory process cannot by itself give the operational guarantee of its periodicity. If it develops alone, removed from any confrontations, we will be unable to compare it with itself in the different stages of its evolution (except for the summary evaluations resulting from its being integrated into the totality of our daily activities). This does not mean that one cannot and must not in any case use it as a metronome, but simply that we have no way to decide, on the strength of a valid proof of some accuracy, whether we have a good metronome or a bad one.

Multiplication of Specimens

The situation is entirely different if one is in a position to confront this first oscillatory process with other processes of the same type, especially those we might call "copies of itself," in other words, if one is able to realize several specimens of the same process. We must naturally assume that the process in question be such that we can mark their characteristic phases, e.g. the phases most widely removed from a middle phase which in turn is recognizable. One may easily imagine a procedure of comparison permitting us to decide whether two oscillatory processes are synchronous or not. For this purpose we return to the procedure which we have described for two rotatory motions. Assume that for each of these processes a characteristic phase has been marked, and that we are in a position to verify the "temporal coincidence" of these two markings. Let us then wait for the occurrence of a second coincidence, then of a third, a fourth, etc. Meanwhile we shall also have verified that the first marking has appeared l times from the first coincidence to the second, m times from the second to the third, n times from the third to the fourth, and so forth, and that the corresponding numbers for the second marking are l_1, m_1, n_1. The equality of the relations $\frac{l}{l_1}, \frac{m}{m_1}, \frac{n}{n_1} \cdots$ guarantees the synchronicity of the two oscillatory processes.

Our operational hold on the temporal structure of a process is reinforced decisively if we have "identical copies" of this process, especially copies of such a kind that a phase defined as the initial stage of the process may be started at any subsequent moment. It would suffice for us to repeat the remarks made concerning the reaction wheel clock in order to show how an oscillatory process with its identical copies (i.e. a certain number of its copies) could serve as a universal metronome, even if it were not by nature a regular metronome. We would thus achieve the operational definition of a good metronome: A good metronome is one which remains synchronized with its identical copies, even if it is not *phased* with them.

This last definition naturally does not solve the problem of the creation of identical copies. Will it be feasible to realize them without a certain inside knowledge of the phenomenon, a knowledge formulated in its temporal law? How can we be sure of this? The conformity of the various specimens certainly could be ensured by identity of manufacture, if such an identity could be realized. Practically it could never be except in a more or less approximate fashion, the degree of approximation moreover eluding any direct verification. This means that for any verification aiming at accuracy, it will always be necessary to check the conformity; this check in turn inevitably represents a proof of synchronicity. The requirement of precision obviously brings back the operational vicious circle which we must avoid: the circle consisting in basing a proof of synchronicity on the existence of a synchronicity which has not been proved.

In practice the problem is essentially complicated by the fact that for reasons which are not completely given and whose effects are not completely described in advance, the original may very well not remain identical with itself, thus giving rise to more or less different copies, each of which moreover may vary individually. The problem is notably simplified if one has a *procedure of reference* of which one may reasonably suppose that if it varies it does so irrespective of eventual variations of its copies.

The argument may then be conducted as follows: Let us assume first that the process remains synchronized with one of its copies. Do we have to conclude that they have not varied and that neither of them is varying? We certainly can also form the hypothesis that both have varied and still vary. Nothing entitles us to exclude this possibility as being absolutely improbable. But is it plausible? In order to remain synchronous, in spite of their variations, both processes would have to vary in exactly the same fashion and in exact synchronicity. Again, this is not impossible; it is even a very frequent occurrence when the various specimens are in the same place and subject to the same influences. In order that the continued conformity should become significant, everything must be done to insure that the influences to which the various specimens are subject are totally unconnected; it then becomes extremely improbable that all specimens should vary in the same way by accident. By far the most plausible conclusion would then be to assume that all specimens run regularly. If the argument can be extended to more than one copy, the plausibility of the conclusion is thereby reinforced.

Consider now the case where two specimens of the same clock do not remain synchronized. The reason must be that either one or both are affected by irregularities. In the absence of any other information we must leave this matter undecided.

But if through a systematic experimentation bearing on the various specimens, we could expose the causes of variation in such a way that once they are eliminated or compensated, the synchronicity of all specimens is reestablished, we could again conclude in favor of the invariance of all the specimens.

The argument would still remain the same if instead of an original and copies whose synchronicity has been disturbed, we had an original and copies in the process of formation, copies to be made as accurate as possible. If an ensemble of corrections suggested by a differentiated experimentation, bearing on the copies, could bring all copies to mutual synchronicity, in addition to synchronicity with the original, the same conclusions could be drawn once again.

The validity of the argument would certainly be impaired if one would assume that the correction could be applied to each of the copies individually, with the sole intention of having it conform to the original which serves as a model. Its validity remains intact, however, if one demands that the corrections should be inspired by general considerations, to be implemented according to each particular case, if one assumes that moreover the original itself could be put to the test again and should not have a privileged status in anything.

Thus we are now in possession of the following result which was hardly forced on us a priori: If one proposes to elevate a process to the rank of metronome (as universal as possible) it may happen that a systematic experimentation conducted on its copies may confirm this rôle or cancel it.

Confirmed by the experiment, the decision to confer this rôle on the process loses its normative character and assumes an operational one. In this way we turn again to our former remarks about the distinctions which must be made between the normative and the operational.

Return to Astronomical Time: Justification of the Selection of Earth as a Standard

How can the preceding discussion be worked into our operational approach? We intend to use it for reviewing the case of the natural metronome, represented by the apparent rotation of the celestial vault, in its relation to the watchmaking practice. Admittedly there is no question of making a simple and rigid application; we shall rather make a transposition. It is first of all clear that if one installs the apparent motion of the celestial vault in the function of the original metronome, the manufactured watches and clocks could not be faithful copies of it. In many respects the distance between the natural time piece and the artificial ones is so great that the term copy is hardly appropriate.

We shall nevertheless retain the word *copy*. But it is clear that here it loses everything which constitutes its usual signification. We are no longer concerned with the confrontation of

one timepiece with another one of the same type based upon
the same principle, but with the confrontation of one type of
timepiece with a different type. The terrestrial clock exists only
in one specimen; therefore we cannot apply to it the procedure
we have applied to all other types of timepieces, from the hourglass to the water clocks and finally to the balance wheel clock.
Does this mean that it is impossible for us to check the functioning of the terrestrial timepiece in an operational way? This
conclusion would impose itself if each phenomenon had its own
particular time, differing from the time of all the rest. We have
established experimentally that the times defined from different
phenomena coincide, with allowance made for the degree of
precision attained; we can therefore state the hypothesis—which
certainly must be verified—that all phenomena admit of the
same time, and that a universal time exists. If a universal time
does exist, the time of the balance wheel clocks is the same as
that of the earth; we may therefore compare the terrestrial timepiece with other types, especially balance wheel clocks.

One may moreover reason in a slightly different way: The
rotation of the earth is, in a first approximation, a uniform motion; we may verify this by taking the time of the balance wheel
clocks as a reference. The very fact of this uniformity guarantees
—to the degree of precision where this uniformity is itself
guaranteed—the identity of terrestrial time with that of the
balance wheel clock. We therefore can do without the
hazardous hypothesis of the existence of a common time; this
common time is itself guaranteed, to a certain approximate degree, by the comparison between the time given by the balance
wheel clocks and the time given by the terrestrial rotation if one
postulates that this rotation is regular.

Thus we find ourselves in a situation we have discussed several
times: A certain group of timepieces (including the earth) converge in a certain degree of approximation and diverge in a more
extensive approximation. What can we conclude from this?

From the crude convergence we may conclude that the entire
group consists of crudely accurate timepieces; since the earth
and the balance wheel clocks are partly based on different principles and partly subject to very different influences it would be

very improbable that the consonance should be accidental (unless one imagines special circumstances equally valid in the entire terrestrial region and with an identical influence on the rotation of the earth and on the oscillation of the balance wheels, which is rather unlikely).

From the subtle divergence we may conclude that certain timepieces are wrong, but which are? Again we have an option of the two usual diagnostic procedures:

1. We may seek to eliminate the possible causes of variations; if the agreement of the clocks with the earth as a reference is improved in the same measure as the causes of perturbation are more completely eliminated, we conclude that the earth is the better timepiece. One would arrive at the opposite conclusion only if the elimination of the causes of perturbation would result in a stable disagreement, identical for all timepieces, which could not be attributed to a common perturbation.

2. We may compare with each other an entire series of timepieces put into conditions as different as possible. If the timepieces differ among themselves as much as they differ from the earth, we would conclude that there is no reason to withdraw from earth its function as a privileged normative standard. On the other hand, if all the timepieces were in accordance on a common time and the time given by the earth would diverge relative to this common time, one would conclude that the common time of the timepieces is a better time than that of the earth and would not hesitate to adopt this better time as a new reference.

Is the Choice of a Standard Arbitrary?

This procedure—and the answer of experience to this procedure—thus justifies operationally the choice of the earth as a norm, a provisional one since the emergence of a new type of clock more accurate than the earth could lead us to revoke this choice. (This is not just a bold hypothesis but has already happened; the earth already, at this moment, has lost its function of norm in favor of other, more accurate timepieces.) The present procedure eliminates all arbitrariness from the choice of a standard and thus gives short shrift to a certain widely held concept of operationality, according to which the processes which serve to define physical units would be chosen arbitrarily; the linear meter would be the length of a certain ruler, the coulomb the quantity of electricity which deposits a certain amount of silver on an electrode, and so forth.

It is true that the *magnitude* of the unit is arbitrary, but the process which leads to its definition is not. We do not select the standard at random; we select a standard of length, for example, in such a way that its *length* remains constant; it is made of platinum so that it should not change, it is given a certain shape so as to be less flexible, it is maintained at a certain temperature so as not to expand, etc. We select as standards phenomena as constant and as easily reproducible as we can find.

Time Precedes the Standard

But what does this mean? It can mean only one thing, namely that the magnitude which we intend to measure exists prior to the process used for measuring it. We select the most constant phenomena that can be found. Constant relative to what? The fact is that there are, previous to the selection of the standard, means to verify whether a certain phenomenon is constant or not; there are means, previous to the selection of a standard of length, to determine whether a certain ruler has a constant length or not.

To say that the magnitude precedes the standard would perhaps be going too far. It precedes any particular standard and it transcends any particular standard; this is an accurate statement. But we must not conclude that the magnitude is independent of *any* phenomenon. On the contrary it must be stated that it is *common* to all those phenomena which can be taken as standards, and it is in this sense that it transcends the individual standards.

The requirement of operationality is justified; to imagine absolute metaphysical magnitudes, independent of any phenomenon and impossible to discover experimentally, would be a highly hazardous enterprise which could not be justified by anything.

But to justify, in the name of operationalism, a concept where everything is conventional, where it would really be the scientist who would create the magnitude by arbitrarily defining a process in order to measure it, would be going too far. Neither time, nor length, nor temperature are the physicist's creations. The physicist, in his heart of hearts, knows this perfectly well, and he accordingly introduces an absolute temperature scale, which is not connected with a particular thermometer as were the first thermometric scales, but which is defined with the help of data of a Carnot cycle; the data are independent of the agent used. Likewise we see emerge at each step of our study an absolute time, absolute not in the sense that it is independent of the phenomena utilized for measuring it, but in the sense that it is independent of the selection of a specific timepiece based on some particular physical process. One might almost say that there exists a real time, not beyond the phenomena but nevertheless beyond the particular phenomenon selected for measuring it.

It is not a time introduced by convention and maintained in use solely out of respect for its conventions. It is an objective time whose objectivity is constituted and confirmed progressively by the agreement among the methods used for measuring it.

Operational Idealism and Realism

We may thus contrast with each other two concepts of operationality; one emphasizes the liberty of selecting rules and of choosing conventions, while the other stresses that which cannot be the domain of the individual, that which exceeds and limits his liberty of action and cannot be the result of his initiative alone. In order to point out this contrast one is tempted to speak of operational idealism in the first case and of operational realism in the second. Naturally it is the second which is most important, as soon as we depart from the simplicity of the elementary timepieces. This is obviously the case in the complex situation which we have described, where astronomical observations are integrated into a general analysis of precision. As we have already noted, it is this collaboration, and in particular the fact that it is successful, which confers an operational character on the time which is read from the position of the stars. In fact there is no operationality peculiar to this time, with a different operationality valid only for the time of the clocks. For all the timepieces whose pace is connected more or less closely with the sidereal day, there is only one operational approach, that which aims at a common measure from which a special measure would differ only by its lack of precision.*

It is finally time to recall that the apparent motion of the celestial sphere is not absolutely regular. How could we be aware of this in the operational context which we are developing at this moment? It is clear, above all, that the rôle which we have conferred on it (the rôle of guide in our search for precision) is valid only insofar as its regularity remains superior to that of the timepieces which are compared to it. This rôle will terminate as soon as we are assured of being able to manufacture timepieces which run as regularly as the celestial sphere.

Actually it is not absurd to form the hypothesis that the constant progress in the manufacture of timepieces makes them comparable, if not superior, to the sidereal timepiece. Shall we then have reached the limit of specification of operational time? Not yet, but we must invoke a new concept, a new principle permitting us to extract from a general confrontation, at least provisionally, new means of appreciation and a new line of conduct. For this purpose we might resort to probability theory and mathematical statistics. But could we then avoid the mixed method which we intended not to apply? In any case the idea of the operational would have to be modified again and depart still further from its original simplicity. For the moment we shall pause here.

RETURN TO THE TEMPORAL INTERVAL
BETWEEN TWO EVENTS

The investigation of the techniques and procedures which one actually knows how to use to measure a temporal interval is not

---

* The terms in which we are discussing this common measure naturally correspond to the ideal of classical physics. But we do not assume that this ideal could be completely realized. It should be noted that we have described it in the conditional mood. All the questions touched upon here will appear in a different light in relativistic physics and, above all, in quantum mechanics.

completed. We interrupt it at this point but shall take it up again later. The utilization, in the laboratories of time, of the pendulum clocks and the high precision chronometers, controlled by the observation of the apparent motion of the celestial vault, remains below a certain level of precision which our exposé still has to attain. We must therefore return to the study of measured time after the sections which now shall be devoted to intuitive time.

Failure of Pure Operationality

But why do we mark a stop at this point? At the end of the preceding section we have stated that we would not further pursue our attempt to isolate from the actual procedures of measuring time a well-defined operational time. It should be well understood that this was not an arbitrary decision. It was imposed on us by the results of our analysis. The very idea of the operational becomes blurred as the techniques gain in precision. But if this is so, can our progress towards higher accuracy be continued? Must the intention to aim at a "purely operational definition" of time not remain our guideline? The moment has come to show that this is not true. So far we have conducted our study "as if" the search for precision in the measuring of time had to be interpreted as the search for a better "operational definition." In spite of increasing difficulties, we have tried to preserve the hypothesis according to which the practitioner's activity must necessarily be informed, even if he is not conscious of it, by a methodology of measurement, which in turn would be dominated entirely by the tendency towards operationality. It must now be admitted that this hypothesis cannot be retained, that such a methodology of measurement does not suggest itself, and that actual practice is hardly informed by it but derives from an entirely different methodology. The practitioner, as we noted in commenting on the *Treatise on Watchmaking*, applies a mixed method which constantly combines the rational and the operational, the theory and the experiment. It creates from them an active synthesis reminiscent of the discursive syntheses which we have already mentioned, and which give to language its flexibility and effectiveness.

It is precisely in the perspective of this synthetical method-ology that we shall consider the very accurate measuring pro-cedures which were recently perfected by astronomy and modern physics. The time which the practitioner today is able to determine with the highest degree of accuracy is a synthe-tical time, a time for whose definition the tendency towards operationality must be combined with the time of mathematics on the one hand and with intuitional time on the other. While the analysis of the mathematician's time has already been made, the analysis of intuitional time still remains to be done. In order to introduce the third of the great variants of time which the procedures of synthesis employ, our exposé thus must digress at this point.

But before we proceed towards a more thorough study of intuitive time we must once again direct our attention towards a point which has not been sufficiently clarified: the characteri-zation and fixation of a precise instant. This point, as we shall see, is of the greatest importance for the determination (and even conception) of the temporal interval between two events.

The Concept of the Event

One might be somewhat surprised in realizing the difficulties encountered in the attempt to define, in general terms, a pre-cise event and to determine a certain event in particular. It is known in what unexpected peripeties modern physics has in-volved the notion of the object, a notion which seems completely secure at the level of common sense but which becomes utterly problematic at the level of atom and quantum physics. The same is true for the idea of the event, which does not seem to present any problem at the level of common sense. But difficulties arise as soon as the event must be designated and defined with some accuracy.

Integration of the Event into the Unfolding of Time

Certain difficulties already emerge when I propose to de-scribe and to place, for the benefit of another person, a certain event which occurred within my own temporal perspective. For

myself, an event E inserts itself into the unreeling film of instants which I have lived. How does it take its place there, how
is it recognized, and how does it acquire its individuality and
its reality? These are so many questions which we can only
answer in tentative outline, giving summary and open answers
(comparable to the outline-ideas) subject to the corrections and
revisions suggested by a specifying experiment.

What we can affirm already at this point, on the strength of
everything that has been said so far, taking into account, in
particular, the multiple aspects of the notion of time in current
language, is that the events do not find in our consciousness an
autonomous and regular unfolding of time upon which they
could simply inscribe themselves (for us) in a superimposition.
We certainly are able to evaluate temporal intervals without the
benefit of any instrument, to feel and to compare their durations,
consciously to note their sequence and commit it to our memory.
But everything must lead us to believe that if the unfolding of
time which we observe did not remain as it were hooked
to the unfolding of certain exterior facts and to the exercise of
our activities, it would give us a rather inconsistent referential
of time. In order to be inscribed on a film which is my own, the
events must also be acknowledged by a tribunal which likewise
is my own, and they must be reconstituted from their sensorial
symptoms. In particular where events are concerned which must
mark for me the unfolding of my own time, each must appear to
me in its singularity and also as a moment of a consistent and
coherent phenomenal evolution. (The situation is hardly less
complicated if the event is limited to the perception of a simple
sensorial symptom which must be integrated as such into a
temporal perspective.)

Our intention is not to clarify the situation by a phenomenological explanation directed towards ourselves and the scene
of our consciousness. As far as the problem of time is concerned,
this would mean to return to zero and to start the discussion in
a direction where it cannot succeed. The phenomenological explanation represents only a moment of a synthetic explanation
in which we are precisely making an effort to progress. Accordingly we have no aim at the moment besides pointing out the

difficulties facing two interlocutors trying to describe to each other the same event and the same moments.

At the level of common sense their agreement is made possible by their mutual participation in an identical "milieu of events." This milieu assures them of a certain communion of points of reference. Their respective films thus are brought into agreement. In the framework of daily activities this natural agreement is not without effectiveness. But it can only be of limited accuracy, for the following three reasons:

1. Each of the two partners has merely a summary knowledge of the event, i.e. an outline-representation.

2. In the temporal perspective (in the film) of each, the place and the moment of the event are fixated only approximately.

3. Neither of the two is in possession of the means (discursive or otherwise) for designing, either for his partner or for himself, a well-specified event or a well-defined instant.

One might wonder how, under these conditions, the two partners could synchronize their actions to the point of obtaining a rather high degree of effectiveness. But one will not be surprised that in order to attain a solidarity of action of wider scope and more stringent coordination, one must resort to techniques capable of guaranteeing, in a fashion more stable and more precise, the signification of the event and also the measurement of time.

Simultaneousness

The preceding remarks are applicable not only at the level of common sense, but also clarify some of the practical difficulties encountered by the simple verification of simultaneities and consequently the determination of the temporal interval which separates two events.

The first of these difficulties relates to the specification of the events whose simultaneousness one wishes to observe. Let us suppose that two events, A and B, are concerned. Neither one of them is represented as a brute fact intervening suddenly and abruptly in an instant likewise determined in the most accurate manner. Both A and B present themselves, each in its own right, as moments to be grasped in contexts which in some cases must still be specified.

Assume, for example, that *A* is the passage of a star at the meridian of a certain observer, and that *B* is the indication of the corresponding moment by an observation clock. *A* is situated in a naturally specified "astronomical context": the apparent motion of the celestial sphere. All the same, it is necessary, depending on the case, to establish certain distinctions and to specify, for example, that the star to be observed must be a fixed star, some particular fixed star. The expression "passage of a star at the meridian" assumes an exact meaning only through the fact that it can be integrated into the well-organized and multilaterally assured discourse of the astronomer. It is through the intermediary of this discourse that the event *A* may be individually designated. It must be emphasized that this discursive determination of the event *A* becomes effective only in the framework of a certain ensemble of notions which themselves have been coherently formulated.

Of course the designation of the event *A* is only one aspect (the aspect of formulation) of our approach. We must still realize the operational aspect. We must imagine and set up, for this purpose, an entire observation apparatus for the technical details which will not be discussed here. For the event *B* the situation is both analogous and different. This event is likewise inscribed in a context, namely the functioning of the clock. This "watchmaker's context" is not naturally given but is an artificial construction by the watchmaker. Every effort by the latter tends to assure its stability while at the same time it fixates the sequence of instants as distinctly as possible. The watchmaking technique adapts to the level of common sense and of current language the discursive designation of an accurately defined moment of the watchmaking context. The fact that we believe we understand, without any effort, the sense of the words "21 hours, 33 minutes, 55 seconds," must nevertheless not give us illusions about the complexity of the techniques which guarantee it.

Each of the two events, *A* and *B*, may thus be grasped within the context to which it belongs. But in order to state a simultaneity, we cannot stop here. It is still necessary to establish a certain agreement between the two contexts. The latter accordingly should be placed in the same integrating context, where the confrontation of the two may take place in a fashion as immediate as possible.

It is thus evident that our practical observation of a simultaneity is affected by (at least) three factors of error and indetermination:

1. The events *A* and *B* are grasped only with a certain indetermination in their own contexts, which in turn are defined only approximately.

2. Principally the same is true of their insertion into the integrating context.

3. The expression "a confrontation . . . as immediate as possible" must not obscure the problem that the practical realization of this confrontation cannot fail to present.

There was a time when, for the events *A* and *B* which have been discussed, the integrating context was provided by the observer's own film. The observer likewise realized, by directly hearing and seeing, their immediate confrontation. The precision of observation did not then exceed a tenth of a second.

The techniques of electronic recording today have permitted to reduce to the point of insignificance the factors of errors 2 and 3.

The factor 1, however, remains and cannot be progressively reduced except by the application of appropriate techniques permitting us to grasp, in particular, the events entering into an observation.

In order to demonstrate the full importance of this last remark, let us assume that a context *B*, very finely structured (the watchmaker's context of a quartz clock, for example), could be projected, in a truly immediate way, onto the context *A*. One may think that this must suffice for structuring *A* with an equal degree of fineness. But this is not the case. If it should happen that for reasons impossible to avoid, an event of this context could not be fixated with an accuracy greater than a three-hundredth of a second, for example, it would be unimportant that the event of the context *B* could be fixated to a millionth or a hundred-millionth of a second; even in a frame of reference of such accuracy the event *A* could only retain unchanged its margin of indetermination.

This is precisely one of the most embarrassing obstacles encountered in astronomical observation. The motion of the atmosphere constantly causes unpredictable variations in the direction in which the rays from the stars observed reach the instruments of observation. This explains why the observation of an event isolated from the astronomical context can hardly be made today with an accuracy greater than a three-hundredth of a second.

These statements naturally apply also to the determination of the temporal interval separating two events, each of which is given with its proper margin of precision.

The statements do not apply, however, in the same fashion to the determination of the duration of a phenomenon defined in a context, whose exact place in this context does not have to be determined. We shall have occasion to return to this problem in our discussion of the time of the ephemerides.

One last principal remark: An investigation of the difficulties facing the practical statement of a simultaneity contributes no confirmation to the methodologies which give a prominent place to the idea of the "pure statement of fact." It may happen, in fact, that the observation of a simultaneity takes its preciseness only from the combination of technical devices which make of this observation something entirely different from a "pure and simple statement of fact."

Chapter Six

INTUITIVE TIME

INTRODUCTION

As a complement to the two great variants of the notion of time which we have sought to define and to specify, we shall now try to describe a third, namely *intuitive time*. Is this the first time that we are mentioning it? We have on the contrary made frequent references to it during our analysis of mathematical time as well as in our discussion of measured time. We have deliberately kept it in the background, however; the moment has now come to explain it more fully.

After having shown in the abstract the structure of mathematical time we already noted that this structure represents at the same time a gain and a loss relative to consciential time, whose unfolding is a datum of consciousness (later taken hold of by the imagination). The gain is that mathematical time ensures and defines the time of the imagination, providing its coherence and defining its structure. The loss, as we have already emphasized, is that time thus "purified" lacks a certain element of representation, a certain "form" which time has for us when it is the time of our own existence.

On the other hand, while analyzing the variants which current language includes and knows how to employ, invoking more or less distinctly one or the other, we had noted that in one of its variants time presents itself as a duration, felt subjectively as a consciously lived duration; whereas in another variant it designates the time which an event needs for its completion, independent of us and of the knowledge we may have of it; while a third evokes the time of the imagination, the time of which the imagination can unreel a century in some minutes or even seconds.

Intuitive Time, a Form of Arbitration

The intuitive time which we shall now discuss does not completely coincide with any one of the variants which our analysis has attempted to distinguish and to separate from each other as clearly as possible. It must be considered a synthetical time at the level of common sense, a time of arbitration between the variants mentioned before for the purposes of effective activities such as our daily activities. It must be interpretable as a time felt in its accurate duration which our conscious attributes, according to its emotive climate, to a particular event. It also has an aspect of objectivity, but this is not yet the objectivity which could be conferred on it through the intermediary of measure; it is merely what an attentive consciousness allows "to be really present in the world." Finally, it may also be taken up by the imagination, but the latter does not use its liberty to deploy it in a representation capable of being lengthened or shortened; it confers on it its idoneous form, in which it can be connected with the other forms of the world in us, with the other representations which we know how to appropriate as "realities of the world."

In short, intuitive time is the result of an arbitration which seems to take place somewhere in the middle between the authority of sentiment, the liberty of imagination, and the objectivity of perception, for the purposes of effective action.*

Relations with Mathematical Time

Mathematical time, as we have defined it, reduced to its ordering structure, to some extent has thus disengaged itself from the intuitive form which we have discussed. Let us recall our remark concerning this subject: If we had thought it appropriate we could have based the temporal order axiomatically on a less abstract plane, without giving up the *sui generis* form it assumes in the intuitive representation which we make of it. Two entirely analogous procedures are available to us in geometry. We may, if we wish, define axiomatically a linear order on a straight line, without giving up the element of form which is inseparable from any straight line in our intuitive representation of space. But we also may abandon, at least in part, this

* Cf. J.-P. Gonseth: *Théâtre de veille et théâtre de songe.* Neuchâtel, Editions du Griffon, 1950.

intuitive aspect and define a variable x on a straight line, retaining only the latter's structural order, exactly as we have done in the case of the temporal variant t.

Geometrical Analogy

It is moreover this strict analogy on which the possibility is based to represent the uniform course of time through the uniform progress of a point on a line. One must not, however, exaggerate the scope of this geometrical analogy. At the level where this spatialization of time is acknowledged by our consciousness it is merely a scientific artifice. At the level of intuitive representations the temporal and linear orders each have a specificity of their own which does not permit us to consider them identical. What rôle has intuitive time played in the study of the measurement of time, in the specification of measured time? Its rôle is absolutely fundamental. It is precisely to emphasize this that we have spent so much time on the study of the most elementary measuring devices such as water clocks, for example. We repeatedly had to acknowledge that a person intending to manufacture and to use these devices has no guarantees of their accuracy and effectiveness except certain of his own natural representations. This is how, for example, the uniformity of the discharge of water which flows out of the water clock guarantees the uniformity of the flow of time. We had to resort to a series of representations of this type in order to give a certain autonomy to the idea of an operational time. All these representations in turn are linked to the representation of the uniform flow of time. In short, in this as in many other respects, intuitive time includes everything which is being thought, said, and done by the person intending to establish a measurement of time.

We have mentioned the strict analogy which permits us to represent the variable t through a coordinate x carried on a straight line.

Provided that we do not gloss over certain differences it may be useful to deepen this analogy. As soon as we decide to go beyond the knowledge of space expressed in current language and illustrated in our daily activities, it is again in the form of three principal variants that this knowledge is defined. Geometry, a deductive discipline, confers on it its mathematical aspect, the measuring procedures involve it in its experimental aspect, and the natural idea every human being has of space assures it of its intuitive character. We cannot show here how these three aspects can be at the same time distinguished from each other so as not to be confused again and nevertheless remain connected with each other, associated in a synthesis which research re-creates each time it becomes "spatialized." Even while tending to depart from the intuitive vision of dimension, the geometrical approach is based on it and retains its hold on it. Even while tending to achieve its operational autonomy, it is in our natural representations that the intention to measure finds its first guidance and its first guarantees. As in the case of time, the intuitive variant of space continues to include and to sustain its rational and operational variants, even though the latter break away and depart from it.

The Lack of a "Temporal Organ"

As we can see, the analogy may be carried too far. On the other hand, there is one aspect in which it fails almost completely. Our eyesight, our sense of touch (and even our hearing) concur to form in us the representation of space, a place for things and a milieu for beings, a space in which our activity can unfold. Certainly there also exists, for us, a lived aspect of distance, as in walking or running, for example; also, there certainly is a lived component in the mass of the stone which we throw into the lake. We are, on the other hand, capable of walking again, mentally, a certain path we have walked ten days or ten years ago. It is possible for us to sketch in our imagination a figure which we had drawn more or less carefully. We even are capable of creating, in our "inner space," forms never seen before which we perhaps try to realize. The capacity of our inner perspective to remain in agreement with its "exterior signification," however, is preponderant. The batting of an eye is enough to renew and set up in us the image-space of the world, an image whose function it is to be as adequate as possible. In short, as long as the geometrizing activity does not take hold of the aspects of spatiality (within ourselves), the intuitive aspect remains the predominant one. This aspect, to repeat it again, is characterized, as we have already seen in the case of the intuitive aspect of time, by a certain way of being univocally representative of an "exterior space"; this is a form of the world in us. The imagination knows how to use it more freely, to make it pliable, and to relieve it of a certain weight of reality in order to bend it to its own laws. The "approach of reality"—essential moment of the intuitive aspect—nevertheless, at least so it seems to us, is never completely absent.

From this angle, the difference between time and space, forms in us and for us of temporality and spatiality, thus depends on the following fact: The representation we have of space tallies with "qualified" sensorial organs. The importance of sight in the disposition of our mental structure is emphasized by the importance of the site in the brain allocated to the extension and ramifications of the optical nerves. But we do not know any specialized organ on which our representation of time may be based. One might, of course, form the hypothesis that this representation results from a reconsideration of certain characteristics of temporality, inscribed in the impressions collected by the specialized sensory organs, auditory impressions in particular, as well as from a reconsideration of certain rhythms of the human body. But this hypothesis does not penetrate beyond the surface of what has to be explained.

The lack of an organ qualified for the measuring of time presents a problem; it is to know we establish and maintain our "approach of reality" to which intuitive time gives a certain effectiveness. By stating the problem, however, we do not mean to question again our natural capacity to measure time with some precision. One could list numerous proofs for this capacity but we shall give only one example: One could ask of any normal person, not only that he should recognize a rhythm, but that he should observe it and coordinate his action with it. He is quite naturally able to clap, to play, to dance to the rhythm, and even to integrate his own cadence into a more complex one which is not his own. How could a rhythm be universally observed unless the duration of the intervals could be accurately appreciated by everyone? For example, the "regular singing" of hammers used by a group of road workers shows a faculty which we share with them to appraise and realize durations in an intersubjective accord. Every orchestra playing before a public gives multiple evidence of the same phenomenon. More generally, all actions concerted in time could serve as analogous illustrations.

The measurement of time of which we are capable by nature remains, however, rather inaccurate, especially when a duration of some length is concerned. One may thus be surprised that the intuitive representations accorded to it should have so much stability and could provide such sure guarantees for the manufacture of measuring instruments whose "estimate" will be more objective as well as more accurate than ours.

Contrary to what we have noted in the case of space, the objective moment of time in us is not explained neatly and clearly, as opposed to the subjective moment. For this reason it seems useful to us to investigate whether there exist other beings in which the element of objectivity is more clearly evident, beings of which one might say without too much exaggeration that they carry a clock in their system. We first recall that the bees actually are beings of this type. We shall later draw the conclusions from this fact.

TIME AND THE BEES

Above all others, the experiments by von Frisch and his collaborators have elucidated the faculty which the bees have of communicating to each other information of rather surprising accuracy concerning directions, distances, and durations of flight.*

The facts which we expect to utilize are rather closely connected and cannot be well understood except through the mutual support which they lend to each other. We shall first re-

---

* The following data are quoted from the work *Vie et moeurs des abeilles,* Paris, Albin Michel, 1955.

view briefly the facts relating to the structure of the eye and the vision of the bees on the one hand and those relating to their "language" on the other.

The Vision of the Bees

The eye of the bee, like that of the other insects, contains neither pupil, nor iris, nor a genuine crystalline lens. It is true that the bee's retina is comparable to the human one, but the images on it are generated in an entirely different way. The strongly convex eyes are located on the sides of the head. By examining their surface with the help of a powerful magnifying glass, one realizes that an eye consists of an immense number (several thousand) of facets; hence the term "facet eye" used to describe that organ. The exterior aspect of the eye already reveals its curious internal structure. But the latter can be shown clearly only in a section, preferably a symmetrical section, of the eye. The facets themselves consist of chitin, as does the entire armor covering the body of the insect. This covering corresponds to the cornea of the human eye. Each of these particles of cornea tops a conical cavity filled with a crystal-clear liquid. This is the crystal cone, which has the function of bending the light rays towards the tip of the cone, where a retinal rod is located. The ensemble of these rods constitute the retina. The facet, the small conical tube, and the retinal rod belonging to it form what is called an ommatidium. The eye of the bee consists of several thousand cones of this type pressed together, adjacent cones always slightly inclined against each other so that no two cones are exactly parallel. All converge towards the optical nerve, whose function is to transmit the multiple impressions it receives to the central nervous system, which has the task of combining them and integrating them into images. The wall of every ommatidium consists of a black, opaque membrane which absorbs the light.

Let us now assume that a luminous spot is located somewhere in the field of vision. Consider all the light rays which strike the different facets of the eye. The only ones to reach the retinal rod are the rays striking the ommatidium whose axis points towards the source of light. Those rays which enter at a more or less oblique angle in all the rest of the ommatidia, strike the black membrane and consequently are absorbed without reaching the retina.

The retinal rod has a very special structure. Examined under a powerful magnifying lens, a section shows that the rod consists of a group of eight sensory cells whose arrangement resembles that of a flower or a star. Experiments have shown that each of these cells has the function, as far as the light is concerned, of an analyzer of polarization.

Starting from this fact, von Frisch has constructed an artificial ommatidium which is analogous to that of the bee and permits to elucidate some fundamental characteristics of the bee's vision. This is the principle: From a sheet of polaroid material* we cut out some isosceles triangles whose base should be parallel to the vibration plane of the light capable of penetrating it. Let us arrange eight of these triangles in the shape of a star. The eight triangles thus arranged form the artificial ommatidium.

If we look through this "eye" at an area emitting natural light (i.e. light in which no vibration plane is favored), all the triangles will be equally transparent and will appear equally luminous to us. We therefore do not notice that they have polarized the light and thus we do not receive any indication on the composition of the light emitted. But if the area which we are investigating emits polarized light, the triangles in their totality will give a fully contrasted image in which the intensity of the light in each sector depends on the position it occupies relative to the vibration plane of the penetrating light.

An ommatidium cannot catch any except perceptibly parallel rays. The eye of the bee as a whole thus represents a se-

---

* Polaroid sheets are made of a transparent synthetic resin whose body is filled with minute herapathite (quinine iodo-sulphate) crystals having all their axes parallel to each other. One obtains such a sheet by putting the mass, at the moment of solidification, on a stretching rack or under the influence of an electric or magnetic field. With reference to the light the sheet behaves like a single crystal, but its dimensions are practically unlimited. (From the *Grand Larousse encyclopédique.*)

ries of analyzers of polarization, each of which responds only to a very limited "visual field." The full significance of this structure becomes clear if one considers the following fact: If the sun is the primary source of all the rays of light which an eye can accommodate, through the diffusion in the atmosphere, each patch of blue in the sky represents a secondary source of light. An essential fact is that these secondary sources emit polarized light. For each of these sources the state of the polarization of the light emitted moreover depends on the hour of the day, i.e. on the position of the sun. We may conclude that for the bee, a sky which to us appears more or less uniformly blue must produce highly differentiated impressions, each "ommatid" sector being able to assume a different aspect at any time of the day.

At first sight the above remarks have nothing to do with the measurement of time. They are, however, indispensable for the understanding of the experiments which demonstrate the bee's natural ability to evaluate durations.

The Language of the Bees

Following now are some explanations concerning the "language" of the bees. It is not a spoken language but rather a "danced" one, whose basic elements are the *roundelays* and the *wiggling dances.*

When a bee has discovered a good place for gathering honey it makes this known at the beehive by a very characteristic behavior. If the spot is at a distance of only 50 to 100 yards at the most, the bee draws attention to itself by circling around on a honeycomb; it describes, several times in a row and with some agitation, a circle whose diameter does not exceed twice or three times the length of its own body. Soon it is followed in this motion by a number of other bees. The latter then depart in search of the location thus reported. For our own purpose the dances, however, are only of minor interest.

If the place to be signalized is more than 50 or 100 yards away from the beehive, the roundelay is replaced by the wiggling dance. In this case the bee first describes a half-circle of rather small diameter and then, wheeling around, it returns on the diameter in a straight line to its point of departure. From there it describes the other half-circle and returns to its starting point on the same diameter and in the same direction as the first time, and so forth. The wiggling dance differs from the roundelay in the characteristic detail that during the rectilinear trajectory the end of the bee's abdomen is agitated by rapid vibrations.

By means of this dance the bee is able to inform the other bees which will follow it of the direction and the distance of the place to be visited, as well as the importance of the harvest.

Various and repeated experiments have established beyond any doubt that the direction of the flight to be taken is determined by the direction of the rectilinear path, the diameter which the bee travels several times in a row during its dance. In order to effect this "communication" the bee employs two quite distinct methods, depending on whether it executes its dance on a honeycomb placed vertically in the hive, which is the more frequent type, or on a horizontal surface, for example, the take-off board. Let us begin with the second case, which is easier to understand. First we must take into account the rôle of compass which the sun plays for the bee; this rôle is favored by the structure of its eye and has been demonstrated in numerous experiments. If, for example, the bee returning to the hive has the sun to its left side, at an angle of 45° to its line of flight, the same angle relative to the direction of the sun will be shown by the rectilinear course of its dance. The direction of flight thus appears to be well determined at take-off. This procedure, however, is effective only when the bee and its followers can see the sun or at least a patch of blue sky (which likewise may serve as a reference because of the characteristic image guaranteed by the polarizing analysis of the ommatidia).

But if the bees dance inside the hive they must indicate the direction of the loot in a different fashion. Dancing on the vertical surface of a honeycomb, they use the following "code": If the rectilinear trajectory of the dance is directed towards the top, this means that the direction of the take-off is the direction of the sun. Oriented towards the bottom, the same course indicates the opposite direction. An angle of 45° with the perpendicular at left towards the top, for example, sends the bees in a direction of 45° to the left relative to the line of sight of the sun. There is no doubt that the bees following the dancer are able to take note of this communication, even in the semidarkness of the hive, and to interpret it with surprising accuracy.

In a different context this ability to turn up, to note, and to transmit information about the angles formed by certain directions of flight and of aim, would certainly deserve comment. For us it is a basically analogous ability related to durations of time which will be the object of discussion.

But,* if the bees would depart in search of the announced crop without knowing the distance (except whether it is above or below the 50- to 100-yard mark in the direction indicated), the search might be in vain. In fact, the bees *proceed in all directions* as far as several kilometers from the hive. By progressively withdrawing the food available to the bees to the limits of their field of action, a correlation has been shown between the distance that has to be covered and the fashion in which the wiggling dance is executed. This correlation seems to provide the bees and even the human observers with relatively accurate information about the distance to be covered. For a distance of 100 yards the dance is rapid and the turns follow each other in quick succession. The greater the distance, the more measured the dances become; the turns follow each other more slowly and the rectilinear course becomes slower and more pronounced. Checking with a watch one observes that if the announced spot is situated at a distance of 100 yards from the hive, the announcing bee traverses the rectilinear part of its route 9 to 10 times per 15 seconds. For 500 yards this factor drops to 6 times, for 1000 yards to 4 or 5 times, for 5000 yards to 2 times, and for 10,000 yards to barely 1. The same rhythm is invariably observed throughout entire days, months, and even years. It is the same from one colony to the next. This is the more remarkable as the bees do not possess any differentiated organs which could serve as a timepiece to

* Frisch, *op. cit.,* p. 149.

them. But obviously their perception of time is accurate enough for the dancer to move in the required rhythm and for the spectators to recognize this rhythm and interpret it as a real duration.

Observations made during windy weather give some interesting clues about the fashion in which the bees evaluate distances. When the course described must be flown against the wind they indicate (according to the code mentioned above) a greater distance than they would if the air were calm. If the bees must fly with the wind they indicate a shorter course. In calm weather the distance indicated is increased or decreased according to whether the flight will be upwards or downwards. It is thus evident that the distances are evaluated in terms of the durations of flights. Are the latter measured, in turn, by corresponding expenditures of energy? One may form this hypothesis but it would not explain the faculty, of which the bees also give other proofs, of measuring time without any special expenditure of energy. We shall return to this problem shortly.

What seems to us particularly striking, in the observations discussed above, is not that the bees are capable of evaluating durations with considerable objectivity. If they were totally incapable of doing so they would be equally incapable of inserting their activity into the flow of "exterior" events, especially into the daily rhythm. This remark is valid for all creatures whose lives are linked to well-defined activities, including man. What appears to us especially remarkable is that the evaluation of durations can be expressed and recognized with the help of something which, in comparison with our own activities, we shall define as a figuration or even a notation. It is therefore perfectly justified to speak of language in this context. The impressions received through the eyes, combined with the impressions received through the other senses and integrated with them by the central nervous system, must be translated into a certain mode of expression in order to be "announced." This announcement must then be received, understood, and reinterpreted as far as the "sensorial data." All the elements of the process which in the human by analogy would be called awareness and expressive elaboration seem to be present. This is precisely what makes these observations, which we report very succinctly, valuable for us. The complementary information which follows will confirm this.

Orientation Necessitates an Internal Timepiece

As we have noted, following von Frisch and his collaborators, the sun (or any patch of blue sky) may serve as a compass to the bee. This statement immediately raises a problem. The sun does not remain stationary throughout the day, and the "map of the sky" consequently must vary in the representation which, on the basis of its polarized vision, the bee must form of it. Is the bee able to take this factor into account? If this were not the case, the references furnished by the sun or by the characteristic aspect of some point on the "map of the sky" could not have any permanent value. Effective only temporarily, they could soon become deceptive. For a human observer, is this eventuality more probable than the opposite? Is he able to form a preliminary judgment, or should he not rather abandon the attempt, in order to investigate by which experiments it will be possible for him to arrive at a well-founded opinion?

One may attack this question from either end; one may ask what supplementary abilities the bee must have so that the reference points retain for it a permanent validity, i.e. so that they determine an invariable orientation, in spite of the incessant variation to which the reference points are subject. As far as the sun is concerned, the bee must be able to take into account, throughout the hours, the distance which it travels on its apparent trajectory between sunrise and sunset, and must be able again to evaluate as a function of time the variation of the angle which its direction forms with the direction of the flight, which must remain constant. As concerns the reference provided by a patch of blue sky, one should also consider some change of aspect at different hours of the day. Must we not hesitate to assume the bee to be endowed with a sensorial and mental organization of such complexity, so different from our own, which accordingly would strike us almost as a miracle of nature?

Viewed from the other end, the situation may be evaluated in an entirely different way. Systematic observation has enabled man to share, more or less deeply, the knowledge of the sensorial organization of certain animals and its irreplaceable function in the integration of the animal into its milieu. This knowledge often enables the observer to imagine means to surprise and to deceive the animal observed. It must be noted, however, that one rule seems to govern the organization of all living creatures, the rule that all activities deployed in the fight for distances form a coordinated whole. We do not intend to discuss here the why and the how of this rule. It is difficult, however, to disregard it completely. This rule hardly permits us to think that the visual function of the bee could be adapted so remarkably well to the determination of a direction of flight, without compensating functionally for the error which this determination would entail for flights to distant points, by no means an exception in the activity of the bees. From this point of view one should not be surprised that the differentiated aspect of the map of the sky is being inserted through its diurnal variations into the unreeling temporal scale which the bee is carrying within itself.

The Experiments

At any rate, the experiment alone can give us some certainty. As far as we are concerned the experiments made by von Frisch and his associates may be divided into three groups:

1. Those which confirm beyond any doubt the rôle of compass played by the sun or a patch of blue sky in the instantaneous determination of a direction of flight.

2. Those which illustrate the ability of the bees to take into account the progress of time and the variation of the points of reference to determine an invariable direction.

3. Those which establish the existence of a sense of time, a sense which is not limited to the "reading" of the hour on the map of the sky, as one might read it on the dial of a clock.

From the first category we shall mention only the following example which to us seems particularly instructive:

At night the bees remain in the hive, but by day they are better able to find their way than a pilot. We already know that their eyes perceive polarized light and even perceive the direction in which this light is oscillating. By using artificial ommatidia in the fashion of eyeglasses it is possible to understand that the variation of the plane of polarization may be translated, in the vision of the bee, into immediately perceptible differences. Let us recall that the blue sky emits polarized light whose intensity and direction depend on the position of the sun and are, for a given position of the latter, characteristic for the portion of the sky under consideration. One may easily verify this with the help of Polaroid material cut in the shape of a star, mounted in such a way that it can swivel in all directions. By orienting it towards the different portions of the sky one observes a particular image for each of them. (It is the total of these particular figures which we have called the map of the sky.) One may thus verify that the bee in its flight is not limited to the guidance provided by the very small part of its eye directly facing the sun, but that it registers at the same time, through thousands of ommatidia, all the particular images which correspond to the different regions of the sky and whose aspect must change with the position of the sun. Through the total of these visual elements, it is the shape of the entire celestial vault (i.e. the whole map) which the bee sees at each moment and in which it is, so to speak, optically anchored. The most insignificant deviation from the adopted direction is registered a thousand times. It is thus again clear that the bee can find its direction with the aid of a mere patch of blue sky.

This means of navigation is not available in cloudy weather, since the clouds do not emit polarized light. For our own purposes it is unnecessary to explain how the bee can compensate for this deficiency.

Influence of Polarization

We shall now describe the experimental proof for what has been explained.

Assume that, in a beehive under observation, vision would be possible only through a glass pane and only from one side, from the north, for example. Then assume that the glass pane be covered by a board into which a small square opening has been cut. The bees dancing in the hive thus do not receive any except almost parallel rays which are perceptibly polarized in the same way. (The polarization may not be total but the plane of polarization is determined.)

We now place in front of the window a polaroid sheet in the form of a disc, mounted in such a way as to be able to swivel around itself. In each of its positions this disc superimposes on the light penetrating it a well-defined plane of polarization. It is therefore sufficient to turn it to modify the plane of polarization. Now we may make the following observation: The disc can be brought into a position where it does not modify the plane of polarization of the light penetrating it. In this case the dance of the bees is not affected. But if the disc is turned the bees immediately change the orientation of the rectilinear course of their dance and thus indicate a false direction.

This experiment may be further specified. A group of bees "loots" the sugared water from a cup placed at a distance of a few hundred yards from the hive, exactly to the west. The hive is located so that the dancers can see a patch of blue sky in the direction of their loot. The rectilinear course of their dance points westward. We now arrange the polaroid disc in such a way that the light rays coming from the west keep their same plane of vibration: The dance of the bees is not changed. One may say that the aspect of the sky which regulates their dance has not varied. By looking at this part of the sky ourselves, through the artificial ommatidium formed by a star of Polaroid material, we can perceive and determine for ourselves, if not the image seen by the bee (which we could hardly know), at least a corresponding image *I*. This image for us corresponds to the image which the bees have before them during the rectilinear course of their wiggling dance, and which they will also have before them while flying towards their loot.

We now turn the disc 30° in the inverse sense of the hands of a watch. The orientation of the rectilinear course of the dance is immediately corrected and the bees indicate a direction which forms an angle of 34° to the southwest relative to the former direction. This angle may be explained as follows: We will ourselves intercept, through an artificial ommatidium, the rays which the bee now sees in the west. We do not find our image *I* there any longer but a different image *I'*. The decisive fact is this: If we examine the sky again, still through the artificial ommatidium but this time without the intervention of the polarizing disc, we find there the image *I'* in a specific direction, precisely at 34° towards the north.

The bee thus has seen, while it was flying towards its loot, the image *I* ahead of it and the image *I'* at 34° to the right, towards the north. We present to it now, in the direction of the west, an image *I'* modified by the corresponding Polaroid into one which would have—without Polaroid—a patch of sky situated at 34° towards the north. The bee interprets this patch of sky as being situated at 34° towards the north, and it indicates to its followers the direction in which they must see the image *I'* when they fly towards their loot, i.e. at 34° to the right. The bees are not mistaken but they are deceived. Once out of the hive and freed from the Polaroid they will fly in the right direction. But instead of flying in such a way as to have the image *I'*—coming from the western sky—before them, they will fly in such a way as to have the image *I'*—coming from a patch of sky situated at 34° to the north of the westerly direction—at 34° to the right.

This result proves not only that the bee orients itself according to the polarized light emitted by the blue sky, but also that it is capable of orienting itself with the help of a patch of sky other than that which it had taken as a reference point, that it has, as we noted before, a map of the polarized sky where it has marked its direction of flight, and that it is able to find this direction even if shown only some fragment of the map.

This experiment is of methodological interest because of the correspondence which the artificial ommatidium permits us to establish between the human vision and the vision of the bee, a correspondence which could only be demonstrated by experiment.

Modification According to the Hour of the Day

Let us now describe an experiment of the second category, which demonstrates the faculty of the bee to keep track of the diurnal variation of *its* map of the sky.

A group of bees (marked in a way to make them recognizable) has been busy all day emptying a cup filled with sugar water. The cup was placed on a small table situated at about 200 yards to the west of the hive. A few drops of perfume have been sprinkled on the table. Early the next morning, before the bees leave, the hive is closed and transferred over a distance of several miles to an entirely different area. At the four cardinal points at about 200 yards from the hive, four tables exactly like the first are installed with a similar cup of sugar water and a few drops of the same perfume sprinkled on the table. Near each table an observer is stationed who catches all the visiting bees so that no informer should spoil the experiment by signalizing with its dance the position of one of the tables. Despite the lack of topographical references, and although the takeoff hole had been turned in a different direction as a precaution, the great majority of the bees fly towards the western table. Thus they leave in the very direction in which they had returned the day before. We know that the sun and more generally the map of the sky serve them as a guide, but the sun has changed its position; it is now in the east, while the evening before it was in the west. The bees have taken this change of position into account and they have even evaluated it correctly. Could they have done so without a sense of time?

Purely Temporal Adjustment

The experiments of the third group consist above all in drilling the bees to come to draw at the same location (at a considerable distance from the hive) and at the same hours from a cup filled with sugar water. This drill undoubtedly is successful; the bees learn how to come to the exact spot at the favorable times and stay away at the unfavorable times.

An interesting detail is that the drill does not succeed if the division into favorable and unfavorable times within a day is not repeated in a rhythm of 24 hours or a submultiple thereof. It seems therefore as though the bee were in a position to consult a watch which periodically marks the hours from 1 to 24.

The question then arises whether the progress of this watch corresponds to the recording of an external phenomenon or to the unreeling of an internal process in the bee. The possibility of an external phenomenon seems rather remote; the hive may be carried into a completely closed place, lit by a strong electric lamp, where no light from the outside can penetrate; even under these very artificial conditions, where the bee is apparently shielded from external influences, the drill is still successful. If the lighting is not interrupted, the drill may even be extended into the hours of the night during which, in nature, the bees would stay in the hive.

In short, the experiments conducted on bees (shown here only in a few brief glimpses) seem to admit of only one interpretation; the bee must be able to confront the unreeling of its own time with the unreeling of a time objectivated by the regular progress of the sun. Everything takes place in such a way as if the bee were able to relate the indications of a timepiece it carries within itself to the indications given by the apparent rotation of the celestial vault. Moreover, for the bee to deploy all the activities upon which its existence is based, these two timepieces must be able to remain synchronized even during the hours when their direct connection is interrupted, as during the night, for example. It is precisely this connection between individual time and universal time which we wish to emphasize. The example of the bees is a specific illustration of it. The organ or device which we have called the watch, by which the bee "measures" its own time, remains obscure in nature. It is, however, hardly possible to doubt that it exists.

Conclusions

In what respect can the study of the bees' sense of time help us understand our own sense of time more clearly? How can it, in particular, help us better to grasp and to delimit the synthetical variant of our own time, which we call intuitive time?

There are some objections which one is immediately tempted to make against our intended analogy. It will be said, for example, that intuitive time, such as we have tried to explain it, is not simply a time inscribed in the different rhythms of our organism: in the normal rhythm of the heart, in the electric pulsations of the brain, etc. In order that these rhythms remain synchronized and we may speak of their normal frequency, it is necessary that our entire body, taken as a whole, to some extent should be comparable to a clock constructed with the deliberate purpose of realizing a regular rhythm. But intuitive time is not the time deeply and mysteriously lived by our organism, even if we do not pay attention to it. It is a time towards which our consciousness is open. We even must take note of it, as we have said, in the feeling for its just proportion with the time inherent in the evolving phenomena in which we do not participate at all or in such a slight degree that the fact escapes our attention. This taking note, this feeling which must accompany it, are they not distinctive characteristics of *our own* intuitive time? If this is so, if we are concerned with what goes on upon the stage of our consciousness, how should we establish the comparison? Do terms such as "taking note," "areas of consciousness," "consciential time" have any meaning if one speaks of the bee? How can we decide this?

But nothing obliges us to aim so far at the first stroke. It should suffice for us at first to state that certain characteristics of the bee's "temporal behavior" may well be compared to our own.

1. We may doubt, thinking of ourselves, that a living creature without a special organ for measuring durations could

possess a relatively well-developed "sense of time." The case of the bee teaches us that it is possible. We will now be less surprised that we can take note of time in its duration and of time in its flow. It is true that for our understanding of our own consciousness the bee can be of no help to us. But in this respect we are self-sufficient.

2. When the bee has left the hive in order to visit a relatively distant place which it has explored, when it has stayed there for some time and the moment has come for it to return, the sun meanwhile may have described an appreciable arc of its trajectory. We have noted that the bee nevertheless is able to use the sun as a reliable guide. It must therefore know how to evaluate the angle at which the direction of the sun rays has shifted (or, in more global terms, the variations which have occurred on the celestial map). Is the measuring of this variation the immediate result of perception, or is it rather something resembling an immediate perception itself? We know that the bee also measures durations without the intermediary of this perception. At any rate, in a more or less immediate fashion the bee's time is measured according to perceptions which are *not exclusively* temporal.

Are we doing anything different when we measure time by means of a uniform discharge or through the intermediary of a uniform rotation? It is true that, for us, as we have realized, the correlation is achieved through the intermediary of adequate representations. In order to translate into effective activity the connections which we establish between these representations, we must invent adequate instruments. The bee by nature carries within itself the instrument which it needs, or rather, the bee *is* that instrument. One might say that the bee knows nothing about being anything but this instrument, or, from a different viewpoint, about also being this instrument. We have no way of knowing. What we are driving at is that from a certain point of view the fact is unimportant. What is important is that with or without conscious perception, with or without intermediary representations, the bee's sense of time is anchored in the time of the universe. Why should the same not be true of our own sense of time, why should the connec-

tions which we establish between our representations not be
the mental forms of this rootedness?

3. When the bee has returned to the hive and dances to indicate the location of a favorable place, it translates the distance
to be covered (or the duration of flight) into other terms; for
a greater distance the dance is less rapid and the frequency
of the rectilinear courses is lower. Nothing prevents us from
expressing these relations in numerical terms. These numerical
values, as we have noted, are constant from one day to the
next and from one hive to another.

Are we doing anything different when we establish the temporal scale for an instrument? Again, one might say that the
bee has no conscious knowledge of what it is doing and that
for it the transposition is merely the equivalent of an instinc-
tive motion or a reflex, that here the abyss opens between
the "mental" activity of the bee and our own. But again we
have no way of knowing. The bee is able, as we have seen,
to make another translation which we would be willing to define as a symbolic representation if we were making it ourselves. But, for what we seek to understand and to explain,
this is not the problem. With or without conscious knowledge,
with or without intermediary representation, the bee realizes
what we believe we are entitled to call an operational measurement of time. We cannot do the same without instruments. In
a certain sense the qualifier *operational* is synonymous with
the qualifier *instrumental*. For the bee this operational activity is only a form of its natural activity. Is it, in this respect,
superior or inferior to us? One might say it is probably both.

4. But the bee does not dance for itself. What it announces
through its danced language is not intended for its own use.
The structure of its dance is a means of information. This information is addressed to the other bees and is intended to
catch their attention.

But are we doing anything different when we announce, in
words or in numbers, the result of a reading on a time scale?
One might say that for us the moment of the announcement is
clearly separated from the moment of perception, that we are
conscious of it, while the bee must be considered as a mere

translation machine. We could again observe that such an objection precisely bypasses the fact which seems relevant to us, namely that the activity of announcing in the case of the bee is directly anchored in its daily activity. The ability to announce thus assumes the aspect of a natural activity. Why should it be otherwise in the case of our own ability to announce, even if we are conscious of it?

To sum up, the investigation into the sense of time in bees, interpreted through our own temporal behavior, throws a rather vivid light on the synthetic variant of our own natural concept of time, which has been labeled intuitive time. This time is not merely a time lived in a purely personal cadence, nor is it the time with which the imagination plays in almost total liberty, nor even a time shaped by artificial representations, either conventional or accidental. The time lived, the time imagined, and the time figured have, so to speak, a common hinge to which they are linked. They have in common a certain approach to reality, a certain concern for effectiveness, a certain intention of accuracy, and a certain way of being; they share the time of one person, the time of others, and the time of the universe. Synthetic at the level of daily activity, this variant is that of *intuitive time*.

INTERMEDIATE METHODOLOGICAL COMMENTARY

Our study is not yet completed. We shall continue the discussion of the problem of measuring time through new modifications, namely the time of the ephemerides, the quartz clocks, and the atomic clocks. Is this really necessary? We have noted repeatedly that for us, the measurement of time is only one means among others (a means, it is true, which implies the most valid guarantees of objectivity) for progressing towards a vision at the same time clearer and more assured of the methods, and of the method of research. It has never been our intention to give a complete survey of all past and present instruments for measuring time, only out of concern that nothing should be overlooked. Does not the preceding material suffice for our purposes? Has the moment not come to draw from it the methodological conclusion?

Negative Aspect of the Results

This moment has not yet come. It is true that we consider certain results as already established, and we need not discuss them any longer. One is our failure to define an operational time, i.e. a time which would be reduced to certain procedures of measurement. After our repeated and fruitless efforts to establish such a definition, the operational doctrine seems to us condemned.

This statement of position only emphasizes one negative aspect of the results to which we have been led. It is not the only one that must be pointed out. It would likewise be incorrect to imagine that time could be reduced to its mathematical aspect or that according to the function which actually belongs to it, it could suffice to base time on the intuitive representations which refer to it, by eventually linking them to an activity which would remain at the level of pure common sense. There are in this three eventualities which must all be rejected, since each of them turns out to be notoriously inadequate.

But the situation not only implies a negative interpretation. One would commit a new error, albeit of another kind, by presenting it as the opposite of a resolutely positive interpretation. It presents itself in two forms.

Solidarity of the Three Aspects

By confirming that each of the three aspects which we have mentioned is inadequate to explain the fashion in which time participates in the construction of objective knowledge, we do not imply by any means that any of these aspects would be superfluous. What has become abundantly clear, on the contrary, is that they are all indispensable and that none may be completely obliterated in favor of the other two.

Are these aspects in constant correlation? Do we have to assume that whenever time participates in our activity as an ordinating element, the task is always divided in the same way among an intuitive (phenomenological) component, a mathematical component, and a technical component? We would be caught in a fresh error by assuming that there exists something like a whole to be statistically divided between these parties. None of these components is given as a complete entity. The technical component is in constant progress; the mathematical idealization which accompanies and sometimes precedes it is periodically revised, and even the intuitive representations evolve under the pressure of the experience into which they are drawn. The three aspects turn out to be solidarily the object of an effort of construction, invention, and analysis, which, without being able to separate them completely, nevertheless clarifies them and thereby successfully confirms their relative specificity.

In our exposé we have given prominence to this characteristic by putting in between a chapter on mathematical time and one on the time of organisms the first and most decisive part of our analysis of the principles and the devices upon which the measurement of time is based.

Dialectic Synthesis

But we would be far from having exhausted the positive aspects of the results which have already been established by remarking that none of the three aspects we have investigated is superfluous. Our observations in the limited domain of the measurement of time have not been put aside. If, in the most simple instruments, the rôle of our natural representations (which, of course, represent for us the continuing flow of time) is entirely fundamental, they are gradually superseded by a dialogue between the mathematical idealization and the technical realization as the requirements of accuracy increase. We are never in a position, however, to do without the guarantees which they provide for our specified activities. Paradoxically (but the matter is explained, as we know, by a difference of scale), the situation will not be different when these representations are checked against the atomic scale.

Already at this point, without going any further, we thus find again in measured time all the characteristics of what we have called, in the context of geometric magnitudes, a *dialectic synthesis*. There is a dialectic, as should be emphasized, not because the elements forming the synthesis are opposites in the sense that a yes is an opposite of a no, but because they belong to complementary levels which, for the purposes of effective action, must be applied in combination.

What Remains for Us to Examine

We have noted that our study is not yet completed. But had we not assumed that it had no purpose other than to deepen and to confirm the views on methodology and open philosophy stated at the conclusion of the work *La géométrie et le problème de l'espace?*

This aim has been attained according to what has been said so far. Why continue our effort still further? There are two reasons for us to do so, the second being the stronger one. Above all, it is appropriate to dispel certain doubts which might persist concerning the newest and most accurate timepieces. They are essentially the work of the physicist; does not this fact compromise the conclusions at which we would have stopped? We shall verify that this is not the case. The theme of synthesis will even be amplified in an unexpected way because the measurement is a synthetic one, obtained through a combination of timepieces of various types, and is actually at the top of the measurements of high precision.

The second reason has much wider implications. Whether in the context of the time of astronomical tables, the time of the quartz clocks, or the time of the atomic clocks, in each case we will have to cross what we called a threshold of accuracy. And each time we will face the same apparent vicious circle, since we are justifying only by itself a still unpublished method of measuring time. The way out of this methodical paradox is always the same: it consists in organizing the conditions of a proof of effectiveness. We shall thus prepare the way for the *procedure of autofoundation* which will crown the open methodology by incorporating into it first of all the method according to which every scientific discipline can be established as an open discipline and by providing it afterwards with the general model according to which any open discipline may be established and consequently may be its own justification.

Chapter Seven

SYNTHETIC TIME

INTRODUCTION

In the three preceding chapters we have tried to separate from each other, as far as possible, the three variants of the notion of time which play a predominant rôle in the structure of knowledge.

We have conducted our analysis along three different lines; has it attained its purpose? Yes and No, depending on the fashion in which we see this purpose. Let us review the problems in detail:

1. If the problem had been to determine, for the three expressions *mathematical time, measured time,* and *intuitive time,* meanings that are invariable because they are complete and self-sufficient, our threefold study has not succeeded. We have in fact been unable to "specify" to the point of autonomy the three aspects of time designated by these terms.

Concerning mathematical time and the variable *t,* which makes of it a numerical magnitude, we have made it clear that these notions must not be completely stripped of their intuitive form to remain steady to play the rôle according to which they may be defined axiomatically. One may certainly reduce *t* to a mere numerical magnitude having left only the function to designate an element of a linear and continuous structure; but it will assume its meaning of temporal variable only by again taking on the intuitive element which makes of it what it is in our mental universe.

As far as measured time is concerned, our analysis has repeatedly led us to institute instrumental procedures (manufacture and use of measuring instruments) based on a small number of special intuitive representations. The use of these representations alone has saved us from an obvious vicious circle or a definition as precarious as it is conventional.

Naturally one could ask whether, through the search for

measuring instruments of ever-increasing accuracy, measured time could not be freed from its intuitive connotations in order to correspond to the ideal of a purely operational time. If this were possible, the use of this variant of the notion of time would then be guaranteed at the very level of research by the soundness and good functioning of the instruments. At first glance it would not seem unreasonable to hope for it. One would thus avoid for the time being the difficulties inherent in every fundamental analysis. The progress of our study, however, has not confirmed this hope. The very idea of the operational, whose clarifying function seemed necessarily decisive, has become increasingly complicated and obscure. Our search for accuracy has rather engaged us in what we have called a *mixed method.*

2. But one may also form a less ambitious project. In order to confer upon the three expressions in question their effective usage in a language ordered and ordering itself according to the total of experiences acquired and experiences in the process of being acquired, it is not necessary to go as far as the significations of the last tribunal, those constituted once and for all. Everything we have said about the outline-ideas and more generally about the means by which open knowledge succeeds in determining its state of advancement may find its application here. If therefore we had proposed only to characterize the three aspects of temporality which we consider fundamental with enough distinctness so as not to confound them, in order to be able to perceive them in their individual properties and in their common quality at the same time, this undeniably would have been attained.

But what was actually our project? Did we opt in advance for or against complete significations, for or against separate and autonomous aspects? The intention which always has been ours cannot be expressed by such a sharp dilemma. We certainly had foreseen that the eventuality 2 would finally remain as the only one to be worthy of consideration. But we have been careful not to eliminate the eventuality 1 without being forced to do so. We thus had to give this eventuality every chance to succeed, and we had to try hard to isolate the conditions of its realization; we would not discard it except after irreparable failure. We have tried to follow these guidelines. We are now faced by the final phase of this inquiry. While we are again increasing our requirements of accuracy in measurements, we can no longer doubt that it is through a correlation of the three fundamental aspects, by a combination of the means of knowledge which they involve, that this requirement can once more be satisfied.

We will then no longer have the liberty to select between the two eventualities 1 and 2. It will no longer depend on us whether the first can be effectively pursued and sincerely defended. The experiment decides in favor of the second, the mixed method towards which, whether we like it or not, we have been gradually proceeding.

We will now embark upon the last phase of our analysis, but only in relation to prerelativistic time. Once this stage is overcome, and before we engage in the study of temporality as it is presented in relativistic science, we shall have to draw the methodological conclusions from the four preceding chapters.

Formulated as they are in terms of an analysis which has hardly crossed the borderlines of classical science, can these conclusions remain valid in a relativistic or quantic perspective? We shall not approach this question with preconceived opinions but must decide it by means of the experiment.

THE TIME OF ASTRONOMY

Speaking of sidereal time, i.e. the time measured by the apparent motion of the celestial vault or—what amounts to the same thing—the rotatory motion of the earth, we have mentioned that certain factors might alter the uniformity of that motion. We indicated that more precise measurements today permit to evaluate by two or three millionths of a second the variations of the sidereal day. We added, however, that at the moment when we were discussing it, our exposé has not provided us with any indications about the means to be applied for making this evaluation. It is these means which we are now going to analyze.

We return to an idea which we already have found useful before. Every phenomenon may serve as a timepiece under these conditions:

1. It must be possible to observe and to designate the successive phases with some precision.

2. One must know its *temporal law,* i.e. one must be able to indicate, for every phase observed, the time corresponding to it on the time scale.

3. The phenomenon must be capable of repetition or it must be of considerable duration.

The first of these conditions may be compared with our remarks concerning the determination of an instantaneous state in what we have called a phenomenal context.

It is, however, the second condition which involves the fundamental difficulty, a difficulty which we already have encountered many times: How can we establish the temporal law of a phenomenon for the past and for the future? And how can we verify it unless we have, in advance, a clock of sufficient accuracy at our disposal?

We have already made several efforts to overcome this difficulty. But it reappears at every new stage, each time we have to introduce a novel instrument of measurement whose function is not simply reducible to that of instruments previously constructed. And far from lessening, it rather intensifies with each fresh requirement of accuracy.

As the following discussion will show, the mixed method alone will enable us to overcome this difficulty.

The three conditions are approximately satisfied by the apparent motion of the celestial vault. Concerning condition 2 in particular, we shall not review the reasons why we have to assume that this motion is uniform—allowing for the divergence which has been mentioned. Could not astronomy offer us the example of a different motion equally permanent, which might be observed with equal accuracy, and which would invariably unfold according to its own law? Such an example does exist; it is the motion of the earth revolving in its orbit around the sun; it could also be the revolving motion of any other planet around the sun, or of a satellite around its planet.

Without unduly committing ourselves in advance to the study of some of these examples, can we foresee what advantages will be gained by their consideration?

For the purpose of comparison let us go back to the apparent motion of the celestial vault and to the sidereal clock provided through this motion. The factors which affect its regularity (albeit very slightly) are of a geophysical character: the terrestrial globe is not a perfectly rigid body, its form and its moment of inertia around its axis are not absolutely constant, the motions of the seas and of the atmosphere dissipate kinetic energy, etc. These factors are difficult to evaluate because of their unsettled character. They can therefore serve only as a rather hazardous basis for eventual corrections of the functioning of the sidereal clock. But if one abandons the rotatory motion of the earth in favor of its revolving motion around the sun, none of these factors remain relevant. The realities and circumstances must no longer be evaluated according to the terrestrial scale but according to the planetary scale.

This advantage, however, will be accompanied by a very obvious disadvantage; the motion of the earth in its orbit is not uniform and its speed is not constant. The temporal law of this motion is not clearly established; none of our intuitive representations is able to suggest it in an immediate and convincing way.

There can be no question, this time, of avoiding the difficulty which we have just discussed. According to what procedure can the temporal law of the revolving motion of the earth be established and determined? We now must attack the problem directly.

But first we must define the manner in which our observation of a phenomenon which fulfills the three conditions can provide a measurement of time.

The Determination of Parameters

We have spoken of observable *phenomena;* we might as well have used the term of *systems* in evolution, observable systems, of course. In a statement of some accuracy, the state of a system in the process of evolution is determined by the attribution of determinate values to a certain number of variables $\lambda_1, \lambda_2, \ldots \lambda_k$, the *parameters* of the system. To say that this system is observable is to say that for a certain instant which the observer is free to choose at will, the corresponding values of some or all parameters may be determined by the observation of the system. This observation can be direct or indirect; direct, if it bears on the λ_i themselves; indirect, if it bears on other observable magnitudes whose λ_i can be inferred.

To know the temporal law of the evolution of an observable system is to know how to attribute in advance to each observed value of the λ_i a determinate value of the variable t. To the values simultaneously observed for different parameters of course must correspond a single and identical value of t.

Observational and Previsional Tables

Let us now assume that we have observed a system in a systematic fashion. The results of these observations may be registered in a table with double entries. If all the λ's can be observed simultaneously, all the corresponding values will be carried on the same line, at the end of which will likewise appear the value of the variable t corresponding to the instant of observation. The columns of the table will be occupied by the values observed successively for an identical λ, except for the last column which will contain the successive values for the variable t. If it is impossible to observe all the λ's at the same time the lines remain incomplete. Consequently the columns will also contain a number of blank spaces which are distributed irregularly. If necessary, and if the instants of observation follow each other closely enough, these blanks may be filled by interpolation.

A table of this type may be set up for every observable system even if one does not know its law of evolution. But, in that case, the column of the times includes only the moments already passed, and the table does not contain any indication about future moments.

The situation is entirely different when the law of evolution of the system is one of the data of the situation. Instead of drawing a table of values actually observed, one may establish a table of the same kind by arbitrarily choosing a sequence of values of the temporal variable, without making any difference between past and future instants, and by calculating the corresponding values of the λ's. (We naturally disregard the difficulties which this calculation could present in practice. We are concerned here only with an explanation of principle.) We may call the table constructed from real observations an *observational table,* and that derived from the law of evolution a *previsional table.*

A previsional table connected with a device of observation may serve as a timepiece. Let us assume, in fact, that we want to determine the value of t corresponding to an instant which is determined by being the instant of the observation of the value of one or several λ's. Two alternatives are then possible:

1. At least one of the values observed is found in the previsional table. The value sought for the variable t accordingly may likewise be found there, on the same line.

2. Each of the values observed falls between two values of the corresponding column of the previsional table, and the instant to be determined accordingly lies between the two corresponding values of t indicated on the table. In this case the value of t will be determined by interpolation. (One could also complete the previsional tables for this value.)

But how can a previsional table be set up? This is the essence of the methodological problem. The example of *astronomical time* will help us to clarify it.

Provisional Suspension of the Requirement of Autonomy

But first we must examine the methodological situation in which we find ourselves. So far every time we have introduced a new method of measuring time we have sought to confer upon it a certain autonomy. This was necessary while we were pursuing the project of instituting a purely operational time. But this project has involved us in increasing difficulties. We are therefore forced to abandon it and to assume again a certain methodological liberty. The first use we shall make of this liberty regained will be to reconsider the facts in order to examine, without preconceived opinions, how to achieve a very accurate measurement of time.

First of all we must give up the idea of instituting a measurement of time unrelated to any previously established method. It certainly has not been without interest to seek to "define," as far as possible, operational times independent of each other; the possibility of synchronizing these times has then given increasing validity to the idea of an objective time, universal metronome of the phenomena. Attractive as this idea may be (we shall come back to it when we discuss the autofoundation of a discipline), it nevertheless does not authorize us to diverge too far from the methods of the practitioner, whose effectiveness cannot be doubted. We shall moreover find again, in a different form, guarantees of objectivity to which, however, we can no longer refer as directly as before.

The practitioner, in his search for greater precision, never starts from a situation *alpha*, i.e. a situation in which he would be forbidden to measure time with instruments previously developed, whose precision is not equal to the precision which he hopes to attain. He considers it neither necessary nor even useful to make a clean sweep and to dismiss temporality entirely except for its intuitive aspect. The practitioner, on the contrary, starts from a situation in which the techniques of the measurement of time already are somewhat advanced. Does the progress to a more accurate method of measurement necessarily make former methods superfluous? Nothing permits us to make such an assumption. Let us not dwell on the fact that the most refined technique generally is not suitable for every purpose. For some purposes the less refined technique could still be the most convenient and rational one. This is an undeniable fact, but it has nothing to do with our problem. It is more to the point to note that a more refined technique may be based on a less refined one, even if both have the same purpose. In some cases the more refined technique can be applied only on the basis of results reached through the less refined one, and it can operate effectively only in a situation where the less refined technique has already been applied. From the methodological point of view we are no longer concerned with a problem of fundamentals but with a problem of integration.

Procedure of Calculation

We can now undertake to explain how previsional tables may be set up by means of which the revolving motion of the earth in its orbit, or the motion of any other planet, may be utilized as a timepiece.

We now approach the problem by way of celestial mechanics. We set up a theoretical model of the solar system where the sun, the earth and the moon, the other planets and their eventual satellites, in short, all the celestial bodies which we will take into account, are represented by point-masses whose relative motions are governed by Newton's law of universal attraction.

Thus the problem at first presents itself as a mathematical problem. It is the *problem of the* n *bodies,* which is among the most difficult ones. In spite of the immense labors spent on it by many of the greatest mathematicians, its solution is still far from being achieved, even for the case $n = 3$.

Theoretically, if the magnitudes of point-masses are known as well as their positions and their velocities at a given moment, the n bodies form a system whose temporal law, the law of evolution, is perfectly determined—at least as long as no collision occurs. But the fact that neither the masses, nor the positions, nor the velocities at a given moment are determined in advance will add to the difficulties of a purely mathematical character a certain number of other difficulties which can only be solved through experimentation. Viewed thus in its entire scope, the problem appears to be insoluble and may remain so for a long time to come.

The astronomers, however, have succeeded in giving approximate solutions for it, thanks to successive procedures of approximation. In fact, the mathematical problem of the two bodies is easy to solve. It leads to the laws of Kepler. In a first approximation one may suppose that it yields an approximate solution for the revolving motion of the planets around the sun. The mathematician's work, however accurate, of course cannot yield the empirical data which are indispensable for the determination, even in approximate form, of the correct trajectory (i.e. the trajectory which, in the mathematical model, represents the trajectory of the planet under consideration).

These data also appear, as constant factors which have to be determined, in the general theoretical solution.

So far we have introduced only the theorician. But although the rôle of the experimenter has remained obscure, it would be an error to think that his collaboration has not yet been invoked. His share of the work is implicit in the situation from which we have started; the formulation of Newton's law and the law of gravitation already represents the result of an investigation where it would be awkward indeed to decide what belongs to the mathematician and what is the domain of the observer. We shall therefore abandon our project of analyzing our starting situation, limiting ourselves to the remark that theory and experience are tightly interwoven in it.

The explicit intervention of the observer is now necessary to attribute to the parameters, mentioned above, values which conform to reality. We shall not seek to specify by what procedures mathematical formulas may be adequately confronted with the results of observation. In principle every observation presents a condition for the magnitudes which have to be determined. What observations must we make in order to obtain the most favorable conditions? Only a detailed investigation of the problem can enable us to answer this question; as far as we are concerned it is not necessary to pay attention to it.

There is one point, however, which we must not pass over in silence; the observations to be made include measurements of angles between directions of lines of sight, and measurements of temporal intervals between the moments of observation. It is the indispensable character of the latter which must be pointed out. The definition of synthetic time or of the time of astronomy, towards which we are proceeding and which our exposé is gradually elucidating, is to some extent contaminated by a previous definition of a time whose former use turns out to be impossible to eliminate. The situation has nothing that should surprise us, since we have alluded to it a moment ago.

But is not this procedure unsound in principle, is it not capable of perverting the correct use of the last of the times we have defined? The only question arising, as we have already remarked, is that of the coherence of the complete procedure and in particular of the times introduced successively. It suffices at this point (but it is also necessary) that the time introduced in the second place should be interpretable as a corrected time, of which the time introduced in the first place has given an open definition likely to be revised. The following discussion will show that precisely this is the case here. In an open methodological perspective, in which the outline-definitions may take their place alongside the outline-ideas, the procedure in which we must use two times has nothing irregular.

What is the value of this first approximation which consists in reducing the problem of the n bodies to a series of problems of two bodies? Is it possible to adjust the theoretical results to the results of observation? Can this adjustment be made without continuing excessive divergences between the observed and the calculated data? We realize that this is in fact the case. This concordance is explained by the predominance of the mass of the sun.

We may therefore outline the procedure used by the astronomer to determine the future positions of the planets:

1. He computes the orbit of each planet as if it were the only one, according to Kepler's law.

2. Relying on the law of gravitation he may then account, in the case of each planet, for the perturbations caused by the other planets (which are, according to point 1, supposed to obey Kepler's laws) and possibly their satellites. This second approximation provides him with new orbits for all the planets. He may then repeat the operation by computing the perturbations according to these new data, etc.

3. These operations cannot be conducted in the retort, or on a purely mathematical plane, with constants given once and for all with the first approximation. The results of the first ap-

proximations can and must be confronted with the experiment, with the observed positions. This permits a readjustment of the constants which further improves the approximation.

In reality the several phases of the procedure are not clearly marked. One must begin somewhere, and we begin with the Keplerian orbits. But afterwards the calculation and the confrontation with the experiment are inextricably mixed in the elaboration of successive approximations. Here, again, as in all cases where we approach in the least degree the real procedure of the practitioner, we encounter a mixed method in which theory and experiment are combined.*

Principally the sequence of possible approximations is unlimited. In practice a new approximation may remain ineffective when the corrections applied stay within the margin of indetermination which attends every observation. It may also happen that the approximations following each other do not converge because of certain circumstances, two of which shall now be investigated.

What would happen, for example, if Newton's law of gravitation had itself only an approximate value and if Einstein's theory of gravitation (based on relativity in general) would correspond better to the description of actual circumstances? There would be, in this case, a principal error in the general setup of the procedure of approximation, since every step of the latter is again based on the validity of Newton's law of attraction. How would this error of principle become evident? Perhaps the different timepieces provided by the different celestial bodies could not be permanently synchronized. Or perhaps a moment would come after which the work of approximation would no longer show any progress.†

---

* Of course, speaking of planets in general, we have made no exception for the earth. The latter certainly cannot be observed as a star on the celestial vault. But its observation may be replaced by the observation of the apparent motion of the sun on its trajectory (the ecliptic) which it appears to describe in the course of a year.

† G.M. Clemence, in the article "Astronomical Time" seems to favor the first of these two alternatives; according to him the synchronization of the planetary timepieces is possible only by adding to the expressions obtained through the classical methods a term originating from Einstein's theory of

Questioning the Validity of Time as a Reference

The second circumstance which we now want to examine is more closely related to our own project. It must not be forgotten that all the times appearing on the side of observation (in all the tables of observation) are times given by an already existing timepiece which we will call clock H. What would happen if this timepiece would run irregularly or were systematically disturbed? Would we have the means to correct this?

Such a case is not hypothetical. It is the case which presents itself if one seeks to achieve greater accuracy in the measurement of time by using the revolving motion of the earth or any other planet, or the law of the evolution of the solar system as a whole, for a timepiece. In order that this project should make sense one must assume that the clock H, which one cannot avoid using, has not yet attained the degree of accuracy in view of which the entire procedure was started in the first place. It must therefore be assumed that the clock is somewhat irregular. It is precisely for the correction of this irregularity that the entire arrangement must be devised. We can by no means be certain that if H were a bad clock, the adjustment of the values calculated and the values observed would permit us to repeat and to profit by the application of an approximation for the calculation of the following one. Do we have to stop here? We have one last resource, namely to introduce the times given by H into the general effort of adjustment. In other words, we must take the liberty to correct the indications of the "observation clock" is such a way as to protect the coherence and the convergence of the entire procedure.

Nevertheless, the procedure does not assume its full meaning unless H already is a good clock. The situation then presents itself as follows:

Disconnecting Clock H

One forms a system of m clocks, the first of which is clock H (in order to define the images, we shall assume that it is rep-

gravitation, which accounts sufficiently for the divergences between the latter and Newton's law of attraction. *Review of Modern Physics, 29:2–8,* 1957; "The Relativity Effect in Planetary Motions", *ibid., 19:361–64,* 1947.

resented by the rotation of the earth), while the rest are provided by the temporal laws of all the celestial bodies (except
for the sun) for which the procedure of successive approximation must account. The temporal laws of the latter are completely determined, even when they are not completely known.
As far as the clock H of our example is concerned, the situation
is somewhat different. One may certainly consider the time
when it "performs" in its rôle as a variant of the temporal
variable t which must appear in the expression of the law of
its motion. But, taking the terrestrial data into account, this
law probably involves an ineluctable moment of risk. Do we
have the theoretical possibility to do without clock H? Is it
possible to disconnect it from the procedure which through successive approximations defines the planetary timepiece, which
from now on we will call clock S? It is essential for us to
realize that this is possible, even though, for practical reasons,
clock H is not completely discarded. The procedure of successive approximations must then be modified in the following
way:

At the moment when we decide to do without clock H, the
temporal law of the motion of each planet is already more or
less accurately known to us. Each planet thus may be assimilated to a timepiece for which two different times must
carefully be distinguished: One is a correct time, the other is
a provisional and somewhat uncertain time. The correct time
is the one which on the basis of our observations we could infer
from the accurate temporal law or from exact previsional tables. The provisional time is the one which, again, on the basis
of our observations, we can infer from the temporal law such
as we know it or from previsional tables such as have been
established. Our periodic readings from our planetary clocks
thus are only provisional times. Each of these times must be
counted from its own origin. We may assume, however, that
the times O have been coordinated in the process of previous
adjustments.

Assume now that it is possible to observe simultaneously the
positions of two planets, M and V, for example. For each of
the two corresponding planetary timepieces we shall be able to

determine the corresponding provisional times, i.e. time t_m for M and time t_v for V. If these two times were accurate we could have chosen the origins from which they are counted so as never to differ, for new observations as well as for observations already made. But the permanent equality of the provisional times cannot be ensured by the choice of the zero times alone, however carefully it has been made. Accordingly there will be a divergence between them which for this first observation we shall designate ϵ_1.

The Method of Least Squares

Let us now assume that a series of other, similar observations has been made, either between the planets M and V, or between these two planets and the rest, or between two of the latter. In principle each of these operations yields a corresponding divergence ϵ. Let us now do the sum of the squares of all these deviations. If the planetary clocks were all perfectly accurate, this sum would be exactly zero. It is thus advisable to keep it as small as possible. Calculated through the intermediary of the provisional temporal law, these divergences are a function of physical, geometrical, and other magnitudes, which by themselves determine the temporal laws of the motions which we have used. It is thus a condition pertaining to these magnitudes which we shall obtain when we require that the sum of the squares of the divergences should be minimal.

The astronomer, of course, may have reasons for making his observations according to a specific program, or even for proceeding in a random manner. Nothing prevents him moreover from conducting a series of mutually independent observations. By postulating, for each series, that the sum of the squares of the divergences be minimal, he will finally have as many conditions at his disposal as he sees fit. They will all serve in a readjustment of the values provisionally attributed to what shall be designated as the natural parameters of the problem. Once these values are revised, the procedure of successive approximations can enter a new phase. The revised values can in fact serve as a basis for an evaluation, itself corrected, of the law of motion of each planet. In other words, the time scale of each of our planetary timepieces will thereby be revised. For each of them we will have made a step on the provisional time scale towards the correct time scale.

The two phases of the procedure we have just described are naturally complementary; one (despite the computations which inevitably attend it) is primarily of an experimental character, while the other is mathematical. In its totality the procedure is therefore one with a double texture or a double source. We shall soon have to point out the importance of this fact.

Here, again, the procedure of successive approximations cannot be continued indefinitely. Here, too, it comes to a halt as soon as the divergences become small enough so that it can no longer be decided whether or not they result from errors of observation. The margin of uncertainty in a specific category of observations is itself, at any stage in the advancement of the techniques of observation, one of the data of the situation.

This is what we wanted to show; the preliminary clock H can in principle be separated from the procedure of successive approximations. The definition of the time of astronomy may be freed from any reference to this preliminary clock. But we should note that this does not mean that we could equally well do without any previous utilization of this clock. On the contrary, it is only in the course of the process that clock H may be declared as discarded.

Such is the theoretical situation. But does practice permit us to realize this situation clearly? Would it not involve certain circumstances which we have not taken into account and which would make the elimination of clock H less legitimate?

The Previous Clock Remains Indispensable in Practice

In fact, given the actual state of astronomical science, recourse to an observation clock is inevitable. We shall not try to enumerate all the reasons why this is so, but present two which will suffice to illuminate the situation.

1. The observation of the planets as a rule takes place through the determination of their situation relative to a sys-

tem of reference formed by some rather bright fixed stars. One measures the angles of the corresponding lines of sight. Through this process the simultaneous observation of two planets cannot be accomplished. In order to coordinate these observations temporally we must include them in the same temporal context. The latter can be provided only by an already existing clock. The clocks which the astronomer thus cannot do without are nevertheless good clocks. Their irregularities are insignificant enough so that the difference of the times which they show between the instants of two comparison observations may be considered practically as an interval of correct time.

2. While he is making the sightings and measurings of angles necessary for the determination of the position of a planet, the astronomer must take into account that his observatory is anchored in the surface of the terrestrial globe and is being carried along in all the motions of the latter. In his work, beginning with the correction necessitated by the phenomenon of aberration, he must put to use all the means of positional astronomy. In particular he has to inscribe into a temporal context all the motions which he may not disregard (rotation, nutation, precession, etc.).

From this point of view it becomes again clear that a clock H is necessary.

Limitations of Planetary Timepieces

Can planetary clocks be used to advantage? The answer to this question must be preceded by a remark concerning the precision of the observations, especially as far as angle measurements are concerned. Despite the technological progress of the last fifty years, these measurements are still relatively inaccurate. Translated into intervals of sidereal time, their precision hardly exceeds one hundredth of a second. It is accordingly with an inaccuracy of this order that every individual measurement is made which is capable of defining the instants of the beginning and of the ending of an interval of time "previously deducted" in the context of a planetary clock. This precision, of course, is far from sufficient for observing the eventual variations of the sidereal day, the variations from one day to the next, which are of the order of one thousandth of a second.

But if an average duration is concerned, the precision naturally increases with the length of the interval separated from its context, with the number of single days which it contains. Over periods of the order of ten years the duration of an average day may be observed in this fashion with sufficient accuracy to establish beyond any doubt a regular loss of speed in the rotation of the earth around its axis, whose consequence is a lengthening of the average day to the tune of one or two seconds per century.

This suffices, of course, to correct towards the past a factor of systematic error which must be inscribed in the temporal scale of the sidereal timepiece, insofar as this scale has already been fixated or can be reconstituted with the help of certain dated events from history.

But this is certainly not enough to establish beyond any doubt the seasonal variation of the average day which we already had occasion to discuss, or other systematic variations verified over periods of some months only. The planetary timepieces alone do not permit us to achieve this goal. We must resort to other devices which will be discussed shortly.

Which Is the Best Clock?

There remains one point, however, which must be discussed because it is of principal importance. We recall the confrontation of rather lengthy periods on the temporal scale of the sidereal timepiece and that of the planetary timepieces. The observation shows that the two scales are not synchronized, that the speed of one of the timepieces is less than that of the others. This is an undeniable fact, but it admits of two, or even three, possible interpretations:

1. The planetary timepieces are accurate and the sidereal clock is slow.

2. The sidereal clock is accurate and the planetary timepieces are the ones which deviate.

3. None of the timepieces are accurate.

Following the astronomers, we have given preference to the first of these three eventualities. This choice is certainly not an arbitrary one. What are its guarantees? Here we are again faced with a question which we have asked before in basically analogous situations. If we had at our disposal a clock *H* more accurate than those we are comparing, and means to confront its indications with those of the latter, the problem of a correct choice would not arise. The choice would be simply a matter of verification. But (and this is true for all situations where one must go beyond the degree of precision available in the already established clocks), the fact is that we do not have a sufficiently accurate control clock at our disposal.

The difference between a planetary timepiece and a water clock is immense; all the same, in order to justify our choice, we do not have to invent a method other than the one we have already used at the start of our study of measured time—a method other than that of the integrating context.

The integrating context, valid in this new case, involves the fact that the loss of kinetic momentum by the terrestrial globe revolving around its axis may reasonably be explained by geophysical factors, in particular by losses of energy due to the motions of the seas and of the atmosphere. This context, on the other hand, includes nothing that could explain to us a uniform acceleration of all the revolving motions in the solar system while, as an incomprehensible exception, the rotatory motion of the earth would remain unchanged. In making our selection, we cannot fail to take into account that the revolving motions are unaffected precisely by those factors (geophysical ones in the case of the earth) which are capable of influencing the rotatory motions. In the integrating context of the solar system it is thus much less risky to choose eventuality 1 than it would be to choose 2 or 3.

If instead of causes acting on all the planetary timepieces at the same time we had to consider causes of variation for each of them in particular, their agreement would seem very unlikely.

Our choice will finally receive supplementary and decisive confirmation in the integrating complex where we shall introduce the quartz clocks and the atomic time scales.

THE QUARTZ CLOCKS

Principle of the Quartz Clock

We have seen that in every mechanical clock there are four fundamental elements:

a) an animated regulatory organ, generally with a periodic motion;

b) a device providing the energy which maintains this regulator in motion;

c) an integrating device counting the number of periods, turns, and so forth.

d) connective devices between *a* on the one hand and *c* on the other, which have the function of

d_1) transmitting the maintenance energy to the regulator as a function of the very motion of the latter, and

d_2) "informing" the integrator about the functioning of the oscillator.

In principle each of these devices could be imagined and realized for itself, as long as one observes the condition that together they must function as a whole. We have seen, however, that in the mechanical clocks the maintaining and the integrating devices use the same mechanism, and the escapement assumes the functions d_1 and d_2 at the same time.

We will find a very similar functional scheme in the quartz clocks. Their oscillations are produced by a mechanical device; it is a sheet of vibrating quartz whose own frequency is determined by the distribution of the masses and the elastic properties of the sheet. On the other hand, the connection of this regulator with the other elements of the clock is not achieved by mechanical means, as in the case of the balance wheel clocks, but electrically. From the functional viewpoint, such a timepiece, except for the integrating device, is similar to an electric bell. We know how the latter functions; a spring to which a small mass is attached becomes an oscillator possessing its own frequency, which is determined by the elastic properties of the spring and the characteristics of the mass. The oscillation of the spring may be maintained by the periodically repeated attraction of an electromagnet. These attractions must

be produced exactly at the right moment if one wants the oscillation not to be disturbed but, on the contrary, to be continually reinforced. This is achieved by their being controlled
through the oscillating system itself, which closes a contact
each time it is in a certain position. In a modified form, we
find here the idea of the escapement. Could this concept not
be used in the manufacture of a clock? Such a method would
not be without inconvenience. The contacts introduce perturbations in the oscillating system; moreover they oxidize rather
rapidly, especially if high voltages are used. They could be replaced by a lamp with three electrodes or by a transistor. We
know that it suffices to charge the grid of such a lamp nega-
tively, which necessitates only a very feeble current, to interrupt the much stronger current from the filament to the plate.
Let us assume that we produce, starting from the mechanical
oscillator and through the intermediary of an electromechani-
cal or piezoelectrical system, a relatively feeble alternating current of which we may correctly and conveniently say that it
"sounds" the oscillator. In this way a much stronger current is
created from the filament to the plaque; this current varies in
the rhythm of the oscillator and consequently may be utilized
to maintain the vibrating state of the latter. This last operation
in turn may be effected through an electromagnetic or piezoelectric system, which will not necessarily differ from the one
already employed in the production of the sounding current.
This is a device which functionally corresponds very closely
to the one used in the mechanical pendulum or balance wheel
clocks. We have noted that the latter contain a regulating device, a maintenance device, a device of integration, and a connective device. The system we are now describing contains the
same elements: a mechanical oscillator, a maintaining device
which provides energy derived from a battery or an electric
current, an integrating device which we shall discuss later, and
finally, a connective element which most deserves our attention. The latter, in fact, involves one more problem than the
mechanical clocks, since the mechanical oscillations have to be
transformed into electrical ones, which in turn would have a
double function to perform. In the first place they would have

to control the transformation of electrical energy of maintenance into mechanical impulses compensating the losses of the mechanical oscillator, and secondly to inform the integrator about each of these oscillations. The transformation from the mechanical to the electrical and vice versa is achieved by means of a single element, either magnetic or piezoelectrical.* The control of the maintaining energy is achieved either by a contact or by a lamp with three electrodes or a transistor.

Besides its very high, ultrasonic—often very highly ultrasonic—frequency, the quartz clock presents the following peculiarity: The quartz crystal serves at the same time as a mechanical vibrator and as a mechano-electric transformer. From the fact of its mechanic properties, its mass, and its elasticity, the sheet of quartz vibrates with a frequency which is peculiar to it; by virtue of its piezoelectric properties it gives rise or responds to an electrical vibration of the same frequency. The integrating device has no special interest for us; let us simply say that a division of frequency is effected by electronic means, and a current of sufficiently low frequency is thus obtained to feed a synchronous motor or a recording device. The actual technique moreover gives us the possibility of direct comparison of high frequencies.

Devices Applied

It has become obvious by now how complex the devices are which are used in the manufacture of such a clock. We have firmly dismissed any intention of analyzing all of them in the hope of isolating the elements of what we have often called an "operational definition." We know, having attempted it several times under less difficult circumstances, that this is a task impossible to accomplish. But now we must extend our renunciation even further. In the case of astronomical time we were able to understand rather clearly how theory and experimentation

---

* Certain anisotropic crystals have the property of contracting in one direction under the influence of an electric field, or of producing an electric current when compressed in a certain direction. We thus have a means for transforming mechanical vibrations into electrical ones and vice versa.

mutually and progressively aid each other in securing the accuracy of the measurement of a certain duration. With the accuracy thus attained, this time may be called synthetic. It is not understood through a reduction to any one of its fundamental aspects whose specificity we have isolated to some extent. This is not the purely mathematical time as a function of which the theory is expressed; it is not the time which some specific instrument would be capable of defining through a simple measurement, and it is not the intuitive time, the time whose representation is a part of our natural means of knowledge. It is a time which we can use, with the required accuracy, only through a synthesis of its different aspects, through a dialectic synthesis capable of drawing them together or pulling them apart according to the purpose we have in mind. Analysis, however, rather clearly illuminates the aspects which the dialectic system brings into play. From this point of view the planetary timepiece may be considered as a privileged case.

The same is not true of the quartz clocks. An extraordinary patience would be necessary to develop all the contexts, theoretical as well as practical, in which the exhaustive analysis of its manufacture would necessarily have to engage. Everything indicates that at every point we would be faced by a more or less analogous synthetizing dialetic. But is there any chance that these contexts could develop independent of each other without mutual reference? Nothing permits us to assume this. The entire question will be discussed again in the chapter on autofoundation. There it will find an answer whose methodological importance will be decisive. We shall then see how, in answer to the requirements of increasing accuracy, the synthetic character of our grasp on time, as well as the other fundamental notions which are used in an exact investigation, is extended and accentuated.

We shall therefore not seek to draw a complete perspective in which the synthetic character of the time of the quartz clocks would be made evident through an exhaustive analysis of the notions and the practices which concur in its determination. Such an enterprise would be entirely useless. All the same we could not abandon some of these contexts without at the same time giving up the idea of understanding certain aspects of the problem of measuring time which have not yet been clarified.

Defects of the Quartz Clock

Do the quartz clocks whose functional scheme we have analyzed give satisfactory results right from the beginning? First of all they have revealed themselves as very sensitive to changes in temperature, which modify the mechanical properties of the crystal. Attempts, of course, have been made to correct this deficiency by maintaining the temperature as constant as possible. Since this measure was not successful, an attempt was made to solve the problem by using certain cuts of quartz in which the effects due to temperature changes cancel each other out almost completely. The frequency curve of a blade of quartz compensated in this fashion goes through an extremum in the neighborhood of a determinate temperature, 30° Centigrade for example, near which the curve is practically flat. This means that variations of temperature in the vicinity of this special temperature have a very weak impact.

Other irregularities depend on the amount of time during which the quartz has already been functioning. They correspond to a group of phenomena called aging. These are the problems which, for an accurate use of the quartz clock, pose the most typical problems. During a first period the frequency varies rather rapidly. Afterwards this variation is stabilized and becomes practically linear, i.e. proportional to the duration of the functioning. This phenomenon is called the drift of the clock. It may happen that the drift finally accelerates after a certain period of normal behavior. One may moreover expect erratic divergences due to minor unchecked variations in the system. We must admit without hesitation, however, that in spite of its defects the quartz clock attains a precision which far surpasses that of the best mechanical clocks and even that of the terrestrial clock.

We have noted that during the period defined as that of the normal behavior of the quartz clock the variation of its frequency is linear, i.e. proportional to the amount of time during which the clock has been functioning. But what instrument was used to measure this duration? Was it done by means of a previously manufactured observation clock, a mechanical clock, for example? In this case the measurement of the drift would not have the accuracy which the installation of the quartz clock should precisely permit us to attain. The most accurate possible use of the latter, which should imply a correction, also as accurate as possible, of the effects of the drift, would invariably be affected by it. In a new form this is again the situation which presents itself each time one crosses a "threshold of precision." Practice might permit us, within the limits of a well circumscribed use, to disregard the consequences of the relative imprecision of the observation clock, or the evaluation of the drift may be certified by a two-way system of successive approximations. But, however justified they may be, these remarks do not offer a clear solution to the methodological problem posed in a very general way by our crossing a threshold of precision. The problem is to base the manufacture and the use of a new instrument, with the guarantees of precision belonging to it, at the very level of that precision. We have already discussed this problem for the time of astronomy, showing how in principle we can eliminate or "disconnect" the observation clocks whose precision must be surpassed.* It is not superfluous to do this once more, taking into account the rather peculiar circumstances prevailing in the case of the quartz clocks.

As we had done for the other clocks, we must above all institute a time of the quartz clocks, which would not owe anything to other types of clocks. The taking into account, or rather the elimination, of the drift raises rather difficult problems analogous to those which we have faced in the case of the simple water clock. This was likewise a "slowed-down" clock since, everything else being equal, the speed of discharge can diminish only at the rate at which the water level in the

---

* As we have already noted but consider useful to repeat, this problem will again be discussed in general terms in Chapter Eight of the present study. The methodological solution we offer can be expressed in the single term of *auto-foundation.*

clock goes down. The simple water clock, however, has an important advantage; it may be set back, if desired, at its initial stage; it may be set at zero as often as required. One may moreover assume that each time the water clock functions from the same level, its drift again takes exactly the same form. In the case now before us these advantages are denied to us; the quartz clock is analogous to a water clock which would empty itself in an irreversible fashion and which, consequently, could never be set back at zero. The drift moreover is a rather mysterious and unpredictable phenomenon. Nothing permits us to assume a priori that a certain crystal will have some specific drift; the latter may be determined only through the experiment. The methodological vicious circle to which we have often called attention again seems to close here in a particularly rigorous way; it appears that we cannot determine the drift without invoking a standard clock superior to the quartz clock. When the first quartz clocks were made there existed no better clocks. But, if one intends to elevate a particular quartz clock to the rank of a standard clock, he must first of all determine its drift; how could this be done without the help of another standard clock? We can hardly see a way out of this dilemma.

Model of a Clock with Drift

Nevertheless we shall once more manage to escape from the vicious circle. But in order to show clearly how this is done, we shall first, according to the method which emerges more and more clearly, develop a model of the clock with drift, or rather of a group of such clocks.

Schematically we can imagine this clock as a disc animated by a rotating motion whose number of turns τ can be counted; τ is not necessarily a whole number. We shall designate as ω the derivative of τ in relation to the mathematical time t, and we shall call it the frequency of the clock at the time t. Concerning the drift, one may hesitate between two definitions. In one the drift is equal to the derivative of ω relative to the time t; in the other it is equal to the derivative of the same ω relative to τ. For reasons of a physical nature we choose the second and posit, calling this drift α; α is equal to $d\omega/d\tau$.

Now let H_1 and H_2 be two clocks of the group in question and let τ_1 and τ_2 be their respective number of turns. Assuming that one can read both by one and the same observation, we establish between them a functional relation $\phi\ (\tau_1,\ \tau_2) = 0$. We shall also assume that this relation could be solved in accordance with either one of the two variables and that each of them can be developed following the powers of the other, all the terms of the development becoming negligible after the fourth. Accordingly we posit:

$$\tau_2 = a_{1,2} + b_{1,2}\ \tau_1 + c_{1,2}\ \tau_1^2 + \ldots$$

where the terms indicated by the points of suspension do not play any further rôle.

In this MacLaurin formula, the coefficients $a_{1,2}$, $b_{1,2}$, and $c_{1,2}$ have the following significance: $a_{1,2}$ is equal to the value of τ_2 for $\tau_1 = 0$; $b_{1,2}$ is the derivative of τ_2 relative to τ_1, for the same value of τ_1, $\tau_1 = 0$. Thus

$$b_{1,2} = \frac{d\tau_2}{d\tau_1} = \frac{\dfrac{d\tau_2}{dt}}{\dfrac{d\tau_1}{dt}} = \frac{\omega_2}{\omega_1} \text{ for } \tau_1 = 0$$

Finally, $c_{1,2}$ is equal to half of the second derivative of τ_2 relative to τ_1 for $\tau_2 = 0$. Thus

$$c_{1,2} = \frac{1}{2}\frac{d^2\tau_2}{d\tau_1^2} = \frac{1}{2}\frac{d}{d\tau_1}\left(\frac{d\tau_2}{d\tau_1}\right) = \frac{1}{2}\frac{d}{d\tau_1}\left(\frac{\omega_2}{\omega_1}\right) = \frac{1}{2}\frac{\omega_1\dfrac{d\omega_2}{d\tau_1} - \omega_2\dfrac{d\omega_1}{d\tau_1}}{\omega_1^2}$$

Putting

$$\frac{d\omega_1}{d\tau_1} = \alpha_1 \text{ and } \frac{d\omega_2}{d\tau_1} = \frac{d\omega_2}{d\tau_2}\cdot\frac{d\tau_2}{d\tau_1} = \alpha_2\frac{\omega_2}{\omega_1}$$

one obtains

$$c_{1,2} = \frac{1}{2}\frac{\omega_2}{\omega_1}\left(\frac{\alpha_2}{\omega_2}\cdot\frac{\omega_2}{\omega_1} - \frac{\alpha_1}{\omega_1}\right) = \frac{1}{2}\frac{\omega_2}{\omega_1}\cdot\frac{\alpha_2 - \alpha_1}{\omega_1}$$

In principle three simultaneous readings of τ_1 and τ_2 would yield three linear equations for the coefficients $a_{1,2}$, $b_{1,2}$, and $c_{1,2}$. They should thus suffice to determinate them. In practice one will make many observations and calculate for each of them an average value by applying the method of least squares.

It will be noted that in this way the only quantities which may be calculated are, besides $a_{1,2}$ which simply can be put $= 0$, the relations

$$\frac{\omega_2}{\omega_1} \text{ and } \frac{\alpha_2}{\omega_2} \cdot \frac{\omega_2}{\omega_2} - \frac{\alpha_1}{\omega_1}$$

It is clear that as long as no unit has been chosen for the variable t, the values of ω_1 and ω_2 at the time $t_1 = 0$ cannot be indicated numerically. Conversely, to choose the value of ϕ_1, for example, amounts to choosing a unit of time. Supposing that this has been done, what was said before makes it clear that the only quantities which could then be defined by the simultaneous observation of the clocks H_1 and H_2 are the frequency ω_2 (for $\tau_1 = 0$) and the difference of the drifts $a_2 - a_1$ (we do not add for $\tau_1 = 0$ since in practice a_1 and a_2 are to be considered as constants).*

Momentary Failure

It will thus be noted that by this procedure neither a_1 nor a_2 can be calculated in isolation. Now we shall see that for a drift clock to be really able to serve as a clock (determining the time t), its drift necessarily must be known.

Can the conditions of the calculation be improved by the introduction of a third clock H_3 and the simultaneous observation of the three clocks H_1, H_2, and H_3? The procedure would consist in adding to the development of τ_2 as a function of τ_1, that of τ_3 as a function of τ_2, and that of τ_3 as a function of τ_1. The simultaneous observations would permit us to calculate the nine coefficients of the following table:

$$
\begin{array}{ccc}
a_{1,2} & b_{1,2} & c_{1,2} \\
a_{2,3} & b_{2,3} & c_{2,3} \\
a_{1,3} & b_{1,3} & c_{1,3}
\end{array}
$$

---

* In the application which is made of these considerations to the quartz clocks, the relation $\Phi(\tau_1, \tau_2) = 0$ is approximately linear and the above hypotheses are very sufficiently adequate.

One may, in order to simplify, fixate the zero point of the three numbers of turns by a simultaneous observation and put accordingly:

$$a_{1,2} = a_{2,3} = a_{1,3} = 0$$

The values of the six remaining coefficients will then yield six equations containing the ratios of the six constants ω_1, ω_2, and ω_3 on the one hand and α_1, α_2, and α_3 on the other.

Our hope of thus encircling the numerical value of each of the constants a_1, a_2, a_3 or each of the ratios α_1/ω_1, α_2/ω_2, and α_3/ω_3 is nevertheless futile. There exists in fact, between the six coefficients $b_{i,k}$ and $c_{i,k}$ a *law of composition* analogous to that of a group of transformations. One may verify without difficulty that, for example, $b_{1,3}$ and $c_{1,3}$ are expressed in the following way starting from $b_{1,2}$ and $c_{1,2}$ on the one hand and $b_{2,3}$ and $c_{2,3}$ on the other:

$$b_{1,3} = b_{1,2} \cdot b_{2,3} \text{ and } c_{1,3} = b^2_{1,3} \, c_{2,3} + b_{2,3} \, c_{1,2}$$

Attempt at a Different Procedure

In order to succeed in the determination of the drifts themselves we must therefore resort to a different procedure.

We return to the two clocks H_1, H_2 and to the relation which is established by a series of simultaneous observations between their respective numbers of turns τ_1 and τ_2. Our knowledge of the coefficients $b_{1,2}$ and $c_{1,2}$ permits us, as we have noted, to determine the ratios of the three quantities ω_2, ω_1, and $\alpha_2 - \alpha_1$, or, if one prefers, to determine the value of the ratios

$$\frac{\omega_2}{\omega_1} = \rho \text{ and } \frac{\alpha_2 - \alpha_1}{\omega_1} = 0$$

At any moment of observation corresponding to the number of turns $\Delta\tau_1$ of the first clock, the ratio ρ^* of the frequencies ω_2^*/ω_1^* is given by the formula $\rho^* = \rho \, (1 + \sigma\Delta\tau_1)$.

Let us assume that the clock H_1 has made the number of turns $\Delta\tau_1$ in question. Then take the end of this first interval $\Delta\tau_1$ as the start of a second interval $\Delta\tau_2$, and repeat the procedure which has been described. The comparison of the two known values $(\alpha_2 - \alpha_1)/\omega_1$ and $(\alpha_2 - \alpha_1)/\omega_1{}^*$ yields the ratio of $\omega_1{}^*/\omega_1$; now, $\omega_1 + \Delta\omega_1$ is equal to $\omega_1 + \alpha_1\Delta\tau_1$. Thus we obtain the value of the ratio of α_1 to ω_1.

One might raise the following objection against this procedure: The difference of $\alpha_2 - \alpha_1$ being very small and the frequencies relatively high, the ratios $(\alpha_2 - \alpha_1)/\omega_1$ and $(\alpha_2 - \alpha_1)/\omega_1{}^*$ are relatively ill-defined by the observation and consequently their ratio itself is ill-defined. It could thus happen that the ratio α_1/ω_1 itself would be affected by a rather perceptible indertermination.

One might therefore prefer to use a different procedure, one which involves the stopping of only one clock, clock H_1, for example. During a rather brief first phase in which the frequencies practically do not vary, one determines the ratio ω_2/ω_1. The clock H_1 is then stopped, whereas clock H_2 continues to run during a rather long span of time, at the end of which its frequency will have the value $\omega_2{}^*$. Clock H_1 is then set back in motion and the ratio $\omega_2{}^*/\omega_1$ is determined. Starting from ω_2/ω_1 and $\omega_2{}^*/\omega_1$ one finally defines the ratio $\omega_2{}^*/\omega_2$.

Now, the drift α_2 being constant, the difference between $\omega_2{}^*$ and ω_2 is equal to the product of this drift into the number of turns effected by clock H_2 during the time when clock H_1 was stopped. The first and third phases of the procedure must be rather short in order to enable us to assume that during the observation the ratios of the frequencies do not vary. In practice 100 seconds suffice for the ratios to be measured. The second phase, on the other hand, must be rather long for the difference between ω_2 and $\omega_2{}^*$ to be perceptible. In the first of the two procedures under consideration, it is the two intervals of observation which must be relatively long.

We have thus explained how, if we had at our disposal two clocks corresponding to our theoretical hypotheses, we could establish a program of observation permitting us to determine the constants through which the motion of one of the clocks may be evaluated as a function of the motion of the other. These constants determine the physical characteristics of this pair of clocks.

Construction of a Uniform Clock

But it is clear that this can only be an intermediary result. What we intend is to turn the hypothetical clocks into real ones which do not drift. This is achieved from the theoretical side by the following operation: Let us consider a new pair of clocks which we call H and T. The first might as well be clock H_1 as clock H_2. We say in a general way that it is a clock which marks a number of turns designated τ, that its frequency for $\tau = 0$ is equal to ω, and that we know the ratio α/ω of the drift, which is constant at this frequency. Of T we assume that it is a clock without drift whose number of turns must be equal to the mathematical time t, and whose frequency therefore is equal to 1 and whose drift equals 0. After replacing H_1 by H and H_2 by T, the relation expressing τ_2 as a function of τ_1 becomes

$$T = T_0 + \frac{\tau}{\omega} - \frac{\alpha}{2}\left(\frac{\tau_2}{\omega_2}\right)$$

We know, as we have noted, how the constant α/ω can be determined for every clock satisfying our theoretical conditions; by defining the value of ω, we also choose a unit of time T.

Combining this expression of T with the clock H we turn the latter into a *real clock* marking a *correct time t*.

Our exposé about the measurement of time by the quartz clocks must include three parts. The first two have already been treated. The first has explained on what physical bases and according to what pattern a quartz clock is constructed; it has posed the problem of the measurement of a correct time through the intermediary of a phenomenon with drift. The second has shown how, starting from a theoretical model, the solution to this problem may be given. The third finally must return from theory to practice in order to examine how they can be brought into agreement.

Construction of a Battery of Good Clocks

It should be emphasized that we are not merely concerned with determining to what extent a specific quartz clock may be

considered a good realization of the theoretical scheme. The
problem facing the designer is, of course, to guarantee the manufacture of good clocks, i.e. clocks as consistent as possible
with the theoretical ideal of the clock with constant drift. But,
given the fact that a quartz clock with a natural quartz conforms to this ideal only during a certain period of time whose
beginning and end cannot be predicted with accuracy, and
given the additional fact that even during this period unforeseeable erratic divergences are to be feared, the problem at
this point would be to construct a battery of good clocks from
which the unsuitable ones would be continuously eliminated.

We must recall that, principally, we have denied ourselves
the use of a previous time, i.e. a time measured by clocks of
a different type. In the second part of our explanations, on the
other hand, we have seen that it is exclusively by a program
of simultaneous observations of at least two drift clocks that
the corrective equations of the latter can be established. It
follows that, for verifying the correctness of a battery of drift
clocks, the expedient most direct and conforming to the theory
is to compare the corrected times of these clocks two at a
time. To do this we have a very clear procedure which we
might already have used for all other types of clocks in the
cases where we had to determine which were the best in a
comparison of several clocks. One carries on an ordinate the
(naturally corrected) time of all the clocks taking as a reference, as abscissa, the time of any one among them. This operation is then repeated, the reference being the time of each
of the other clocks respectively. Let us assume that all the
clocks are good clocks; the curves obtained by comparing the
times of the clocks two by two will all be straight lines. Conversely, if the graphs are all presented in this form we will not
hesitate to conclude that the clocks are good, since it may be
considered extremely improbable that eventual irregularities of
one among them could be exactly compensated by corresponding irregularities in all the rest.

But suppose, taking as an example the times of the clocks
2 and 5, that the curves corresponding to a certain group of
other clocks all show the same hump in the graph 2 and the

same trough in the graph 5. One will naturally conclude that the clocks 2 and 5 have presented irregularities. The reasoning which leads to this conclusion is the same as before; we have used it often before and the moment has come for us to give it a more precise form.

Reasoning Through the Improbable

What is the essence of this reasoning which might be called the reasoning through the improbable? Mr. Polya, in his book on *Probable Reasoning,* gives a form to it which seems to us very clear and very satisfactory. Let it be assumed that we have made an exhaustive enumeration of the possible hypotheses. Assume that a certain event is very improbable in all the hypotheses except one. Assume, finally, that the event does occur. The occurrence of the event may then be considered as a confirmation of the hypothesis in which it was probable. In other words, and more briefly, a hypothesis is the more strongly confirmed by the result of an experiment as this result was more probable in this hypothesis and less probable in the competing ones.*

* One may imagine a probabilistic model of this reasoning; for the sake of simplicity suppose that we have only two hypotheses H_1 and H_2, represented in the model by two urns, U_1 and U_2, both of which contain red and white balls. Let p_1 be the probability one has to draw a red ball from urn U_1 and p_2 the corresponding probability for urn U_2. Let π_1 be the probability of drawing a red ball from urn U_1 and π_2 the corresponding probability for urn U_2. It is then easy to calculate the probability of drawing a red ball from urn U_1, relative to all the eventualities in which one draws a red ball; it is

$$\pi_1{}^1 = \frac{\pi_1 \, p_1}{\pi_1 \, p_1 + \pi_2 \, p_2}$$

Assume now that our situation is as follows: A red ball has been drawn but it is not known from which urn it was taken. The following question arises: what is the plausibility of the hypothesis according to which it came from urn U_1? The answer merely applies a principle valid in all analogous cases; this plausibility is strictly measured by the probability π_1 one had to draw a red ball from urn U_1 relative to drawings of red balls only. From the study of the value of $\pi_1{}^1$ one may easily conclude that $\pi_1{}^1$ is greater than π_1 when p_1 is greater than p_2 and even more strictly that $\pi_1{}^1$ is much greater than π_1 if p_1 is much greater than p_2. This result may be translated as follows: A red ball having been drawn, the plausibility $\pi_1{}^1$ of the hypothesis according to which it would come from

In the preceding discussion we have left aside the problem of erratic errors. Their influence may be eliminated by replacing the individual time of each clock by the *time of the battery*, i.e. by a mean time calculated according to a general synchronization as rigorous as possible.

In order to bring theory and practice into agreement we have insisted especially on the construction of a battery of clocks through the comparison of two by two in their corrected times. This is, of course, not the only procedure that may be applied. One might, for example, transform into a testing procedure the method permitting to calculate the ratio of the drifts to the frequencies by means of two series of successive observations.

On the other hand, we have not tried to establish or even to know all the contexts in which we would have to engage in order to reach the fundamental roots of all the knowledge and of all practices to be applied. We have repeatedly noted that if we wanted to include everything we would face a task of generalized elucidation. What are the principles according to which such a task may be undertaken? This is the question in which, throughout constantly renewed peripeties, culminates the study of the measurement of time. This question will not remain unanswered. Our answer which we shall give in the last two chapters of the present work will likewise represent a culmination, that of the test to which we have subjected the principles of open methodology. We already have emphasized that in order to maintain clearly the direction of our project, we must show by what procedure a battery of drift clocks could be used to measure a time without drift, while we do not resort to a different type of clock. This has

---

urn U_1 is greater than the probability one had of drawing it from this urn at the moment when the probability of drawing red from the first urn is greater than the corresponding probability for the second urn.

But π_1 is the measure of the plausibility of the hypothesis H_1 before the drawing, and π_1^1 is the plausibility of the same hypothesis after the drawing. The resulting rule is the following: When, given two concurrent hypotheses H_1 and H_2, an event is more probable in the hypothesis H_1, the plausibility of H_1 is reinforced if the event comes to pass.

been done; we have shown how practice and theory must support each other to reach this aim.

Of course this does not mean that introduced into a specific situation as an instrument of precision, the battery of quartz clocks must not be combined with other clocks. The reasons which we have, in the framework of the present study, to show that the battery of quartz clocks can be set up and can function as a closed system, do not affect in any way the person who must measure time with all possible precision. Such a person, for example, does not have to defend himself for making use of heterogeneous time, of a synthetic time in whose measurement the quartz clocks must collaborate with the planetary timepiece which was mentioned in connection with astronomical time and with the atomic clocks, which will be discussed later. It is enough that he has his own reasons for doing so. We shall come back to this subject at the end of the following section.

The following concrete specifications are from the chronometrical observatory of Neuchâtel (Switzerland).

The short-term stability of a quartz clock is $1,5 \cdot 10^{-11}$. The drift may be, for example, 10^{-10} of relative variation of the frequency per 24 hours. Unfortunately we do not have accurate data for the long term stability of the quartz clock with corrected drift.

THE ATOMIC CLOCKS
Limitations of the Other Clocks

Before we begin our explanation of the principles on which the construction of the atomic clock is based, let us briefly recall the circumstances which guarantee for the measurement of astronomical time and of the time of the quartz clocks a precision superior to that of the terrestrial timepiece.

The rotatory motion of the earth around its axis is affected by certain irregularities, some of which may be understood rather easily while others are still unexplained. The motion includes, for example, a secular drift whose cause could be the loss of kinetic energy due to disturbances of the seas and the atmosphere; the motion presents seasonal fluctuations which may be attributed at least in part to variations of the moment of inertia of the terrestrial globe, produced by phenomena such as the transfer of ice from the northern to the southern hemisphere and vice versa, etc. The explanations which may thus be given have a common characteristic: They introduce events and phenomena which are located on the earth itself and which because of their accidental character can hardly be evaluated.

Now, if one proceeds from the rotatory motion of the earth around its axis to its revolving motion around the sun, i.e. if one proceeds from the terrestrial timepiece to the planetary one, the influence of these factors disappears. The value of terrestrial and planetary constants on which the law of evolution of the planetary system around the sun depends, seems practically unaffected by the phenomena responsible for the irregularities of the terrestrial timepiece. Consequently, if we knew the exact laws of the progress of the stars on the celestial vault, and if it were possible for us to observe them with absolute accuracy, we would thereby possess a clock whose irregularities would be negligible. But we know that, in certain respects, perfection could not be attained. The unforeseeable motions of the atmosphere in particular introduce an element of chance into all results of our observations. It follows, as we have already said, that only the determination of rather long durations of time attains a relative precision which justifies the use of astronomical time.

Quartz clocks are far from exhibiting the stability of the planetary timepiece. The drift affecting them is not constant at first and then remains so only during a certain span of time. The theoretical aspect of their law of aging eludes us almost completely. These clocks moreover present erratic and totally unforeseeable irregularities. How can these highly unfavorable conditions be overcome? The first point is that the simultaneous observation of a certain group of quartz clocks permits us to eliminate the bad clocks and to determine the constant characteristics of the remaining good ones. The calculation of the average time of a battery of clocks thus constituted moreover permits us to weaken and even to eliminate the influence of the erratic irregularities. While the planetary timepiece does not offer us any hold for the experiment, the quartz clocks lend themselves to it to the extent of their ability to compensate mutually their factors of irregularity. What especially characterizes the quartz clock, as compared with clocks with medium or long periods, is the structural fineness of the oscillatory phenomenon utilized by it. It is true that this utilization requires an entire apparatus of electronic supplement, but this is a circumstance which we had decided not to dwell upon.

The planetary timepiece and the quartz clock thus offer very different advantages; one might ask whether a clock could be imagined which would combine them. In other terms, are there no oscillatory phenomena of a much greater stability than that of the quartz oscillators and of a structural fineness comparable to theirs? The answer is positive. We have today at our disposal a family of devices, the *masers* (Microwave Amplification by Stimulated Emission of Radiation), which satisfy both these requirements. We shall now explain how some of the masers can be utilized.

Principle of the Atomic Clocks

We shall not plunge into the details of execution, however, which pose numerous delicate problems to the specialists of time measurement. What we consider most important is to find again the outline of the procedure by which one can utilize a phenomenon or a group of phenomena in order to make a clock.

Let us first note that in principle a stationary electromagnetic wave of sufficient energy and proper frequency may immediately give rise to a timepiece; it suffices to erect an antenna on it which converts the electromagnetic oscillation into an electric oscillation of the same frequency, which an electronic apparatus will transform into a rotatory motion as in a quartz clock. The electronic apparatus involves a certain inertia. As a result the frequency of the oscillation must not exceed the limit of the ultra-short hertzian waves.

Suppose that the technical problems relating to this aspect

of the procedure have been properly solved. It remains to be explained how one can produce an adequate frequency of very high stability and impose it on an electromagnetic oscillation of sufficient energy.

Let us now examine the production of this frequency. Theoretical considerations at first are predominant. We invoke a fundamental principle of quantum physics, which may be expressed as follows:

Certain material structures (atoms, molecules, etc.) are capable of more or less instantaneous mutations characterized by the absorption or the emission of certain corresponding energy quanta. Of each mutation of this kind we say that the structure passes from one level of energy to another, to a superior level if absorption is concerned and to an inferior one in the case of emission.

Let Δe be the quantum of energy liberated by the transition from a superior level to an inferior one; the quantic theory of emission attributes it to a photon affected by a frequency v determined through the following relation: $\Delta e = hv$, in which h represents the famous constant of Planck.

It is known that neither energy nor frequency are scalar quantities, i.e. quantities which remain unchanged if one switches from one system of reference to another. On the contrary, we are concerned in both cases with the fourth component of a quadridimensional vector of four-dimensional space from the Minkowski universe used in relativity theory. It is therefore necessary, for the preceding definitions to make univocal sense, to define clearly to which system of reference the corresponding energy and frequency are attributed. There is only one possibility for designating without ambiguity the energy quanta which a specific material structure is capable of emitting or absorbing, namely to put them univocally defined into the appropriate system of reference of the material structure. The frequencies emitted or absorbed may then be considered as the natural constants of that structure.

This precise attribution may also be considered when one must evaluate these frequencies in the system of reference of an observation device to which the material structures are not invariably linked. This is the case especially if we are concerned, not with a material structure taken in isolation, but rather with an ensemble of similar structures whose systems proper are not all at rest relative to each other. All have the same eigenfrequency but nevertheless do not necessarily deliver frequencies equal to the system of the observing device respectively. Compared to their natural values the frequencies observed will thus appear to have undergone some dispersion. They will be distributed on a band of a certain width.

Here are some examples of "transitions" which certain transmitters already are utilizing:

1. Passage of the nitrogen atom from one side to the other of the ammonia molecule.

2. Lines of the hyperfine structure of the caesium and rubidium atoms.

Projects exist to utilize others which would permit a still greater accuracy:

3. Thallium lines.

4. Hydrogen lines.

5. Carbon monoxide lines.

After these reminders, there are two more points to be elucidated: how to prepare a "population" of oscillators each of which would be ready to emit in its own system a photon corresponding to one of its own natural frequencies; to explain how the photons thus emitted concur in maintaining a stationary electromagnetic wave of the same frequency.

The emissions in the domain of the microwaves, in contrast to the emissions in the domain of optics, are not spontaneous; the population of the two levels of energy being perceptibly equal, the frequency emitted by those in the higher state of energy is immediately absorbed by those in the lower state. In order that the emission should be strong enough and consequently should not be troubled too much by background noise, one must somehow increase the proportion of atoms in the higher state. This may be done by various methods: optical pumping causing the atoms to pass to the higher level, or elimination of atoms from the lower level with the help of a magnetic or electrical field. The atoms thus prepared could then furnish the necessary energy of maintenance to a stationary electromagnetic wave coordinated with the frequency of their emission.

Concerning this stationary wave there is one last principal question to be elucidated. The entire apparatus is designed to produce a particularly stable frequency. It finds it in the natural frequency of the elementary transmitters selected for this purpose. In order to be observable, the former must be collected. Is it not paradoxical to attempt this through the intermediary of a wave whose frequency would in advance be adapted to the one which is to be observed? If this wave can be produced, is it not unnecessary to resort to the population of elementary emitters? As a matter of fact, this wave is not produced in advance. It is the wave of resonance of a reflecting cavity and may be regulated with extreme precision; the wave can be produced by the spontaneous emission of only a few of the photons produced by the injected emitters.

Briefly, the theoretical scheme of an atomic clock thus conceived contains three essential parts: The first is, after suitable preparation, the emission of a well-defined frequency; the second is the manifestation of this frequency by the wave of resonance of a well-regulated cavity, and the third is the reception of the latter wave by a receiving post capable of counting and adding up its oscillations.

The realization of this program naturally involves numerous and considerable difficulties of a technical order. To explain how they can be surmounted, we would have to establish numerous contexts, theoretical as well as practical. In order to achieve this, we would not only have to do the work of a specialist; in addition, starting from the specialist's position, we would have to go into all the explanations which a complete analysis of this position would require. It is clear that again this is a task which nobody would like to undertake. But for our purposes the setting up of these contexts would have only a secondary importance. We know in advance, as we have noted on other occasions, the situation to which each of them would inevitably lead us; concerning any specific other fundamental notion, we would only encounter problems analogous to those treated in connection with time. We therefore turn our attention to those among these problems which are brought into focus in particular through the examination of atomic clocks.*

Let us return to the main intention which informs the project of manufacturing an atomic clock according to the scheme we have explained. The problem is to produce, for the purpose of measuring time, an especially fine and stable oscillation. The question of fineness of structure of a phenomenon, an oscillation in particular, has already been evoked in the context of the quartz clocks; we will therefore not discuss it here. It remains for us to discuss the question of stability. We shall then find another opportunity for some principal remarks concerning the methodology of research.

Stability

It is convenient to distinguish between the theoretical and the observational aspects of stability. This fact cannot surprise us; it is in accordance with the principle of duality according to which an investigation concerning the real world could not be reduced either to its rational or to its observational aspects. Let us first consider the theoretical side.†

We return to the example of the emission of a quantum of energy of the corresponding frequency by an elementary transmitter. We have said that for a specific transmitter (determined not individually but through the characteristics of the theory applied), and in the eigensystem of this transmitter, the frequencies which the latter is capable of emitting are completely determined. But, to be able to speak with such incisive simplicity, the theory isolates the transmitter in its own universe. One will have to go back to his first statements in order to revise and complete them, taking into account the circumstances of the insertion of the elementary transmitter into an

---

* We might recall that as a whole the question will be taken up again in the chapter on the autofoundation of the disciplines of science.

† It is obvious that at each of its stages our exposé lends itself to certain observations concerning the method of research. Thus we proceed towards an experience whose total evaluation will be made in our two last chapters, especially in our methodological commentaries.

enlarged context. This is the case, for example, if one imagines that this system is integrated into a field of gravitation; the more intensive the field, the more the ensemble of possible frequencies is deviating "towards the red," i.e. the more each of these frequencies decreases. The same is true if one imagines that the eigensystem of the transmitter is the seat of an electric or electromagnetic field; entering into reaction with these, the phenomenon of emission undergoes certain effects, the Zeeman effect in particular.

The phenomenon of the emission thus is not completely determined (and consequently, perfectly stable) except in an ideally simplified case.

Can the affirmation of stability be maintained in the other cases? How should it be defined? One may say that a phenomenon, otherwise determinate, is stable if its development and its characteristics vary only very little if certain circumstances capable of influencing them vary perceptibly. (By pressing the matter more closely one might introduce a *degree of stability*, provided that the theory would sufficiently dominate the circumstances to be taken into consideration. In the practice of research one does not generally stop to make a preliminary theoretical study of the phenomena under consideration; one judges them taking into account at the same time theoretical considerations and the results of observation. For what we have seen of this, it is nevertheless important to keep the theoretical and the observational aspects of the question as neatly separated as possible.)

Does the phenomenon of emission remain stable in the enlarged sense which we have just considered? Let us say, so as to be on the safe side, that the specialists of atomic clocks know how to avoid the cases in which the answer would not be clearly in the affirmative.

In our preceding remarks the particular case which occupies our attention has remained at the center of discussion. We believe, however, that it would by no means be difficult to transfer the essence of what has been said to any other case.

Let us now turn to the observational aspect. The definition of stability may remain the same, but the words in it do not retain the same sense. What, for example, from the observational viewpoint, is a well-determined phenomenon? It is naturally not enough that it should be conceived with all the precision which the theory may imply; it also must be realized with the guarantees of an experimentation sufficiently exact and assured. And how does one actually establish the connection of this phenomenon with an eventual experimental context capable of influencing it? We are faced here again with all the problems into which we have run each time when we had to cross a threshold of accuracy.

With the guarantee of the analyses which we have made so far, and the results which we have already obtained, we nevertheless cannot question everything again. The control of a stability does not present hitherto unknown difficulties, if one stays within the scope of easy-to-make observations and if one is content with the precision proper to a certain group of instruments and devices which have already been tested. But the same is not the case if one goes to the limits of this precision, especially if one intends to attain a superior precision. One will then find himself again in a situation analogous to the one which we have described several times before, namely in the situation where he plans to measure time with an accuracy not offered by any of the clocks already in existence. We have given various examples of how this difficulty may be solved.

In our case the situation presents itself as follows: From a strictly observational viewpoint one can only verify relative stabilities. It is always in relation to standards which are considered as stable that a specific experimental result may be interpreted as a proof of stability. It may happen, however, that the connection with an overall situation can be more important than a connection which can be observed with one of its parts. But how do we have to operate in the area where we plan to use a phenomenon more stable than all those which have already been realized through our observational activity? How can we give an operational basis to these claims? Is this not an insoluble problem?

As we know, the problem is not insoluble. The situation is

analogous to that in which we had to show how bad quartz clocks may be eliminated without the use of clocks of a different type. It was sufficient to have a group of quartz clocks at our disposal and to be able to compare them with the required precision, the justification of the entire procedure being given by what we called the reasoning through the improbable.

It is clear that the problem of observational guarantees of stability could be treated in the same fashion if the following conditions were fulfilled:

1. *The element* through which the stability must be guaranteed must be able to be produced and reproduced repeatedly.

2. It is not necessary that all the devices and all the phenomena which are used for this purpose should be identical, but it is necessary that the relative stability of each of these cases relative to all the rest could be verified with the desired accuracy.

3. Finally it is necessary that the techniques of manufacture be sufficiently advanced so that the case of the relative stability should not be improbable.

In the device which we have shown schematically, *the element* whose stability is being discussed is the frequency of the resonance wave. Supposing that the latter could be produced in a way to satisfy the exigencies which have been described, it would be unimportant if it were produced in a different fashion. It could play the rôle which belongs to it in our plan. There is one question in particular which could be disregarded: to know whether the frequency realizes precisely that of the elementary transmitters which the entire apparatus is designed to realize.

Accuracy

The problem of accuracy, or fidelity of realization, is thus distinct from the problem of stability. This is not surprising. The way in which the latter presents itself in our case shows clearly with how much additional attention it must be viewed. On two points, among others, the realization of the scheme will introduce an indetermination which was not contained in the scheme. This concerns above all the frequency of injected transmitters. The conditions under which we might speak for all at the same time of one and the same frequency are not fulfilled. This is not a frequency determined with the utmost precision, but rather a band of frequencies proposed to the amplification by the resonance of the cavity. On the other hand, the frequency of resonance is not specified either in a completely accurate way: For the cavity itself there exists a certain band of possible resonances. How should we formulate the problem of accuracy under these conditions? One might be tempted to give up this project, because it may seem that the search for a *true* frequency, whose realization with a maximum of accuracy would be of practical interest, can only lead to an arbitrary decision. It is certainly remarkable that this is not the case. We shall not enter into the details of all the measures taken to ensure the singleness and the stability of the frequency which will be said to be the most exact possible under the conditions of the experiment. It seems not to be in doubt that these measures cannot be understood and justified except through the intention of realizing with precision a privileged frequency, the one which is isolated from the entire apparatus to be proposed to the resonance.

Let us now try to discern the perspective in which all the elements necessary for the determination of an atomic time articulate each other. Have the theoretical views which are part of it already found their definitive basis elsewhere and in advance? This is impossible, because time enters into it, and consequently they could not be supposed as being valid without an observational guarantee in which time could play a part. But, as far as time in particular is concerned, none of the previous guarantees equals the manufacture, the setting in motion, and the synchronization of two atomic clocks, or better still, of a battery of atomic clocks. But can this manufacture, this setting in motion, and this synchronization operate in any way other than by being informed by these theoretical views, as plausible hypotheses of which we must make the most correct use? And this most correct use, does it not mean to rely on them without ignoring the fact that by thus involving them in the adventure of the measurement of time, we subject them to the most exacting test?

In short, it is the totality, the theoretical views as well as the technical inventions and the experimental procedures, which are involved all at the same time and finally justified in the success of the enterprise.

For the moment, what has been said nevertheless must be treated with a certain reserve; many technical difficulties have to be solved before the atomic clocks can function continuously during extended periods of time. For the moment their specific importance is mainly their function as a standard of frequency.

Pragmatic Synthesis at the Level of the Measured Times

We have not failed to emphasize that the three variants of the measurement of time, discussed under the common title of *"Synthetic Time,"* do not all offer the same advantages. The time of astronomy is suitable for long periods and then provides a long-term verification for the time of the quartz clocks; the quartz clocks are especially suitable for short and medium lengths of time, provided that they are given regular frequency checks through atomic clocks; in their rôle as standards of frequency the atomic clocks are irreplaceable. Thus we see being "defined," with the aid of techniques as different and as diversely founded as those which have been discussed, a synthetic time whose precision surpasses the precision of any one of all the times measured separately.

The following fact must be emphasized because it is highly important for a just appreciation of what constitutes the objectivity of knowledge: It is not towards a dispersion of the times measured separately that their comparison leads, but to a convergence towards a time more precise and more broadly based than each of them separately.

The chronometric observatory of Neuchâtel writes on the subject: "The following is a very succinct chronological outline of the fashion in which the problems of the accurate measurement of time have presented themselves to us since the construction

of our first atomic clocks. These few data permit us to understand that in practice the development of methods and procedures must follow the concern for increasing effectiveness."

In 1957, *the second* was officially defined as a well-determined fraction of the tropical year. This definition was still
valid on January 1, 1964. The corresponding temporal scale was
that of *astronomical* time. Its origin is conventionally fixated
precisely at the beginning of the year 1900 of our calendar.
The determination of *instants* is based on the observation of
the planets and of the moon in relation to the fixed stars. In
practice, astronomical time is obtained by applying a correction Δ to the universal time determined by a previous method,
such as the passage of stars at the meridian, for example. The
adoption of astronomical time is justified by the fact that if one
identifies it with the variable t of the equations of celestial mechanics, one obtains for the solar system a better adjustment
of the observations to the calculations.

The temporal scale thus established, however, has a grave
defect; it is the difficulty and the delay with which it carries
an instant, as well as a certain inaccuracy which results from
the limited precision of the observations as well as from the
imperfect exactness of the computations through successive approximations.

When in 1957 it appeared possible to substitute a more uniform temporal scale for the former universal time, quartz
clocks were being used which, in the space of one year, were
equal in accuracy to the "universal clock," being superior to
it over shorter durations of time and less exact over longer
durations.

The first atomic clocks essentially were *standards of frequency*. Their stability was so precarious that it was out of the
question to let them run without interruption in order to count
their oscillations one by one from a determinate starting point
in order to establish a new time scale. Quartz clocks were
therefore used as *balance wheels*, their frequency being verified from time to time, every hour, for example, by comparison with atomic frequencies. By reporting the frequencies thus
obtained as ordinates, one obtained a graph representing, as a

function of time, the variation of the frequency of a specific quartz clock. (The question of knowing which time had to be reported as abscissa was without practical importance.) Under the hypothesis that the functions thus obtained are integrable, one finds that their integral from a specified origin represents for each quartz clock the correction capable of converting the time of this clock into what we have called an atomic time.

For us, the principal justification of this procedure consisted in the fact that the times thus corrected from different quartz clocks diverged very little from each other. We have been able to show in this fashion that the error introduced by the use of quartz clocks as balancing wheels was negligible relative to the fluctuations of the atomic standards themselves. We have in effect been able to determine these fluctuations, or at least their minimal value, from the moment when we had at our disposal several standards whose frequencies could be compared. The situation is therefore entirely different from that prevailing in the field of astronomy; there the test for the quality of a time scale is the agreement between the computation and the observation; for a physical scale the test is the agreement between the various experiments.*

From 1957 to the present, atomic times established with the help of quartz clocks as balance wheels have been preserved in all the laboratories having atomic standards at their disposal. A common starting point has been conventionally determined for them (atomic time = universal time on January 1, 1958), and an arbitrary numerical value has been attributed by general agreement to the frequency utilized, that of the caesium atom. The comparison of these atomic scales, by means of radioelectric signals, equally makes evident that the error introduced by the quartz clocks is negligible relative to the other errors of measurement.

Since 1957 the atomic standards have been improved considerably:

1. Above all, atomic clocks were constructed in which the quartz clock was incorporated, the motion of the latter being

---

* In our perspective these two tests reveal two aspects of the procedure of autofoundation.

corrected through an auxiliary mechanism in such a way as to show the atomic hour directly.

2. The relative stability of the laboratory standards has successfully progressed from 10^{-9} to 10^{-10}, and as far as 10^{-12}.

The performances of the quartz clocks moreover have been improved sufficiently so that these clocks could continue to absorb the frequencies of the atomic standards without introducing any appreciable error. It is only quite recently that the discovery was made that at the precision of 10^{-12} the frequency of the best quartz clocks is a discontinuous function in each of its points.

Equally recently, other types of atomic standards were developed (hydrogen *masers*, for example) which represent a new fundamental advance; they are active oscillators, i.e. oscillators indicating their frequency at each moment; they function so accurately that they can remain active without interruption over long periods of time. Thus the *masers* combine the two functions which formerly were filled by the quartz clocks for the determination of the atomic hour, namely to give signals and to serve as a balance wheel.

A certain development is thus completed. Nevertheless it remains true that the combined uses of different types of clocks, corresponding to the means one has at his disposal and the aims he has in mind, retains its complete legitimacy.

Chapter Eight

METHODOLOGICAL COMMENTARY
AND CONCLUSIONS

AUTOFOUNDATION

We might have decided not to wait until now to present some methodological conclusions concerning the fashion in which an exact experimental science can be established.

Classical Mechanics Cannot Be Established
Without Measuring Instruments

Take the example of classical mechanics. If one keeps to its theoretical and consequently to its mathematical aspect, it may be constructed deductively from a certain number of fundamental notions and basic principles. Time necessarily is one of the fundamental notions, and the principle of inertia (or any other principle equivalent to it) is one of the basic principles. But time is not simply and exclusively the variable t which occurs, for example, in Lagrange's equations; this variable must be capable of a practical interpretation which makes of it a measurable magnitude. The same is true for all the other variables which determine the state of a particular mechanism whose evolution one wishes to describe. To the question, "How does the variable t have to be interpreted?" we remember having heard the following reply: "It is simply the time which your watch shows to you." This answer is of course inadequate, since there are not only good watches, such as show the time with infallible precision. The answer therefore should at least have been modified by the following reservation: ". . . provided that you have a good watch." It is true that this would only have provoked a new question: "How does one know and prove that a watch is good?" From question to answer to question, it is finally the problem of the manufacture itself of the good watch which remains unsolved.

But the Construction of the Instrument Invokes the Theory

We have seen the outlines of the solution. Let us remember this: The development of the watchmaking craft may be explained in terms of an ideal and of a solution; the ideal is that of the isochronal oscillatory system, while the intention is materially to realize this ideal as best we can, with the highest precision possible. The ideal has taken the form of the theoretical balance wheel in which the conditions of a perfectly elastic oscillation are assumed to be satisfied. The intention has tended concretely to realize these conditions, going so far as to create the metallurgy of especially adapted steels, viz. the *invar* and its derivatives. For what we wish to explain now, it is important to emphasize that it is the study of the theoretical balance wheel which orients our appreciation of the causes for which the watch emerging from the watchmaker's shop is still deviating from its ideal model, and our search for ways to remedy this situation. Now the study (not necessarily theoretical) of the perfectly isochronous balance wheel explicitly presents itself here as a special application of the laws of classical mechanics as an already established discipline. In short, the manufacture of a good watch thus turns out to be based on two foundations: the knowledge and application of the laws of classical mechanics on the one hand and experimental research and the testing of the best materials and procedures on the other. It is therefore clear that the watch which is consulted does not give, to someone wishing to explain how mechanics can be established as a discipline at the same time coherent and effective, a previously determined interpretation of the variable t assured without the help of mechanics.

Taking this statement into account, one must therefore say that, as far as time is concerned, mechanics is *autofounded*. This statement throws a rather unexpected light on the problem of the foundation of a discipline which, as we have noted, is supposed to be both coherent and effective. (By an "effective" discipline we mean a discipline which can be successfully applied and satisfy certain requirements of precision in some particular area of our activity.) Having encountered so

many examples, we know by now that the coherence of the
theoretical formulation does not in itself represent an adequate
guarantee of effectiveness. Such a guarantee is achieved only
through the experiment. The theory must be put to the test
in the very interpretation one intends to give to it. "If that is
all," we might be told, "it will suffice to mount an adequate
device of observation and make the required measurements.
Once these are made and interpreted, the situation will no
longer contain any equivocation. From a merely coherent statement the testimony of the experiment will make, or not make,
an effective and consequently admissible statement. Is it not
always so that, in the sciences aiming at the exploration of
reality, the discursive and the experimental must mutually complete each other in order to form the double web of objective
knowledge?"

The Problem of the Instrument

Certainly not! This is not the way, from the point of view
of a correct method, in which things must be judged. It is
not enough to have the intention of effecting a series of decisive measurements in order to be able to do so. In order
to measure, one must have the indispensable measuring instruments. Does one have the right (methodologically) to pass over
in silence the question of the source of these instruments? Leaving this question aside, as if it did not raise any problems,
seems to imply that the experimenter will have no trouble acquiring the instruments he needs, and that they are available
to him in advance. But in general the observer is in an entirely different situation. It may happen that in forming the
project of measuring a magnitude with some degree of precision, he does not have any instrument which he could use
for this purpose. In the course of our study we have found
ourselves more than once in this situation. In particular, this
was the case each time we prepared to cross a "threshold of
precision." We have seen the problem of the instrument gradually assume its full dimension together with the problem of
accuracy. It now takes its place in the dialogue which must
be established between the theoretical statement and the ex-

perimental proof. The idea of what a normal situation is, as held by someone who engages in research, is fundamentally influenced thereby. This situation is the following: Having to verify the correctness of a theoretical statement about a certain physical reality—its interpretation, which in itself is given only in practice, i.e. with some degree of stability and precision—the practitioner is not automatically in possession of the indispensable measuring instruments. The obligation to invent and to produce these instruments is then integrated into the research program. The measuring instrument has the function of managing the encounter between the theories announced and the realities observed. In two cases at least, the production of an original instrument presents itself as a preliminary condition for the progress of the investigation:

1. It may happen that the already existing instruments do not imply the degree of precision required for an observation to be decisive.

2. It may also happen (the transition from classical physics to relativistic physics offers a prime example) that the measuring instruments at one's disposal have been conceived and constructed in accordance with theoretical views whose inadequacy has been revealed by the experiment and for which one intends to substitute new and more exact theoretical concepts.

This situation appears in its whole acuity when the new theories are still awaiting their test while the latter cannot be conducted without the help of new instruments, whose manufacture is not yet accomplished.

We have just said that in a very conventional and superficial way of conceiving the method of the experimental sciences, no mention is made of the problem of the instrument, as if one always had in advance the measuring instruments without which the confrontation of the experiment with the theory could never take place. The second of these eventualities clearly shows how incorrect this concept is. It is totally incapable of expressing, especially in the "acute" case which has been discussed, how one can effect correctly, in a given experimental context, the substitution of one theory for another when these two theories are not logically compatible. Now this acute case is by no means a somewhat artificial "method-ological invention." It is on the contrary something which is proposed most urgently by contemporary physics for a method-ical analysis.

It is true that at first sight the project of integrating the problem of the instrument with the problem of the verification (or interpretation) of the theories appears to be unrealizable. This is so unless one discards a certain group of much too simplistic ideas about the fashion in which scientific research creates the connection between the laws announced and the facts observed. But it is not so for one who knows how to distinguish from them the solution concerning the example which we have just given, the autofoundation of classical me-chanics through the intermediary of the watch. We have noted that the processes of manufacture of a good watch have not been developed in a stage preceding any setup of theoretical mechanics. The study of these procedures on the contrary has brought into focus the involvement of the theory in the prac-tice of manufacture. Classical mechanics is a structure whose being tested through the experiment cannot be considered su-perfluous; such a test can be made only by the intermediary, among other things, of an instrument for measuring time. Thus the watch, to whose manufacture mechanics contributes, in turn contributes to the foundation of mechanics as a confirmed discipline, with the degree of precision required in experimen-tation.

A Vicious Circle?

Is there not, in this give-and-take from mechanics to the watch and from the watch to mechanics, something analogous to a vicious circle? This would certainly be the case if it were merely a matter of definition. But mechanics and its theoretical setup on the one hand, and the watch and its practical manu-facture on the other, form a whole which is involved as such in the test, in an activity whose criteria are failure or success. For both, their common success is that time, for which the watch provides the measure, may be interpreted as a realization of the variable t of mechanics. It is sufficient for this that the interpretation makes of the latter an effective discipline, i.e. a discipline permanently applicable.

The success of the testing of the whole thus ensures two essential results. The first concerns the watch whose good quality it ensures, the quality of a watch capable of accurately measuring the time which will be used in the applications of mechanics; the second concerns the mechanics to which it guarantees its character of effective discipline.

To someone who is troubled about the significance of the variable t which appears in the formulations of the laws of mechanics, one may thus answer: It is the time measured by the good watches. But it should be added immediately that if this is so, the reason is that the watches have been manufactured according to this purpose, complying in advance, to the full extent of their possibilities, with the laws which they serve to make visible. It should also be added that by abandoning the idea of an instrument constructed and calibrated in advance in a stage previous to that of the decisive application, whose legitimacy is established together with that of mechanics, one does not commit any methodological error. We recognize that by letting the watch contribute to the test of mechanics, we are making an experiment which in turn puts the watch to the test. This does not mean that we have discovered a gap or a weakness of the method; we only put into place, by conferring on it its inalienable importance, the rôle of the test of effectiveness—a test in which the measuring instrument is likewise involved. The discipline proves valuable by even involving the instrument as an organizer of an activity capable of questioning it again. The demonstration towards which it proceeds is not a demonstration of logics but a demonstration by the fact; the reason that the activity which it organizes actually eludes the sanction of failure is that the discipline is validly established.

Generality of These Remarks

Throughout classical mechanics the preceding considerations concern, as we have noted, the very method of scientific research, especially as far as concerns the knowledge of the world

which is called "the world of the physical realities." One may
easily imagine how this first example of autofoundation could
be adapted to other situations and circumstances; the example
is so clear that the generalization offers itself spontaneously. It
seems useful to us, however, to make some supplementary remarks which the case of classical mechanics naturally suggests.

The variable *t* is not the only independent variable which
appears in the formulation of the laws of mechanics; *t* certainly
is a privileged variable, since it is the only one which furnishes
the referential into which is inscribed the temporal structure of
the evolution of any mechanical system. The thought strikes one
immediately, however, that what has been said of time and its
measurement must be able to find its application in a more or
less strict analogy for all the other magnitudes defining the state
of the system. The first of these magnitudes that come to mind
are of course the geometric magnitudes, viz. distances and
angles. For each of these, i.e. for the variable designating it,
whether it be *x, y, z, ϕ, ψ,* or *θ,* one may equally demand that
it should be their interpretation from the angle of applied mechanics. And if one would answer that these are simply the
values furnished by the corresponding instruments of measurement (with a more or less narrow margin of precision) we
could not fail to decide, as we have for the watch and for the
variable *t,* that this way of answering is inadequate. It is so because it passes over in complete silence everything relating to
the manufacture and to the use of these instruments. It presupposes in particular that the latter could be constructed without involving the laws in whose verification they might be used.
As we know by now this is a hazardous presupposition, whose
soundness cannot be taken for granted without a thorough
study of the instruments themselves, the principles and procedures of their manufacture, as well as the conditions and
the circumstances of their repeated use. What appears plausible,
as soon as our attention has been directed towards the problem
of the instrument, is not that the latter can be constructed on a
theoretical and technical level to some extent inferior or anterior
to that of mechanics and ever answer afresh to the exigencies of
a ceaselessly increasing precision. It is not even that the theo-

retical and technical level where the production of the instrument really takes place is that of mechanics itself. On the contrary, it is that one must (as in the case of radar installations) go beyond the level of mechanics to stop only at a superior level, the level of an area of physics where mechanics is no more than a special sector.

This statement should not surprise us; it was already inevitable throughout the chapter in which we have analyzed the modalities of the collaboration, in the determination of the actually most accurate time, between astronomical observations, quartz clocks, and atomic clocks. Does not the consideration of this fact modify the fashion in which the methodological problem must be formulated?

Let us not rush to extreme conclusions. It is true that in the production of measuring instruments for geometrical magnitudes, the stage where the theoretical and technical means of classical mechanics could suffice is already past. It is not forbidden, however, to return to it in our imagination. If we could maintain ourselves at this stage, the methodological situation in principle would not present any new problem. It would suffice to repeat everything we have said about the rôle of the watch and its manufacture in the process of autofoundation of mechanics, and to apply it to the ensemble of instruments of measurement indispensable for the test of validity so often mentioned before. This last remark casts a new light on what we have called the problem of the instrument. We have been able to show that this problem is not completely separable from that of the autofoundation of the discipline, that it is incorporated into it and illustrates only one of its aspects. It becomes evident at this point that the problem of the instrument does not concern the instrument capable of measuring a specific magnitude, such as time, for example. In the open perspective of a search for an ever-improved precision, the production of this type of instrument is not independent of the production of the instruments intended for measuring other magnitudes with which the autofoundation of the discipline associates them. We have emphasized, in the context of the watch, the give-and-take between it and mechanics. We now discover that the same must be said, at least in principle, of all the other instruments involved in the test of validity of the discipline. This fact establishes between them a solidarity of destination and of justification which no longer permit us to imagine how each of the magnitudes involved together could be the object of a separate "operational definition."

The solidarity of which we are speaking may be underscored by a comparison with the axiomatic method, which could also show how different, in spite of certain analogies, the procedure of autofoundation is from a procedure of axiomatization.

Does the Axiomatic Method Suffice?

In order to found a discipline axiomatically one chooses a certain ensemble of fundamental notions (of which one has reason to assume that they are adequate) and one interposes between them a certain ensemble of fundamental relations (the axioms of the discipline, of which one has reason to believe that they will never be found inadequate). The rest, i.e. the deployment of the discipline, is then solely a matter of definition and deduction.

In the most recent version of the axiomatic method the axioms are not to be considered as statements each of which would command recognition by its own evidence. They are statements to be used in combination, even though, for reasons of clarity, they are introduced in isolation. The only condition which an axiomatic system must satisfy in order to be admissible is that it should not create contradictions. In the absence of a method capable of deciding, according to the axioms, that this condition is actually satisfied, the axiomatic system cannot be withdrawn from the test of validity represented by its own construction. As far as the theoretical and mathematical aspect is concerned, the testing of a discipline through the intermediary of the activity which it deploys thus compels immediate recognition. We wish, however, to emphasize the following point: In the practice of axiomatization which we are discussing, the fundamental notions must not have other properties than to satisfy the announced axioms. The latter thus give for them an implicit definition. The notions defined in this way therefore are so all at the same time, not each individually. Their participation in one and the same axiomatic structure establishes among them an essential solidarity of signification and capacity of engagement.

The quality of being, or not being, axiomatically developed concerns only the theoretical aspect of a discipline such as mechanics. The test of validity which we have discussed does not transcend this aspect. It must not be confounded with the other test of validity which the discipline undergoes when, by engaging it in an ensemble of interpretations, one turns it into an applied theory. The success of the second test is not a necessary consequence of the success of the first. The first takes place in what may be called the horizon of the theoretical enunciation, the second in that of experimental activity. But in spite of this (essential) difference the recall of the fashion in which the theoretical aspect may be constructed axiomatically permits us to return with greater precision to the circumstances which prevail at the foundation of the doctrine endowed with its full significance.*

* The geometric magnitudes have been cited among the number of magnitudes whose measurement is indispensable for the test of the validity of mechanics. Engaging them thus in the procedure of the autofoundation of the latter, one makes, of course, of geometry a special chapter of mechanics. There is no doubt that geometry can be treated in this fashion. It is even necessary to do so if one wishes that geometry, which must be utilized by mechanics, should have, in the same way as the latter and with the same degree of precision, the character of a proven discipline. The fact remains nevertheless that geometry, earlier than mechanics, has found its status of rational and applied science. It is true that the question of the adequacy of geometry, an abstract discipline, for the description of the real world has often been brought up and discussed. It has often been noted that the following two circumstances have given it a particular acuteness: The discovery of the noneuclidean geometries could not fail to cast doubt on the adequacy of classical geometry as a science of real or physical space; the conversion of the entire physical science to the atomic viewpoint and later to the quantic viewpoint, on the other hand, inevitably leads to the result that only limited precision is accorded to actually effected geometrical measurements. With few exceptions the function of the instrument in the foundation of geometry as a discipline concerned with reality does not seem to be recognized. The fact has not been noted that the measuring instrument itself is inevitably engaged in the test of validity. We shall mention at this point the exceptions to which we have alluded.

When giving a historical account of the noneuclidean geometries, one often

On the other hand, in order that we may speak of a real implicit definition of the fundamental notions, the rôle itself of the axioms must be well defined. Their unique function must be to establish the purely formal relations which, in their totality, will confer their meaning on the notions thus defined. At the moment when an axiom is imposed on the mind it is often endowed with an evidence derived from its involvement in one of its possible realizations. It is a carrier of preliminary information which turns it into something entirely different from a simple structural exigency to be utilized. To be included in a formal system the axioms must therefore be free of any preliminary signification. One must somehow cut the flow of information which they express. Thus separated from any anterior validity, whether intuitive or experimental, it is from the noncontradictory deployment of their consequences that they will derive their legitimacy. And it is through this slant that an element of experimentation will be carried into the very axiomatic setup of the discipline.

---

leaves unexplained what makes the essential difference between the geometric doctrine of Bolyai, for example, and that of Lobachevsky. For Lobachevsky, geometry is not established as true by the single fact of its logical coherence (which, however, seems assured to him by the translation of geometry into analytical geometry). This truth is of the order of effectiveness; it could not be affirmed in the absence of an explicitly given body of procedures and instruments of measurement. Put in their historic context the views of Lobachevsky cannot fail to strike the reader by their profoundness and their originality.

But how does the connection between rational geometry and its applications function according to the usual tradition? One certainly speaks of measuring instruments for distances as well as for angles. But one imagines them *more geometrico*. They are ideal models imagined at the geometric level to which are attributed the properties characteristic of geometrical entities. It is true that in order to effect an actual measurement in a concretely defined situation one could not avoid replacing these ideal instruments by more or less faithful realizations. But the measurement is effected according to the following tacit assumption: if the measuring instrument were perfect, i.e. perfectly conformable to its ideal model, and if its application were perfectly correct, the measurement itself could not but be perfectly correct. This hypothesis is the equivalent of a certain theory of the measurement of geometric magnitudes and the structure of measurable matter. In this respect it only has a very limited validity. Thus it may be explained that the problem of the instrument could have been passed over in silence. It was implicitly attacked by assumptions which common sense entertains but which the progress of knowledge has already proved false.

But this explanation of axiomatization as a procedure of implicit definition does not have its intrinsic aim here. It must serve us exclusively as a term of comparison. Could it not suggest to us a more or less analogous explanation of the operational definition starting from the procedure of autofoundation? The situation would then be as follows:

The Axiom Is Not Yet a Natural Law

1. The theory to be founded in its integral signification would be present in its theoretical form as an axiomatized structure.

This naturally implies that the theory should be considered as complete and furnishing the complete list of the notions, i.e. the magnitudes, to be defined. It implies likewise that these magnitudes are solidarily engaged in the procedure which would exhaustively define their meaning. It finally implies that the theory is complete, that it is not presented merely as a part of a more comprehensive theory which would include it. Under this double aspect the axiomatized theory is closed, although

---

We have emphasized in the text and in the above the solidarity which is established between geometry and mechanics through the fact that the latter's validity necessitates the measuring of certain geometric magnitudes. But cannot geometry be founded for its own sake, apart from this solidarity? Of course this could only be the autofoundation of a geometry assuming the integral totality of its aspects.

In our work, *La géométrie et le problème de l'espace*, we have studied especially the "internal" structure of such an integrated geometry; we have shown the interplay in which its three aspects, the theoretical, the experimental, and the intuitive, can or must be connected or disconnected, identified with, or distinguished from, each other. In these investigations no use has yet been made of the term autofoundation, and the function of the instrument is not yet illuminated with the care we are applying here. But although the word is not used there, the idea is everywhere present. Explaining in particular the intuitive representations and the manipulations through which one can manufacture a series of "geometric objects" permitting to subject the statements of geometry to an experimental test, the author actually develops the program of a genuine autofoundation. Already at this level the conclusions with which he finishes his discussion prepare and prefigure those to which the concern for the highest accuracy gives their full prominence; already in the most elementary perspective the three aspects under which geometry presents itself are recognized as connected and lend mutual support to each other.

Cf. *La géométrie et le problème de l'espace, Cahier 2: Les trois aspects de la géométrie.* Neuchâtel, Editions du Griffon, 1947.

capable of being deductively deployed. It is to be feared that
this closedness may limit the scope of the power of definition
with which the theory will remain invested when it must be
connected with other elements necessarily involved in the situation of autofoundation.

2. Through the intermediary of a certain interpretation, the
statements invested with an axiomatic validity will have to assume a second signification and undergo a second test of validity—this time as natural laws governing a certain group of
phenomena.

It is convenient thus to put the emphasis on the interpretation
which makes of the axiomatized discipline a discipline aiming
at a special reality. But how can such an interpretation be
given, not only in principle but in a way to be able really to
serve at the experimental level? It is totally useless to imagine
a connection between the axiomatic level and an empty experimental level. There cannot be any interpretation except
through the intermediary of adequate realizations. The axiomatic formulations must be realized as natural laws in a certain
ensemble of phenomena, and one must be able to judge to what
extent they are. (The word *phenomenon* must be taken here in
a rather wide sense to designate the ways of existence of a "real
object.") But again, how can the phenomenon be given so as to
be the object of an experiment of some precision?

Assume that we have natural phenomena, given in the same
way as the movements of the planets and the comets on the
celestial sphere, for example. They offer themselves naturally
to observation, but this does not mean that they are natural
carriers of an interpretation which would permit us to read
there the statement of Newton's law of universal attraction. The
observer must be in a position to determine the stages whose
succession constitutes the evolution of such a phenomenon. He
must know how to discern the magnitudes between which the
natural law must establish the link of a solidary variation. But
we must not deceive ourselves; even the most immediate phenomenal appearances do not at first deliver the phenomenon or
the group of phenomena on which the axiomatic statements will
be tested for their secondary validity. These appearances are

like the traces from which the phenomenon must be recon-
structed. But how can it be? Precisely by the fact that these
traces may be incorporated in an interpretation. Thus one falsi-
fies the real data of the problem by assuming that the phenomenon on which the interpretation must project itself can be
given in reality previous to any interpretation, and by also assuming that an interpretation could be imagined on the mere
sight of the phenomenal appearances and independent of any
theorizing activity. Behind the problem of interpretation we
thus find again the whole problem of autofoundation. Knowing
well that we shall engage in an excessively simplified hypothesis,
we nevertheless believe that the situation in which we imagine
ourselves involves an interpretation which should be utilized.
Concerning the phenomenal appearances, however, we shall
remember that the problem of their accurate observation is not
solved in advance.

3. Supposing that we possess a ready-made interpretation to
be used in an ensemble of naturally given phenomena, the
correctness of this interpretation could not in advance be taken
for granted. However plausible it may otherwise be, the decisive
argument for it can only come from the test. Now the latter is
not conducted once and for all with ultimate precision, but
rather at a level of precision which is not designated in any
way as being the ultimate possible.

Several times already we had to take into account the problem
of precision whose increasing importance is revealed by the
analysis. This time again we must give it its rightful place. But
we must at the same time be careful not to substitute artificial
conditions for the real conditions of its introduction. The testing
of the interpretation does not simply consist in opposing to each
other well-formulated statements on the one hand and well-
determined phenomena on the other, without excluding in
advance the possibility of certain disparities. It is in the very
determination of the phenomena, or rather in their degree of de-
terminedness, that the degree of accuracy of the means at our
disposal can be judged. What counts is not the determination of
the phenomenon as such (it would be rather pointless to make
any specific hypotheses about it here), but its degree of de-

terminedness at the observer's level, in the knowledge which he can have of it. But at this level, under this aspect, immediate observation in general is not enough. However slight the requirements may be, the natural situation must be complemented by certain technical devices. Among these one must of course first mention the use of instruments of observation and measurement. We are thus back, for both, at the remarks which we have made earlier concerning measuring instruments only. They must be invented, manufactured, regulated, applied, and corrected. All this is not done in a universe foreign to that of their utilization. The interpretation which they must serve to prove is inscribed in them; it has directed their manufacture which had to be based on it, and it continues to direct their use. What is put to the test therefore is not merely a more or less clearly formulated or formulable interpretation; it is at the same time the totality of the means by which to test it.

Such is the situation in its great outlines when the interpretation aims at realizing the theoretical statements through naturally given phenomena. But it is known that modern science does not keep to situations of this type. It produces phenomena which it intends to study in order to confer upon them, among other things, a higher degree of determination, if it is not concerned with unpublished phenomena. To the technical devices relating to observation and measurement of the phenomena one must therefore add those which necessitate their production and their repetition. Everything we have said before concerning the former must now be repeated concerning the latter. It may even be that the analysis of this case, which appears more and more as the normal case, could carry us well beyond the observations which we have put on record so far. But the latter suffice for our purposes at this point.

In all the cases there is one characteristic which profoundly affects the situation in which one undertakes to invest an axiomatically valid statement with a tested experimental significance: the reason being that, the technical means remaining what they are, the precision of the totality of processes and instruments through which an interpretation is tested does not exceed a certain ceiling which thus turns out to be one of the essential characteristics of the situation.

The situation thus analyzed and delimited, we shall now seek to pursue the idea of the implicit definition into the field of experimentation. We have noted that, at the axiomatic level, the condition for speaking meaningfully of an implicit definition of the fundamental notions through the intermediary of the axioms is the closedness of the system towards any anterior or exterior information, and the fact that the process through which this closedness operates is that of total formalization.*

The Operational Definition

Is it possible to imagine a more or less analogous closedness on the experimental side? There is one that rather naturally comes to mind, but whose artificial character is recognized immediately. Taking as a model the deployment of a formal system, one could define as "closed" an activity having the following two characteristics:

1. It includes a certain number of well-defined operations whose complete list has been given in advance.

2. It would then be deployed by the execution of "programs" composed on the basis of fundamental operations.

If the manufacture of the devices and the setting up of the apparatus which must serve to produce, observe, and measure the phenomena and all the admissible methods of utilizing them, could take place within a closed system, it would be advisable to let ourselves be guided by the analogy of the situations in order to extend the idea of the definition implicit in the phenomenal interpretations of the magnitudes of the axiomatized theory.

But is such an hypothesis plausible? It is not, at any rate, if the activity thus channelled into a program would, while it remains closed, also remain engaged in the project of ensuring

---

* We shall not consider at this point the reservations which may be made against the idea of a formalization which would strip the axiomatized statements of *any* anterior meaning. See "General Evaluations" on this subject.

greater accuracy for itself. Nothing, in effect, permits us to affirm that the execution of this project should not be linked to a modification of the basic situation (i.e. the defining situation), a modification following the production and introduction of new technical devices, if not the substitution of a new axiomatized theory for the old one. Everything we know, and everything our analysis has brought to light, prompts us to believe that a modification of this type is precisely the event which the closedness of the system is supposed to prevent.

Does the hypothesis become plausible in the case where such an eventuality is excluded? Nothing could be less certain. We may, however, excuse ourselves from making the test, because for a real investigation which has not attained its ultimate goal, this case has no interest.

However this may be, the physical magnitudes upon which the interpretation projects the theoretical magnitudes cannot be defined with a precision greater than that of the defining situation.

Let us pause here in our attempt to constitute an "integrated defining situation" in which the theoretical magnitudes and the corresponding physical magnitudes would be both definite and implicit at the same time. It is now clear that this endeavor cannot succeed. The analysis of the situation and the factual conditions under which an interpretation is actually given do not leave any doubt in this regard.

Lessons To Be Learned from This Failure

Is the present analysis therefore useless? The answer is no, because the analysis has enabled us to illuminate the elements which essentially must be retained in a correct view of the situation.

The first element relates to what might be called the doctrine of interpretation. The datum of an interpretation is effected by a correlation between the theoretical level and the phenomenal level, the two levels facing each other in an irreducible perspective of duality. This datum thus is part of the conditions under which, on the experimental side, a reality may be grasped; this can never be done with complete precision. The testing of an interpretation therefore is never a mere attempt to offer a proven realization at a certain level of precision.

The second element relates to the irreducibly evolutive character of the integrated situation. One may certainly imagine that the production and the setup of all the necessary experimental devices (means of observation assembled to ensure the apparition of the phenomena) have attained a certain stage of convenience and perfection which guarantees some stability for them. This must even be the case if the test of the integrated situation is to offer any real interest. But this stability could not be assumed with certainty without sterilizing the investigation, even if it were only a search for greater precision. The fact of excessive duration could be taken as a symptom of stagnation. Principally, the integrated situation thus remains open in all its parts towards the eventuality of modifications more or less radical and more or less dearly acquired.

The third element relates to the solidarity in the testing of all the elements of the integrated situation. We are concerned here with a first aspect of the organic character of the total of known facts constituted at a specific moment. We shall return to this point shortly.

The fourth element, finally, relates to the necessarily limited character of the precision of the means employed on the side of experimentation. It follows that the search for means capable of ensuring greater precision (the often difficult gain of an additional certified decimal, for example) is not separable from the activities whose totality constitutes "the investigation." There is no "investigation of reality" which could be deployed without being an aspect of it in the same way as all the others. Thus there is introduced into the practice of research an element of technicality which the method of science could not disregard without changing its nature.

It seems to us rather striking that these four points illustrate precisely the four fundamental principles of open methodology, viz. duality, revisibility, integrality, and technicity.

Our analysis, however, is not complete. In continuing it we

will be able better to delimit the meaning of the last two of these four principles.

The Solidarity Revealed by the Instrument

Let us return to the situation where the theory and all the experimental devices are solidarily engaged in the test of effectiveness through which the discipline is autofounded. This situation—as we have noted—may take on a certain stability. The fact, however, that a specific level of precision is attached to it as a characteristic, renders this stability precarious. In the perspective of autofoundation every gain in precision must be paid for by a revision of the situation in its totality. The example of geometry will permit us to illustrate the point we intend to emphasize. The Eleventh General Conference on Weights and Measures has undertaken the revision of the unit of length. Up to that time this unit had been defined as being the length of the standard meter made of platinum (90%) and iridium (10%) deposited at the International Bureau of Weights and Measures at Sèvres. The definition is now the following:

The meter is the length equalling 1,650,763.73 wave lengths in the vacuum corresponding to the transition between the levels $2p_{10}$ and $5d_5$ of the krypton atom 86. *

* The following details, which we reproduce with the kind permission of the *Bulletin technique de la Suisse romande*, illustrate in a particularly striking fashion the two principles whose importance we have emphasized, viz. the principles of technicity and of solidarity.

"The first general Conference on Weights and Measures established in 1889 the new prototype of the legal meter as being the distance separating the axes of the extreme markings of an international standard, traced upon a rod of metal alloy consisting of 90% platinum and 10% iridium, at the temperature of melting ice, i.e. 0°C. At the time 30 similar rods were cast, and number 6, selected as the international prototype, was enclosed, with three other samples, in the vault of the BIPM at Sèvres.

"The science of metrology, in constant evolution, was not to be satisfied for long with this definition of the meter; in 1954 it was in fact proposed that the meter should be defined in terms of the lengths of light waves. The detailed studies which were then undertaken in this new direction have resulted precisely in the important decision taken by the XIth General Conference on Weights and Measures, viz., that the meter henceforth should be defined by

For us the transition from the first of these definitions to the second represents a genuine change from the "perspective of foundation." It is true that the total of the devices to be applied in the first transcends the limits of simple geometric devices. One may admit, however, that optics does not occur in it except as geometrical optics, not as undulatory optics. The latter, on the other hand, will be part of those contexts without which the second definition would be inexplicable. The transi-

---

a natural and indestructible standard, and would be equivalent to 1,650,763.73 times the length of the wave of red-orange color of the isotope of krypton emitted in the vacuum by radiation (this wave length is equivalent to 0.6057 .... μm).

"In order to compare the old standard with the new, an apparatus of the highest precision was required. BIPM entrusted the *Société genevoise d'instruments de physique* with the task of setting up a sufficiently accurate comparator, based on an idea formulated by Mr. Volet, director of the BIPM. The S.I.P. has gloriously acquitted itself of the delicate task, realizing an interferential photo-electric comparator, which permits the reading of marks with an accuracy of some millionths of a millimeter.

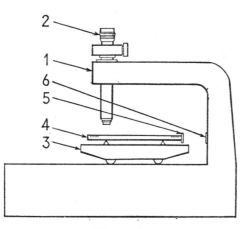

FIGURE 1.

"The new apparatus combines with an *interferometer*—an instrument which utilizes the undulatory nature of light for the purposes of metrology—an especially sophisticated *longitudinal comparator;* this comparator notably contains two photo-electric microscopes. The connection between the interferometer and the comparator has posed difficult problems which have required original solutions.

"Figure 1 illustrates the method of comparison of the marked ruler with the interferences. The support (1) of the microscope (2) is a part of the

tion from the first definition to the second thus is marked in
the following way: In the first definition the designation of the
meter could only take place solidarily with that of a certain
group of other fundamental magnitudes. It has thus partici-
pated in the autofoundation of a part of physics including, in
particular, geometry as one of its first chapters. To use a convenient image, one might say that the standard meter is at the
centre of a certain area of solidarity which the accuracy with

---

structure upon which the carriage (3) moves; the latter carries the standard
ruler (4), which is equipped with a movable mirror (5) at one extremity;
the fixed mirror (6) is fastened to the support of the microscope. The temperature of course must remain stable, lest the length of the ruler or that of
the support vary, and it must be accurately known (the temperature is
measured with a precision of the order of a thousandth of one degree). The

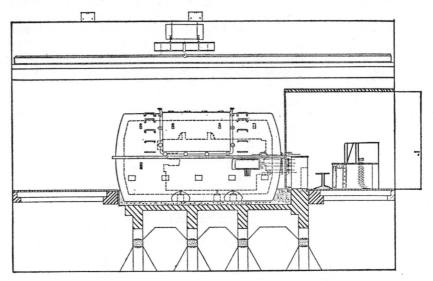

FIGURE 2.

coefficient of refraction of the air, which depends on the temperature, the
atmospheric pressure, and the composition of the air, must likewise remain
constant, lest the wave length vary, and it must be known exactly relative
to the vacuum (a control interferometer is provided for this purpose to the
apparatus of the S.I.P.) Furthermore, since the interferences have turned
out to be highly sensitive to mechanical perturbations, the least vibration and
the slightest instability must be avoided. For all these reasons, the comparator,
steered from a distance, is enclosed in a closed space, consisting of an isolated
thermal chest which is rigid and tight and placed on an extremely stable
foundation in an air-conditioned room.

which it may be designed essentially contributes to determine. In the second version the unit of length determines a new domain of solidarity more extensive than the first, which is only a part of it. This example casts a very vivid and very unexpected light on the problem of precision in general.

One would like to imagine that the search for greater precision in the determination of a specific physical magnitude must be able to be operated in isolation, independent of all

---

"Figure 2 represents the air-conditioned room and the enclosure. Inside the room a constant temperature of about 0.1 degree Centigrade variation is maintained; the thermic damping effected by the isolation of 20 cm of plastic foam around the enclosure guarantees, inside the enclosure, a maximal variation of the temperature of the order of 0.001 degree Centigrade. One may note in the illustration that the foundation beams are equipped with a layer of isolating material, in order to eliminate any 'heat bridge' and thus to avoid the effects of thermal conduction. The apparatus within the enclosure weighs about 3,500 kilograms and the enclosure weighs again as much.

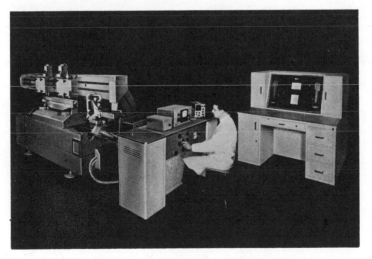

FIGURE 3.

"Figure 3 shows the complete installation before being set up within the enclosure. One notices the comparator itself, which will be placed in the enclosure, the command desk, where the operator is installed, as well as the reading desk.

"Figure 4 reproduces a detailed view of the comparator; one distinguishes
1. the support,
2. the left slide runner,
3. the right slide runner,

the other magnitudes, each of which could in turn be the object of an analogous investigation. As we can see, reality is entirely different: the more the precision increases with which a physical magnitude may be measured the more this measurement depends on that of other magnitudes and on the accuracy with which they in turn may be determined. This is perhaps the most fundamental meaning of the principle of integrality of open methodology.*

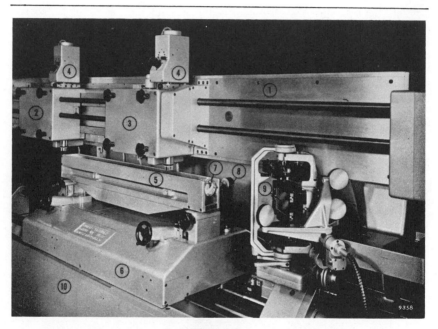

FIGURE 4.

4. the two photo-electric microscopes,
5. the ruler carriage,
6. the movable carriage,
7. the movable mirror (fastened to the extreme end of the ruler),
8. the counterweight of the movable mirror,
9. the compensator of the interferometer,
10. the support which rests on the socket by means of three ball-bearings."
From *Bulletin technique de la Suisse romande*, 87,7:94–95, 1961.

* The four governing principles of open methodology have already been explained on several occasions, notably in the reports of the *Entretiens de Zurich*, which have appeared starting from 1947 in the periodical *Dialectica*. The explanation of the principle of revisibility is the author's principal concern in the work *Philosophie néoscolastique et philosophie ouverte*, in the first series

In the same context the principle of technicity is explained as follows: The increasing precision of our objective knowledge must be guaranteed by an ensemble of technical improvements which turn out to be increasingly solidary among themselves.

The Problem of Induction

One more remark, in conclusion, about the relation of the above discussion with the traditional problem of induction. It is, in its logical aspect, the problem of proceeding from one group of particular statements to a general statement which includes all the former ones. Under its scientific aspect, it is the problem of extracting, from a certain body of observations relating to a phenomenon, the law of this phenomenon.

The presuppositions which these statements imply are in complete contradiction to the guiding principles mentioned before. The observations, for example, do not figure in it as observations actually made, with all the risks of imprecision and even error with which they would then invariably be tainted. The observations in question are idealized as if they could be unconditionally correct. Between this idea of observation and the one resulting from our analysis there is an insuperable "methodical distance."

The same would have to be said of the presuppositions concerning the way in which a phenomenon may be given and its law of evolution determined. Accordingly the crucial experiment, which should enable us to decide about the reliability of specific observations, whether a specific law is verified or

---

of his dialogues at the *Centre romain de synthèse et de comparaison,* whereas the volume *La métaphysique et l'ouverture à l'expérience,* in the second series of the same dialogues, especially illuminates the principle of duality (PUF, Paris, 1954 and 1960).

The function of the four principles as guiding principles of an open methodology has been explained in the conclusions of the work, already mentioned, *La géométrie et le problème de l'espace, cahier 6: Le problème de l'espace.* Neuchâtel, Editions du Griffon, 1956.

In this work the author moreover presents the open methodology as the one which imposes itself if one intends to base on its integrity and validity, theoretically and practically, a discipline such as geometry.

not, is still only the project of an experiment whose execution is not even outlined.

Of course we do not mean to say that this project must be forever unrealizable, because no mention is made of the means which should enable us to realize it. What we do mean to say is that the question of these means is not so banal as to be simply passed over in silence. But this is precisely what one does by assuming as unconditionally acquired the possibility of deciding whether or not an observation verifies the statement of a law. It is precisely this question of the means which has been illuminated by a rather unexpected light during the progress of the discussion of the "problem of precision." Essentially we can formulate the results of this discussion as follows: The process of autofoundation of a discipline is precisely the one through which the program of the induction finds its concrete realization. If we elaborate the "inductive intention" taking into account the actual conditions to which the experimentation must submit and adapt, taking into account, above all, the fact that every experimental situation has a ceiling of precision proper to it, we arrive at the perspective of autofoundation.

This is also the final goal of our analysis of the measurement of time. It is within the framework of the autofoundation of the integrated total of the disciplines which concur in the measurement of time in a definite situation and by the very means of this autofoundation that, as far as possible, we may define the answer to the question, What is the time which we measure?

METHODOLOGICAL COMMENTARY

We have consistently conducted our exposé as a work of research. Thus we have taken from the start a methodological attitude which was to inform our entire work. We have not sought to sketch or justify this attitude in advance; by doing so we would have been fatally caught in the paradox of the beginning which, as we know, leads nowhere, except to a doctrine of absolute evidences whose introduction into real research becomes increasingly problematic. The methodological attitude which one takes at the beginning of an investigation of method (and this is precisely what our study is intended to be) could not be anything but an option which appears as the best, considering everything which one already knows and again uses in the investigation, so that it should become more accurate, more certain, unless the necessity of revision arises.

We are now in a position to project a light backwards on the premises involved in the simple intention to "conduct an exposé like a work of research."

The Beginning of Research

As a rule an investigation is not an end unto itself. It does not represent a closed whole, which would contain the essence of its own significance. If the experiment has meaning, it comes from its insertion into a context which the experiment merely puts to the test.

It is certainly true that the first information which one collects by making an experiment is the fact that the experiment can be made. Thus the experiment always starts by contributing evidence about itself, or rather about the idea which one had of it before it was made. If anyone doubts, for example, that it is possible to conduct an experiment which is being described to him, he still has the liberty—at least in principle—to try it himself. Attempted and carried out successfully, the experiment is then its own witness of its capacity of actualization. Every experiment inevitably involves this somewhat elementary aspect, but nevertheless one should not consider as a limit case the one in which the finality of the experiment stops there without tending towards other aims. In all these cases the experiment which is effected by means of our exposé differs from it so radically that it is of no further interest to us.

Let us therefore return to our analysis in order to ask whether an activity which must serve as an experiment for something other than itself must not present, because of this very fact, certain typical characteristics.

The Temptation of the "Protokollsätze"

The first point to be emphasized is that an activity of this type must be engaged, in two very dissimilar ways, in two con-

texts, which are very different themselves. Take as an example
the determination of the instant when a planet passes the meridian, made as accurately as possible on an observation clock.
Let us not say anything as yet about the intention in which
such an observation could be made. This will enable us to
work out clearly the distinction between the two contexts in
which it participates. The first of these contexts may be called
observational. The activity of the observer is inserted into it in
an unproblematic way. The question may be, for example, to
note in the most accurate way possible the position of the hand
on the dial of the clock at the moment when the apparent
edge of the planet will touch the image of a thread spanned
across the field of vision of a telescope. The fact has often been
stressed that observations of this type may be systematically
reduced to the verification of certain coincidences whose immediate judges, in the simplest cases, are the eye and the ear.
We have noted that, in the observational context, or at the
observational level, the observation of these coincidences is not
problematic. This does not mean, of course, that they may be
verified with absolute precision. They are on the contrary affected by a certain margin of imprecision which may depend
on many intersubjective factors, having to do with the structure of the sensorial apparatus, which to some extent is the
same for all observers, as well as subjective and personal factors which vary from one observer to the next. Thus we do
not say that the verification of coincidences does not pose any
problem; the problem of the superior accuracy in particular will
always be present. Let it suffice for us to recall here the rôle
it has constantly played throughout our exposé, especially the
fashion in which it has appeared in the last section in the procedure of autofoundation of every discipline involved with
experimentation. The observational situation which has been
discussed could be improved if its level of accuracy could be
perceptibly raised through the use of automatic (especially
electronic) recording instruments far more sensitive and reacting
in a far more immediate way than the cerebrosensorial system
of an observer. Nevertheless, whatever the equipment with which
the observational situation may be fortified, the problem of

superior precision is never totally eliminated. As we have already said, an observational situation, whatever it may be, inevitably involves a certain level of precision which is a characteristic typical of this situation.

Under these circumstances, is it not paradoxical to claim that the observer's activity in such a situation would not appear problematic? Here is an essential point to be grasped. In any given observational situation, taking into account the margin of imprecision it involves, there is no sense at all in casting doubt on the effectiveness of some simple actions, the truth of some direct statements, and the objectivity of some immediate verifications. In other words, it makes no sense to imagine that two normally qualified observers, placed in the same observational situation, could be in disagreement about what they are doing, observing, and verifying. What is not problematic is thus a certain immediate and effective rapport between the observer and the observational situation.

For example, after taking the usual precautions and making the normal verifications, one will not stop to question the validity of an "announcement of observation" such as the following: "At the moment when the planet's rim touched the thread, the hand of the clock showed exactly 2:15 o'clock." The term "exactly" moreover will not be taken literally but will be interpreted according to the level of precision which the observational situation implies. The main fact is that there exist observational situations which give rise to statements of this kind, to statements whose somewhat elementary validity would not be improved by being questioned again. Does this fact require a demonstration whose strictness would compel recognition by itself? This is out of the question. We are concerned here with a fact of experience pledged on the one hand by the total of our actions at the level of common sense and guaranteed, on the other hand, by the function which it has in the structure of scientific knowledge. To recognize and accommodate it as such is merely an aspect of the option which we have already mentioned. This time again it is clear that we are concerned with an option which sums up and anticipates, which sums up everything we know about the fashion in which scientific experimentation is based on the possibility of isolating primary observational situations, and which anticipates the results to be obtained from this procedure. Modern man is not in a nondescript situation, where it would be optional for him to disregard or to put into parenthesis the crushing testimony of the existence and increasing effectiveness of scientific research. Whether he is happy about it or not, man profits from a situation in which this evidence is inevitably incorporated. Our situation in history does not permit us to disregard it in good faith.*

Elementary Statements Are Not Enough

We must, however, be careful not to overestimate the nonproblematic content of the information expressed and conveyed by the observational statements. There is no reason, as we have noted, to contest the validity of the affirmation according to which the hand of the clock, at the moment of a specific, well-designed coincidence, is placed on a specific section of the dial. There is nothing to be gained by doubting that this statement is correct. But have we thereby made a correct measurement of time? It is clear that the correctness of the

---

* It is known what fundamental rôle logical empirism has tended to attribute to elementary statements of observation. According to the opinions of that school, the elaboration of knowledge from such statements would be reduced to the building of a system of logical relations to which it would give a starting point. We have never been able to endorse this viewpoint, and the following explanations will justify us for not having done so. But there is one point on which the doctrine of logical empirism was fundamentally correct: it has illuminated our inevitable need to make use of primary observations and, according to what their purpose was, the unproblematic nature of these observations.

Nevertheless, the conclusions which supposedly could be drawn from these statements have always seemed premature to us. In order to utilize the observational statements it is not enough to collect their evidence as primary statements, avoiding to transcend the observational level. The statements must on the contrary be involved in a second level of validity, as we will show in an instant.

On the other hand, even before engaging the observational statements on their second level of validity, it is proper further to specify and even to reduce the nonproblematic contents of the information which it yields. This point especially will be discussed later.

first statement, elementary though it may be, does not imply the correctness of the measurement of time thus effected. The correct elementary statement is a correct measurement only if the clock itself is adequate. How can this requirement be satisfied? This is precisely what our entire exposé has been supposed to show. But what could be the use of stating the elementarily incontestable verification of an incorrect time? The observational statements thus assume their elementary and nonproblematic value only if they in turn are guaranteed by the correctness and objectivity of the entire apparatus utilized, whether this apparatus be a natural or an artificial one.

From whichever side the problem is attacked, it is clear that the problem of the instrument cannot be eliminated. One cannot avoid making this statement by remarking that an adequate instrument is not recognizable as such without a systematic test, and that the latter must inevitably invoke a group of elementary observations. It cannot be denied that the manufacture of an adequate instrument requires the utilization of corresponding observational situations. But by emphasizing this, one does not reduce the complex question of the dependable instrument to a simple autonomous and preliminary practice of the elementary observation. One merely makes clear their interdependence from the opposite side. As carriers of the only information which their participation in a given observational situation confers on them, the observational statements by themselves thus do not yet assume the significance in view of which they had been formulated.*

Explaining how an axiomatically established statement may be invested with an experimental significance, we have stressed the fact that such a statement is involved at two levels of

---

* The reservations which have just been made concerning the information content of the observational statements may still be reinforced. For certain instruments the reading of their indications must be systematically corrected; the correct reading of these indications becomes so only after correction. To do this one must sometimes resort to the theory of this instrument. Thus a new context is opened, into which the utilization of certain observational situations must invariably be integrated. It may even occur that the corresponding elementary observations develop their content of information only across several interpretive stages.

validity; one is the axiomatic structure and the other is the experimental activity. If we had ever believed that the procedure through which a deductive system receives a phenomenal interpretation consists in making elementary observations and interconnecting them logically, we would now be undeceived.

The investigation of the procedure of autofoundation made in the preceding section on the one hand, and our investigation of observational situations on the other, irrevocably dispel the notion that the problem could be solved in a simple way. We shall now depart from the elementary notions and show how they in turn must be given a second signification in order to be able to play their informational rôle. We therefore return to our example.

We were concerned, as we may recall, with the determination of the instant when a planet passes the meridian. In making this statement, we have deliberately overstepped the limits of the observational level. At the level of elementary statements it is not a planet which we are observing but rather a small luminous spot. And it is not the apparent contour of this planet which touches the image of the thread spanned across the field of vision; it is the rim of this luminous spot. We proposed not to comment as yet on the intention in which such elementary statements may be made. We have not strictly adhered to our instructions. Why not? Our purpose was to show how easy and natural it is to confuse the elementary event belonging to the observational level with its interpretation.

Having said this, we may dismiss the fiction according to which the elementary statements made in an observational situation would take on their own meaning spontaneously, independent of the totality of the experiment. Let us review in its proper perspective the intention in which these elementary statements could have been made. There might be, for example, a particular observation contained in a program of observations serving to advance the calculation through successive approximations of the "real" trajectory of a specific planet. In order not to settle for an appearance of simplicity, it is moreover indispensable to explain what is intended by "the real trajectory of a planet." This is the trajectory of the planet in a frame of reference whose origin is at the centre of the sun. It is this frame of reference into which the observational situation must be integrated so that the experiment may develop its informational content. The same may also be done by enlarging the observer's natural horizon (of which the observational horizon is an integral part) in such a way that the frame of reference linked to the sun is part of it and may be imagined in it, animated by its own motion.*

Either one or more likely both these frames of reference form the second level of validity of the elementary statements, in which they must receive their second signification. At this point we must anticipate a possible error of interpretation which would be extremely embarrassing. Speaking of a second level of validity and of a second signification, we do not mean to imply that they are of a secondary order or importance. It is on the contrary this second level which "takes the shape" of the real world, and it is the second signification which must effectively participate in the process of our acquisition and elaboration of knowledge about this world. Neither in its intention nor in its execution does the experiment have its starting point in the elementary statements. The action of the experiment starts at the level where the questions emerge, participates in an observational situation, and returns to its starting point with an information which will receive only here its decisive evaluation. The elementary statements are what they are only for answering questions not formulated at the level of the observational situation, and the answers they provide assume their meaning only after being retranslated into the language of the questions. In the first place, therefore, the observational level is an integral part of the global level of research, where the object of research has the value of reality. It is through the special way in which it is integrated that it acquires its natural unproblematic character, at the level of per-

---

* It is above all in the frame of reference of the observer that the planet will be considered to occupy a definite position, and it is in the frame of reference linked to the sun that the trajectory will be computed.

ception and of the use of the instrument. This unproblematic character is of the order of facts by which we profit or have been able to do so.

We therefore discard as unfounded and even arbitrary the notion that an observational horizon could form a little universe unto itself, and that the elementary statements to which it gives rise could assume in it a definitive meaning, a meaning which later might be utilized by being projected on the level of the experiment. We endorse on the contrary as the most plausible one the notion that the observational level must remain open to the consequences in return for the progress of knowledge through research, a progress for which it has been the starting point. In our opinion this fact must be emphasized especially. We shall illustrate it by returning once more to our example.

Let us assume that it is not a planet but rather a fixed star which the observer decides to check during its passage at its meridian, and let us further assume that he observes the event over a long period of time, a year, for example. The observer may expect that the event will repeat itself with the greatest regularity, the limit regularity implied by the precision of his instruments. (We might add that if this were the case he would incorporate into his observational situation an element of outside information; he would presuppose that the rotatory motion of the celestial sphere around its polar axis involves precisely this regularity. Will he go so far as to assume that this is only an apparent motion whose cause must be sought in the rotatory motion of the earth around its axis, and will he assume as a certainty that the latter must be extremely regular? If he did so the outside contribution to what the observational situation has to offer in immediate information would only be increased. It is therefore clear that the observational level is not a small closed universe containing the information of which it gives evidence. It is on the contrary an incomplete system capable of receiving and assimilating a specific piece of information which comes to it from a different field of experience.)

An observer who would take such regularity for granted would be mistaken, and the more accurate his data the greater his error would be. He might observe other fixed stars, compute means to eliminate the divergences due to incidental factors of observation; the result of his recordings will only be strengthened thereby; in the case of all fixed stars, either obviously or imperceptibly, there will be an annual oscillation of the times of arrival in his findings, whereas the arrival times of a mean (and artificial) event appear with the regularity which had been expected in the first place. Is the task of the observer thus completed? Certainly not. He will be unable to avoid the problem of interpretation facing him at this point. Is the annual variation, confirmed beyond any doubt, due to a corresponding variation of the speed of rotation of the celestial sphere? If this were so the amplitude of the variation would have to be the same for all fixed stars. This hypothesis must therefore be rejected. But it is obviously not from a combination of elementary statements that the solution will result. We must try to imagine the real world in such a way that the traces imprinted on the observational situation are those which the observer verifies.

We shall not explain here how the annual variation of the times of arrival of the observed signal may first be translated into a variation of the direction of arrival in the observational horizon of the light ray emitted by the star, and how finally this latter variation may be explained by the variation (especially in direction) of the speed of the earth during its annual revolution around the sun. This is the phenomenon of *aberration* to which Einstein has made a particularly convincing application of the theory of relativity.

Establishing the Observational Level

The preceding considerations show that, isolated from the context where they must be interpreted, the elementary statements remain incomplete regarding the meaning they will assume and the rôle they will play. This meaning and this rôle will be defined only through the integration of the operational situation into the level of reality of research, in such a way that the elementary statements can be considered as the traces of the world of research in the restricted universe of the observer. That under these circumstances the great changes of perspective which take place in the field of knowledge can influence even the meaning to be given to the elementary statements should hardly be doubted any longer. This is precisely what establishing the observational level amounts to.

The following, briefly, are the characteristics of a well-conducted experiment, as we have tried to define it in the preceding discussion:

1. As a rule, an experiment is not an end unto itself.

2. The experiment benefits by an operational situation where the person who makes the experiment is in a position to make a group of elementary or guaranteed statements. At the restricted observational level to which they belong and within the framework of the experiment, these statements do not have a guarantee more reliable than themselves. In this sense and at least provisionally, they are thus unproblematic.

3. In order to be utilized these elementary statements must be integrated, together with the observational situation which has generated them, into the normal level of research. Here they must be reinterpreted in such a way as to be no more than the traces of events of this last level. Their meaning thus participates in all the changes of perspective which, as we know, may take place at the level of research.

4. The unproblematic character of the elementary judgments at the level of the experiment does not imply that the observational level is closed. On the contrary it remains open, including even the meaning of the elementary recordings and their consequences, in return for their engagement in the frontline of research.

These four points may be summarized into the following brief formula: To opt for the experiment means to opt for openness. On the other hand, is it possible to opt against the experiment unless it were in the hope for a still more decisive experiment? (Note that we thus irrevocably move away from logical empirism on the very track which the latter was intended to use.)

The Experiment of the Experiment

The experiment certainly is not merely a pure and simple elementary statement. Look again at a remark we already have found necessary to make in this context. In order to evaluate the true size of an object seen through a microscope, we could not do without a certain amount of information about the latter. We must know above all what its magnifying power is. Such data can only be obtained through the activities which have to do with the manufacture of a good instrument. But we know (since we have verified it in the case of the watches and clocks) how many interrelated contexts must be established for this manufacture, contexts in each of which some experimentation is inevitable. Valid for the case of the microscope, our last remark could also be applied to the telescope or any other instrument which must be used with some accuracy. In a hypothetical way we may certainly imagine an experiment whose related contexts would all have been deployed to the point of illustrating all the elementary recordings on which they would be based. An experiment thus analyzed and taken apart might be called integrally reduced. In fact, however, this is not the way in which to proceed. At an observational level where a specific elementary statement is made one does not at the same time uncover all the observational situations which the integrally reduced experiment would have to include. One applies, on the contrary, together with the information derived from the immediate recordings, an ensemble of outside information which is considered as guaranteed although one does not have the pattern of their integral reduction. By seeking to clarify this pattern one would merely fall back upon the procedure of autofoundation, which was the subject of the preceding chapter, and in which the elementary recordings as a whole participate. Thus anyone who makes an experiment benefits by a certain situation of knowledge and a certain activity based on it. Concerning the development of the experiment itself there is no reason whatever

to doubt the former or to question the effectiveness of the
latter. Why should the experimentor disregard the fact that the
history of knowledge does not begin with him? The experiment
which he makes will only be a small part of a much greater
experiment which was made without him, which has been in
progress for thousands of years, and by which he benefits,
the experiment of the experiment. Will he decide that it has
no relevance for him and that he must act as if such a development had never taken place? He may consider and even intend to adopt such an attitude. But he has neither the liberty
nor the capability to realize this project. It is impossible for
him to disengage himself from the common experience, in
which after so many others he participates with his entire being. He is engaged in this experience as a natural being, as
a creature among creatures; but he also participates in it as
a conscious and knowing being, as a person situated at a definite stage of the most real and irreplaceable of all experiments,
*the experiment of the effectiveness of the knowledge based on
the experiment.* Does this mean that anyone who finds himself
caught in this experiment remains forever a prisoner of the
experiment of the past? This is certainly not so, but if he doubts
the experiment it is in the name of a protracted experiment,
including the former as an experiment of failure. In sum, the
project not to participate in the experiment, or to participate
only under constraint, refusing to recognize it in order to
accommodate himself to it, is an illusion; the conditions of the
activity of which we are capable, even if it is only in thought,
do not enter into it with their full significance.

The Situation of Knowledge, Context of the Test

Do these considerations reduce the value and the scope of
the observational statements? Yes and no. Yes, because one
must recognize that these statements contribute only part of
the information which makes the experiment fully significant,
because the observational situation where they originate cannot be taken as evidence except after being inserted into a

situation of knowledge which it is impossible to analyze completely. But we must add immediately that by setting up the observational situation, one isolates a local level and defines a limited activity whose unproblematic character is particularly obvious. Thus the observational statements, in the situation of the scientific experiment, enjoy a status of privileged security; this is the reason why an experiment in which they play a decisive rôle may be considered an example of a well-conducted experiment.

But one could not expect that in order to be valid, every experiment should be of this type. In order to be valid as evidence, it suffices that at its starting level it benefits, or *could* benefit, from a relatively proven ensemble of practices and informations. Isolated from any context the conclusions drawn as interpretation of an experiment of this type would often inspire very little confidence. But the experiment in the general sense is not composed of single experiments foreign to each other. By mutually completing, checking, and verifying each other the several experiments form a texture whose solidity is incomparably greater than that of the sum of its component parts.

For an explanation we must not turn to the observational situations and their unproblematic character, but should rather undertake an analysis of probability. This will be an entirely new context, although we have often alluded to it throughout our exposé. One may define as an integrating experiment one which is effected through the combination of various particular experiments capable of checking each other. The integrating experiment is the prototype of the scientific experiment. It is to this characteristic as well as to its rootedness in certain observational situations that scientific research owes its extraordinary effectiveness.

But there exists a reinforced type of integrating experiment; it is the "crossed" experiment. This is the one which, in order to obtain results of a methodological or philosophical order, assembles and crosswise exchanges information coming from sometimes very diverse and widely separated sectors.

The Option of Openness Towards the Experiment

To opt for the experiment means to determine, as we have explained, certain essential points of a preliminary doctrine of research and knowledge. We shall not explain again why the choice of such a doctrine is not arbitrary but is at the same time based on a previous experiment and directed towards a future one. But are our remarks not rather appropriate for observational situations? Do we not have to assume that what is valid for an integrally reduced experiment is also valid for all other forms of experiment, including the integrating or even the crossed experiment? The answer cannot be in doubt; the farther the situation in which an experiment is conducted is removed from a purely observational status, the less the observations to be made are perceptions of simple coincidences, and the less resistance does the starting situation offer to the penetration and integration of the information which comes from the front of research. In some cases the value of an integrating experiment results less from the dependability of the statements upon which it is based than from the convergence of the interpretations to which the latter give rise. Under these conditions it is normal and even favorable that the starting situation involves a certain degree of malleability, a certain dimension of indetermination or, in other words, a certain capacity for openness.

In all these forms the option for the experiment thus involves an always renewed option for openness towards the experiment.

We had begun these conclusions with the statement that we have conducted our exposé as an experiment. We have just seen how far and in which direction the simple intention of this procedure has led us. In retrospect we shall now investigate how well we have succeeded, how the projected experiment has been carried out and what its results are.

It is clear that our experiment could not be based everywhere in any well-defined observational situation. In many instances in our text, especially where manufacture is concerned, such as the regulation and use of watches and clocks, we admittedly have emphasized not elementary observations but rather indications concerning their use. But they merely form the backdrop of our exposé. Our experiment is not an experiment of physics but rather a methodological experiment. Involving items of information as diverse as those concerning "Time in Language," "The Measurement of Time," and "The Time of the Bees," it cannot be anything but a crossed experiment.

The Analysis of Language Through Language

From the methodological viewpoint, let us examine how an analysis of language may be adapted to an experiment, what kind of results may be expected and what assurances are given for them.

At first glance this question appears difficult to deal with because language is involved in it in several ways which we must try to distinguish from each other. First there is the language or discourse of the exposé which we are in the process of developing. On the one hand this language is everybody's language, but on the other hand it is influenced by the situation elaborated through our study, which it presently serves by isolating its conclusions. Discussing time, e.g. the representation and the notion of time, the variants under which the latter are presented in language, the temporal order and the temporal character of certain relations of succession, and so forth, we do not use the term as "everybody" does any longer. Our discourse is informed by the experiment we have just made and which, at least provisionally, has reached its conclusion. It is out of the question for us to challenge its results, as if we did not have the right to integrate it into our ways of speaking. If we therefore return briefly to our method of analysis, we will do so in our own language.

What guarantee can we give for the language of our own discourse, the language we are now using for the purposes of our exposition? As we have noted, we cannot guarantee that it is exactly the same as that which we used at the beginning of our study. Let it be agreed that we thus have passed from language π_1 to language π_2. Are the guarantees of the adequate use of the latter superior to those of the former? The unfolding of our exposé and its conclusion certainly assure us that this is true.

But, what were the guarantees for π_1? To analyze them is not a simple matter. In one respect it was "everybody's language"; we shall soon face again the problem of the guarantees for any language "of wide communication." Nevertheless we were not without information on how our study would be oriented and what results we might expect. By anticipation π_1 accordingly has already profited from the results of the inquiry which was to be developed. There is no vicious circle in the procedure of anticipation, testing, and subsequent confirmation of which this is an example; this method conforms to the general procedure of research which we have repeatedly explained under the name of the procedure of the four phases.*

Having stated this we now proceed to the analysis of language such as we have practiced it. The language analyzed is neither the variant π_1 nor the variant π_2 of our explanatory discourse. It is not so banal and so simple a language that it could be the very language of common sense; one may doubt that such a language exists in a separate state. Nevertheless our language is a language "of wide communication," the language of the rather numerous linguistic community for which the *Littré* is intended. This language was introduced into our investigation only through some specially selected examples. We call it the basic language, or language β. Principally language β could be chosen in a different fashion. We expect of it only that it should lend itself to analysis such as we have practiced it.

The Method of the Contexts

The following is our method in the simplest case. It permits us to discuss what we have called the problem of acceptation.

---

* See especially the conclusions, already cited, of *La géométrie et le problème de l'espace, cahier 6;* also "De l'homme, médecine et philosophie," *Praxis*, 1960; the article by Feibleman in *Dialectica* 1953, p. 208, and the remarks following it (*ibid.*, p. 226).

This is the method of contexts. Let us assume that we have to define the significations, admissible in the language β, which a specific word may assume. This problematic word is introduced in a text which is as brief as possible, in an expression, for example, whose meaning is not problematic. And if the expression thus selected remains problematic one introduces it into a more extensive text whose meaning is better assured, etc. In carefully selected cases the meaning of the problematic word is univocally* determined by the context into which it is thus inserted.

Our intention to apply such a method may seem surprising; how can a text which contains certain problematic elements not be problematic itself? The undeniable and even obvious fact, however, is that the method can be applied successfully; witness the example of the *Littré,* and with it all the dictionaries in the world. There is in this a fact of experience which it is entirely legitimate to utilize. The guarantee of the method of the contexts is therefore not to be sought in some previous theory of language but is simply provided by a practice widely tested over a long period of time. This fact of experience is translated into a criterion of correctness; any theory of language that would not be established in such a way as to take it into account would be inadequate.

We shall soon return to the question of what can be the object of an investigation conducted in this fashion, taking the result of our own analysis as an example. But before doing so it seems useful to us to emphasize again the experimental character of the method of the context, drawing attention to the fact that it is merely a variant of a still simpler method whose relation to the experiment is obvious. Assume that we propose to study the rôle of the adverb in the "discursive formulation" of the temporal order. This is, as should be emphasized, a problem very different from the problem of acceptation which was mentioned above. The task is approached in the simplest way according to the general procedure of the four phases.

---

* The univocity of the meaning thus determined is not absolute but depends on the exigencies of the analysis.

The Procedure of the Four Phases

The first phase is the one where the problem emerges and the object of the investigation is being defined.

The second phase, after more or less numerous tentative efforts, results in the formulation of a hypothesis. In the case which serves us as an example we shall admittedly make a hypothesis of the unifying rôle of the adverb which we have so greatly emphasized while discussing the "Discursive Synthesis at the Level of the Verb and the Adverb."

The third phase is the testing of the hypothesis. In our particular case this will be done precisely according to the very simple and even banal method which we have described.

The fourth phase, finally, is the one where interpretations are made and one evaluates the success or failure of the testing of the hypothesis.

Positive Semantic Analysis

As far as our purpose is concerned, the entire procedure is now concentrated on the means we have to effect this test. They may be summarized as follows: We propose texts as brief as possible, mere sentences or even incomplete statements, fragmentary expressions whose meaning is undetermined, which might serve in an unproblematic way as examples or counterexamples for the hypothesis to be tested. It is clear that the validity of this method is based entirely on the possibility of finding such examples which would immediately and undeniably be relevant to the problem in hand.

It is again sufficient to confirm this through the experiment. The example, *After some thought I decided to leave after sunset,* perfectly answers all requirements of this method. It is irrelevant whether the statement which it contains is true or false, and whether the elements mentioned in it are real or fictional. The statement by itself does not permit us to decide these questions. It evokes a situation which, even though it might be imaginary, offers the same guarantees as a real situation would for our purposes. It contributes, without the help of an intermediary and without possible question, the proof that adverbial expressions based on the preposition *after* (*after* some thought, *after* sunset) may function in a perspective of subjectivity as well as in one of objectivity.

This statement clearly supports our hypothesis. By itself and made for itself such a statement would have no interest. One might compare it to the observation of a coincidence made in isolation and without ulterior motive. More generally, for an immediate observation to take on its full value it is necessary that it can be interpreted in the framework of an investigation which, as we have seen, is not reducible to its observational traces; from this point on, the analogy appears to us to be obvious. The formulation and investigation of any example similar to the preceding one may be correlated to the preparation and execution of an elementary observation. In order to be valid these examples nevertheless must be multiplied systematically, in order to be able to answer the requirements of determined research; in our case it would in fact be simple to multiply the examples, all composed for the same purpose, namely to test the hypothesis which we formulated earlier about the unifying rôle of the adverb.

It is true that this has been done while we were taking some liberties with the pattern now under consideration. The hypothesis has been confirmed, in our opinion, with a high coefficient of plausibility. On the other hand, the information thus assembled forms only one of the foundations of a crossed experiment concerning the capacity of the adverb to contribute to the dialectic of time which involves, besides other dialectics, every language of "wide communication."

Using a special example, we have thus presented our method of the analysis of language and defined the guarantees which are offered for it. These guarantees are all based on an experiment which includes all the experiences in which words are used, i.e. the experience common to all humans possessing a normally constituted language of being able to formulate statements which, for the purpose intended, have no problematic aspect.

One might make the objection that in the very sense of the

method we have just proposed, the latter is not sufficiently corroborated by the single example given above. This objection certainly would be fully justified if we did not have more examples at our disposal. But we cannot repeat here the multitude of examples we have used especially in studying the function of the verb in the constitution of the dialectic of time at the level of current language. Moreover, beyond the experiment, in our opinion entirely positive, which is represented by our exposé, there is also, as a fundamental guarantee for the method, the experience which everybody is making every day.

Discussing observational situations in which certain immediate observations may be made, we have noted that in the framework of a determinate investigation these situations are not given in advance but must be isolated. In the method of analyzing language which has just been mentioned, every well-chosen example creates an analytical situation in which certain statements may be made without difficulty by anyone to whom the example is clear. In the analogy which we are using here to illustrate our method, these statements may be compared to elementary statements. We thus find again emphasized the irreducible character of a certain utilization of experience, an experience which every person makes through the intermediary of language.

Results of the Analysis of Language

Is it possible to define the results to which this method may lead? In our preceding discussion we have given two examples, one involving the definition of acceptations, the other involving the unifying function of the adverb in discourse. In our exposé one will find numerous other examples which all have the same purpose, namely to clarify the function, or rather the functions, of language by means of an example treated in depth. This example, of course, is the example of *Time*.

Let us return to the *problems of acceptation* such as they present themselves in the perspective of our method. Does this method enable us to isolate, for a specific word such as the word *time,* for example, a well-defined acceptation in a definitive way? It disproves, on the contrary, in the most categorical fashion the notion that behind every word in current usage there exists a complete, closed, and unchangeable acceptation. It rather shows that the acceptations remain in a state of incompleteness and indetermination. They are open and capable of absorbing the information coming from the many-sided experiment in which they are involved. This result undermines the legitimacy of any analytical method that would postulate in principle the existence of acceptations perfectly settled as such. But in order to assume all its acuity, this *critique* must be considered in the context of the following notes.

Carried to the level of the adverb and the verb, our analytical method has shown beyond any doubt that what language can express is only partially due to significations inherent in the words. The words take on part of their meaning through their being part of special expressions, idiomatic forms, combinations, and multiple and various plays upon words. Language institutes dialectics, a dialectic of time, for example, which in turn is only an approximation of the mathematical theory of time seen as a linear continuum.

Consider this last statement for a moment. The dialectic of time instituted by language through the intermediary of the verb is still only an outline of what the mathematician, pursuing the work of language, is capable of building in forms of far greater precision. This means that a speaker is not faced with a universe of beings, things, and facts given before the command of language and independent of it, and that the function of language would merely be to grasp and to express for all according to the rules of truth, i.e. in full adequation with what they are. Neither the "fashion of being for us" of everything that might be said, nor the language capable of giving it its discursive form is given to us in a separate state. The formation of language in children, for example, is only one aspect of their integration into their *milieu*, an integration at the same time active and passive into a familial, social, and natural *milieu*. Language does not exist for its own sake; it is an aspect *sui generis* of the activity through which are expressed, but also shaped and reshaped, the ways of being in the world and the modalities of our being in the world. The capacity of language to express our thoughts comes from the fact that its formation and evolution follow the formation and evolution of our capability to think. Everything we have in this respect of strength or weakness, correctness or incorrectness, effectiveness or indetermination language assumes to the extent to which it is capable of remaining faithful to our thoughts. Every principle discovered in the search for a knowledge capable of formulation is reflected in language. Our analysis therefore does not permit us to entertain the notion that a significant discourse could be formed from "elementary propositions"* each of which would contain a clear and complete meaning in itself. This hypothesis seems to be inspired by an analogy with the hypothesis which proposes to make of the statement of knowledge a compound of simple observational statements.

The Principle of Integrality Extended to Language

The *critique* which we have given of the opinion according to which the normal experiment would be of the type of an integrally reduced experiment, makes this analogy entirely questionable. Or rather, if we elect to use the more precise language of a specific scientific discipline in order to derive from it suggestions concerning the study of language in general, we do not have to establish the comparison with an unrealizable ideal. On the other hand, the analogy is made very suggestive if we try to transfer to the study of language the principles of integrality and of technicity which emerge so clearly in the construction of a science open to the search for higher precision. The principle of integrality extended to language accounts for the fact that the meaning of the words which compose a text and the meaning of this text itself may be more or less strongly shaded, defined, and even modified

---

* This hypothesis, of course, must be accompanied by a complementary hypothesis concerning rules of combination, the syntax of connection of the elementary (or atomic) parts of speech. This approach leads to the assumption that this syntax can be identified with the rules of formulation of a formalized system. Our explanations give the reason why the second part of the hypothesis is still less plausible than the first.

through the solidarity of interpretation which the text establishes between the words. This solidarity is not only syntactic but is also a solidarity of signification glancing back to the words from the signification which the text itself can assume in the milieu where it finds its interpretation. Viewed from this angle, the method of contexts, which we have seen as being capable of defining the meaning of a word through its insertion into a suitably selected context, is but an application of the principle of integrality extended to language. The principle of technicity accounts for the fact that the meaning of a word or of a text is specified in proportion as this word or this text are interpreted at the level of a knowledge which in turn is well defined.

Following our analysis of the experiment, we have very resolutely moved away from the doctrine of science (and the corresponding theory of knowledge) which primarily stresses the observational statements and syntactic rules according to which the former must or might be put together. The fiction of the integrally reduced experiment had seemed to us especially questionable. Continuing the analogy which we have used before, it is now the fiction of an integrally reducible text which it seems to us necessary to reject. (An integrally reducible text would be such that an analytical investigation would recognize it as totally equivalent, from the point of view of its meaning, to a combination of a certain number of elementary statements. The combination would have to be effected according to the well-defined and exhaustively formulated rules of syntax. The elementary statements would correspond to the description which we have given above.)

Continuing still further, we categorically put in doubt every method of analysis or every analytic doctrine which would be "closed" in the following sense: We would declare as closed every doctrine which claims to be able to state through its own authority the definitive criteria of its validity—without reserving the eventuality of a revision which its involvement in an open activity might entail.

How should we name the analytical method which we have used? In discussing language one sometimes makes a very sharp distinction between the syntactic viewpoint and the point of view of semantics. According to the first, language is considered under the angle of its own structure, independent of what it has to signify. According to the second, language is studied from the point of view of significations, with attention to the ways of connecting, in the manner of a code, a grammatically and syntactically correct statement to the perfectly ordered elements of a certain sector of reality. It is above all clear that these definitions, taken quite rigorously, are fundamentally incompatible with our method, in its practice as well as in its results. Our analysis goes from certain texts to their signification and from there back to the texts, sometimes causing the renewed investigation of the validity of certain syntactic structures. This would not be possible if syntax and semantics had to exercise themselves each on its side on levels independent of each other. In fact, seeing the actual state of our knowledge, in particular our aptitude of knowing the world of realities and our capacity to formulate what we have learned, the presuppositions which would give a meaning to the preceding definitions appear very arbitrary; if we had to take them quite seriously they would resist any extension, *mutatis mutandis,* of the principles of integrality and technicity to the study of language. We shall therefore not maintain them in their rigorous tenor. But we shall nevertheless retain the distinction between syntactic and semantic aspects; this distinction will serve as a sketch which in our efforts to use it will be retouched and made more meaningful. In this sense it does not seem to us out of place to call our method a positive semantic analysis.

Let us now return to our former discussion and recall the distinctions which we have already made between the different forms under which language is introduced into an exposé such as the present one. We have termed π_1 and π_2 the two variants which we have used and are using in our own explanatory discourse.

We have then introduced, under the name of language β, the language which is analyzed and which serves as a milieu or a basis for analysis. For the sake of completeness one must naturally also mention the analyzing language which serves as the instrument of analysis. We shall call it the language δ, carrier of the *dialectic of the analysis*. The language β is determined, at least in the examples which are borrowed from it; the language δ is not in the same degree. Like the language π it is a language of explanatory discourse, but of a discourse more restricted and more compressed. What are its guarantees? We shall not develop all aspects of this question. We have done so, admittedly very briefly and summarily, in our discussion of the language π. By entering into the details we would only encounter again, albeit in a somewhat different perspective, the elements of appreciation which we have already stressed.*

Enlargement of the Experiment

The analysis aimed at disengaging from language the discursive aspects of what is interpreted as a temporal aspect was designed mainly for one purpose: to give a valid justification to a philosophy of research. On the other hand, lest our study disintegrate, we have chosen to concentrate our attention upon a well-defined subject, viz. the problem of time. We have explained our reasons for this choice at the beginning of our work. This also explains that the pursuit of our main purpose has at first taken a special form and that we had been obliged to use an analytical method which does not involve too much arbitrariness, i.e. too many factors of indetermination. In a somewhat complementary fashion the entire problem of language has been placed in a different light, together with the special problem of time in language.

These results could have been researched for their own sake, and we have just seen that they force us to challenge the validity of certain inadequately established analytical methods. They do not, however, represent more for us than intermediary

---

* In a certain sense the language δ may be compared to a *rhetorical discourse* in the new and generalized sense which Ch. Perelman gives to this expression. Like the languages π, the language δ is not simply a means of intersubjective communication; it is the means of a certain experiment which may be made in common and to which we shall return towards the end of the present conclusions.

results, on which we had to rely for the pursuit of our main purpose.

In the second part of our work this purpose has been deployed on a broader scale. The discussion has clearly taken on the form of a crossed experiment, of a constructive experiment, in the manner of the discursive syntheses which play such an important rôle in the functioning of language, but transferred into a much more rigorous climate.

The transition from the first part to the second part of the present work is in fact marked by the introduction of certain requirements of precision and objectivity. These requirements have informed the elaboration of the three great principal aspects under which time appears in scientific research: the intuitive aspect, the mathematical aspect, and the experimental aspect.*

We must not think that the *three variants* in question are created from a vacuum, as a result of the simple intention to use them in a scientific investigation. They are already present, prefigured, or more or less clearly outlined in every prescientific language. But, in order to conform to the exigencies of research, each of them must be defined and specified.

We have seen how, at the level of the adverb and the verb, language involves a certain structure and a certain dialectic of time. But for this structure to be clearly conceived and for this dialectic to be conducted coherently, the mathematician must take them in hand again, think them over, create them again, confer on them a different mode of existence, in a word, make of them mathematical realities. Can the time considered in this fashion be considered, as such, to be the true scientific time? Is scientific time reducible to it? One of the results of our study is to show that this is not the case.

Facing mathematical time there is the time whose flow is inscribed as a duration in a living organism. It is the existence of such a time at the level of the organism which we have

---

* In *La géométrie et le problème de l'espace*, we have already shown that these are also the three aspects under which space appears in the construction of a geometry taking on its full meaning. Compare also what has been said concerning its autofoundation.

sought to prove while discussing the time of the bees. It is also certain that this time may be known by human beings.

The Situation ε

The analysis of language towards which we have proceeded has placed us in a "situation of information and knowledge" whose degree of accuracy must be evaluated correctly. It is not a situation of full certitude, a situation α, to use again a technical term which we have already employed on several occasions.*

But the very method which has permitted us to disengage it also permits us to assert that this is not a nondescript situation but one already highly elaborated through the crossed experiment whose lines intersect on it. For the convenience of our explanations we shall call it the situation ε.

But why was this situation chosen as the starting-point for the second phase of our investigation? Was this choice inevitable? Was it not possible, and would it not have been simpler, to enter this second phase at the same level, our only concern being to utilize information of a scientific character? This is not an unnecessary question; in order to answer it we are forced to return to what we have called our "fundamental option," on which the entire structure of our exposé depends, and on which also depends the structure of the open methodology, for which this exposé claims to be no more than an illustration.

Let us go back once more to the analytical method which we have called a positive semantic analysis in order to emphasize its connection with this experiment. This method is merely a *form of realization* of our fundamental option. By selecting elementary texts in order to anchor the analysis in them (i.e. texts whose signification is not problematic, for the purpose they are to serve, at the level of their interpretation), we only isolate a number of points where the analysis guarantees the support of an already tested experiment. Does the method have no other justification? It could not be defended if it were not

---

* See, for example, the article "Pour commencer," *Revue Internationale de Philosophie*, Bruxelles, 1960.

also tested through its own results. It would merely be an incomplete form of the fundamental option. The same must also be said of any other way of particularizing the latter, which, it should be remembered, is but the option of openness towards experience. This experience, being renewed in each of its realizations and particularizations, is the basis for the general coherence of all the activities inspired by it.

Does this also entitle us to reject every analytical approach to language (and, more generally, every analytical philosophy) which would not recommend itself by the same fundamental option? The fact is that in practice, and regardless of the doctrine on whose authority it rests, an analysis inevitably invokes specific forms and specific results of the experiment. The practice thus must be unfaithful to the doctrine, unless the latter is principally integrated with a certain openness towards experience.

In sum, a practice in agreement with the option of openness could never claim to utilize in full confidence a situation of complete certainty; conversely, an analytical practice could not remain true to a doctrine which would not imply any openness towards experience.

What has been said particularly concerns the analytic method which we have used. But it is clear that the option of openness does not apply in this particular case. To limit it in this way would make it meaningless. It has value only when its scope is not limited in advance. How could we justify that any order of research be closed to it, unless we invoke the experience made of the closedness of this investigation? This justification moreover would open the domain where the option should have remained ineffective. There is no option of closedness except through a choice which would carry its own justification independent of experience. As we have already noted, we do not have to make, or rather we are not entitled to make such a choice at this point.

If therefore we had proposed to enter upon the scientific phase of our study at the same level, we would not have been exempt for this reason alone from utilizing the exigencies deriving from our fundamental option. We specify only two of these exigencies which may easily be transferred from the particular case of our analytical method to any method of research:

1. Research must be given a guaranteed starting situation, not of complete certainty, but of some security.

2. The method must moreover include a certain ensemble of tested means whose application permits us to develop the starting situation and thereby realize a certain progress of research.

The first of these requirements naturally does not determine the situation univocally, and the second does not determine in a satisfactory way the means capable of developing it. Concerning the second phase of our investigations we have chosen as a starting situation precisely the situation ϵ which the semantic analysis of the first phase has enabled us to isolate. We shall shortly return to the procedures which have permitted us to ensure its development.

From here on, even without going into the details, we can thus present the method according to which the second phase of our investigations has evolved as a new "form of realization" of our fundamental option.

An Implicit Philosophy of Time

Continuing our commentary, we must thus return to the situation ϵ and ask what our analysis, acting as an indicator, reveals in it. Under two inseparable and mutually complementary aspects, we have seen emerge the outline of a preliminary doctrine of time, of a philosophy of time which current language implicitly contains, which is part of it and informs its use. The simplest way to evoke this twofold aspect is to take up again the idea of the sketch in the strong sense which we have used before. A sculptor sketching a statue may at the same time seek better to imagine what must take form and seek the form capable of giving expression to it. That which is taking form and the form thus achieved together advance towards completion.

The same is true of the implicit philosophy of time and its discursive formulation. Nothing suggests that we are concerned here with a special example; the same relation probably exists between anything which contains meaning on the one hand and its form of expression on the other.

What are the essential characteristics of this implicit philosophy of time? At the level of current language, time does not intervene as a clear and distinct idea which would represent the proper and well-defined meaning of the word *Time,* and which could be invoked in its totality for us to take full cognizance of it. It is neither a complete and fully delimited notion, nor is it a representation perfectly formed and defined forever. In a language "of wide communication" time is not at first introduced with an essential and final signification, to which well-defined significations would subsequently be attributed to express exactly all that has to be said. In other words, time is not subject to the laws of Aristotelian logic. According to the circumstances of the discourse, it appears on the contrary only under the aspect of "variants" which are specialized as yet only in a summary fashion. They certainly are specific enough for us to distinguish them from each other, for example, and not to confound the subjective time evoked by a specific part of the discourse with the objective time evoked by another. We say that these distinctions are established only in a summary fashion. They are firmly established when the conditions of interpretation are not problematic or hardly so. But they may lose their "separating power" and become wholly uncertain if they are introduced without precautions into certain domains of research very remote from common sense.*

Do these variants remain isolated from each other, and does there not exist, on a higher level, a time which unifies them and through which they enter into correlation and interaction? This is certainly the case, but we must note and emphasize that the unifying power manifests itself at the very level of discourse, and that the coherence proper to it (in the evocation of particular circumstances) is in itself a means of unification and generates a time more general and more universal.

---

* The word "variant" invites criticism because it might suggest that we are concerned with somehow parallel variants, for which the general case is still undecided.

As we have shown, it is not by isolating the proper and final meaning of a word that the unity of the different variants revealed through the analysis is constituted. This unity is the effect of the discursive synthesis which, by means of the same text, lets its variants share in a common effort of expression. We have given several examples of this, first at the level of nouns and adjectives and later at the level of verbs and adverbs. To the power of separation of the analysis the discursive synthesis opposes its power of correlation and unification. According to the purposes which the discourse has or which are prescribed for it, the discursive action will disperse, as a prism dispersing the colors, the meanings which the word *time* may assume, or it will unite them, working towards a collective meaning, as the colors of the rainbow combine in the formation of white daylight.

This, then, is what our analysis has brought to light in the situation ε, concerning the philosophy of time which current language implicitly involves. It is part of our method not to force the interpretation of results thus obtained. It is nevertheless clear that every philosophy of language and every philosophy of time must take note of it and take it into account. What follows from this at first is a double caution. In fact, nothing in the results obtained supports the hypothesis that time should be reducible to its subjective aspect, or the opposite hypothesis that it should be reducible to its objective aspect. At the level where our analysis takes place and has formed its guarantees, neither of these hypotheses is confirmed. The situation ε does not offer any pledge of validity for them. The action of the discursive synthesis, on the contrary, disproves them decisively. Does this double caution find its confirmation through the study of the other "side" of the question, the side of the discursive formulation? It suffices, to account for it, to recall what we have said about the system of the verb and the dialectic of time outlined in it.

In the system of the verb, time may be the time of the phenomenon as well as the time of the self. The dialectic of the times outlined therein is not at all limited to a dialectic of durations and does not imply in any way the Bergsonian thesis

according to which time is entirely in duration as an immediate datum of consciousness. But neither does anything confirm
the opposite thesis, according to which time in its totality can
be grasped without reference to the duration of the time lived.
In the discursive formulation that which is expressed is neither
a purely subjective time nor a totally objective one, but a combination of both.

From the Situation ϵ to the Situation θ

This is how matters present themselves in the situation ϵ.
But this situation must only be the starting-point of an evolution towards a situation (which we shall call the situation θ)
of which we may say with some confidence that it is more
advanced than the former. The transition from one of these two
situations to the other inevitably gives rise to a new series of
questions in the face of which we should maintain our principal
attitude, i.e. always keep in mind the guarantees by which we
must be supported in order to give valid answers. We note the
following four questions, among others:

1. What means do we have at our disposal for developing
the situation ϵ to approach the situation θ?

2. Is this evolution likely to involve a corresponding evolution of the philosophy of time, which has turned out to be im-
plictly connected with the situation ϵ?

3. Is it not possible that, in the philosophy of time connected
with the situation θ, the temporal variants become clearly separable, with one of them even becoming predominant? Or, if
this is not the case, by what synthetic procedure should the
procedure of discursive synthesis be replaced?

4. Does the special case of time give us any insights on a
general method of research, of scientific research in particular?

Is there no reason for hope that such insights might in turn
suggest and even guarantee the great outlines of a philosophy
of knowledge, into which a tested method of research would
thus be incorporated?

These four questions certainly represent only a sample, albeit
a characteristic one, of all the questions that come to mind.

The first is a methodological question. It is so even in a double sense, since it concerns at the same time the method according to which the present exposé was conducted, and the method according to which the results on which it is based may be guaranteed objectively. It is an extension of the method of the contexts. This method takes a word, an expression, or more generally an element of discourse whose meaning is still open (i.e. suspended in the two meanings in which the outline in the strong sense is suspended) and engages it in contexts whose meaning is not doubtful.*

* Let us underscore once more that the method of the context is in disagreement with the notion that the meaning of a text cannot be certain if the meaning of any of the discursive elements contained in it is not assured to the same extent, but that this disagreement does not compromise its factual validity. On the other hand, the method is in perfect agreement with a methodology intended to utilize to its very principles the fundamental option of openness towards experience and presenting itself as a form of realization of the latter.

This method may be considered as a special case of a more general procedure, which consists in engaging the elements to be tested, defined, or modified in an activity subject to certain requirements of validity or effectiveness; in order to participate in a valid fashion the elements involved must themselves satisfy certain conditions whose effect is often to define them more precisely or even to modify them. The elements in question no longer are necessarily elements of discourse. They may be more or less clear views and representations, ideas or textures of more or less coherent ideas, or even more or less imaginative hypotheses, any elements, in short, through which a thought takes on form and power. But it would mean restricting the scope of the procedure too much if one would limit its application to what might be called the elements of knowledge. Nothing prevents its extension to all forms of activity open to the sanction of failure. This fashion of limiting its activities and incorporating them into an activity already recognized as effective may be called a procedure of agreement.

The axiomatic method certainly was not deliberately imagined as a special application of this procedure. But nothing prevents us in retrospect from considering it as such. It involves a certain ensemble of notions and a certain number of relations between them in the exigencies of the deductive activity. The same may be said, in a more general way, about any attempt to establish a certain order and to set up certain guiding principles of coherence in any domain of knowledge. Still more generally, every attempt to utilize a crossed experiment depends on the procedure of agreement; the various components of the experiment are involved in a synthetic effort which in turn limits everything which must be an element of synthesis.

As far as we are concerned, we have used the method in a constant as well as diversified way. We have started to explain its functioning by describing the procedure of the contexts. But we might as well have started with the

The positive semantic analysis has put us in possession of a certain ensemble of informations on the subjective aspect of the dialectic of time incorporated in current language. The activity in which we have engaged these informations in order to test and complete them has none of the rigor of mathemat-

---

positive semantic analysis and the discursive syntheses. More or less visibly the procedure of agreement thus was already in the background of the entire first phase of our exposé. But it was in the course of the second phase that its rôle has been systematically confirmed and that it has assumed its function as a means par excellence for securing the progress of our undertaking. We have first applied it to the dialectic of time, which the analysis of the functions of the adverb and the verb had brought to light in the situation ϵ. Viewed as an outline to be completed, and subject to the exigencies of mathematical rigor, this dialectic has given rise to the linear temporal continuum and the group of mappings of it onto itself, a group through which is realized the displacement of the origin of time to an unspecified instant of the past or the future. The mathematical time thus obtained achieves the discursive synthesis of the subjective time with the objective time. This is no longer a time lived as a duration through a personal consciousness, nor is it a metronome of all natural phenomena. It is a time of the imagination, an ideal model of subjective as well as of objective time. It is this time which will participate as a theoretical and irreplaceable component in the synthesis in which we seek to emphasize the requirements of an increasing precision.

In order that the application of the procedure of agreements in question may correspond to the model proposed above, the mathematical activity must be designed as a tested activity whose aspirations of coherence do not risk the sanction of failure. For it is precisely in the success of the mathematical activity that the procedure of agreement finds its guarantees in any particular case.

We readily admit that anyone who has not fundamentally understood the character of a method designed to correspond to the fundamental option of openness towards experience might raise objections. He will not understand, for example, that the mathematical activity may be invoked and guaranteed without in turn having found the ultimate guarantee of being demonstrably noncontradictory, whereby the risk of producing a paradox would be eliminated forever. In order to reply to this objection, would it not be necessary to open the entire context of the research on the foundations of mathematics and "liquidate" at least the question of noncontradiction? But this expedient would be impracticable; every demonstration requires a mathematical practice concerning which the same objection could be raised again.

In the framework of open methodology, to which the procedure of agreement belongs, the noncontradictory nature of mathematics being of the order of facts, at the level of the activities which in practice enter into the process, its test does not overtake at once but rather accompanies the evolvement of mathematics. In the final analysis, it is in the procedure of autofoundation that the objection is answered.

ics. It requires more common sense and alertness than accuracy, more patience and method than strictness, more comparison than deduction. But above all it must be informed by a certain vision of what we can hardly avoid calling the relation of finality of living beings with their natural habitat (we are using the term finality in a sense comparable to that which it has in cybernetics). Our viewpoint is that of a specialist studying the behavior of certain animals, of the bees in our case. Does it provide the guarantees of security required by the application of the procedure of agreement? This is doubtless the case and we do not want to be dragged into a discussion of all the contexts which would have to be opened in order to account for it. We would again be led to a procedure of solidary autofoundation.

A bee, as we were able to state in our conclusions, is at the same time a watch and a compass. We have thus established beyond any doubt that certain organisms carry within themselves the capacity of connecting a relatively accurate estimate of durations with the estimate of certain data of place and position. It is therefore conceivable that no living creature is completely without this same capacity. There may be a great difference between the organic structures which are involved here and the mental structures capable of being projected into the consciousness as intuitive *representations;* nevertheless a connection has been established with those which henceforth appear trustworthy within a certain natural area, without having to assume absolute certainty.

The most important of our applications of the procedure of agreement, however, is the one where we have applied the variant of objectively measured time to the investigation of the procedures of the manufacture of watches and clocks, taking the search for ever-increased precision as a guideline. We shall later return to the most striking result of this phase of our study.

We have asked what means we have at our disposal to develop the situation ϵ towards the situation θ. The answer is now abundantly clear; we first have applied the procedure of agreement three times in a row. We have then introduced the

results thus obtained into a crossed experiment, an experiment
of synthesis.

The Dialectic Synthesis

We have just explained how the transition from the situation ϵ to the situation θ may be effected.

Two opposing elements contribute to this: the procedure of
agreement on the one hand, being a procedure of specification; and, on the other hand, the crossed experiment, being a
synthetic experiment. These two elements maintain between
themselves a dialectic interplay which recalls the discursive
synthesis, as well as the dialectic syntheses thanks to which
geometry can retain the totality of its significations. But it was
above all the synthetizing element which was illuminated
through our remarks; the system of the time integrated into the
situation θ now includes three variants evolved and defined
more precisely, viz. intuitive time, mathematical time, and
measured time. We still have to emphasize the synthetizing factor, taking up again the second of our four questions. Could
it not happen, we have asked, that the transition from the situation ϵ to the situation θ defines and specifies the different
variants to the point of separating them completely and mak-
ing them autonomous, and must we not expect that one of
these well-defined variants assumes by itself all aspects of time,
all the other aspects becoming reducible to it? The answer to
this question has been prepared carefully, through multiple episodes, throughout our entire study of the measurement of time;
it is negative. At the same time and by the very fashion in which
our study was conducted, we have been led to take a position more and more firmly opposed to the operationalistic thesis. The latter, as we know, gives a predominant significance
to the physicist's time, asserting moreover that this time can
and must be fixated through a purely operational definition.
In the simplest cases this thesis appears to be defensible, provided that the defining power of the instrument be completed
by that of certain intuitive representations connected with the
flow of time, as well as certain principles of common sense,
in particular the principle of sufficient reason. Whereas, in the

simplest cases, the use of these representations and principles is not problematic, the question cannot be settled as easily when the operational definition must correspond to increasing requirements of precision. In fact, the manufacture of watches and clocks and the practice of the measurement of time do not correspond at all to the operationalistic hypothesis. The project to defend and to utilize it leads us into increasingly insuperable difficulties where it soon loses its plausibility.

On the contrary, as we progress towards high precision it becomes strikingly evident that the time of effective action is a synthetic time. We have shown this twice in two very different ways. The first time we have proposed to use each instrument for a strictly operational definition of time, and each time we had to admit, after having realized our inability to pursue this project, that the very manufacture of the instrument, as well as its adjustment, inevitably and unconditionally require the joint application of mathematical, technical, and (intuitive) phenomenological aspects of our efforts. In the chapter on synthetic time we have again faced the same fact. It actually seems that the most accurate measurement of time feasible results from the combined use of three types of measurements, for each of which the preceding remarks are equally valid.

We thus have elucidated the synthetizing factor of the dialectic action through which our grasp of time is functioning.

It remains for us to answer the last two of our four questions. We shall do so in the next section while at the same time presenting some methodological and philosophical conclusions.

CONCLUSIONS

What is the methodological and philosophical result of our investigation, which has now reached its conclusion? Our intention has not been to present a ready-made doctrine, but rather to make an experiment from which this doctrine would result. The experiment was made with the help of a discourse, the discourse of our exposé. But, except for some of its parts, it was not an experiment of discursive character. Language had the rôle of a general milieu of projection, representation, and correlation proper to it. If language speaks of the physicist's activity, for example, it certainly does not make physicists of us. All the same, it actually does give us an aspect of the physicist's activity, more particularly that which we need. Made through the intermediary of language, our experiment thus was to be anchored in a multitude of experiences actually made. Charged with constantly renewed information for which it was only partly accountable, language could become the agent of our own methodological approach.

But is this not the usual form of any investigation intended to yield results of a methodological or philosophical order? If language were not capable of exercising this function, the very material of any systematic reflection on what we are capable of doing would be missing. It would thus be impossible to set up a methodological level. But such is not the case, and the function of language through which it operates cannot be questioned. There is in this an essential fact to be remembered and accommodated, but not to be justified in advance.

Must the aim of methodological reflection be to isolate, formulate, and install a well-defined method, i.e. an ensemble of precise rules and indubitable criteria which offer a sufficient guarantee for the effectiveness of research and the correctness of its results?

Some people have thought and may still think so. We have never considered it possible to explain a method which could be sufficiently guaranteed by being stated, and nothing in the course of our study has ever led us towards such a concept. We certainly have had occasion to present and to propose a specific procedure, the procedure of the four phases, for example, as a normal procedure of research. But we have never claimed the right to assert its correctness by dissociating it from the test of effectiveness which it had undergone and to which it has remained subject. On the other hand, it is a fundamental aspect of method which we have illustrated by showing that the procedure of autofoundation is inevitably that of every discipline in which the concern for accuracy is not a mere affair of words. But the fact of being inevitable would not suffice as a justification unless it were combined with effectiveness. Wherever we have seen the method taking shape and being defined sufficiently for us to explain it in certain of its aspects, we also have seen it each time involved in the test of its own validity. The power which it has to aim at experience it derives above all from experience, and it never receives it in a definitive way. The method does not represent a last tribunal beyond which there would be no appeal; it is itself merely a form of realization of a certain purpose and remains liable to be revoked through the very exigencies involved in the pursuit of this intention. What, then, can the latter be?

During our investigation we have been faced many times by the necessity to be open towards experience, to go beyond an already consolidated situation in order to invoke new elements of appreciation and knowledge. We have finally realized that the method by which we have proceeded may be viewed as a sequence of responses, or even as one consistently renewed response to a dominant intention, to the option of openness towards experience. But are we concerned only with the method of our own exposé? As we have noted before, the latter takes on its meaning only by being anchored and grounded in the entire field of experience it invokes. It is thus through our own experience that the general method of research, scientific research in particular, is being approached and, at least in part, understood. The method of science and the method by which it may be studied have a common background, corresponding to a common intention; they are constituted, under the pressure of the experiment, in such a way as to be able, to the full extent of their possibilities, to make room for the new experiment. This is, very briefly, the methodological result of our undertaking. It follows that there is no point in trying to establish a method and to formulate criteria which would derive their justification only from themselves. They receive their meaning from incorporating and deploying the fundamental option according to the circumstances and the situations. The important and decisive fact is that an entire methodology can be defined and progressively explained as a response to such a fundamental option.

One may remind us, meaning to raise an objection, that it is not so much at the end of the analysis, but already at the very beginning of our exposé, that we have come out for openness towards experience, and that we have remained faithful to this attitude throughout; that, consequently, it is by no means surprising or convincing if we find again this same option of openness in the function of a prime organizer. The answer is easy: Our choice at the beginning certainly was not arbitrary; it was an informed choice of which we were almost certain that it would not turn out to be a mistake. But this is not the essential fact, and even if our choice had been a pure accident, our conclusions would remain the same nevertheless. What must be emphasized is that our guiding idea has proved to be correct, that it has again and again compelled recognition and finally has taken the form in which we now know it, as a guiding and organizing concept of research. The objection is therefore invalid; what it underscores, on the contrary, is the most authentic proof that could be found for the option of openness, the proof given according to the procedure of autofoundation.

To sum up, our approach has been of a methodological and philosophical order. We have sought to present its methodological aspect in its most basic form, as succinctly as possible. But it is clear that the concern for method is at the core of every philosophy of knowledge, and that every philosophy when approached from a certain angle presents itself under the aspect of a philosophy of knowledge. For us there can be no doubt that the option of openness towards experience and its procedures of application and realization, the crossed experiment in particular, can, in the entire field of philosophic research, play the same rôle as it does in the diversified field of research we have just travelled through. The outline of an open phenomenology has already been accomplished.* The first traces of an outline for an open aesthetic may already be discerned.†

---

* See *Théâtre de veille et théâtre de songes; Essai de dialectisation de la conscience.* By Dr. J.-P. Gonseth. Neuchâtel, Editions du Griffon, 1950.

† See Eric Eméry's work, *La gamme et le language musical.* Paris, 1961.

We believe that we have shown by many examples in the preceding discussion how the option of openness towards experience may guide the synthetic and dialectic functions of the most diverse aspects of our activity, of our philosophic activity in particular.

Do not our lives have to be illuminated by an option of openness towards everything which is given us to live? What seems certain to me is that a philosophy, of whatever kind it may be, puts into discursive form the deployment of certain fundamental options. But if it lacks the option of openness towards experience, nothing can save it from closing itself on an ensemble of statements whose meaning cannot be renewed and which will increasingly assume the character of arbitrary declarations.

INDEX

A

Aberration, 415
Académie Française, 20
Acceptation, 18, 22 ff., 43, 50, 81, 422, 426 open, 27
Accuracy, 376
  threshold of, 332
Adverb, 88 ff.
Adverbial, 91
Adverbs, of time, 97
Aging, 356
Agreement, procedure of, 441
Amplitude, 281
Analysis
  closed, 429
  of language, v, 36–7, 76, 78 n., 167, 421, 427, 434
  semantic positive, xi, 424, 426, 440
Analytic philosophy, x
Arbitrariness, v, 270, 296
Autofoundation, procedure of, 332, 441
Autofounded, 383
Autonomy, 339
Axiomatization
  schematizing, 185
  structuring, 184

B

Balance wheel clock, 275
Balance wheel spiral, 281
Bees
  experiments on, 320 ff.
  language, 315 ff.
  time of, 318, 324, 327
  vision of, 313
Bergson, 60, 63
Bolyai, 392 n.
Bossuet, 59, 63, 71

C

Carnot cycle, 298
Cause, 241
Causality, principle of, 159
Chandler, 263, 264
Change, 238
Clemence, G.M., 344 n.
Clepsydra, 199; see also Water Clock
Clock
  atomic, v, 367 ff.
  balance wheel, 275 ff.
  pendulum, 275
  quartz, 352 ff.
  uniform, 363
  water, 199, 217, 222; see also Clepsydra
  with drift, 358
Common sense, operational, 248
Completion, 102
Condillac, 63, 64
Conjugation, 120 ff., 145
Context, procedure of, 28, 30–3, 46, 423, 429, 439
Continuum, 178, 181–4
Correctness, 220, 229
Crystals, anisotropic, 354 n.

D

Day
  increase of average, 266
  of ancients, 202
  mean solar, 260
  sidereal, 259
  solar, 259
  variation in length of, 266
Defossez, L., 227 n., 279 n.
Desiderative, 106
Determinate, 23–4

449